THE CLASSIC 1000 LOW-FAT RECIPES

Carolyn Humphries

foulsham
LONDON • NEW YORK • TORONTO • SYDNEY

foulsham

The Publishing House, Bennetts Close,
Cippenham, Berks SL1 5AP

ISBN 0-572-02804-0

Copyright © 2002 Strathearn Publishing

Printed in Great Britain by St. Edmundsbury Press, Bury St. Edmunds, Suffolk.

Contents

Introduction

We've all been advised to reduce our fat intake – especially animal fats, which can lead to high blood cholesterol levels and, in turn, lead to heart disease. It may be that you are simply a little overweight or just want to change to a healthier lifestyle. Alternatively, you may have a particular medical problem and have been advised by your doctor to change to a low-fat diet. But even if you haven't any significant health worries, you know it makes sense to eat wisely.

This book is designed to give you a healthy and enjoyable eating plan that won't mean depriving you of your favourite foods – you can still have chocolate cake or roast potatoes if you cook them my way! The recipes I have created for you will not only considerably lower your fat consumption in the most delightful way possible, but will also give you an all-round healthy diet. This way you can enjoy your cooking and eating and feel confident that you are taking positive steps to stay healthy.

A Healthy Low-fat Diet

Eating should be a pleasure but it is important to have a balanced diet. Every day you need to have foods from all the main food groups and in the correct proportions.

Carbohydrates for Energy

There are two types of carbohydrate – complex and simple. The complex ones are all the starchy foods such as all types of bread, pasta, rice and cereals (including breakfast ones, but choose wholegrain ones and avoid those coated in sugar) and potatoes. Eat plenty for energy. The simple ones are sugars, found naturally in many foods from fruit to milk but also manufactured commercially in various forms – all the granular sugars, syrups, black treacle (molasses) and honey. You get plenty in natural foods so all the extra you sprinkle on or put in cakes and puds just pile on unwanted calories, so keep added sugars to a minimum. I often use honey for sweetening as it is naturally sweeter than sugar so you need less.

Proteins for Body Growth and Repair

The best sources of protein are lean meat, poultry, game, fish, eggs and dairy products, pulses and manufactured vegetable proteins like soya protein, tofu (bean curd) and quorn. Eat two or three small portions a day.

Vitamins and Minerals for General Well-being

The best sources of vitamins and minerals are fruit and vegetables, ideally fresh but frozen or canned in natural juice or water are fine too. Eat at least five portions a day.

Fibre for Healthy Body Functioning

Eat plenty of fruit and vegetables, wholegrain cereals and skins on potatoes. But if you have had a low-fibre diet until now, you should take it slowly. For instance, start by having some wholemeal bread and some white, or a mixture of high- and lower-fibre cereal for breakfast, then gradually increase the amount of the higher fibre foods.

Fat for Warmth and Energy

Yes, even though you want to reduce your fat intake, you do need some to keep healthy. But most people in the Western world eat too much fat – it's about 40 per cent of our daily calorie (energy) intake on average and it is recommended that we all cut this down to 35 per cent or less. All the fat you need is found naturally in foods, so you don't need to add any when you are cooking or preparing foods. There are plenty of simple tips for cutting down on pages 10–11, and learning how to balance the type of fat you eat can also help.

Are All Fats the Same?

All fats are made up of three different fatty acids in differing quantities:

- **Saturated fatty acids:** The main sources of these are animal fats. They are solid at room temperature and are particularly found in meat, dairy products and many margarines. However, palm oil and coconut oil – obviously both from plants – also solidify at room temperature and are high in saturated fatty acids.
- **Polyunsaturated fatty acids:** These are mainly found in vegetable oils such as corn and sunflower oil and also in polyunsaturated margarines. Oily fish such as tuna and mackerel are also high in polyunsaturates. But you should be aware that a product labelled 'vegetable oil', may not be high in polyunsaturates; if the label says 'hydrogenised vegetable oil', the fatty acids will have been changed chemically from polyunsaturated fatty acids to saturated fatty acids.
- **Monounsaturated fatty acids:** The main sources of these are olive oil, avocados and rapeseed oil.

Dietary Recommendations

It is now widely recommended that no more than 10 per cent of your diet should be derived from saturated fats as they can raise your blood cholesterol level. Polyunsaturated fats can lower your blood cholesterol level but should be used only in moderation. And if you overheat polyunsaturated fat – by using the same corn oil for deep-frying several times, for instance – the composition changes and the benefits will be lost.

Monounsaturates do not affect blood cholesterol levels so are a good substitute for animal fats. Perhaps that is why people in Mediterranean countries, where they use olive oil all the time, seem to live so long!

Low-fat Spreads

Because you need to reduce your fat intake overall, it makes sense to use low-fat spreads instead of ordinary butter, margarine or oils. There is an enormous range on the market now but they are not all suitable for all purposes. Here are a few words of advice:

- Some low-fat spreads are still high in saturated fats, even if there is less fat overall than in a conventional margarine.

- Many are not suitable for baking or frying (sautéing) because of their high water content – check the labels.

- Don't be lured into thinking that because your spread is low in fat you can have lots of it.

- Some taste better than others.

My personal preference is for reduced-fat olive oil spreads, which are low in saturated fat, lower in calories, taste very good and can be used for baking or frying. So choose either one of these or a reduced-fat sunflower spread for spreading and baking.

Cutting Down Fat Made Easy

Obviously all the recipes in this book will help you cut down significantly on your fat intake. But here are some general tips:

- Use skimmed (preferably) or semi-skimmed milk rather than whole milk.

- Chose the lowest-fat yoghurts, cheeses and creams you can find. Read the labels – virtually fat-free ones are ideal.

- Remove all skin and fat from meat and poultry.

- Grill (broil) rather than fry (sauté).

- Use only the minimum of fat for cooking.

- Use non-stick cookware and baking parchment. If you have to grease a tin or a pan, use a reduced-fat spread suitable for baking and frying. Melt it first, then use a brush to coat the surface as thinly as possible.

- Add only a scraping of reduced-fat spread to bread and don't add any extra to vegetables before serving.

- When browning meat, dry-fry rather than use added fat and pour off any excess fat (but not the juices) before continuing with the recipe.

- Choose canned fish and vegetables in water or brine rather than oil.

- If you have to buy biscuits (cookies) and other snacks, choose reduced fat, salt and sugar ranges.

- Avoid eating fatty, salty snacks such as crisps (chips) and roasted peanuts. For a treat try one of the virtually fat-free savoury snacks (pages 287–306).

Other Tips for a Healthy Eating Plan

● Keep salt to a minimum. Don't add it at the table and use as little as possible in cooking.

● Drink alcohol only in moderation – a maximum of 14–21 units a week for a woman and 21–28 units a week for a man. A unit is a small sherry, a glass of wine, a single measure of spirits or 300 ml/½ pt of ordinary strength beer.

● To reduce your calorie intake further, choose reduced-sugar and sugar-free varieties of jams (conserves), marmalades, jellies (jellos) and sauces and always choose canned fruit in natural juice rather than syrup.

● Take regular exercise.

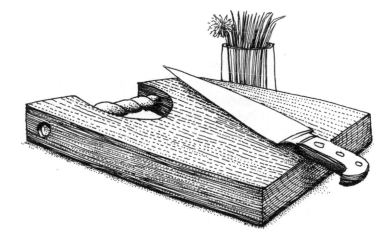

Feel the Difference in Just Seven Days

Here are menus for a week to get you in the mood for your new lifestyle.

Monday

Breakfast	A glass of pure orange juice
	Raisin and Cinnamon Breakfast Muffins (page 26)
	Coffee or tea
Lunch	Velvety Chicken Liver Pâté (page 97)
	Wholemeal toast
	A piece of fresh fruit
Snack	Light Digestive Biscuit (page 370)
Dinner	Chinese Beef Bowl (page 212)
	Apricot Floating Islands (page 330)

Tuesday

Breakfast	Half a grapefruit
	Herby Mushrooms on Toast (page 34)
	Tea or coffee
Lunch	Red Lentil and Tomato Soup with Basil (page 59)
	Virtually fat-free fruit fromage frais
Snack	A slice of Teacup Loaf (page 360)
Dinner	Spaghetti Bolognese (page 204)
	Spiced Poached Pears with Dates (page 327)

Wednesday

Breakfast	A glass of pure orange juice
	Apple Oat Bran Cereal (page 20)
	Tea or coffee
Lunch	Peperonata (page 101)
	French bread
	A piece of fresh fruit
Snack	A slice of Jam Sponge (page 372)
Dinner	Scotch Lamb Stew (page 190)
	Vanilla Ice (page 344)

Thursday

Breakfast	A glass of pure grapefruit juice
	Devilled Kidneys (page 37)
	Tea or coffee
Lunch	Mushroom Quichette (page 102)
	Virtually fat-free fruit yoghurt
Snack	Vanilla Tea Biscuit (page 373)
Dinner	Cottage Pie (page 203)
	Fresh Fruit Salad (page 331)

Friday

Breakfast	Half a grapefruit
	Cranberry Porridge (page 19)
	Tea or coffee
Lunch	Chicken and Corn Chowder (page 56)
	A piece of fresh fruit
Snack	Ginger Drop (page 374)
Dinner	French-style Cod (page 128)
	Steamed Chocolate Cherry Pudding (page 327)

Saturday

Breakfast	A glass of pure orange juice
	Baked Mushroom-stuffed Tomatoes (page 35)
	Tea or coffee
Lunch	Minestrone (page 54)
	A piece of fresh fruit
Snack	A slice of Chocolate Indulgence (page 373)
Dinner	Pork Stroganoff (page 214)
	Marbled Honey Fruit Fool (page 332)

Sunday

Breakfast	A glass of pure grapefruit juice
	White Fish Kedgeree (page 29)
	Tea or coffee
Lunch	Roast Chicken Dinner (page 164)
	Apple Strudel (page 328)
Snack	Oven-fresh Scone (page 357)
Supper	Spiced Carrot Soup (page 57)
	A piece of fresh fruit

Basic Food Hygiene

A hygienic cook is a healthy cook – so please bear the following in mind when you're preparing food.

- Always wash your hands before preparing food.

- Always wash and dry fresh produce before use.

- Don't lick your fingers.

- Don't keep tasting and stirring with the same spoon. Use a clean spoon every time you taste the food.

- Don't put raw and cooked meat on the same shelf in the fridge. Store raw meat on the bottom shelf, so it can't drip over other foods. Keep all perishable foods wrapped separately. Don't overfill the fridge or it will become too warm.

- Never use the same cloth to wipe down a chopping board you have been using for cutting up meat, for instance, then to wipe down your work surfaces – you will simply spread germs. Always thoroughly wash your cloth in hot, soapy water and, better still, use an anti-bacterial kitchen cleaner on all surfaces as well.

- Always transfer leftovers to a clean container and cover with a lid, clingfilm (plastic wrap) or foil. Leave until completely cold, then store in the fridge. Never put any warm food in the fridge.

- When reheating food, always make sure it is piping hot throughout, never just lukewarm.

- Don't refreeze foods that have defrosted unless you cook them before freezing again.

- Never reheat previously cooked food more than once.

Notes on the Recipes

- All spoon measures are level: 1 tsp = 5 ml; 1 tbsp = 15 ml.

- Do not mix metric, imperial and American measures. Follow one set only, never a combination.

- Eggs are medium unless otherwise stated.

- Wholemeal flour is plain unless otherwise stated.

- When baking and frying (sautéing), use a suitable low-fat spread (read the labels).

- All herbs are fresh unless dried are specifically called for. If substituting dried, use only half the quantity or less as they are very pungent, but chopped, frozen varieties are a better substitute than dried.

- Always wash, dry, peel, core and seed, if necessary, any fresh produce before use.

- All cooking times are approximate and are intended as a guide only.

- All calorie counts are based on average-sized portions. Most have been rounded up to the nearest 5 calories for convenient counting – that means you'll have had a few calories less than you think at the end of the day! But please note, they do not include serving suggestions.

- All recipes are marked with an indication of the quantity of fibre; high, fairly high, medium, fairly low and low.

- A thick slice of crusty bread contains about 100 calories, depending on the type of loaf. Pitta breads contain about 250 calories per 100 g/4 oz.

- When a recipe calls for a low-fat ingredient, use a virtually fat-free variety where available.

Complete Breakfasts

Breakfast is probably the most important meal of the day. It is when you need to re-fuel to give you the energy to perform whatever tasks you have throughout your waking hours. Lack of food means lack of energy, which means you won't function efficiently, so never skip breakfast. Apart from anything else, it will simply mean you'll be tempted to nibble during the morning – and probably at the foods that are least good for you!

Serve any of the following recipes with a glass of pure unsweetened fruit juice or half a grapefruit, a slice of melon or a piece of any other fresh fruit (the vitamin C will help your body absorb the iron in cereals) and a cup of coffee or tea, either black or with skimmed milk. Note too that the cooked breakfasts are also great as light lunches or suppers.

Luxury Muesli

MAKES 10 SERVINGS

175 g/6 oz/1½ cups rolled oats
25 g/1 oz/½ cup wheat bran
25 g/1 oz/¼ cup sesame seeds
25 g/1 oz/¼ cup chopped hazelnuts
(filberts)
50 g/2 oz/⅓ cup raisins
50 g/2 oz/⅓ cup sultanas (golden
raisins)
50 g/2 oz/⅓ cup ready-to-eat dried
prunes, stoned (pitted) and chopped
50 g/2 oz/⅓ cup dried banana slices
A good pinch of ground cinnamon
Skimmed milk, to serve

Mix the oats and bran in a bowl. Toast the sesame seeds and hazelnuts under the grill (broiler) or in a frying pan (skillet), turning frequently to prevent burning. Add to the bowl with the remaining ingredients and mix well. Store in an airtight container. Serve with enough skimmed milk to moisten.

* **195 calories per serving**
* **High fibre**

Winter Muesli

MAKES 10 SERVINGS

Prepare as for Luxury Muesli but substitute a 225 g/8 oz packet of dried fruit salad, chopped and any stones (pits) discarded, for the raisins, sultanas, prunes and dried banana.

* **195 calories per serving**
* **High fibre**

Banana Bran Muesli

SERVES 6

175 g/6 oz/1½ cups rolled oats
50 g/2 oz/1 cup all bran cereal
50 g/2 oz/⅓ cup dried banana slices
50 g/2 oz/⅓ cup raisins
1.5 ml/¼ tsp mixed (apple-pie) spice
30 ml/2 tbsp light brown sugar
Skimmed milk, to serve

Mix together the dry ingredients and store in an airtight container. Serve with enough skimmed milk to moisten.

* **220 calories per serving**
* **High fibre**

Real Oatmeal Porridge

You can, of course make quick porridge with rolled oats, but this creamy concoction is far superior.

SERVES 4

1.2 litres/2 pts/5 cups water
150 g/5 oz/1¼ cups medium oatmeal
1.5 ml/¼ tsp salt
Skimmed milk and clear honey, to
serve

Bring the water to the boil in a heavy-based saucepan. Add the oatmeal in a steady stream, stirring all the time. Bring back to the boil, then turn the heat down as low as possible, cover and simmer very gently for 10 minutes, stirring occasionally. Add the salt, stir again, cover and simmer very gently for a further 10–15 minutes, stirring occasionally, until smooth and creamy. Spoon into bowls, add skimmed milk and drizzle a little honey over the surface.

* **190 calories per serving**
* **High fibre**

Cranberry Porridge

SERVES 2

50 g/2 oz/⅓ cup dried cranberries
300 ml/½ pt/1¼ cups water
40 g/1½ oz/⅓ cup porridge oats
Clear honey, to taste
Skimmed milk, to serve

Put the cranberries in a pan with the water and leave to soak overnight. In the morning, stir in the porridge oats. Bring to the boil, stirring, then reduce the heat and simmer for 3–5 minutes, stirring occasionally. Sweeten to taste with honey. Spoon into bowls and serve with a little skimmed milk poured over.

* 210 calories per serving
* High fibre

Raisin Porridge

SERVES 2

40 g/1½ oz/⅓ cup porridge oats
300 ml/½ pt/1¼ cups water
50 g/2 oz/⅓ cup raisins
Skimmed milk, to serve

Put the porridge in a pan with the water and stir in the raisins. Bring to the boil, reduce the heat and simmer for 3–5 minutes, stirring all the time. Spoon into bowls and serve with a little skimmed milk poured over.

* 210 calories per serving
* High fibre

Apricot Porridge

SERVES 2

40 g/1½ oz/⅓ cup porridge oats
300 ml/½ pt/1¼ cups water
50 g/2 oz/⅓ cup ready-to-eat dried
*   apricots, chopped*
Clear honey, to taste (optional)
Skimmed milk, to serve

Put the porridge in a pan with the water and stir in the apricots. Bring to the boil, reduce the heat and simmer for 3–5 minutes, stirring all the time. Spoon into bowls, drizzle with a little honey, if liked, and serve with skimmed milk poured over.

* 180 calories per serving
* High fibre

Sunshine Porridge

SERVES 2

15 ml/1 tbsp chopped hazelnuts
*   (filberts)*
25 g/1 oz/¼ cup rolled oats
15 ml/1 tbsp clear honey
150 ml/¼ pt/⅔ cup low-fat plain
*   yoghurt*
Finely grated rind and juice of
*   1 orange*
50 g/2 oz strawberries, sliced

Heat a non-stick frying pan (skillet). Add the nuts and oats and cook, stirring, until golden brown but do not allow to burn. Transfer to a bowl and leave to cool. Stir in the honey, yoghurt and orange rind and juice. Mix well. Spoon into serving bowls and top with sliced strawberries.

* 160 calories per serving
* High fibre

Apple Oat Bran Cereal

SERVES 8

225 g/8 oz/2 cups porridge oats
50 g/2 oz/¹/₃ cup raisins
50 g/2 oz/¹/₃ cup sultanas (golden raisins)
50 g/2 oz/1 cup bran flakes
60 ml/4 tbsp bran
50 g/2 oz dried apple rings, chopped
Skimmed milk, to serve

Spread out the porridge oats on a baking (cookie) sheet and lightly toast under a moderate grill (broiler) until golden, stirring frequently. Do not over-brown. Leave to cool. Mix with the remaining ingredients and store in an airtight container. Serve with skimmed milk poured over.

* **190 calories per serving**
* **High fibre**

Sweet Potato Crescents

You can use a large, drained can of sweet potatoes for speed. If you want to cook the crescents fresh in the morning, once shaped leave them in the fridge overnight to rise slowly.

MAKES 16

1 large sweet potato, peeled and diced
175 g/6 oz/1¹/₂ cups wholemeal flour
175 g/6 oz/1¹/₂ cups strong plain (bread) flour
25 g/1 oz/2 tbsp low-fat sunflower or olive oil spread
1 sachet of easy-blend dried yeast
25 g/1 oz/2 tbsp light brown sugar
1 large egg, beaten
175 ml/6 fl oz/³/₄ cup hand-hot water
Low-fat sunflower or olive oil spread, to serve

Cook the sweet potato in boiling, salted water until tender. Drain well. Turn into a food processor and purée until smooth. Add the flours, low-fat spread, yeast and sugar and run the machine until well mixed. Add the egg and, with the machine running, add enough of the hot water to form a soft but not too sticky dough. Run the machine for a further minute to knead the mixture. Turn the mixture into a lightly oiled plastic bag and leave in a warm place for 1 hour until doubled in size.

Re-knead the dough, then divide into eight equal pieces. Roll out each piece to a 15 cm/5 in square. Cut diagonally into halves to form triangles. Dampen with a little water. Starting at the long edge, roll up each triangle, then curve the points round to form crescents. Transfer to a non-stick baking (cookie) sheet, cover with lightly oiled clingfilm (plastic wrap) and leave in a warm place for about 20 minutes to rise.

Remove the clingfilm and bake in a preheated oven at 230°C/ 450°F/gas mark 8 for about 15 minutes until risen and golden and the bases sound hollow when tapped. Serve warm with a scraping of low-fat spread.

* **100 calories per crescent**
* **Fairly high fibre**

Crunchy Pecan Rolls

You can buy brown bread mix with sunflower seeds already in. If you use this, omit the sunflower seeds in the recipe.

MAKES 8

---

283 g/10¼ oz/1 packet of wholemeal bread mix
25 g/1 oz/2 tbsp low-fat sunflower or olive oil spread
50 g/2 oz/½ cup pecan nuts, roughly chopped
15 ml/1 tbsp sunflower seeds
175 ml/6 fl oz/¾ cup hand-hot water
Low-fat soft cheese, to serve

Empty the bread mix into a bowl and rub in the low-fat spread. Stir in the nuts and sunflower seeds and mix with the water to form a firm dough. Knead gently on a lightly floured surface for 5 minutes. Divide into eight pieces and shape into balls. Place well apart on a non-stick baking (cookie) sheet. Cover loosely with lightly oiled clingfilm (plastic wrap) and leave in a warm place for about 45 minutes until doubled in size.

Remove the clingfilm and bake in a preheated oven at 200°C/400°F/gas mark 6 for about 10–12 minutes until golden and the bases sound hollow when tapped. Serve warm or cold, split and spread with a scraping of low-fat soft cheese.

* 190 calories per roll
* High fibre

Pain Perdu

SERVES 4

---

2 eggs
30 ml/2 tbsp skimmed milk
Salt and freshly ground black pepper
5 ml/1 tsp clear honey
4 slices of bread, crusts removed
25 g/1 oz/2 tbsp low-fat sunflower or olive oil spread
100 g/4 oz fresh strawberries, sliced
15 ml/1 tbsp caster (superfine) sugar
15 ml/1 tbsp chopped mint

Beat the eggs with the milk, a little salt and pepper and the honey. Soak the bread slices in this. Fry (sauté) the soaked bread, a piece at a time, in a little of the low-fat spread in a non-stick frying pan (skillet) until golden on each side. Drain on kitchen paper (paper towels). Transfer to warm serving plates and top with the strawberry slices. Mix the sugar with the mint and scatter over. Serve straight away.

* 110 calories per serving
* Medium fibre

Hot Pepper Corn Buns

MAKES 8

50 g/2 oz/¹/₂ cup self-raising (self-rising) flour
2.5 ml/¹/₂ tsp salt
5 ml/1 tsp baking powder
50 g/2 oz/¹/₂ cup cornmeal
5 ml/1 tsp clear honey
120 ml/4 fl oz/¹/₂ cup skimmed milk
1 egg
1 jalapeño pepper, seeded and finely chopped
50 g/2 oz frozen sweetcorn (corn), thawed
50 g/2 oz/¹/₂ cup low-fat Cheddar cheese, grated
Freshly ground black pepper

Sift the flour, salt and baking powder into a bowl and stir in the cornmeal. Whisk together the honey, milk and egg and stir into the mixture. Add the chopped pepper, corn and cheese and a good grinding of black pepper. Mix well. Line eight sections of a muffin tin (pan) with paper cake cases (cupcake papers) and spoon in the sweetcorn mixture. Bake in a preheated oven at 230°C/450°F/gas mark 8 for 15 minutes until risen and golden brown. Serve warm or cold.

* **95 calories per bun**
* **High fibre**

Pan-cooked Seeded Soda Bread

MAKES 8 WEDGES

450 g/1 lb/4 cups plain (all-purpose) flour
225 g/8 oz/2 cups wholemeal flour
5 ml/1 tsp bicarbonate of soda (baking soda)
5 ml/1 tsp cream of tartar
5 ml/1 tsp salt
25 g/1 oz/2 tbsp low-fat sunflower or olive oil spread
300 ml/¹/₂ pt/1¹/₄ cups cultured buttermilk
30 ml/2 tbsp caraway seeds
Low-fat fromage frais and clear honey, to serve

Mix together the flours, soda, cream of tartar and salt in a bowl. Add the spread and rub in with the fingertips. Mix with the buttermilk and caraway seeds to form a soft but not sticky dough. Shape into a 20 cm/8 in diameter round and cut into eight wedges. Heat a non-stick, heavy-based frying pan (skillet) and add the wedges. Cook for about 15 minutes on each side until risen and golden and the bases sound hollow when tapped. Serve hot with a scraping of low-fat fromage frais and honey.

* **320 calories per wedge**
* **High fibre**

Multi-cereal Cottage Loaf Rolls

MAKES 6

225 g/8 oz/2 cups strong plain (bread) flour
75 g/3 oz/³/₄ cup wholemeal flour
75 g/3 oz/³/₄ cup barley or rye flour
50 g/2 oz/¹/₂ cup oat bran
2.5 ml/¹/₂ tsp salt
10 ml/2 tsp easy-blend dried yeast
15 g/¹/₂ oz/1 tbsp low-fat sunflower or olive oil spread
15 ml/1 tbsp clear honey
300 ml/¹/₂ pt/1¹/₄ cups hand-hot water
90 ml/6 tbsp low-fat fromage frais and cherry jam (conserve), to serve

Mix together the flours and bran in a bowl. Stir in the salt and yeast and rub in the low-fat spread. Blend together the honey and water and mix into the flour mixture to form a firm dough. Knead well on a lightly floured surface until smooth and elastic. Return to the bowl, cover with a damp cloth and leave in a warm place for about 1 hour until doubled in size.

Re-knead the dough, then divide into six equal pieces. Take a third off each piece and roll into a ball. Roll the larger pieces into balls. Place the larger pieces well apart on a floured non-stick baking (cookie) sheet. Top each with a smaller ball then, using a floured finger, plunge down through the small ball into the larger ball to form the traditional cottage loaf shape. Leave in a warm place for about 30 minutes until doubled in size.

Bake in a preheated oven at 230°C/450°F/gas mark 8 for about 15 minutes until risen, golden and the bases sound hollow when tapped. Cool on a wire rack. Serve warm or cold with the fromage frais and a little cherry jam.

* **300 calories per roll**
* **High fibre**

Almond Sultana Bread

MAKES 1 LOAF

450 g/1 lb/4 cups self-raising (self-rising) flour
5 ml/1 tsp salt
15 g/¹/₂ oz/1 tbsp low-fat sunflower or olive oil spread, plus extra to serve
75 g/3 oz/¹/₃ cup caster (superfine) sugar
100 g/4 oz/1 cup chopped almonds
75 g/3 oz/¹/₂ cup sultanas (golden raisins)
1 egg
300 ml/¹/₂ pt/1¹/₄ cups skimmed milk
Apricot jam (conserve), to serve

Sift the flour and salt into a bowl. Add the spread and rub in. Stir in the sugar, nuts and sultanas. Beat together the egg and milk and mix into the flour mixture to form a soft but not sticky dough. Knead gently on a lightly floured surface, shape into a loaf and place in a 900 g/2 lb loaf tin (pan), lined with non-stick baking parchment. Bake in a preheated oven at 200°C/400°F/ gas mark 6 for about 1 hour or until risen, golden and firm to the touch. Turn out on to a wire rack, remove the paper and leave to cool. Serve sliced with a scraping of low-fat spread and a little apricot jam.

* **220 calories per thick slice**
* **High fibre**

Apricot and Pecan Loaf

MAKES 1 LOAF

100 g/4 oz/1 cup self-raising (self-rising) wholemeal flour
350 g/12 oz/3 cups self-raising white flour
25 g/1 oz/2 tbsp low-fat sunflower or olive oil spread
45 ml/3 tbsp clear honey
75 g/3 oz/½ cup no-need-to-soak dried apricots, chopped
100 g/4 oz/1 cup pecan nuts, chopped
325 ml/11 fl oz/1⅓ cups skimmed milk
5 ml/1 tsp bicarbonate of soda (baking soda)
Low-fat sunflower or olive oil spread, to serve

Mix together the two flours in a large bowl. Rub in the sunflower spread, then stir in the honey, apricots and nuts. Mix a little of the milk with the bicarbonate of soda and add to the bowl with enough of the remaining milk to form a soft dough. Turn into a non-stick 900 g/2 lb loaf tin (pan), base-lined with non-stick baking parchment. Bake in a preheated oven at 200°C/400°F/gas mark 6 for 1 hour or until risen, golden and a skewer inserted into the centre comes out clean. Allow to cool slightly, then turn out on to a wire rack, remove the paper and leave to cool completely. Serve sliced with a scraping of low-fat spread.

* **250 calories per thick slice**
* **High fibre**

Country Cobs

MAKES ABOUT 16

225 g/8 oz/2 cups plain (all-purpose) flour
A pinch of salt
1.5 ml/¼ tsp baking powder
50 g/2 oz/¼ cup low-fat sunflower or olive oil spread, plus extra to serve
1 egg
Skimmed milk
Yeast extract, to serve

Sift the flour, salt and baking powder into a bowl. Rub in the low-fat spread. Beat the egg and add to the flour with enough milk to form a firm dough. Knead gently on a lightly floured surface. Roll out to 2 cm/¾ in thick and cut into rounds using a 5 cm/2 in biscuit (cookie) cutter. Transfer to a non-stick baking (cookie) sheet and bake in a preheated oven at 220°C/425°F/gas mark 7 for 10 minutes. Remove from the oven and, using oven-gloved hands, pull the rolls in half through the middle. Return the halves to the baking sheet, torn sides up, and bake for a further 10 minutes or until crisp and lightly golden. Transfer to a wire rack to cool. Store in an airtight container. Serve with a scraping of low-fat spread and yeast extract.

* **70 calories per piece**
* **Medium fibre**

English Muffins

To serve these freshly cooked for breakfast, after shaping and placing on the baking (cookie) sheet covered with clingfilm (plastic wrap), store in the fridge overnight ready to cook in the morning. When cooked, they also reheat well in a microwave, allowing about 20 seconds per muffin.

MAKES 6

100 g/4 oz/1 cup strong plain (bread) flour
75 g/3 oz/³/₄ cup plain (all-purpose) flour
10 ml/2 tsp easy-blend dried yeast
5 ml/1 tsp low-fat sunflower or olive oil spread, plus extra for greasing
60 ml/4 tbsp skimmed milk
About 60 ml/4 tbsp hand-hot water
Cornflour (cornstarch), for dusting
90 ml/6 tbsp low-fat fromage frais
60 ml/4 tbsp strawberry jam (conserve)

Sift the flours into a bowl and stir in the yeast. Heat the spread in the milk in a small saucepan. When hand-hot, stir into the flour mixture with enough of the hot water to form a very soft, sticky dough. Use a wooden spoon, then work with the hands until it is smooth and elastic (it should be too wet to knead). Cover the bowl with clingfilm (plastic wrap) and leave in a warm place for about 1 hour until the mixture has doubled in size. Knock back (punch down) to its original size, then divide into six equal pieces. Using hands dusted with cornflour, shape the mixture into balls and place on a non-stick baking (cookie) sheet, dusted with cornflour. Cover with clingfilm dusted with cornflour, and leave in a warm place for about 40 minutes to rise. Very lightly grease a heavy frying pan (skillet), or two if you want to cook all the muffins at once. Heat the pan over a moderate heat. Carefully transfer three muffins to the hot pan and cook gently for about 8 minutes on each side until pale golden. Allow to cool slightly on a wire rack. Split and spread each half lightly with the fromage frais and top with 5 ml/1 tsp jam.

* **250 calories per muffin**
* **Medium fibre**

Blueberry Breakfast Muffins

MAKES 16–18

300 ml/¹/₂ pt/1¹/₄ cups boiling water
75 g/3 oz/¹/₂ cup dried blueberries
40 g/1¹/₂ oz/3 tbsp low-fat sunflower or olive oil spread
60 ml/4 tbsp clear honey
225 g/8 oz/2 cups self-raising (self-rising) wholemeal flour
5 ml/1 tsp baking powder
Finely grated rind of ¹/₂ lemon
A pinch of grated nutmeg
1 egg, beaten

Mix the water with the blueberries and low-fat spread and leave to soak until the mixture is just warm. Stir in the remaining ingredients. Turn into the sections of tartlet tins (patty pans) lined with paper cake cases (cupcake papers) and bake in a preheated oven at 180°C/350°F/gas mark 4 for about 20 minutes until risen and the centres spring back when pressed. Transfer to a wire rack to cool. Store in an airtight container. Serve warm or cold.

* **150 calories per muffin**
* **High fibre**

Carroty Yoghurt Muffins

MAKES 16

2 large carrots, grated
90 ml/6 tbsp clear honey
100 g/4 oz/1 cup wholemeal flour
225 g/8 oz/2 cups oat bran
5 ml/1 tsp baking powder
2.5 ml/½ tsp bicarbonate of soda
(baking soda)
50 g/2 oz/½ cup walnuts, finely
chopped
75 g/3 oz/½ cup raisins
2.5 ml/½ tsp mixed (apple-pie) spice
30 ml/2 tbsp melted low-fat sunflower
or olive oil spread
120 ml/4 fl oz/½ cup low-fat plain
yoghurt
250 ml/8 fl oz/1 cup skimmed milk
2 egg whites

Line 16 tartlet tin (patty pan) sections with paper cake cases (cupcake papers). Mix together all the ingredients thoroughly. Spoon into the cases and bake in a preheated oven at 200°C/400°F/ gas mark 6 for about 20 minutes until risen and the centres spring back when pressed. Cool on a wire rack.

* **180 calories per muffin**
* **High fibre**

Raisin and Cinnamon Breakfast Muffins

MAKES 16

300 ml/½ pt/1¼ cups hot black tea
100 g/4 oz/⅔ cup raisins
40 g/1½ oz/3 tbsp low-fat sunflower
or olive oil spread
30 ml/2 tbsp clear honey
175 g/6 oz/1½ cups self-raising (self-
rising) wholemeal flour
5 ml/1 tsp baking powder
2.5 ml/½ tsp ground cinnamon
1 egg, beaten

Mix the tea with the raisins and low-fat spread and leave to soak until the mixture is just warm. Stir in the remaining ingredients. Turn into 16 tartlet tin (patty pan) sections, lined with paper cake cases (cupcake papers) and bake in a preheated oven at 180°C/ 350°F/gas mark 4 for about 20 minutes until risen and the centres spring back when pressed. Transfer to a wire rack to cool. Store in an airtight container. Serve warm or cold.

* **200 calories per muffin**
* **High fibre**

Carob Morning Rolls

MAKES 12

450 g/1 lb/4 cups strong plain (bread) flour
5 ml/1 tsp salt
A good pinch of ground cinnamon
15 g/½ oz/1 tbsp low-fat sunflower or olive oil spread
10 ml/2 tsp easy-blend dried yeast
1 egg, beaten
10 ml/2 tsp clear honey
300 ml/½ pt/1¼ cups hand-hot skimmed milk
50 g/2 oz/½ cup carob chips
Icing (confectioners') sugar, for dusting

Sift the flour, salt and cinnamon into a bowl and rub in the low-fat spread. Add the yeast and mix well. Reserve a little of the egg to glaze, then mix in the remaining egg, the honey and enough of the milk to form a firm dough. Knead gently on a lightly floured surface for about 4 minutes until smooth and elastic. Return to the bowl, cover with a damp tea towel (dish cloth) and leave in a warm place for 45 minutes until doubled in size. Re-knead the dough and knead in the carob chips. Shape into 12 rolls and place well apart on a non-stick baking (cookie) sheet. Leave to rise again for 15 minutes. Brush with the reserved egg to glaze. Bake in a preheated oven at 220°C/425°F/gas mark 7 for about 12–15 minutes until risen, golden and the bases sound hollow when tapped. Dust with a little sifted icing sugar and cool on a wire rack.

* **135 calories per roll**
* **Medium fibre**

Scottish Oatcakes

MAKES ABOUT 12

175 g/6 oz/1½ cups medium oatmeal
100 g/4 oz/1 cup plain (all-purpose) flour
1.5 ml/¼ tsp salt
15 ml/1 tbsp caster (superfine) sugar
25 g/1 oz/2 tbsp low-fat sunflower or olive oil spread, melted, plus extra to serve
1 egg, beaten
Jam (conserve) or marmalade, to serve

Mix together the oatmeal, flour, salt and sugar in a bowl. Stir in the melted low-fat spread and the egg and mix to form a soft but not sticky dough, adding a little water if necessary. Knead gently on a lightly floured surface. Roll out and cut into 5 cm/2 in rounds, using a biscuit (cookie) cutter. Transfer to a non-stick baking (cookie) sheet and bake in a preheated oven at 180°C/350°F/ gas mark 4 for 12–15 minutes until crisp. Leave to cool, then store in an airtight container. Serve with a scraping of low-fat spread and a little jam or marmalade.

* **110 calories per oatcake**
* **High fibre**

Malted Breakfast Loaf

MAKES 1 LOAF

175 g/6 oz/1½ cups self-raising (self-rising) flour
7.5 ml/1½ tsp baking powder
2.5 ml/½ tsp bicarbonate of soda (baking soda)
75 g/3 oz/¾ cup any muesli (page 18 or use bought)
50 g/2 oz/⅓ cup sultanas (golden raisins)
20 ml/1½ tbsp black treacle (molasses)
15 ml/1 tbsp golden (light corn) syrup
45 ml/3 tbsp low-fat malted milk powder or granules
25 g/1 oz/2 tbsp low-fat sunflower or olive oil spread
175 ml/6 fl oz/¾ cup skimmed milk

Wet a 450 g/1 lb loaf tin (pan) and line with non-stick baking parchment. Mix together the flour, baking powder, bicarbonate of soda, muesli and sultanas in a bowl. Warm the remaining ingredients together until the low-fat spread melts. Pour into the dry ingredients and mix well. Turn into the prepared tin and bake in a preheated oven at 160°C/325°F/gas mark 3 for about 45 minutes or until risen, golden and just firm. Allow to cool in the tin for about 10 minutes, then remove from the tin, peel away the paper and cool on a wire rack.

* **135 calories per thick slice**
* **High fibre**

Chocolate Malted Breakfast Loaf

MAKES 1 LOAF

Prepare as for Malted Breakfast Loaf, but substitute low-fat chocolate malted milk powder or granules for plain.

* **135 calories per thick slice**
* **High fibre**

Banana and Chocolate Malted Breakfast Loaf

MAKES 1 LOAF

Prepare as for Chocolate Malted Breakfast Loaf, but substitute crushed dried banana slices for the sultanas.

* **140 calories per thick slice**
* **High fibre**

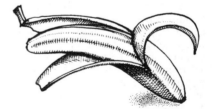

Salmon Kedgeree

SERVES 4

175 g/6 oz/³/₄ cup brown long-grain
  rice
50 g/2 oz frozen peas
175 g/6 oz salmon tail fillet, skinned
5 ml/1 tsp curry powder
60 ml/4 tbsp skimmed milk
30 ml/2 tbsp chopped parsley
A pinch of salt
Freshly ground black pepper
2 tomatoes, cut into neat chunks
5 ml/1 tsp lemon juice
Lemon wedges, to garnish

Cook the rice in plenty of boiling water for about 30 minutes or until tender, adding the peas for the last 5 minutes. Drain and return to the pan. Meanwhile, dust the fish with the curry powder and place in a shallow pan with the milk. Cover and cook gently for 6–8 minutes until just tender and the fish flakes easily with a fork. Break the fish into neat pieces. Add the fish and its cooking liquid to the cooked rice with half the parsley, the salt and lots of pepper, the tomatoes and lemon juice. Toss over a gentle heat until piping hot. Pile on to hot plates, sprinkle with the remaining parsley and garnish with lemon wedges before serving.

* **260 calories per serving**
* **High fibre**

White Fish Kedgeree

SERVES 4

175 g/6 oz/³/₄ cup long-grain rice
750 ml/1¼ pts/3 cups water
225 g/8 oz white fish fillet, skinned
  and boned
50 g/2 oz frozen peas
2.5 ml/½ tsp ground cumin
1.5 ml/¼ tsp grated nutmeg
Salt and freshly ground black pepper
30 ml/2 tbsp chopped parsley
30 ml/2 tbsp skimmed milk
Lemon wedges and parsley sprigs, to
  garnish

Put the rice in a large saucepan with the water. Bring to the boil and stir once. Cook for 10 minutes, then add the fish and peas. Re-cover tightly, reduce the heat and cook gently for 10 minutes until the rice is tender and has absorbed the liquid. Add the remaining ingredients and toss gently to break up the fish. Pile on to warm plates and garnish with lemon wedges and parsley sprigs.

* **215 calories per serving**
* **Medium fibre**

Tuna Kedgeree

SERVES 4

Prepare as for White Fish Kedgeree but substitute 185 g/ 6½ oz/1 small can of tuna in brine or water, drained, for the white fish fillet. Add to the mixture with the seasonings after the rice and peas are cooked, then toss to heat through.

* **210 calories per serving**
* **Medium fibre**

Haddock and Eggs

SERVES 4

4 small undyed smoked haddock tails,
*   about 100 g/4 oz each*
½ small bay leaf
10 ml/2 tsp lemon juice
4 eggs
2 slices of wholemeal bread

Put the fish in a large frying pan (skillet) with the bay leaf and just cover with water. Bring to the boil, cover with a lid or foil, reduce the heat and cook for 5 minutes or until the fish flakes easily with a fork. Meanwhile, put about 2.5 cm /1 in water in a second frying pan with the lemon juice. Bring to the boil, reduce the heat, then gently slide in the eggs and poach until cooked to your liking – about 3 minutes for firm whites and soft yolks. Toast the bread and cut into triangles. Lift the fish out of the water with a fish slice and transfer to warm plates. Top each with a poached egg and put two triangles of toast on the side of each plate.

* 200 calories per serving
* Medium fibre

Jugged Kippers

SERVES 2

2 kippers
Lemon wedges, to garnish
2 thin slices of brown bread with a
*   scraping of low-fat sunflower or*
*   olive oil spread*

Put the kippers in a jug, tails up, and top up with boiling water. Cover and leave to stand for 5 minutes. Drain, transfer to two plates, garnish with lemon wedges and serve each with a slice of brown bread.

* 280 calories per serving
* Medium fibre

Scotch Woodcock

SERVES 2

8 canned anchovy fillets
15 g/½ oz/1 tbsp low-fat sunflower or
*   olive oil spread*
2 eggs
2 egg whites
30 ml/2 tbsp skimmed milk
Freshly ground black pepper
15 ml/1 tbsp chopped parsley
2 slices of bread
5 ml/1 tsp capers
4 tomatoes, sliced

Rinse the anchovy fillets under cold water and dry on kitchen paper (paper towels). Melt the low-fat spread in a saucepan. Remove from the heat and whisk in the eggs, egg whites, milk and a little pepper. Add the parsley. Cook over a gentle heat, stirring all the time, until scrambled but still creamy. Do not allow to boil. Meanwhile, chop four of the anchovies. Toast the bread and place on two warm plates. Stir the chopped anchovies into the scrambled egg. Spoon on top of the toast and garnish each with two anchovy fillets in a cross and a few capers. Arrange tomato slices round the toast and serve.

* 215 calories per serving
* Medium fibre

Egg and Mushroom Cases

SERVES 2

2 large open mushrooms
10 ml/2 tsp lemon juice
2 small eggs
1 English muffin (home-made, page
*   25, or use bought)*
10 ml/2 tsp chopped parsley

Peel the mushrooms and place in a small frying pan (skillet) with 90 ml/6 tbsp water. Cover and simmer gently until the mushrooms are tender. Meanwhile, put about 2.5 cm/1 in water in a second frying pan with the lemon juice. Bring to the boil, then reduce the heat to a simmer. Gently slide in the eggs and poach until cooked to your liking – about 3 minutes for firm whites and soft yolks. Meanwhile, halve and toast the muffin. Place each half on a plate. Spoon the mushroom juices over, then lay a mushroom on each muffin half. Carefully lift out the eggs with a fish slice and place one in each mushroom. Sprinkle with the parsley and serve.

* **160 calories per serving**

* **Medium fibre**

Egg and Tomato Muffins

SERVES 4

2 English muffins (home-made, page
*   25, or use bought)*
Low-fat sunflower or olive oil spread
1 beefsteak tomato, cut into 4 thick
*   slices*
4 eggs
5 ml/1 tsp lemon juice
15 ml/1 tbsp snipped chives

Halve the muffins, toast under a preheated grill (broiler) and spread with a thin scraping of low-fat spread. Place a tomato slice on each half and return to the grill until hot through. Meanwhile, put about 2.5 cm/1 in water in a frying pan (skillet) with the lemon juice and bring to the boil. Reduce the heat to a simmer, then gently slide in the eggs. Poach until cooked to your liking – about 3 minutes for firm whites and soft yolks. Transfer the muffins to warm plates. Carefully lift out the eggs with a fish slice and slide on top of the tomatoes. Sprinkle with the chives and serve.

* **160 calories per serving**

* **Medium fibre**

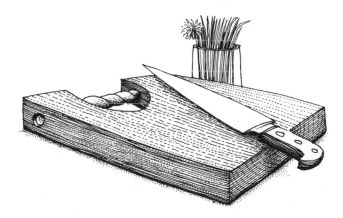

American Hash Browns

SERVES 4

1 large onion, finely chopped
25 g/1 oz/2 tbsp low-fat sunflower or
olive oil spread
4 large floury potatoes, cooked and
diced
2.5 ml/½ tsp ground cumin
2.5 ml/½ tsp paprika
Salt and freshly ground black pepper
Grilled (broiled) tomatoes and brown
table sauce, to serve

Fry (sauté) the onion in the low-fat spread in a non-stick frying pan (skillet) for 3 minutes to soften. Add the cooked potato, the spices and a little salt and pepper. Fry over a high heat, pressing and stirring with a fish slice, until golden brown and the potato is becoming mushy. Spoon on to warm plates and serve with grilled tomatoes and brown table sauce.

* **250 calories per serving**
* **Fairly low fibre**

Potato and Bacon Cakes

MAKES 12

450 g/1 lb potatoes
25 g/1 oz/2 tbsp low-fat sunflower or
olive oil spread
50 g/2 oz/½ cup wholemeal flour
2 rashers (slices) rindless, extra-lean,
unsmoked back bacon, diced
15 ml/1 tbsp snipped chives
15 ml/1 tbsp caraway seeds
3 tomatoes, each cut into four slices

Peel the potatoes and cut into even-sized pieces. Boil in water until tender. Drain and mash with the low-fat spread, then beat in the flour. Meanwhile, dry-fry the bacon in a non-stick frying pan (skillet) until cooked through. Remove from the pan and drain on kitchen paper (paper towels). Add to the potato mixture with the chives and mix well. Wipe out the pan to clean it thoroughly. Shape into 12 cakes and flatten slightly, pressing a few caraway seeds into the surface of each. Heat the frying pan thoroughly, then cook the rounds for 3 minutes on each side until golden brown and slightly puffy. Meanwhile, place the tomato slices on a flameproof plate and warm briefly under the grill (broiler). Top each potato cake with a slice of tomato before serving.

* **75 calories per cake**
* **Fairly high fibre**

Onion Potato Cakes

MAKES 12

450 g/1 lb/2 cups cooked mashed potato
50 g/2 oz/¹/₄ cup low-fat sunflower or olive oil spread
1 onion, grated
50 g/2 oz/¹/₂ cup wholemeal flour
Salt and freshly ground black pepper

Beat the potato well and work in all but 15 g/¹/₂ oz/1 tbsp of the low-fat spread, the onion and the flour, seasoning with salt and pepper. Turn the dough out on to a lightly floured surface. Pat out to a round about 1 cm/¹/₂ in thick, then cut into rounds using a 7.5 cm/3 in biscuit (cookie) cutter. Re-knead the trimmings and cut again. Heat a heavy non-stick frying pan (skillet) and cook for about 3 minutes on each side until golden brown. Spread the top of each very lightly with the remaining low-fat spread and serve.

* **75 calories per cake**
* **Fairly high fibre**

Bacon and Sun-dried Tomato Scones

MAKES 12

50 g/2 oz sun-dried tomatoes, soaked in hot water then drained
3 rashers (slices) rindless lean smoked streaky bacon
225 g/8 oz/2 cups self-raising (self-rising) flour
5 ml/1 tsp baking powder
5 ml/1 tsp mustard powder
7.5 ml/1¹/₂ tsp paprika
A good pinch of salt
2.5 ml/¹/₂ tsp dried thyme
25 g/1 oz/2 tbsp low-fat sunflower or olive oil spread, plus extra to serve
120 ml/4 fl oz/¹/₂ cup skimmed milk

Chop the sun-dried tomatoes. Grill (broil) the bacon until really crisp, drain on kitchen paper (paper towels), then snip into small pieces. Sift the flour, baking powder, mustard, paprika and salt into a bowl and stir in the thyme. Rub in the low-fat spread, then add the tomatoes and bacon. Mix with enough of the skimmed milk to form a soft but not sticky dough. Knead gently on a lightly floured surface. Roll out and cut into 12 rounds using a 5 cm/2 in biscuit (cookie) cutter. Transfer to a non-stick baking (cookie) sheet. Brush with a little more milk to glaze and bake in a preheated oven at 200°C/400°F/gas mark 6 for about 15 minutes until well risen, golden and the bases sound hollow when tapped. Serve the scones (biscuits) warm, split with a scraping of low-fat spread.

* **100 calories per scone**
* **Medium fibre**

Herby Mushrooms on Toast

SERVES 2

100 g/4 oz button mushrooms
30 ml/2 tbsp water
Freshly ground black pepper
A pinch of paprika
15 ml/1 tbsp chopped parsley
15 ml/1 tbsp snipped chives
2 slices of wholemeal bread
10 g/¼ oz/2 tsp low-fat sunflower or olive oil spread

Wipe the mushrooms to remove any dirt and trim the bases of the stalks, if necessary. Place in a saucepan with the water, a good grinding of pepper, the paprika and half the herbs. Bring to the boil, cover with a lid and simmer gently for 5 minutes, stirring or shaking the pan occasionally. Remove the lid and boil rapidly, if necessary, to evaporate any remaining liquid. Meanwhile, toast the bread and spread with the low-fat spread. Place on warm plates, top with the mushrooms, sprinkle with the remaining herbs and serve.

* **110 calories per serving**
* **Fairly high fibre**

Baked Eggs in Tomatoes

SERVES 4

4 beefsteak tomatoes
Salt and freshly ground black pepper
1 spring onion (scallion), very finely chopped
4 eggs
20 ml/4 tsp low-fat crème fraîche
20 ml/4 tsp grated low-fat Cheddar cheese
4 thin slices of bread
Low-fat sunflower or olive oil spread and yeast extract, to serve

Cut a slice off the top of each tomato on the rounded side and scoop out the seeds. Sprinkle with salt on the insides, turn upside-down and drain for 30 minutes on kitchen paper (paper towels). Transfer to individual shallow ovenproof dishes. Season the insides with pepper and add the chopped spring onion. Carefully break an egg into each tomato. Spoon over the crème fraîche and season again. Sprinkle with the cheese. Bake in a preheated oven at 180°C/350°F/ gas mark 4 for 15–20 minutes until just set. Meanwhile, toast the bread and spread very thinly with low-fat spread and yeast extract. Cut into fingers and arrange beside the tomatoes to serve.

* **220 calories per serving**
* **Medium fibre**

The Lean English Breakfast

SERVES 4

4 rashers (slices) rindless extra-lean
back bacon
2 tomatoes, halved
Freshly ground black pepper
25 g/1 oz/2 tbsp low-fat sunflower or
olive oil spread
2 slices of bread
100 g/4 oz button mushrooms
30 ml/2 tbsp water
2 whole eggs
4 egg whites
45 ml/3 tbsp skimmed milk
A pinch of salt

Put the bacon and tomato halves under the grill (broiler) and sprinkle the tomatoes with pepper. Spread half the low-fat spread on both sides of the bread and cut into halves. Lay them on the grill rack. Grill (broil) until cooked to your liking, turning once. Remove the foods as they are cooked and keep warm. Meanwhile, put the mushrooms in a saucepan with the water and season with pepper. Cover and cook gently for 5 minutes until tender. Melt the remaining low-fat spread in a non-stick saucepan. Whisk in the eggs and egg whites with the milk and salt and a good grinding of pepper. Cook over a gentle heat, stirring all the time, until scrambled. Do not allow to boil. Serve all together on warm plates.

* **190 calories per serving**
* **Fairly low fibre**

Baked Mushroom-stuffed Tomatoes

Prepare the night before, then just cook before breakfast.

SERVES 4

4 beefsteak tomatoes
100 g/4 oz mushrooms
1 slice of wholemeal bread
1 large sprig of parsley
10 ml/2 tsp Worcestershire sauce
1 egg
Freshly ground black pepper
30 ml/2 tbsp water
Small sprigs of parsley, to garnish

Cut a slice off the rounded end of each tomato and reserve. Scoop the seeds out into the bowl of a food processor or blender goblet. Run the machine and gradually drop in the mushrooms, bread and parsley until finely chopped. Stir in the Worcestershire sauce, the egg and a good grinding of pepper. Stand the tomato shells in a baking tin (pan). Spoon the stuffing inside and top with the 'lids'. Add the water to the tin. Bake in a preheated oven at 190°C/375°F/gas mark 5 for 20–25 minutes until tender but still holding their shape. Serve straight away, garnished with small sprigs of parsley.

* **100 calories per serving**
* **Medium fibre**

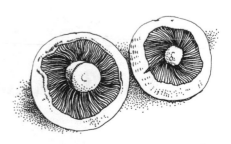

Devilled Kidneys

SERVES 4

8 lambs' kidneys
15 g/¹/₂ oz/1 tbsp low-fat sunflower or
*   olive oil spread*
5 ml/1 tsp mustard powder
5 ml/1 tsp curry powder
10 ml/2 tsp tomato ketchup (catsup)
10 ml/2 tsp Worcestershire sauce
30 ml/2 tbsp water
Chopped parsley, to garnish
4 slices of wholemeal toast, cut into
*   triangles, to serve*

Remove any skin from the kidneys, snip out the central cores with scissors and discard. Snip the kidneys into quarters. Heat the low-fat spread in a saucepan and brown the kidneys for 2 minutes. Stir in the mustard and curry powder and cook for 1 minute, stirring. Stir in the ketchup, Worcestershire sauce and water. Simmer for 2 minutes, stirring, until the kidneys are tender. Spoon into warm bowls, sprinkle with parsley and arrange the toast triangles round the edge.

* **200 calories per serving**
* **Fairly high fibre**

Devilled Mushrooms

SERVES 4

1 large onion, finely chopped
15 g/¹/₂ oz/1 tbsp low-fat sunflower or
*   olive oil spread*
350 g/12 oz button mushrooms
4 tomatoes, skinned and chopped
20 ml/1¹/₂ tbsp tomato ketchup
*   (catsup)*
20 ml/1¹/₂ tbsp Worcestershire sauce
A few drops of Tabasco sauce
4 slices of wholemeal toast and a little
*   chopped parsley, to serve*

Cook the onion in the low-fat spread for 3 minutes, stirring, until softened and slightly browned. Add the mushrooms and tomatoes and cook, stirring, for 2 minutes. Add the remaining ingredients, cover and cook for about 7 minutes, stirring once or twice, until the mushrooms are just cooked. Pile on to wholemeal toast, sprinkle with chopped parsley and serve.

* **150 calories per serving**
* **Medium fibre**

Tomatoes and Basil on Toast

SERVES 4

4 slices of granary bread
45 ml/3 tbsp low-fat soft cheese
4 ripe beefsteak tomatoes, sliced
Freshly ground black pepper
12 basil leaves, torn into small pieces

Toast the bread on one side only. Turn over and spread the soft side with the cheese. Top with the tomato slices, a good grinding of pepper and the torn basil leaves. Grill (broil) until the tomatoes are hot, then serve straight away.

* **140 calories per serving**
* **Fairly high fibre**

Potato and Sausage Stir-fry

SERVES 4

8 extra-lean pork chipolata sausages
10 g/¹/₄ oz/2 tsp low-fat sunflower or olive oil spread
450 g/1 lb cooked new potatoes, cut into walnut-sized pieces, if necessary
A good pinch of dried mixed herbs
Freshly ground black pepper
Brown table sauce, to serve

Cut each sausage into four pieces. Heat the low-fat spread in a non-stick frying pan (skillet) and fry (sauté) the sausages for 5 minutes, stirring, until brown all over. Add the potatoes, the herbs and a good grinding of pepper and continue to stir-fry until piping hot and golden brown. Pile on to warm plates and serve with brown table sauce.

* **220 calories per serving**
* **Low fibre**

Savoury Chicken Liver Toasts

SERVES 4

200 g/7 oz/scant 2 cups chicken livers, thawed if frozen
10 g/¹/₄ oz/2 tsp low-fat sunflower or olive oil spread
5 ml/1 tsp chopped sage
15 ml/1 tbsp chopped parsley, plus extra to garnish
5 ml/1 tsp Worcestershire sauce
A pinch of salt
Freshly ground black pepper
4 slices of granary bread, toasted

Trim any membranes from the livers and cut into bite-sized pieces. Melt the low-fat spread in a non-stick saucepan. Add the livers and toss over a gentle heat for 4–5 minutes until tender and just cooked. Do not overcook. Stir in the herbs, Worcestershire sauce, salt and lots of pepper. Pile on to the toast and sprinkle with a little extra chopped parsley before serving.

* **160 calories per serving**
* **Fairly high fibre**

Baked Bean Soufflé Omelette

SERVES 2

1 egg
Salt and freshly ground black pepper
3 egg whites
10 g/¼ oz/2 tsp low-fat sunflower or olive oil spread
225 g/8 oz/1 small can of baked beans

Beat the whole egg with a little salt and pepper until blended. Whisk the egg whites until stiff, then fold into the beaten egg with a metal spoon. Heat the low-fat spread until sizzling in a non-stick omelette pan. Add the egg mixture and cook until the base is set and golden brown. Slide out on to a plate. Add the beans to the pan and heat through, stirring with a wooden spoon. Carefully invert the omelette on top and cook for 3 minutes more until set. Cut in half and serve on warm plates.

* **160 calories per serving**
* **High fibre**

Mushroom Soufflé Omelette

SERVES 2

75 g/3 oz button mushrooms, sliced
30 ml/2 tbsp water
1 egg
Salt and freshly ground black pepper
3 egg whites
10 g/¼ oz/2 tsp low-fat sunflower or olive oil spread

Put the mushrooms in a saucepan with the water. Cover and cook for 3–4 minutes until soft. Meanwhile, beat the whole egg with a little salt and pepper until blended. Whisk the egg whites until stiff, then fold into the beaten egg with a metal spoon. Heat the low-fat spread in a non-stick omelette pan. Add the egg mixture and cook until the base is set and golden brown. Scatter the mushrooms over. Place under a hot grill (broiler) until fluffy and golden. Cut in half and serve straight away.

* **85 calories per serving**
* **Low fibre**

Tomato Soufflé Omelette

SERVES 2

1 egg
Salt and freshly ground black pepper
3 egg whites
10 g/¼ oz/2 tsp low-fat sunflower or olive oil spread
2 ripe tomatoes, sliced
6 basil leaves, chopped

Beat the whole egg with a little salt and pepper until blended. Whisk the egg whites until stiff, then fold into the beaten egg with a metal spoon. Heat the low-fat spread in a non-stick omelette pan. Add the egg mixture and cook for about 3 minutes until the underside is set and golden. Lay the tomato slices on top and place under a preheated grill (broiler) until puffy and golden brown. Scatter the basil leaves over, cut in half and serve straight away.

* **100 calories per serving**
* **Fairly low fibre**

Piperade

SERVES 4

*15 g/½ oz/1 tbsp low-fat sunflower or
  olive oil spread*
1 green (bell) pepper, sliced
1 red pepper, sliced
1 onion, thinly sliced
4 large ripe tomatoes, roughly diced
3 eggs
30 ml/2 tbsp skimmed milk
Salt and freshly ground black pepper
Wholemeal toast, to serve

Heat the low-fat spread in a non-stick frying pan (skillet). Add the peppers and onion and fry (sauté) for 5 minutes, stirring, until tender. Add the tomato and cook for a further 2 minutes. Beat the eggs and milk with a little salt and pepper and add to the pan. Cook, stirring gently, over a gentle heat until the egg is lightly scrambled. Serve straight from the pan with wholemeal toast.

* **140 calories per serving**
* **Fairly high fibre**

Fluffy Steak and Eggs

SERVES 4

*175 g/6 oz fillet steak, cut into very
  thin strips*
*15 g/½ oz/1 tbsp low-fat sunflower or
  olive oil spread*
2 eggs
15 ml/1 tbsp milk
4 egg whites
Salt and freshly ground black pepper
4 slices of granary bread
*15 ml/1 tbsp chopped parsley, to
  garnish*

Fry (sauté) the steak in the low-fat spread for 3 minutes, stirring, until browned. Beat the whole eggs with the milk. Whisk the egg whites until stiff, then fold into the beaten eggs with a metal spoon. Add to the steak with a little salt and pepper and cook over a gentle heat, stirring, until lightly scrambled. Meanwhile, toast the bread on both sides. Pile the mixture on to the bread and sprinkle with parsley before serving.

* **220 calories per serving**
* **Medium fibre**

Macedonian Fruits

Ideally, prepare the night before and chill in a plastic container with a lid.

SERVES 4

2 nectarines, sliced
1 ripe galia melon, scooped into balls or diced
100 g/4 oz strawberries, sliced
100 g/4 oz raspberries
Pure pineapple juice, chilled
Low-fat plain yoghurt, to serve

Layer the fruits in a glass dish. Pour over just enough pineapple juice to cover the fruit. Serve very cold, topped with a dollop of plain yoghurt.

* **85 calories per serving**
* **Medium fibre**

Tropical Compôte

SERVES 6

45 ml/3 tbsp clear honey
150 ml/¹/₄ pt/²/₃ cup water
2 pomegranates
1 passion fruit
2 oranges
1 mango
2 kiwi fruit
1 small pineapple

Put the honey and water in a saucepan. Bring to the boil and boil for 2 minutes. Meanwhile, halve the pomegranates and passion fruit and squeeze out the juice as you would for a lemon. Strain the juice into the syrup. Holding the oranges over the saucepan to catch the juice, cut off all the rind and pith, then slice and halve the slices. Peel the mango and cut all the flesh off the stone (pit) in long strips. Halve if very big and add to the syrup. Peel and slice the kiwi fruit and add to the syrup. Cut all the skin off the pineapple, slice the fruit, then cut into chunks, discarding any hard core. Mix all together and leave until cold. Chill overnight.

* **100 calories per serving**
* **Medium fibre**

Hot Winter Morning Fruit

SERVES 4

75 g/3 oz/¹/₂ cup dried figs
50 g/2 oz/¹/₃ cup dried dates, stoned (pitted)
450 ml/³/₄ pt/2 cups apple juice
1 large red eating (dessert) apple, quartered and sliced
1 large green eating apple, quartered and sliced
3 bananas, thickly sliced
15 ml/1 tbsp lemon juice
3 clementines, segmented
2 pieces of stem ginger in syrup, chopped
15 ml/1 tbsp ginger syrup from the jar

Soak the figs and dates in the apple juice for at least 6 hours or overnight. Place in a saucepan, bring to the boil and simmer gently for 5 minutes. Toss the apple and banana slices in the lemon juice and add to the pan with the remaining ingredients. Bring to the boil again and simmer for 3 minutes. Serve hot.

* **235 calories per serving**
* **High fibre**

Breakfast in a Glass

SERVES 1

1 ripe banana
100 ml/3½ fl oz/scant ½ cup skimmed
    milk
125 g/4½ oz/1 small pot of low-fat
    vanilla yoghurt
15 ml/1 tbsp oat bran

Peel the banana, break into small pieces and place in a blender or food processor. Add a little of the milk and process until smooth. Add the remaining milk, the yoghurt and bran and run the machine until smooth. Pour into a glass and serve.

* 190 calories
* High fibre

Mango Smoothie

SERVES 2

1 small ripe mango
1 banana
120 ml/4 fl oz/1 cup pineapple juice
170 g/6½ oz/1 small can of low-fat
    evaporated milk, well chilled
Lemon juice, to taste

Peel the mango, cut all the flesh off the stone (pit) and place in a blender or food processor. Peel the banana, break into pieces and add to the mango. Add half the pineapple juice and purée until smooth. Blend in the remaining juice. Meanwhile, whisk the evaporated milk until thick and doubled in volume. Whisk in the fruit mixture, add lemon juice to taste, then pour into glasses and serve.

* 150 calories per glass
* Medium fibre

Berry Yoghurt Shake

SERVES 1

75 g/3 oz ripe strawberries
75 g/3 oz raspberries
75 ml/5 tbsp thick low-fat plain
    yoghurt
150 ml/¼ pt/⅔ cup ice-cold skimmed
    milk
Clear honey, to taste (optional)

Purée the strawberries and raspberries in a blender or food processor. Add the yoghurt and milk and run the machine until frothy. Sweeten, if liked, with honey. Pour into a glass and serve.

* 120 calories
* Medium fibre

Nectarine and Banana Yoghurt Shake

SERVES 1

1 ripe nectarine, peeled and stoned
    (pitted)
1 small ripe banana
75 ml/5 tbsp thick low-fat plain
    yoghurt
150 ml/¼ pt/⅔ cup ice-cold skimmed
    milk

Chop the fruit and purée in a blender or food processor. Add the yoghurt and milk and run the machine until frothy. Pour into a glass and serve.

* 200 calories
* Fairly high fibre

Peach and Prune Yoghurt Shake

SERVES 1

1 ripe peach, peeled and stoned
 (pitted)
4 ready-to-eat prunes, stoned
75 ml/5 tbsp thick low-fat plain
 yoghurt
150 ml/¹/₄ pt/²/₃ cup ice-cold skimmed
 milk

Chop the peach and purée with the prunes in a blender or food processor. Add the yoghurt and milk and run the machine until frothy. Pour into a glass and serve.

* **190 calories**
* **Fairly high fibre**

Tomato Wakener

SERVES 1

3 ripe tomatoes, quartered
60 ml/4 tbsp pure orange juice
A good pinch of chilli powder
A dash of reduced-salt soy sauce
Freshly ground black pepper
30 ml/2 tbsp low-fat fromage frais
Ice cubes, to serve

Purée the tomatoes in a blender or food processor. Add the remaining ingredients and blend again. Pour over ice cubes in a tall glass and drink straight away.

* **105 calories**
* **Low fibre**

Soups

Soups make wonderful, nutritious, easy-to-eat and filling meals when served with some crusty bread. They can, of course, also double as starters before a light main course.

Stock Pot

Use this as a substitute for any recipe that calls for vegetable stock made with stock cubes.

MAKES ABOUT 1.2 LITRES/2 PTS/5 CUPS

1.2 litres/2 pts/5 cups water, plus extra
as needed
1 bouquet garni sachet
Scrubbed thickish peel from 6 potatoes
1 large carrot, scrubbed and roughly
chopped
1 celery stick, roughly chopped
1 large onion, quartered
1 turnip or a small piece of swede
(rutabaga), roughly chopped
A pinch of salt
Freshly ground black pepper

Put all the ingredients in a large saucepan. Bring to the boil, reduce the heat, cover and simmer for 1½ hours, topping up with water as necessary to keep the vegetables covered. Strain into a clean airtight container and allow to cool. Store in the fridge for up to four days, or freeze (preferably in two or four containers) to use as required.

* **10 calories per serving**
* **No fibre**

Potch Soup

SERVES 6

Prepare as for Stock Pot, but when cooked, discard the bouquet garni sachet, purée in a blender or food processor, then pass through a sieve (strainer) to remove any strings from the celery. Reheat and serve garnished with chopped parsley.

* **20 calories per serving**
* **High fibre**

Haricot Bean and Ratatouille Soup

SERVES 6

1 onion, finely chopped
1 garlic clove, crushed
15 g/½ oz/1 tbsp low-fat sunflower or
olive oil spread
1 aubergine (eggplant), diced
1 red (bell) pepper, diced
1 green pepper, diced
1 courgette (zucchini), diced
425 g/15 oz/1 large can of haricot
(navy) beans, drained and
thoroughly rinsed
400 g/14 oz/1 large can of chopped
tomatoes
1 vegetable stock cube
15 ml/1 tbsp tomato purée (paste)
2.5 ml/½ tsp dried mixed herbs
A pinch of salt
Freshly ground black pepper

Fry (sauté) the onion and garlic in the low-fat spread in a large saucepan for 2 minutes, stirring. Add all the remaining ingredients. Fill the tomato can with water and add to the pan. Repeat with a second canful of water. Bring to the boil, reduce the heat, part-cover and simmer for 30 minutes until the vegetables are really tender. Ladle into warm soup bowls and serve.

* **75 calories per serving**
* **High fibre**

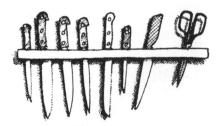

Flageolet and Green Pepper Soup

SERVES 6

Prepare as for Haricot Bean and Ratatouille Soup, but substitute 2 extra green (bell) peppers for the aubergine (eggplant) and courgette (zucchini), and a can of flageolet beans for the haricot (navy) beans.

* 75 calories per serving
* High fibre

Kowloon Soup

SERVES 4

100 g/4 oz pork fillet
5 ml/1 tsp cornflour (cornstarch)
15 ml/1 tbsp reduced-salt soy sauce
2 carrots, coarsely grated
5 cm/2 in piece of cucumber, coarsely grated
1.2 litres/2 pts/5 cups chicken stock, made with 2 stock cubes
15 ml/1 tbsp medium-dry sherry

Slice the pork thinly, then cut the slices into thin strips. Place in a bowl. Toss in the cornflour, then add the soy sauce and toss again. Leave to stand for 10 minutes. Put in a saucepan and stir in the remaining ingredients. Bring to the boil, reduce the heat and simmer for 8 minutes until the pork is really tender. Taste and add a little more soy sauce, if liked. Ladle into soup bowls and serve.

* 45 calories per serving
* Medium fibre

Brown Onion Soup

SERVES 6

900 g/2 lb onions, thinly sliced
40 g/1½ oz/3 tbsp low-fat sunflower or olive oil spread
10 ml/2 tsp light brown sugar
900 ml/1½ pts/3 cups beef stock, made with 2 stock cubes
Salt and freshly ground black pepper
45 ml/3 tbsp grated low-fat Cheddar cheese, to serve

Put the onions in a large saucepan with the low-fat spread. Cover and sweat gently, stirring occasionally, for 5 minutes. Remove the lid, turn up the heat, add the sugar and fry (sauté), stirring, for 10 minutes until soft and richly browned. Add the stock and some salt and pepper, bring to the boil, reduce the heat and simmer gently for 20 minutes. Ladle into warm bowls and sprinkle with the grated cheese before serving.

* 110 calories per serving
* Medium fibre

French Onion Soup

SERVES 6

Prepare as for Brown Onion Soup, but when ready to serve toast four slices of French bread on one side only. Turn them over, top each with 10 ml/2 tsp grated low-fat Cheddar cheese and toast until bubbling. Float one in each bowl of soup instead of serving with grated cheese.

* 150 calories per serving
* Medium fibre

Danish Pea Soup

SERVES 6

15 g/½ oz/1 tbsp low-fat sunflower or
  olive oil spread
1 large onion, finely chopped
75 g/3 oz/½ cup yellow split peas,
  soaked overnight in cold water
75 g/3 oz/scant ½ cup pearl barley,
  soaked overnight in cold water
1.2 litres/2 pts/5 cups vegetable or
  chicken stock, made with 2 stock
  cubes
30 ml/2 tbsp tomato purée (paste)
Salt and freshly ground black pepper
150 ml/¼ pt/⅔ cup skimmed milk
15 ml/1 tbsp snipped chives
15 ml/1 tbsp chopped parsley

Heat the low-fat spread in a saucepan and cook the onion gently for 3 minutes, stirring, until soft but not brown. Drain the peas and barley and add to the saucepan with the stock. Bring to the boil, skim the surface, part-cover and simmer gently for 1½ hours. Purée in a blender or food processor with the tomato purée. Return to the saucepan and season to taste. Stir in the milk and chives and heat through. Ladle into warm bowls and sprinkle with chopped parsley before serving.

* **90 calories per serving**
* **High fibre**

Rich Mushroom Soup

SERVES 6

1 small onion, chopped
350 g/12 oz button mushrooms,
  roughly chopped
15 g/½ oz/1 tbsp low-fat sunflower or
  olive oil spread
150 ml/¼ pt/⅔ cup chicken or
  vegetable stock, made with
  ½ stock cube
30 ml/2 tbsp plain (all-purpose) flour
450 ml/¾ pt/2 cups skimmed milk
A pinch of salt
Freshly ground black pepper
30 ml/2 tbsp finely chopped parsley
30 ml/2 tbsp low-fat fromage frais

Cook the onion and mushrooms in the low-fat spread gently for 3 minutes, stirring, until soft but not brown. Add the stock, stir, cover, reduce the heat to low and simmer gently for 10 minutes, stirring occasionally, until tender. Blend the flour with a little of the milk and stir into the mushrooms with the remaining milk. Bring to the boil and cook for 2 minutes, stirring. Purée in a blender or food processor and return to the saucepan. Add the salt and pepper to taste, then stir in the parsley and fromage frais. Reheat but do not boil. Ladle into warm bowls and serve straight away.

* **55 calories per serving**
* **Low fibre**

Cock-a-leekie Soup

SERVES 6

2 large leeks, thinly sliced
2 chicken portions, skin removed
75 g/3 oz/scant ¹/₂ cup pearl barley
1 bouquet garni sachet
1.75 litres/3 pts/7¹/₂ cups chicken
stock, made with 3 stock cubes
A pinch of salt
Freshly ground black pepper
8 prunes, quartered and stoned (pitted)
30 ml/2 tbsp chopped parsley

Put all the ingredients except the prunes and parsley in a large saucepan. Bring to the boil, reduce the heat, part-cover and simmer gently for 1 hour. Add the prunes and cook for a further 30 minutes until the barley and chicken are tender. Lift the chicken out of the soup, take all the meat off the bones and cut into small pieces. Return to the pan and simmer for a further 5 minutes. Taste and re-season, if necessary. Discard the bouquet garni sachet. Stir in the parsley and serve.

* **140 calories per serving**
* **High fibre**

Golden Root Soup

SERVES 8

1 onion, chopped
15 g/¹/₂ oz/1 tbsp low-fat sunflower or
olive oil spread, plus extra for
spreading
¹/₂ small swede (rutabaga), diced
1 potato, diced
1 small parsnip, diced
1 large carrot, diced
¹/₂ small celeriac (celery root), diced
1.5 litres/2¹/₂ pts/6 cups vegetable
stock, made with 2 stock cubes
1 bay leaf
A pinch of salt
Freshly ground black pepper
2 slices of wholemeal bread
5 ml/1 tsp paprika
30 ml/2 tbsp chopped parsley

Fry (sauté) the onion in the measured low-fat spread for 2 minutes, stirring, until soft but not brown. Add the remaining vegetables, the stock, bay leaf, salt and a little pepper. Bring to the boil, part-cover, reduce the heat and simmer for 30 minutes. Remove the bay leaf and purée the mixture in a blender or food processor. Return to the pan and re-season, if necessary. Heat through. Meanwhile, spread the bread with a very thin scraping of sunflower or olive oil spread and cut into small cubes. Dust with the paprika. Dry-fry in a frying pan (skillet), tossing until crisp and brown. Ladle the soup into warm bowls. Sprinkle with the parsley before serving with the croûtons handed separately.

* **75 calories per serving**
* **Fairly high fibre**

White Vegetable Soup

SERVES 4

15 g/¹/₂ oz/1 tbsp low-fat sunflower or
   olive oil spread
1 onion, finely chopped
450 g/1 lb frozen diced mixed
   vegetables
300 ml/¹/₂ pt/1¹/₄ cups vegetable
   stock, made with 1 stock cube
1 bay leaf
600 ml/1 pt/2¹/₂ cups skimmed milk
30 ml/2 tbsp cornflour (cornstarch)
Salt and white pepper

Heat the low-fat spread in a large
saucepan. Add the onion and fry
(sauté) for 2 minutes, stirring, until
softened but not browned. Add the
vegetables, stock and bay leaf. Bring to
the boil, part-cover, reduce the heat
and simmer for 15 minutes until really
tender. Blend a little of the milk with
the cornflour, then stir in the
remaining milk. Add to the pan, bring
to the boil and cook for
2 minutes, stirring, until slightly
thickened. Season to taste. Remove the
bay leaf and serve hot.

* **120 calories per serving**
* **Medium fibre**

Flageolet and Almond Soup

SERVES 6

100 g/4 oz/1 cup dried green flageolet
   beans, soaked overnight in cold
   water
2 litres/3¹/₂ pts/8¹/₂ cups water
1 bunch of spring onions (scallions),
   finely chopped
1 garlic clove, crushed
15 g/¹/₂ oz/1 tbsp low-fat sunflower or
   olive oil spread
2 celery sticks, finely chopped
2 vegetable stock cubes
100 g/4 oz/1 cup ground almonds
A pinch of salt
Freshly ground black pepper
30 ml/2 tbsp chopped parsley
30 ml/2 tbsp toasted flaked (slivered)
   almonds

Drain the beans and place in a
saucepan with half the water.
Bring to the boil and boil rapidly for
10 minutes. Part-cover and simmer
gently for about 1 hour or until the
beans are tender. Add the remaining
ingredients except the parsley and
toasted almonds and simmer for
30 minutes. Taste and re-season, if
necessary. Ladle into warm soup bowls
and sprinkle with the parsley and
toasted almonds before serving.

* **205 calories per serving**
* **High fibre**

Clear Garlic Broth with Noodles

SERVES 6

2 potatoes, scrubbed and chopped
2 carrots, scrubbed and chopped
2 outer celery sticks, chopped,
    including any leaves
1 large onion, chopped
1 small bay leaf
Salt and freshly ground black pepper
1.5 litres/2½ pts/6 cups water
1 garlic bulb, separated into cloves and
    peeled
1 large sprig of fresh thyme
6 sage leaves
75 g/3 oz vermicelli, broken into small
    pieces

Put the potatoes, carrots, celery and
onion in a large saucepan with the
bay leaf, a little salt, lots of pepper and
the water. Bring to the boil, part-cover,
reduce the heat and simmer for
2 hours. Strain and return to the
rinsed-out saucepan. Add the
remaining ingredients except the
vermicelli, bring back to the boil, part-
cover, reduce the heat and simmer
gently for 30 minutes. Strain again,
return to the heat and add the
vermicelli. Simmer gently for about
5 minutes or until the pasta is tender.
Taste and re-season, if necessary. Serve
in colourful bowls with no garnish.

* **120 calories per serving**
* **Medium fibre**

Clear Vegetable Strand Soup

SERVES 4

1 small carrot, cut into thin
    matchsticks
1 celery stick, cut into thin
    matchsticks
1 onion, halved and thinly sliced
900 ml/1½ pts/3¾ cups chicken or
    vegetable stock, made with 2 stock
    cubes
¼ small green cabbage, thinly
    shredded
100 g/4 oz frozen shelled baby broad
    (fava) beans
8 basil leaves, shredded
Salt and freshly ground black pepper

Put the carrot, celery and onion in a
saucepan with the stock. Bring to
the boil and simmer for 5 minutes.
Add the cabbage and beans and
simmer for a further 5 minutes or until
the vegetables are tender. Add the basil
and season to taste. Ladle into warm
bowls and serve hot.

* **40 calories per serving**
* **High fibre**

Chinese Mock Seaweed Soup

SERVES 4

225 g/8 oz curly kale
1.2 litres/2 pts/5 cups chicken stock,
made with 2 stock cubes
1 bunch of spring onions (scallions),
chopped
15 g/¹/₂ oz/1 tbsp low-fat sunflower or
olive oil spread
45 ml/3 tbsp reduced-salt soy sauce
A pinch of ground ginger
30 ml/2 tbsp sherry
Freshly ground black pepper
1 egg white
A pinch of salt
15 ml/1 tbsp snipped chives

Discard any thick stalks from the kale and shred the leaves. Bring the stock to the boil, add the kale and cook for 5 minutes. Meanwhile, fry (sauté) the spring onions in the low-fat spread for 3 minutes, stirring. Add to the kale and the stock and simmer for a further 30 minutes. Purée in a blender or food processor. Return to the pan and stir in the soy sauce, ginger, sherry and lots of pepper. Reheat. Whisk the egg white with the salt until stiff, then fold in the chives. Ladle the soup into flameproof bowls and put a spoonful of the egg white on top of each. Flash under a preheated grill (broiler) for about 2 minutes to brown and set the egg white. Serve straight away.

* **50 calories per serving**
* **High fibre**

Sherried Chicken and Pasta Soup

SERVES 4

1 small skinless chicken breast, cut
into thin strips about 2.5 cm/1 in
long
900 ml/1¹/₂ pts/3³/₄ cups chicken
stock, made with 2 stock cubes
4 spring onions (scallions), chopped
100 g/4 oz small button mushrooms,
sliced
50 g/2 oz soup pasta shapes
1 bouquet garni sachet
Salt and freshly ground black pepper
60 ml/4 tbsp medium-dry sherry

Put all the ingredients except the sherry in a saucepan. Bring to the boil, reduce the heat and simmer for 10 minutes. Stir in the sherry, taste and re-season, if necessary. Ladle into warm bowls and serve hot.

* **65 calories per serving**
* **Medium fibre**

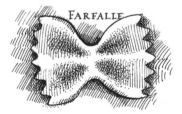

FARFALLE

Red Onion and Cabbage Soup

SERVES 6

*15 g/½ oz/1 tbsp low-fat sunflower or
olive oil spread*
3 large red onions, thinly sliced
1 garlic clove, crushed
*1 very small red cabbage (about
350 g/12 oz), shredded*
*1.2 litres/2 pts/5 cups vegetable stock,
made with 2 stock cubes*
1 bay leaf
5 ml/1 tsp light brown sugar
15 ml/1 tbsp red wine vinegar
Salt and freshly ground black pepper
60 ml/4 tbsp low-fat plain yoghurt
10 ml/2 tsp snipped chives

Heat the low-fat spread in a large saucepan. Add the onions and fry (sauté), stirring, for 5 minutes. Add the garlic and cabbage and cook for 3 minutes, stirring. Add the stock, bay leaf, sugar, vinegar and some salt and pepper. Bring to the boil, reduce the heat and simmer for 40 minutes until the cabbage is really tender. Taste and re-season, if necessary. Discard the bay leaf. Ladle into warm bowls and top each with 10 ml/2 tsp yoghurt and a sprinkling of chives.

* **45 calories per serving**
* **High fibre**

Super Slimmer's Cabbage Soup

SERVES 4

1 onion, finely chopped
*25 g/1 oz/2 tbsp low-fat sunflower or
olive oil spread*
*1 small green cabbage, thinly
shredded*
*600 ml/1 pt/2½ cups vegetable stock,
made with 1 stock cube*
Salt and freshly ground black pepper
A good pinch of grated nutmeg
20 ml/4 tsp low-fat crème fraîche
5 ml/1 tsp caraway seeds

Fry (sauté) the onion in the low-fat spread in a saucepan for 2 minutes, stirring. Add the cabbage, stock, a little salt and pepper and the nutmeg. Bring to the boil, reduce the heat, part-cover and simmer gently for 15 minutes. Taste and re-season, if necessary. Ladle into warm bowls, top each with 5 ml/ 1 tsp low-fat crème fraîche and sprinkle with caraway seeds before serving.

* **50 calories per serving**
* **High fibre**

White Bean and Cauliflower Soup

SERVES 6

15 g/½ oz/1 tbsp low-fat sunflower or
   olive oil spread
1 onion, finely chopped
1 potato, peeled and diced
1 small cauliflower, all green
   discarded, cut into small florets
1 litre/1¾ pts/4¼ cups vegetable
   stock, made with 2 stock cubes
1 bay leaf
Salt and white pepper
30 ml/2 tbsp skimmed dried milk
   powder (non-fat dry milk)
425 g/15 oz/1 large can of cannellini
   beans, drained, rinsed and drained
   again
6 coriander (cilantro) leaves, to garnish

Heat the low-fat spread in a saucepan. Add the onion and potato and fry (sauté) for 2 minutes until softened slightly but not browned. Add the cauliflower, stock, bay leaf and a little salt and pepper. Bring to the boil, reduce the heat, part-cover and simmer gently for 20 minutes. Remove the bay leaf. Purée in a blender or food processor with the milk powder. Return to the saucepan and stir in the cannellini beans. Heat through. Taste and re-season, if necessary. Ladle into warm bowls and garnish each with a single coriander leaf.

* **105 calories per serving**
* **High fibre**

White Bean and Broccoli Soup

SERVES 6

Prepare as for White Bean and Cauliflower Soup but substitute broccoli for the cauliflower and use a bouquet garni sachet instead of a bay leaf.

* **105 calories per serving**
* **High fibre**

Cider Apple Bisque

SERVES 4

15 g/½ oz/1 tbsp low-fat sunflower or
   olive oil spread
3 green eating (dessert) apples,
   peeled, cored and chopped
2.5 ml/½ tsp ground cinnamon or
   cloves
300 ml/½ pt/1¼ cups apple juice
300 ml/½ pt/1¼ cups dry cider
150 ml/¼ pt/⅔ cup low-fat crème
   fraîche

Heat the low-fat spread in a saucepan. Add the apple and cook gently, stirring, for 3 minutes. Add the spice, apple juice and cider. Bring to the boil, reduce the heat, part-cover and simmer for 15 minutes until the apple is tender. Purée in a blender or food processor and return to the pan. Stir in the crème fraîche and heat through. Ladle into warm bowls and serve very hot.

* **105 calories per serving**
* **Low fibre**

Oriental Crab and Sweetcorn Soup

SERVES 6

900 ml/1¹/₂ pts/3³/₄ cups chicken stock, made with 2 stock cubes
2 thin slices of fresh root ginger
1 garlic clove, halved
320 g/12 oz/1 medium can of naturally sweet sweetcorn (corn)
200 g/7 oz/1 small can of crabmeat
30 ml/2 tbsp dry sherry
15 ml/1 tbsp reduced-salt soy sauce
1 spring onion (scallion), very finely chopped
15 ml/1 tbsp cornflour (cornstarch)
30 ml/2 tbsp water
Salt and white pepper

Put the stock in a saucepan with the ginger and garlic. Bring to the boil, cover, reduce the heat and simmer for 5 minutes. Remove the ginger and garlic with a draining spoon and discard. Add the remaining ingredients except the cornflour, water and seasoning. Bring to the boil, reduce the heat and simmer gently for 3 minutes. Blend the cornflour with the water and stir into the soup. Simmer for a further 2 minutes, stirring. Season to taste with salt and pepper and add a little extra soy sauce, if liked. Ladle into warm bowls and serve.

* **90 calories per serving**
* **High fibre**

Oriental Chicken and Sweetcorn Soup

SERVES 6

Prepare as for Oriental Crab and Sweetcorn Soup, but substitute 100 g/ 4 oz/1 cup cooked chicken, all skin removed and finely diced, for the crab.

* **90 calories per serving**
* **High fibre**

Garlic Soup with Bay

SERVES 4

900 ml/1¹/₂ pts/3³/₄ cups chicken stock, made with 2 stock cubes
4 large garlic cloves, crushed
2 large bay leaves
Salt and freshly ground black pepper
30 ml/2 tbsp chopped parsley
Croûtons, to serve

Put the stock, garlic and bay leaves in a saucepan. Bring to the boil and simmer for 10 minutes. Turn off the heat and leave to infuse for at least 1 hour, preferably longer. Strain and return to the saucepan. Season to taste, then reheat, ladle into warm bowls, sprinkle with parsley and serve with croûtons handed separately.

* **35 calories per serving**
* **Low fibre**

New-Age Partan Bree

SERVES 6

900 ml/1½ pts/3¾ cups water
50 g/2 oz/¼ cup brown rice
2 chicken stock cubes
1 large cooked crab
90 ml/6 tbsp skimmed dried milk
    powder (non-fat dry milk)
5 ml/1 tsp anchovy essence (extract)
10 ml/2 tsp tomato purée (paste)
A pinch of salt
White pepper
10 ml/2 tsp cornflour (cornstarch)
30 ml/2 tbsp skimmed milk
150 ml/¼ pt/⅔ cup cultured
    buttermilk or low-fat crème fraîche
15 ml/1 tbsp chopped parsley, to serve

Put the water and rice in a saucepan with the stock cubes. Bring to the boil, reduce the heat and simmer for about 40 minutes until the rice is tender, stirring occasionally. Pick all the brown and white meat out of the body and small legs of the crab and place in a food processor or blender. Crack the large claws, remove the meat, cut into neat pieces and set aside. Add the cooked rice and liquid to the crab meat in the blender or food processor and blend to a purée. Add the milk powder, anchovy essence and tomato purée and run the machine again until well blended. Return to the saucepan. Season to taste. Blend the cornflour with the milk and stir in. Bring to the boil and cook for 1 minute, stirring. Stir in the buttermilk or crème fraîche and the claw meat. Taste and re-season, if necessary. Ladle into warm bowls and sprinkle with the parsley before serving.

* **115 calories per serving**
* **High fibre**

Minestrone

SERVES 4

1 small onion, grated
1 carrot, grated
1 small parsnip, grated
1 potato, grated
¼ small green cabbage, finely
    shredded
50 g/2 oz frozen peas
25 g/1 oz quick-cook macaroni
400 g/14 oz/1 large can of chopped
    tomatoes
2.5 ml/½ tsp dried mixed herbs
A pinch of salt
Freshly ground black pepper
20 ml/4 tsp grated Parmesan cheese,
    to garnish

Put the prepared vegetables in a saucepan with the peas, macaroni and chopped tomatoes. Fill the tomato can with water and add to the saucepan. Repeat with a second canful. Add the herbs, salt and lots of pepper. Bring to the boil, reduce the heat, part-cover and simmer gently for 10 minutes or until the vegetables and pasta are tender. Ladle into warm bowls and sprinkle each with 5 ml/ 1 tsp Parmesan.

* **100 calories per serving**
* **High fibre**

The Whole Caboodle Pea Soup

SERVES 4

450 g/1 lb fresh peas in their pods
1 bunch of spring onions (scallions),
    roughly chopped
1 potato, diced
750 ml/1¼pts/3 cups water
15 ml/1 tbsp chopped mint
A pinch of grated nutmeg
A pinch of salt
Freshly ground black pepper
45 ml/3 tbsp low-fat crème fraîche
A little chopped mint, to garnish

Roughly chop up the pea pods and place in a saucepan with the remaining ingredients except the crème fraîche. Bring to the boil, reduce the heat, part-cover and simmer gently for 30 minutes. Purée in a blender or food processor, then pass through a sieve (strainer) to remove the membranes. Return to the heat and stir in the crème fraîche. Season with more pepper, if liked, and serve hot sprinkled with a little chopped mint.

* **100 calories per serving**
* **Fairly high fibre**

Thai Noodle Soup

SERVES 4

1.2 litres/2 pts/5 cups chicken stock,
    made with 2 stock cubes
5 cm/2 in piece of lemon grass
1 garlic clove, halved
5 ml/1 tsp reduced-salt soy sauce
75 g/3 oz vermicelli, broken into short
    lengths
4 nasturtium flowers or a few rose
    petals, to garnish

Put the stock in a saucepan. Bruise the lemon grass with a heavy weight or a rolling pin and add to the stock with the garlic halves and soy sauce. Bring to the boil, add the vermicelli and simmer for 5 minutes until the noodles are tender. Remove the lemon grass and garlic. Ladle into bowls and float a nasturtium flower or a couple of rose petals on each.

* **80 calories per serving**
* **Medium fibre**

Mushroom and Courgette Soup with Thyme

SERVES 4

2 courgettes (zucchini)
350 g/12 oz button mushrooms, finely chopped
15 ml/1 tbsp paprika
5 ml/1 tsp Worcestershire sauce
300 ml/¹/₂ pt/1¹/₄ cups water
7.5 ml/1¹/₂ tsp chopped thyme
A pinch of salt
Freshly ground black pepper
30 ml/2 tbsp plain (all-purpose) flour
450 ml/³/₄ pt/2 cups skimmed milk
Lemon juice, to taste

Cut four thin slices off one of the courgettes and reserve. Grate the remainder. Place in a saucepan with the mushrooms, paprika, Worcestershire sauce, water, thyme, salt and a good grinding of pepper. Bring to the boil, reduce the heat, cover and simmer gently for 15 minutes. Blend the flour with a little of the milk, then stir in the remaining milk. Add to the pan, bring to the boil and cook for 2 minutes, stirring all the time, until thickened slightly. Spike with lemon juice to taste and add a little more pepper, if liked. Ladle into warm bowls and garnish each with a reserved courgette slice.

* **70 calories per serving**
* **Medium fibre**

Chicken and Corn Chowder

SERVES 4

1 chicken portion, all skin removed
450 ml/³/₄ pt/2 cups water
1 bunch of spring onions (scallions), chopped
2 potatoes, finely diced
A pinch of salt
Freshly ground black pepper
320 g/12 oz/1 medium can of naturally sweet sweetcorn (corn), drained
300 ml/¹/₂ pt/1¹/₄ cups skimmed milk
30 ml/2 tbsp skimmed dried milk powder (non-fat dry milk)
30 ml/2 tbsp chopped parsley

Put the chicken portion in a pan with the water. Bring to the boil, reduce the heat, part-cover and simmer gently for 45 minutes. Carefully lift out the chicken, remove all meat from the bones, chop and reserve. Add the spring onions, potatoes, salt and some pepper to the chicken stock and simmer for 10 minutes. Add the chopped chicken, the corn and the milk. Bring to the boil and cook for 2 minutes, stirring all the time. Stir in the parsley and season with more pepper, if liked. Ladle into bowls and serve hot.

* **210 calories per serving**
* **Fairly high fibre**

Spiced Carrot Soup

SERVES 4

450 g/1 lb carrots, chopped
1 onion, chopped
750 ml/1¼ pts/3 cups vegetable
*   stock, made with 2 stock cubes*
5 ml/1 tsp ground coriander (cilantro)
2.5 ml/½ tsp dried mixed herbs
A pinch of grated nutmeg
Salt and freshly ground black pepper
15 ml/1 tbsp snipped chives, to garnish

Put the carrots, onion and stock in a saucepan with the coriander, herbs and nutmeg. Add a good grinding of pepper and bring to the boil. Reduce the heat, part-cover and simmer gently for 30 minutes. Purée in a blender or food processor, then return to the saucepan. Reheat, season with salt and a little more pepper, if liked, and serve garnished with snipped chives.

* **45 calories per serving**
* **Fairly high fibre**

Spiced Parsnip Soup

SERVES 4

Prepare as for Spiced Carrot Soup, but substitute parsnips for the carrots and use half ground cumin and half ground coriander (cilantro) instead of all coriander.

* **50 calories per serving**
* **Fairly high fibre**

Spiced Sweet Potato Soup

SERVES 4

Prepare as for Spiced Carrot Soup, but substitute sweet potatoes (or half ordinary potatoes and half sweet potatoes) for the carrots and add a handful of sultanas (golden raisins) after puréeing.

* **60 calories per serving**
* **Fairly high fibre**

Quick Minted Pea and Ham Soup

SERVES 4

1.2 litres/2 pts/5 cups ham or chicken
*   stock, made with 2 stock cubes*
225 g/8 oz frozen peas
1.5 ml/¼ tsp dried mint
50 g/2 oz/½ cup lean cooked ham,
*   finely chopped*
60 ml/4 tbsp skimmed milk
Salt and freshly ground black pepper

Bring the stock to the boil in a saucepan. Add the peas and mint and simmer for 3 minutes. Purée in a blender or food processor. Return to the saucepan. Stir in the ham, milk and a little salt and pepper. Reheat until piping hot and serve.

* **50 calories per serving**
* **High fibre**

Tomato and Citrus Soup

SERVES 4

1 orange
150 ml/¼ pt/⅔ cup water
1 onion, roughly chopped
15 g/½ oz/1 tbsp low-fat sunflower or
    olive oil spread
400 g/14 oz/1 large can of tomatoes
300 ml/½ pt/1¼ cups vegetable stock,
    made with 1 stock cube
30 ml/2 tbsp tomato purée (paste)
Finely grated rind and juice of
    ½ lemon
5 ml/1 tsp caster (superfine) sugar
Salt and freshly ground black pepper
15 ml/1 tbsp snipped chives

Thinly pare the rind from the orange and cut into thin strips. Squeeze the juice and reserve. Boil the rind in the water for 3 minutes. Carefully lift the rind out of the water with a draining spoon and reserve. Meanwhile, in a separate pan, fry (sauté) the onion in the low-fat spread for 2 minutes, stirring, until softened but not browned. Add the orange cooking water, orange juice and the remaining ingredients except the chives. Break up the tomatoes with a wooden spoon. Bring the soup to the boil and simmer for 5 minutes. Turn into a blender or food processor and purée until smooth. Return to the pan, season to taste and reheat. Ladle into soup bowls, garnish with the reserved orange rind and the chives and serve straight away.

* **55 calories per serving**
* **Medium fibre**

Curried Lentil and Pepper Warmer

SERVES 6

175 g/6 oz/1 cup green lentils
1.2 litres/2 pts/5 cups boiling water
1 onion, finely chopped
1 carrot, finely chopped
1 green (bell) pepper, finely chopped
1 red pepper, finely chopped
1 small red or green chilli, seeded and
    finely chopped (optional)
1 bay leaf
15 ml/1 tbsp curry powder
15 ml/1 tbsp tomato purée (paste)
10 ml/2 tsp mango chutney
Salt and freshly ground black pepper
15 ml/1 tbsp chopped coriander
    (cilantro)

Rinse the lentils thoroughly, then place in a saucepan and cover with the boiling water. Stir and leave to stand for 1 hour. Add the remaining ingredients except the salt, pepper and coriander. Bring to the boil, reduce the heat, part-cover and simmer very gently for 1¼ hours or until the lentils are really tender. Season to taste with salt and pepper and stir in the coriander. Ladle into warm bowls and serve hot.

* **140 calories per serving**
* **High fibre**

Red Lentil and Tomato Soup with Basil

SERVES 6

175 g/6 oz/1 cup split red lentils
900 ml/1½ pts/3¾ cups water
1 leek, finely chopped
3 large carrots, finely chopped
1 garlic clove, crushed
400 g/14 oz/1 large can of chopped tomatoes
15 ml/1 tbsp tomato purée (paste)
150 ml/¼ pt/⅔ cup dry white wine
A pinch of salt
Freshly ground black pepper
30 ml/2 tbsp finely chopped basil

Put all the ingredients except the basil in a large saucepan. Bring to the boil, reduce the heat, part-cover and simmer gently for about 35 minutes until really tender. Purée in a blender or food processor with the basil and return to the saucepan. Heat through and serve straight away.

* **145 calories per serving**
* **High fibre**

Mediterranean Tuna Soup

SERVES 4

300 ml/½ pt/1¼ cups fish or vegetable stock, made with 1 stock cube
400 g/14 oz/1 large can of chopped tomatoes
1 small red (bell) pepper, grated
185 g/6½ oz/1 small can of tuna in brine or water
A pinch of salt
Freshly ground black pepper
15 ml/1 tbsp chopped parsley
15 ml/1 tbsp chopped basil

Put all the ingredients in a saucepan, reserving half the herbs for garnishing. Bring to the boil, reduce the heat, part-cover and simmer gently for 3 minutes. Ladle into warm bowls and sprinkle with the remaining herbs to garnish.

* **70 calories per serving**
* **Medium fibre**

Portuguese Sardine Soup

SERVES 4

Prepare as for Mediterranean Tuna Soup, but substitute 110 g/4½ oz/ 1 small can of sardines, well drained and finely chopped (discard the bones if preferred but they are very good for you!). Sprinkle with a little finely grated lemon rind as well as the parsley before serving.

* **100 calories per serving**
* **Medium fibre**

Borsch

SERVES 6

2 carrots
1 onion
2 celery sticks
4 cooked beetroot (red beets)
900 ml/1½ pts/3¾ cups beef or
vegetable stock, made with 2 stock
cubes
15 ml/1 tbsp red wine vinegar
Salt and freshly ground black pepper
20 ml/4 tsp low-fat crème fraîche
15 ml/1 tbsp snipped chives

Grate the carrots, onion, celery and beetroot and place in a saucepan. Add the stock and vinegar and bring to the boil. Reduce the heat, cover and simmer gently for 20 minutes until the vegetables are tender. Season to taste. Ladle into warm soup bowls and put a little crème fraîche on top of each. Sprinkle with the chives and serve. Alternatively, leave the soup to cool, then chill before serving.

* **35 calories per serving**
* **High fibre**

Curried Parsnip Soup

SERVES 6

450 g/1 lb parsnips, sliced
1 onion, roughly chopped
15 g/½ oz/1 tbsp low-fat sunflower or
olive oil spread
15 ml/1 tbsp curry powder
600 ml/1 pt/2½ cups vegetable stock,
made with 1 stock cube
300 ml/½ pt/1¼ cups skimmed milk
Salt and freshly ground black pepper
15 ml/1 tbsp chopped coriander
(cilantro)
Naan bread, to serve

Put the parsnips in a saucepan with the onion, low-fat spread and curry powder. Cook, stirring, over a moderate heat for 2 minutes. Add the stock, bring to the boil, reduce the heat, part-cover and simmer gently for 15 minutes or until the parsnips are really tender. Purée in a blender or food processor, then return to the saucepan. Stir in the milk, season to taste and stir in the coriander. Heat through. Ladle into warm soup bowls and serve hot with naan bread.

* **65 calories per serving**
* **Fairly high fibre**

Verdentia

SERVES 4

450 g/1 lb spinach
15 g/½ oz/1 tbsp low-fat sunflower or olive oil spread
1 onion, roughly chopped
175 g/6 oz fresh, shelled or frozen broad (fava) beans
A good pinch of grated nutmeg
A good pinch of dried thyme
600 ml/1 pt/2½ cups vegetable stock, made with 1 stock cube
300 ml/½ pt/1¼ cups skimmed milk
Salt and freshly ground black pepper

Wash the spinach thoroughly under running water. Remove any thick stalks and tear the leaves into pieces. Heat the low-fat spread in a large saucepan. Add the onion and fry (sauté) for 2 minutes, stirring. Add the spinach and stir until it softens slightly. Add the beans, nutmeg, thyme and stock. Bring to the boil, reduce the heat, part-cover and simmer gently for 15 minutes until the beans and spinach are really tender. Purée in a blender or food processor. Return to the saucepan and stir in the milk. Season to taste. Ladle into warm soup bowls and serve very hot.

* **110 calories per serving**
* **High fibre**

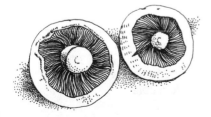

Mushroom and Corn Chowder

SERVES 4

1 onion, finely chopped
15 g/½ oz/1 tbsp low-fat sunflower or olive oil spread
1 large potato, finely diced
225 g/8 oz button mushrooms, fairly finely chopped
300 ml/½ pt/1¼ cups vegetable stock, made with 1 stock cube
320 g/12 oz/1 medium can of naturally sweet sweetcorn (corn)
300 ml/½ pt/1¼ cups skimmed milk
Salt and freshly ground black pepper
15 ml/1 tbsp chopped parsley, to garnish

Fry (sauté) the onion in the low-fat spread in a saucepan for 2 minutes, stirring, until softened but not browned. Add the potato, mushrooms and stock. Bring to the boil, reduce the heat, part-cover and simmer gently for 15 minutes until the potatoes are tender. Stir in the sweetcorn and milk and season to taste. Heat for 2 minutes, then ladle into warm soup bowls and sprinkle with chopped parsley before serving.

* **180 calories per serving**
* **High fibre**

Cheese and Corn Chowder

SERVES 4

Prepare as for Mushroom and Corn Chowder but omit the mushrooms. Stir in 50 g/2 oz/½ cup low-fat strong Cheddar cheese when adding the corn, then continue as before.

* **210 calories per serving**
* **Fairly high fibre**

61

Fresh Watercress Soup

SERVES 6

2 bunches of watercress
15 g/¹/₂ oz/1 tbsp low-fat sunflower or
olive oil spread
1 large onion, roughly chopped
1 large potato, peeled and diced
600 ml/1 pt/2¹/₂ cups vegetable stock,
made with 1 stock cube
Salt and freshly ground black pepper
300 ml/¹/₂ pt/1¹/₄ cups skimmed milk

Wash the watercress and cut off and discard the feathery stalks. Reserve four tiny sprigs for garnish and chop the remainder. Heat the low-fat spread in a saucepan. Add the onion and fry (sauté), stirring, for 2 minutes until softened but not browned. Add the watercress and potato and cook for 1 minute, stirring. Add the stock and a little salt and pepper. Bring to the boil, reduce the heat, part-cover and simmer gently for 15–20 minutes until the potato is really soft. Purée in a blender or food processor and return to the pan. Stir in the milk and heat through. Taste and re-season, if necessary. Ladle into warm soup bowls and garnish with the reserved sprigs of watercress. Alternatively, after puréeing, turn into a bowl, leave until cold, stir in the milk, re-season and chill until ready to serve cold in bowls, garnished with the watercress.

* **65 calories per serving**
* **Fairly high fibre**

Sherried Consommé with Mushrooms

SERVES 4

50 g/2 oz button mushrooms, thinly
sliced
30 ml/2 tbsp water
295 g/10¹/₂ oz/1 medium can of
condensed beef consommé
30 ml/2 tbsp medium-dry sherry

Put the mushrooms and water in a saucepan. Cover and simmer gently for 3 minutes. Add the consommé, water (according to the can directions) and the sherry and heat through. Ladle into warm bowls and serve.

* **20 calories per serving**
* **Low fibre**

Italian Consommé

SERVES 4

40 g/1¹/₂ oz conchiglietti or other soup
pasta, or vermicelli broken into
very small pieces
295 g/10¹/₂ oz/1 medium can of
condensed beef consommé
30 ml/2 tbsp red vermouth
20 ml/4 tsp grated Parmesan cheese

Cook the pasta in plenty of boiling, lightly salted water until just tender. Drain and return to the saucepan. Add the consommé, water (according to the can directions) and the vermouth. Heat through, stirring. Ladle into warm soup bowls and sprinkle each with 5 ml/1 tsp grated Parmesan cheese before serving.

* **70 calories per serving**
* **Medium fibre**

Watercress and Prawn Soup

SERVES 6

Prepare as for Fresh Watercress Soup (page 62) but add 75 g/3 oz cooked peeled prawns (shrimp), chopped, after puréeing and garnish each bowl with a whole unpeeled prawn on the side of the dish.

* 80 calories per serving
* Fairly high fibre

Consommé Julienne

SERVES 4

1 small carrot, cut into very thin matchsticks
1 celery stick, cut into very thin matchsticks
150 ml/¹/₄ pt/²/₃ cup water
150 ml/¹/₄ pt/²/₃ cup dry white wine
295 g/10¹/₂ oz/1 medium can of condensed beef consommé

Cook the carrot and celery in the water in a covered pan for 5 minutes until tender. Add the wine and consommé and heat through. Ladle into warm soup bowls and serve.

* 25 calories per serving
* Fairly high fibre

Consommé with Brandy and Peas

SERVES 4

50 g/2 oz frozen peas
300 ml/¹/₂ pt/1¹/₄ cups water
295 g/10¹/₂ oz/1 medium can of condensed beef consommé
15 ml/1 tbsp brandy

Cook the peas in the water for 4 minutes. Add the consommé and heat through. Stir in the brandy and serve very hot in warmed bowls.

* 20 calories per serving
* Fairly high fibre

Light Leek and Potato Soup

SERVES 4

2 large leeks, well washed and sliced
15 g/¹/₂ oz/1 tbsp low-fat sunflower or olive oil spread
1 large potato, diced
300 ml/¹/₂ pt/1¹/₄ cups chicken or vegetable stock, made with 1 stock cube
1 bouquet garni sachet
Salt and freshly ground black pepper
300 ml/¹/₂ pt/1¹/₄ cups skimmed milk
Snipped chives, to garnish

Cook the leeks in the low-fat spread in a saucepan, stirring, for 3 minutes until softened but not browned. Add the potato and cook, stirring for 1 minute. Add the stock, the bouquet garni sachet and a little salt and pepper. Bring to the boil, part-cover, reduce the heat and simmer gently for 20 minutes. Remove the bouquet garni sachet. Purée in a blender or food processor and return to the saucepan. Stir in the milk. Taste and re-season, if necessary. Either reheat or cool, then chill before serving sprinkled with snipped chives.

* 100 calories per serving
* Medium fibre

Pumpkin Pottage

SERVES 6

750 g/1½ lb pumpkin, diced
600 ml/1 pt/2½ cups vegetable stock,
  made with 1 stock cube
600 ml/1 pt/2½ cups skimmed milk
Salt and freshly ground black pepper
15 ml/1 tbsp light brown sugar
A good pinch of grated nutmeg
15 ml/1 tbsp chopped parsley

Cook the pumpkin in the stock in a large saucepan for 20 minutes until tender. Purée in a blender or food processor. Return to the pan, stir in the milk, salt and pepper to taste, the sugar and nutmeg. Reheat but do not boil. Ladle into warm bowls and sprinkle with parsley before serving.

* **60 calories per serving**
* **Medium fibre**

Yoghurt Salad Soup

SERVES 4

400 g/14 oz/1 large can of tomatoes
5 cm/2 in piece of cucumber,
  quartered
1 red (bell) pepper, quartered and
  seeded
1 garlic clove, crushed
15 ml/1 tbsp Worcestershire sauce
A few drops of Tabasco sauce
150 ml/¼ pt/⅔ cup low-fat plain
  yoghurt
Salt and freshly ground black pepper

Empty the contents of the can of tomatoes into a blender or food processor. Add the cucumber, pepper and garlic and run the machine until well blended. Add the sauces and yoghurt and blend again. Season to taste. Chill until ready to serve.

* **50 calories per serving**
* **Medium fibre**

Chilled Smooth Tomato Soup

SERVES 4

400 g/14 oz/1 large can of tomatoes
15 ml/1 tbsp red wine vinegar
45 ml/3 tbsp low-fat crème fraîche
60 ml/4 tbsp apple juice
2.5 ml/½ tsp Dijon mustard
5 ml/1 tsp dried thyme
Salt and freshly ground black pepper

Rub the tomatoes through a sieve (strainer) to remove the seeds. Stir in the remaining ingredients and chill until ready to serve.

* **30 calories per serving**
* **Low fibre**

Russian-style Chilled Consommé

SERVES 6

3 x 295 g/3 x 10½ oz/3 medium cans
  of condensed beef consommé,
  chilled
45 ml/3 tbsp vodka
A few drops of Tabasco sauce
60 ml/4 tbsp low-fat crème fraîche
50 g/2 oz/1 small jar of Danish
  lumpfish roe

Mix the jellied consommé with the vodka and Tabasco sauce. Spoon into serving bowls. Top each with 10 ml/2 tsp crème fraîche and a spoonful of lumpfish roe and serve cold.

* **40 calories per serving**
* **No fibre**

Summer Raspberry Soup

SERVES 4

450 g/1 lb raspberries
100 g/4 oz/¹/₂ cup granulated sugar
900 ml/1¹/₂ pts/3³/₄ cups skimmed milk
4 small sprigs of raspberry leaves and a few extra fresh raspberries, to garnish (optional)

Heat the fruit and sugar in a saucepan until the juice runs. Purée in a blender or food processor, then pass through a sieve (strainer) to remove the seeds. Meanwhile, bring the milk slowly to the boil, then allow to cool. Stir into the purée and chill until ready to serve. Ladle into soup bowls and place the bowls on plates. Arrange a small sprig of raspberry leaves and a few berries on the plate at the side of each bowl, if liked.

* **220 calories per serving**
* **Low fibre**

English Strawberry Soup

SERVES 4

Prepare as for Summer Raspberry Soup, but substitute ripe strawberries for the raspberries and garnish with strawberry leaves and strawberries.

* **220 calories per serving**
* **Low fibre**

Blackcurrant and Mint Soup

SERVES 4

Prepare as for Summer Raspberry Soup, but substitute blackcurrants for the the raspberries. Put a large sprig of mint in the milk before heating and remove when the cold milk is added to the fruit purée. Garnish with a sprig of mint on the side of each bowl instead of the fruit leaves.

* **220 calories per serving**
* **Low fibre**

65

Blushing Beetroot and Orange Soup

If you don't want to use wine, use pure orange juice instead and spike it with an extra 5 ml/1 tsp wine vinegar

SERVES 4

2 cooked beetroot (red beets), roughly chopped
300 ml/¹/₂ pt/1¹/₄ cups vegetable stock, made with 1 stock cube
300 ml/¹/₂ pt/1¹/₄ cups dry white wine
10 ml/2 tsp white wine vinegar
Finely grated rind and juice of 1 orange
Salt and freshly ground black pepper
300 ml/¹/₂ pt/1¹/₄ cups low-fat plain yoghurt

Put all the ingredients in a blender or food processor and run the machine until smooth. Taste and re-season, if necessary. Chill until ready to serve.

* **100 calories per serving**
* **Fairly high fibre**

Cooling Cucumber and Dill Soup

SERVES 4

1 cucumber
Salt
10 ml/2 tsp dried dill (dill weed)
30 ml/2 tbsp cider vinegar
Freshly ground black pepper
300 ml/¹/₂ pt/1¹/₄ cups low-fat plain yoghurt
300 ml/¹/₂ pt/1¹/₄ cups skimmed milk

Cut four thin slices off the cucumber and reserve for garnish. Coarsely grate the remainder into a bowl. Sprinkle with salt and leave to stand for 10 minutes to draw out the moisture. Squeeze out and drain off all the moisture. Stir in the dill, vinegar and a good grinding of pepper, then stir in the yoghurt. Chill for at least 1 hour. Just before serving, stir in the milk, ladle into soup bowls and float a slice of cucumber on each.

* **65 calories per serving**
* **Medium fibre**

Cooling Cucumber, Tomato and Mint Soup

SERVES 4

Prepare as for Cooling Cucumber and Dill Soup but use ½ a cucumber and add 3 tomatoes, skinned, seeded and chopped, after squeezing out the moisture from the cucumber. Flavour with dried mint instead of dill (dill weed).

* **65 calories per serving**
* **Medium fibre**

Middle Eastern Sultana Soup

SERVES 4

100 g/4 oz green seedless grapes, halved
75 g/3 oz/¹/₂ cup sultanas (golden raisins)
300 ml/¹/₂ pt/1¹/₄ cups water
150 ml/¹/₄ pt/²/₃ cup dry white wine
150 ml/¹/₄ pt/²/₃ cup low-fat plain yoghurt
5 ml/1 tsp clear honey
1.5 ml/¹/₄ tsp ground cinnamon
Melba Toast (page 351), to serve

Purée all the ingredients in a blender or food processor. Chill until ready to serve with Melba Toast.

* **30 calories per serving**
* **Fairly high fibre**

Spanish Summer Soup

SERVES 4

1 slice of fresh bread
5 ml/1 tsp olive oil
15 ml/1 tbsp lemon juice
150 ml/¼ pt/⅔ cup iced water
1 shallot, roughly chopped
1 small garlic clove, chopped
1 small red (bell) pepper, roughly
    chopped
½ small cucumber, roughly chopped
400 g/14 oz/1 large can of tomatoes
15 ml/1 tbsp tomato purée (paste)
5 ml/1 tsp caster (superfine) sugar
Salt and freshly ground black pepper
Snipped chives, to garnish

Break up the piece of bread and place in a bowl with the oil, lemon juice and 30 ml/2 tbsp of the water. Leave to soak for 5 minutes. Place in a blender or food processor with the remaining ingredients except the remaining water and the seasoning. Run the machine until smooth. Stir in the iced water and season to taste. Ladle into soup bowls and garnish with snipped chives before serving.

* **75 calories per serving**
* **Fairly high fibre**

Chilled Guacamole Soup

SERVES 6

2 large ripe avocados
1 shallot, grated
15 ml/1 tbsp lemon juice
10 ml/2 tsp Worcestershire sauce
1.5 ml/¼ tsp Tabasco sauce
300 ml/½ pt/1¼ cups vegetable
    stock, made with 1 stock cube and
    cooled
450 ml/¾ pt/2 cups skimmed milk
5 cm/2 in piece of cucumber, very
    finely chopped
2 tomatoes, finely chopped
Salt and freshly ground black pepper
30 ml/2 tbsp snipped chives, to
    garnish

Peel the avocados, discard the stones (pits) and place in a blender or food processor with the shallot and lemon juice. Run the machine until smooth. Add the Worcestershire and Tabasco sauces and the cooled stock. Run the machine again. Turn the mixture into a bowl and stir in the remaining ingredients. Chill until ready to serve. Ladle into bowls and sprinkle each with snipped chives before serving.

* **190 calories per serving**
* **Medium fibre**

Fragrant Melon Soup

SERVES 4

*50 g/2 oz/¹/₄ cup caster (superfine)
  sugar*
90 ml/6 tbsp water
90 ml/6 tbsp apple juice
1 cantaloupe melon
Finely grated rind and juice of 1 lime
15 ml/1 tbsp chopped mint
15 ml/1 tbsp chopped basil
*Fresh Herb Baguette (page 350), to
  serve*

Put the sugar and water in a saucepan and heat until dissolved. Stir in the apple juice and leave to cool. Halve the melon and scoop out the seeds. Using a melon baller, cut out 20 balls (or cut 20 dice) and reserve. Scoop the remaining flesh into a blender or food processor. Add the prepared liquid and the lime rind and juice. Purée until smooth. Turn into a bowl and stir in the mint and basil. Chill until ready to serve. Ladle into soup bowls, garnish with the reserved melon pieces and serve with Fresh Herb Baguette.

* **30 calories per serving**
* **Low fibre**

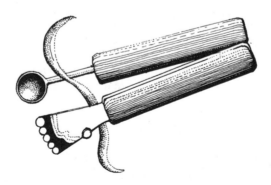

Starters and Light Meals

All of these make wonderful appetisers at the beginning of a special main meal. They also make perfect light lunch or supper dishes when served in slightly larger portions with, perhaps, some crusty bread, rolls or a side salad where appropriate.

Westphalian Beans with Pears

SERVES 6

4 cooking pears, cored and thickly sliced
450 ml/³/₄ pt/2 cups vegetable stock, made with 1 stock cube
Thickly pared rind of ¹/₂ lemon
450 g/1 lb French (green) beans, cut into short lengths
30 ml/2 tbsp light brown sugar
15 ml/1 tbsp cider vinegar
Salt and freshly ground black pepper
2.5 ml/¹/₂ tsp dried tarragon
2 thin slices of Westphalian ham, all fat removed, cut into thin strips
Light rye bread, to serve

Cook the pears in the stock with the lemon rind for 10 minutes. Discard the lemon rind. Add the beans and continue cooking for 5 minutes. Add the sugar and vinegar with a little salt and pepper and the tarragon. Boil rapidly until well reduced and syrupy. Spoon on to warm plates and sprinkle with the ham before serving with light rye bread.

* **60 calories per serving**
* **High fibre**

Parma Pears

SERVES 2 OR 4

2 wholemeal English muffins
20 ml/4 tsp low-fat sunflower or olive oil spread
2 thin slices of lean Parma (or similar) ham, all fat removed
2 ripe eating (dessert) pears, peeled, halved and cored
6 basil leaves, torn
50 g/2 oz/¹/₂ cup low-fat Mozzarella cheese, grated
Freshly ground black pepper
4 small sprigs of basil, to garnish

Split and toast the muffins, then spread with low-fat spread. Lay half a slice of Parma ham on each muffin half. Place on two or four flameproof plates. Cut a thin slice off the rounded sides of the pears so they will stand up. Place the pears, cored sides up, on the muffin halves and put the pear slices in the core holes. Sprinkle with the torn basil leaves and top with the cheese. Add a good grinding of black pepper, then flash under a hot grill (broiler) until the cheese has melted. Serve each garnished with a sprig of basil.

* **280 or 140 calories per serving**
* **High fibre**

Mint and Tarragon Pears

SERVES 6

Lollo rosso lettuce leaves
6 ripe pears
150 ml/¹/₄ pt/²/₃ cup low-fat crème
 fraîche
15 ml/1 tbsp lemon juice
5 ml/1 tsp clear honey
15 ml/1 tbsp chopped tarragon
15 ml/1 tbsp chopped mint
Salt and freshly ground black pepper
A few sprigs of tarragon and mint, to
 garnish

Arrange the lettuce leaves on six plates. Peel, halve and core the pears. Put two halves, rounded sides up, on each plate. Blend together the remaining ingredients and spoon over. Garnish with the sprigs of herbs and serve.

* **125 calories per serving**
* **Medium fibre**

Salade Niçoise

SERVES 4 OR 6

225 g/8 oz French (green) beans, cut
 into thirds
2 tomatoes, cut into small wedges
5 cm/2 in piece of cucumber, cubed
1 small onion, sliced and separated
 into rings
12 black olives
185 g/6¹/₂ oz/1 small can of tuna in
 brine or water, drained
15 ml/1 tbsp chopped parsley
Low-fat French Dressing (page 380)
1 hard-boiled (hard-cooked) egg,
 chopped

Cook the beans in lightly salted water for about 5 minutes until just tender. Drain, rinse with cold water and drain again. Place in a bowl and add the remaining ingredients except the egg. Toss gently. Spoon on to plates and sprinkle with the chopped egg before serving.

* **140 or 95 calories per serving**
* **High fibre**

Grilled Oysters with Jalapeño Salsa

SERVES 6

1 jalapeño chilli, seeded
3 ripe tomatoes, skinned
200 g/7 oz/1 small can of pimientos,
*   drained*
15 ml/1 tbsp tomato purée (paste)
15 ml/1 tbsp red wine vinegar
5 ml/1 tsp clear honey
Salt and freshly ground black pepper
18 fresh oysters in their shells

Put all the ingredients except the salt and pepper and the oysters in a blender or food processor. Run the machine until fairly smooth. Season to taste. Turn into a small saucepan and heat through. Open the oysters and remove the top shells. Add a good grinding of pepper to the oysters. Carefully put the oysters in their shells on the grill (broiler) rack and grill (broil) for about 3 minutes until the oysters sizzle. Transfer to plates, spoon a little salsa over each and serve.

* **50 calories per serving**
* **Medium fibre**

Corn Cobs with Soft Cheese and Chives

SERVES 4

4 sweetcorn (corn) cobs
50 g/2 oz/¹/₄ cup low-fat soft cheese
30 ml/2 tbsp skimmed milk
30 ml/2 tbsp snipped chives
Salt and freshly ground black pepper

Remove the leaves and silks from the corn. Cook in boiling, lightly salted water for about 20 minutes until tender. Drain and place on warm plates. Insert corn cob holders, if you have them. Meanwhile, put the cheese, milk and chives in a saucepan and heat gently, stirring, until blended and piping hot. Do not boil. Season to taste and spoon over the corn cobs.

* **185 calories per serving**
* **High fibre**

Corn Cobs with Soft Cheese, Tomatoes and Basil

SERVES 4

Prepare as for Corn Cobs with Soft Cheese and Chives but add 2 skinned, seeded and chopped tomatoes to the cheese mixture and substitute chopped basil for the chives.

* **190 calories per serving**
* **High fibre**

Tiger Prawns with Garlic Dip

SERVES 4

24 raw tiger prawns (jumbo shrimp),
heads removed
15 ml/1 tbsp olive oil
15 ml/1 tbsp lemon juice
1 large sprig of rosemary
Freshly ground black pepper
45 ml/3 tbsp low-calorie mayonnaise
45 ml/3 tbsp low-fat plain yoghurt
1 large garlic clove, crushed
15 ml/1 tbsp chopped parsley
Lemon wedges and sprigs of rosemary,
to garnish

Lay the prawns in a shallow dish. Whisk together the oil and lemon juice and pour over the prawns. Add the rosemary and a good grinding of pepper. Cover and chill for 2–3 hours, turning occasionally. Mix the mayonnaise with the yoghurt, garlic, parsley and a good grinding of pepper. Turn into a small bowl, cover and chill until ready to serve. Thread the marinated prawns on to four soaked wooden skewers. Grill (broil) for about 4 minutes, turning occasionally and brushing with any remaining marinade, until completely pink. Transfer to plates, garnish with lemon wedges and sprigs of rosemary and serve with the Garlic Dip.

* **130 calories per serving**

* **Low fibre**

Artichokes with Fragrant Vinaigrette

SERVES 6

6 globe artichokes
10 ml/2 tsp lemon juice
Salt and freshly ground black pepper
45 ml/3 tbsp sunflower or olive oil
30 ml/2 tbsp water
30 ml/2 tbsp white wine vinegar
5 ml/1 tsp caster (superfine) sugar
15 ml/1 tbsp chopped parsley
15 ml/1 tsp chopped basil
15 ml/1 tbsp snipped chives

Twist the stalks off the artichokes. Trim the tips of the leaves, if liked. Bring a large pan of water to the boil with the lemon juice and a little salt. Add the artichokes and cook for about 20 minutes until a leaf can be pulled off easily. Drain and dry on kitchen paper (paper towels). Leave to cool. Meanwhile, put the remaining ingredients with a little salt and lots of pepper in a screw-topped jar. Shake vigorously until well blended. Spoon into six small bowls. Put an artichoke with a bowl of dressing to one side on each of six plates. To eat: pull off the leaves, dip the fleshy end in the dressing, draw between the teeth, then discard. When all the leaves have been pulled off, cut off the hairy 'choke', then eat the base with a knife and fork, dipping it in any remaining dressing.

* **110 calories per serving**

* **Medium fibre**

Artichokes with Honey Nut Dressing

SERVES 6

Prepare as for Artichokes with Fragrant Vinaigrette (page 73), but substitute 2 quantities of Honey Nut Dressing (page 380) for the Fragrant Vinaigrette.

* 130 calories per serving
* Medium fibre

Artichokes with Hot Chilli Salsa

SERVES 6

Prepare as for Artichokes with Fragrant Vinaigrette (page 73), but substitute 1 quantity of Hot Chilli Salsa (page 383) for the Fragrant Vinaigrette.

* 100 calories per serving
* Medium fibre

Italian Crostini

SERVES 4 OR 8

8 diagonal slices from a ciabatta loaf
1 large garlic clove
175 g/6 oz button mushrooms, finely chopped
15 g/¹/₂ oz/1 tbsp low-fat sunflower or olive oil spread
15 ml/1 tbsp dry vermouth
Freshly ground black pepper
50 g/2 oz/¹/₃ cup stoned (pitted) black olives
5 ml/1 tsp lemon juice
15 ml/1 tbsp chopped basil

Lay the slices of bread on a baking (cookie) sheet. Halve the garlic clove and rub the cut surfaces all over the bread, then crush the garlic and reserve. Bake the bread in a preheated oven at 180°C/350°F/gas mark 4 for about 20 minutes until golden. Meanwhile, put the crushed garlic in a saucepan with the mushrooms, half the low-fat spread and the vermouth. Add a good grinding of pepper. Cook gently, stirring occasionally, for 5 minutes until soft. Meanwhile, purée the olives in a blender or food processor, stopping the machine and scraping down the sides, if necessary. Sharpen to taste with the lemon juice. Remove the bread from the oven, spread with the olive paste and top with the chopped mushrooms. Sprinkle with the basil and serve straight away.

* 60 calories per slice
* Medium fibre

Nectarine and Serrano Ham Crostini

SERVES 4

2 nectarines, skinned, halved and
    stoned (pitted)
8 slices of ciabatta
20 g/³/₄ oz/1¹/₂ tbsp low-fat sunflower
    or olive oil spread
4 wafer-thin slices of Serrano ham, all
    fat removed and halved widthways
175 g/6 oz low-fat Mozzarella cheese,
    sliced
Lollo rosso leaves
Low-fat French Dressing (page 380)

Cut each nectarine half into four slices. Spread the ciabatta slices with the low-fat spread. Toast until turning golden on the spread sides. Turn over and top each half with a slice of Serrano ham, then the cheese. Top each with two slices of nectarine and cook until the cheese is beginning to melt. Transfer to plates, add a garnish of lollo rosso leaves with a little Low-fat French Dressing spooned over.

* 120 calories per slice
* Medium fibre

Peach and Sweet-cured Ham Crostini

SERVES 4

Prepare as for Nectarine and Serrano Ham Crostini, but substitute lean sweet-cured ham (all fat removed) for the Serrano ham, and peeled, stoned (pitted) peaches for the nectarines.

* 120 calories per slice
* Medium fibre

Parma Ham and Melon with Herb Croûtons

SERVES 4

2 slices of white bread
Low-fat sunflower or olive oil spread
1.5 ml/¹/₄ tsp garlic salt
2.5 ml/¹/₂ tsp dried mixed herbs
2 small cantaloupe melons
4 wafer-thin slices of Parma ham, all
    fat removed

Spread with bread very lightly with low-fat spread. Cut into very small cubes. Heat a non-stick frying pan (skillet). Add the bread and sprinkle with the garlic salt and herbs. Toss over a moderate heat until golden brown and crisp. Tip on to kitchen paper (paper towels) and leave to cool. Halve the melon and scoop out the seeds. Place in small bowls. Cut the ham into thin strips and mix with the croûtons. Spoon into the cavities and serve straight away.

* 100 calories per serving
* Medium fibre

Champignons à la Grècque

SERVES 6

1 bunch of spring onions (scallions),
    chopped, reserving a little of the
    green for garnish
1 garlic clove, crushed
25 g/1 oz/2 tbsp low-fat sunflower or
    olive oil spread
300 ml/½ pt/1¼ cups red wine
A pinch of salt
Freshly ground black pepper
2.5 ml/½ tsp dried oregano
450 g/1 lb button mushrooms
400 g/14 oz/1 large can of chopped
    tomatoes
5 ml/1 tsp finely grated lemon rind
A pinch of caster (superfine) sugar
Round lettuce leaves
6 slices of lemon, to garnish

Put the spring onions in a large
saucepan with the garlic and oil.
Cook gently for 2 minutes, stirring.
Add all the remaining ingredients
except the lettuce leaves. Bring to the
boil, reduce the heat and simmer for
20 minutes until the mushrooms are
cooked and bathed in sauce. Leave
until cold, then chill. When ready to
serve, line six bowls with lettuce leaves
and spoon in the mushroom mixture.
Top each with a twist of lemon and a
sprinkling of spring onion tops.

* **80 calories per serving**
* **Medium fibre**

Mushrooms with Tuna Mayo

SERVES 6

225 g/8 oz button mushrooms, thinly
    sliced
Low-fat French Dressing (page 380)
85 g/3½ oz/1 very small can of tuna
    in brine or water, drained
6 canned anchovy fillets, drained and
    finely chopped
15 ml/1 tbsp capers, chopped
45 ml/3 tbsp low-calorie mayonnaise
15 ml/1 tbsp lemon juice
Freshly ground black pepper
Parsley sprigs, to garnish
Melba Toast (page 351), to serve

Put the mushrooms in a bowl. Add
the dressing, toss gently and leave
to marinate while preparing the tuna
mixture. Put the tuna in a bowl and
add the anchovies and capers. Stir in
the mayonnaise and lemon juice and
season with pepper. Divide the
mushrooms between six dishes. Top
with the tuna mixture, garnish with
parsley and serve with Melba Toast.

* **70 calories per serving**
* **Low fibre**

Mushrooms with Crab Mayo

SERVES 6

Prepare as for Mushrooms with Tuna
Mayo, but substitute drained,
canned crabmeat for the tuna.

* **75 calories per serving**
* **Low fibre**

Ratatouille

SERVES 6

1 aubergine (eggplant), sliced
Salt and freshly ground black pepper
25 g/1 oz/2 tbsp low-fat sunflower or
*   olive oil spread*
1 onion, sliced
1 garlic clove, crushed
1 red (bell) pepper, cut into thin strips
1 green pepper, cut into thin strips
1 large courgette (zucchini), sliced
4 ripe tomatoes, skinned and chopped
30 ml/2 tbsp tomato purée (paste)
150 ml/¹/₄ pt/²/₃ cup red wine
2.5 ml/¹/₂ tsp dried mixed herbs
5 ml/1 tsp caster (superfine) sugar
30 ml/2 tbsp grated Parmesan cheese

Put the aubergine slices in a colander. Sprinkle with salt and leave to stand for 30 minutes. Rinse well. Heat the spread in a large saucepan. Add the onion and garlic and fry (sauté) for 2 minutes. Add all the prepared vegetables including the aubergine slices and cook, stirring, for 3 minutes. Mix the tomato purée with the wine and add with the herbs and sugar. Season with a little salt and pepper. Bring to the boil, cover, reduce the heat and simmer for 20 minutes until the vegetables are tender. Serve hot, or leave to cool, then chill before serving, sprinkled with a little Parmesan cheese.

* **75 calories per serving**
* **Fairly high fibre**

Cooling Pea Pâté

SERVES 4

225 g/8 oz frozen peas
Salt and freshly ground black pepper
50 g/2 oz/¹/₄ cup low-fat fromage frais
5 ml/1 tsp chopped mint
A small sprig of mint, to garnish
Melba Toast (page 351), to serve

Cook the peas in just enough water to cover for 5 minutes or until tender. Drain, reserving the cooking water, and purée in a blender or food processor with some salt and pepper, the low-fat spread and the mint. Thin with a little cooking water, if necessary, to form a spreadable paste. Spoon into a small dish. Garnish with a small sprig of mint and serve with Melba Toast.

* **50 calories per serving**
* **High fibre**

Smooth Broad Bean Pâté

SERVES 4

Prepare as for Cooling Pea Pâté, but substitute frozen broad (fava) beans for the peas and dried oregano for the mint. Season with a pinch of grated nutmeg as well as the salt and pepper.

* **55 calories per serving**
* **High fibre**

Blended Butter Bean Pâté

SERVES 4

Prepare as for Cooling Pea Pâté (page 77), but use 425 g/15 oz/ 1 large can of butter (lima) beans, drained, instead of the cooked peas and add 1 small crushed garlic clove to the mixture. Flavour with dried mixed herbs instead of mint.

* 55 calories per serving
* High fibre

Waldorf Stuffed Cucumber

SERVES 4

1 large cucumber, halved lengthways
Salt and freshly ground black pepper
1 red eating (dessert) apple, diced
30 ml/2 tbsp walnuts, chopped
1 celery stick, finely chopped
100 g/4 oz/¹/₂ cup low-fat cottage cheese
30 ml/2 tbsp low-calorie mayonnaise
2 stuffed olives, sliced, to garnish

Scoop the seeds out of the cucumber and discard. Cut the halves in half widthways to form four 'boats'. Boil in lightly salted water for 1 minute. Drain, rinse with cold water and drain again. Mix together the remaining ingredients, seasoning to taste, and pile on to the cucumber. Garnish with olive slices and serve cold.

* 80 calories per serving
* High fibre

Jellied Tomatoes

SERVES 4

4 tomatoes
75 g/3 oz/¹/₃ cup low-fat soft cheese
15 ml/1 tbsp skimmed milk
15 ml/1 tbsp snipped chives
15 ml/1 tbsp chopped parsley
Salt and freshly ground black pepper
15 ml/1 tbsp medium-dry sherry
5 ml/1 tsp powdered gelatine
295 g/10¹/₂ oz/1 medium can of condensed beef comsommé
4 small sprigs of parsley

Plunge the tomatoes into boiling water for 30 seconds. Drain and peel off the skins. Cut a slice off the top of each tomato and reserve. Scoop out the seeds and discard. Mash the cheese with the milk, herbs, a little salt and a good grinding of pepper. Spoon into the tomatoes and replace the 'lids'. Place in four ramekin dishes (custard cups). Put the sherry in a small bowl and sprinkle the gelatine over. Leave to soften for 5 minutes, then stand the bowl in a pan of hot water and stir until the gelatine dissolves completely. Stir into the consommé. Spoon over the tomatoes and chill until set. Garnish each with a small sprig of parsley before serving.

* 40 calories per serving
* Low fibre

Barely Bagna Cauda

SERVES 4 OR 6

*15 g/¹/₂ oz/1 tbsp low-fat sunflower or
olive oil spread*
1 small onion, finely chopped
*1 large ripe tomato, skinned and finely
chopped*
5 ml/1 tsp cornflour (cornstarch)
*50 g/2 oz/1 small can of anchovy
fillets, drained, rinsed and finely
chopped*
A few drops of Tabasco sauce
*50 g/2 oz/¹/₂ cup low-fat Cheddar
cheese, grated*
100 g/4 oz/¹/₂ cup low-fat soft cheese
15 ml/1 tbsp skimmed milk
*Carrots, cucumber, green and red (bell)
peppers and celery, cut into
matchsticks, to serve*

Heat the low-fat spread in a flameproof serving dish or fondue pot. Add the onion and tomato and cook gently, stirring, until the onion is softened. Remove from the heat and stir in the cornflour. Add the anchovies and return to the heat. Cook, stirring, until the anchovies form a paste. Stir in the Tabasco sauce, cheeses and milk and simmer gently for 3 minutes. Serve hot with the vegetables to dip in.

* **110 or 75 calories per serving**
* **Low fibre**

Asparagus with Tarragon Vinaigrette

SERVES 6

750 g/1¹/₂ lb thin asparagus spears
Salt
75 ml/5 tbsp white wine vinegar
30 ml/2 tbsp sunflower oil
30 ml/2 tbsp water
Freshly ground black pepper
2.5 ml/¹/₂ tsp caster (superfine) sugar
30 ml/2 tbsp chopped tarragon
15 ml/1 tbsp chopped parsley

Trim off any thick woody ends from the asparagus and tie in two bundles. Stand the bundles in a large pan of boiling water with a pinch of salt added. Bring back to the boil, cover with a lid (or foil if the bunches are too tall). Simmer for 10 minutes. Drain, reserving the liquid for soup or stock if liked. Rinse the asparagus with cold water, drain again and leave until completely cold. Chill. Meanwhile, put the remaining ingredients in a screw-topped jar and add a pinch of salt. Shake vigorously until well blended. Chill. When ready to serve, lay the asparagus on plates. Shake the dressing again and spoon across the stems. Serve cold.

* **75 calories per serving**
* **Fairly high fibre**

Asparagus with Sage and Onion Vinaigrette

SERVES 6

Prepare as for Asparagus with Tarragon Vinaigrette (page 79), but substitute 15 ml/1 tbsp chopped sage for the tarragon and add 1 small finely chopped onion to the mixture.

* 75 calories per serving
* Fairly high fibre

Baby Asparagus Spears

SERVES 4

350 g/12 oz baby asparagus spears, trimmed
Salt and freshly ground black pepper
40 g/1½ oz/3 tbsp low-fat sunflower or olive oil spread
10 ml/2 tsp lemon juice
15 ml/1 tbsp snipped chives
15 ml/1 tbsp chopped parsley

Tie the spears in four small bundles. Stand them in a small saucepan and half-fill with boiling water. Add a little salt. Cover and cook for 6 minutes. Leave the lid on, turn off the heat and leave to stand for 5 minutes. Carefully lift out of the pan and arrange on four small warm plates. Meanwhile, melt the low-fat spread with the lemon juice, herbs and some pepper. Spoon over the asparagus and serve.

* 65 calories per serving
* Fairly high fibre

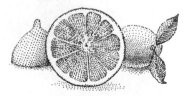

Chilled Baby Asparagus Spears with Smoked Salmon

SERVES 4

Prepare as for Baby Asparagus Spears, but leave the asparagus to cool after cooking, then chill. Use low-fat crème fraîche instead of the low-fat spread and lay a curled slice of smoked salmon to the side of the asparagus on each plate before serving.

* 85 calories per serving
* Fairly high fibre

Mozzarella-topped Aubergines

SERVES 6

1 garlic clove, halved
2 large aubergines (eggplants), sliced
A pinch of salt
Freshly ground black pepper
300 ml/½ pt/1¼ cups passata (sieved tomatoes)
30 ml/2 tbsp tomato purée (paste)
5 ml/1 tsp dried basil
100 g/4 oz/1 cup low-fat Mozzarella cheese, grated

Rub around the sides and bases of six shallow individual ovenproof dishes with the cut garlic, then discard. Cook the aubergine slices in boiling water for 5 minutes until just tender. Drain and arrange in the prepared dishes. Season with the salt and lots of pepper. Whisk the passata with the tomato purée and basil and spoon over the aubergines. Sprinkle with the cheese, then bake in a preheated oven at 200°C/ 400°F/gas mark 6 for 15 minutes until the cheese has melted and is bubbling. Serve hot.

* 65 calories per serving
* Fairly high fibre

Campari Soda Cocktail

SERVES 6

6 oranges
120 ml/4 fl oz/¹/₂ cup Campari
600 ml/1 pt/2¹/₂ cups soda water
6 sprigs of mint

Thinly pare the rind off one of the oranges, cut into thin strips and boil in water for 3 minutes. Drain, rinse with cold water and drain again. Cut all the peel and pith off all the oranges, cut the fruit into slices, then each slice into quarters. Place in a container with a lid, add the Campari and chill until ready to serve. Spoon the oranges and Campari into six wine goblets, top up with soda water, add a sprig of mint to each and serve immediately.

* **95 calories per serving**
* **Low fibre**

Fresh Figs with Bresaola

SERVES 6

6 fresh ripe figs
12 thin slices of bresaola (dried beef)
90 ml/6 tbsp low-fat fromage frais
6 toasted hazelnuts (filberts)

Trim the base of each fig so it will stand up, if necessary. Cut a cross in the top of each fig and gently open up slightly to resemble a flower bud. Lay the bresaola on six plates and place a fig on each plate. Top each fig with a spoonful of fromage frais and garnish with a hazelnut.

* **90 calories per serving**
* **Fairly high fibre**

Fresh Figs with Parma Ham

SERVES 6

Prepare as for Fresh Figs with Bresaola, but substitute Parma ham, all fat removed, for the bresaola and garnish the fromage frais with black olives instead of hazelnuts (filberts).

* **85 calories per serving**
* **Fairly high fibre**

Tomato and Mozzarella Salad

SERVES 4

4 beefsteak tomatoes, halved and
*   thinly sliced*
100 g/4 oz low-fat Mozzarella cheese,
*   sliced*
16 basil leaves, torn
10 ml/2 tsp olive oil
Freshly ground black pepper
Hot crusty bread, to serve

Arrange the tomato slices and Mozzarella attractively on four small plates. Scatter the torn basil leaves over. Drizzle with a very little olive oil and sprinkle liberally with pepper. Serve with hot crusty bread.

* **100 calories per serving**
* **Medium fibre**

Crudités with Tuna Salsa

SERVES 4

185 g/6½ oz/1 small can of tuna in
   brine or water, drained
2 ripe tomatoes, seeded and finely
   chopped
1 shallot, finely chopped
1 small green (bell) pepper, seeded
   and finely chopped
1 small green or red chilli, seeded and
   finely chopped
Freshly ground black pepper
A dash of Worcestershire sauce
2 carrots, cut into matchsticks
½ cucumber, cut into matchsticks
3 celery sticks, cut into matchsticks
4 tiny sprigs of parsley

Flake the tuna thoroughly in a bowl.
Mix in the tomatoes, shallot,
pepper and chilli. Season with pepper
and Worcestershire sauce and chill.
Chill the crudités. When ready to serve,
divide the salsa between four small
pots. Place on plates and arrange the
vegetable sticks around. Garnish the
pots of salsa with small sprigs of
parsley and serve.

* 70 calories per serving
* Fairly high fibre

Crudités with Corn Salsa

SERVES 4

Prepare as for Crudités with Tuna
Salsa, but substitute a 200 g/7 oz/
1 small can of sweetcorn (corn),
drained, for the tuna and mix with the
other ingredients.

* 75 calories per serving
* Fairly high fibre

Iceberg Boats

SERVES 4

½ cucumber, chopped
4 tomatoes, chopped
½ small yellow (bell) pepper, diced
75 ml/5 tbsp low-fat plain yoghurt
5 ml/1 tsp dried mint
1 small garlic clove, crushed (optional)
Salt and freshly ground black pepper
4 large iceberg lettuce leaves
10 ml/2 tsp fennel seeds and
   4 gherkins (cornichons), to garnish

Mix the cucumber, tomato and
pepper with the yoghurt, mint,
garlic, if using, and salt and pepper to
taste. Pile into the lettuce leaves.
Garnish each with a sprinkling of
fennel seeds and a gherkin 'fan' made
by making several cuts from the tip
almost through to the stalk end of each
pickle, then gently opening it up.

* 35 calories per serving
* Medium fibre

Flageolet and Tuna Vinaigrette

SERVES 4

425 g/15 oz/1 large can of flageolet
  beans, rinsed and drained
185 g/6½ oz/1 small can of tuna in
  brine or water, drained
1 small onion, sliced and separated
  into rings
1 small green (bell) pepper, diced
1 garlic clove, crushed
15 ml/1 tbsp olive oil
15 ml/1 tbsp white wine vinegar
15 ml/1 tbsp water
5 ml/1 tsp chopped thyme
A pinch of salt
Freshly ground black pepper
15 ml/1 tbsp chopped parsley

Put the beans in a bowl with the tuna, onion and pepper. Whisk together the remaining ingredients except the parsley. Pour over and toss gently. Cover and chill for 1 hour to allow the flavours to develop. Spoon on to small plates and sprinkle with chopped parsley.

* **150 calories per serving**
* **High fibre**

Haricot Bean and Salmon Vinaigrette

SERVES 4

Prepare as for Flageolet and Tuna Vinaigrette, but substitute haricot (navy) beans for the flageolet beans and canned salmon, all skin and bones removed, for the tuna.

* **170 calories per serving**
* **High fibre**

Aubergine Pâté

SERVES 6

1 large aubergine (eggplant)
5 ml/1 tsp lemon juice
30 ml/2 tbsp low-fat plain yoghurt
1 shallot, finely chopped
100 g/4 oz/½ cup low-fat soft cheese
15 ml/1 tbsp snipped chives
15 ml/1 tbsp chopped parsley
Salt and freshly ground black pepper
Rye bread, to serve

Cut the stalk off the aubergine and discard. Boil in water with the lemon juice added for 10–15 minutes until really tender. Drain and when cool enough to handle, peel off the skin and discard. Purée the flesh in a blender or food processor and then blend in the yoghurt, shallot, cheese, chives and half the parsley. Season to taste. Spoon into small pots, sprinkle with the remaining parsley and chill. Serve with rye bread.

* **45 calories per serving**
* **Medium fibre**

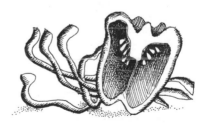

Warm Scallop, Bacon and Apple Salad

SERVES 4

175 g/6 oz ready-prepared mixed salad
  leaves
4 cherry tomatoes, quartered
5 cm/2 in piece of cucumber, diced
1 small red onion, thinly sliced and
  separated into rings
15 ml/1 tbsp olive oil
1 small onion, finely chopped
2 rashers (slices) of extra-lean, rindless
  back bacon, cut into small pieces
1 small red eating (dessert) apple,
  cored and diced
175 g/6 oz queen scallops
60 ml/4 tbsp cider
15 ml/1 tbsp snipped chives
Freshly ground black pepper
30 ml/2 tbsp cider vinegar
15 ml/1 tbsp water
Chopped parsley, to garnish

Arrange the salad leaves on four
plates. Scatter the tomatoes,
cucumber and onion rings over. Heat
the oil in a large frying pan (skillet).
Add the chopped onion, bacon and
apple and fry (sauté) for 1 minute. Add
the scallops and cook, stirring, for
2–3 minutes. Add the cider, chives and
pepper and simmer for 2 minutes. Lift
the scallop and bacon mixture out of
the pan with a draining spoon and
place on the salad. Quickly add the
vinegar, water and another good
grinding of pepper to the juices and
bring just to the boil. Spoon over the
salads and sprinkle with chopped
parsley before serving straight away.

* 110 calories per serving
* Fairly high fibre

Smoked Salmon with Watercress and Orange

SERVES 6

1 bunch of watercress
2 oranges
100 g/4 oz smoked salmon pieces
¼ cucumber, diced
15 ml/1 tbsp olive oil
15 ml/1 tbsp pure orange juice
10 ml/2 tsp lemon juice
Freshly ground black pepper
5 ml/1 tsp horseradish relish

Trim the feathery stalks off the
watercress and separate into
sprigs. Place in a bowl. Holding them
over the bowl, cut all the rind and pith
off both oranges. Separate the fruit into
segments by cutting either side of each
membrane and add to the bowl.
Squeeze the membranes over to
extract any juice. Add the smoked
salmon and the cucumber. Whisk
together the oil, orange and lemon
juice, lots of pepper and the
horseradish. Pour over the watercress,
salmon and orange and toss gently.
Spoon into bowls and serve.

* 80 calories per serving
* Fairly high fibre

Minted Melon with Garlic Cheese Bread

SERVES 6

1 honeydew melon
30 ml/2 tbsp chopped mint
90 ml/6 tbsp apple juice
1 small wholemeal baguette
25 g/1 oz/2 tbsp low-fat sunflower or olive oil spread
75 g/3 oz/^{1}/$_3$ cup low-fat garlic-and-herb soft cheese
30 ml/2 tbsp chopped parsley
Freshly ground black pepper
6 small mint sprigs, to garnish

Halve the melon and remove the seeds. Use a melon baller to scoop the flesh out of the shell (or peel and cut the fruit into dice). Place in a sealable container and add the mint and apple juice. Cover and chill. Cut the baguette into 12 slices, not quite through the base crust. Mash the low-fat spread with the cheese, parsley and lots of pepper and spread between the slices. Wrap in foil, shiny side in. Bake in a preheated oven at 200°C/400°F/ gas mark 6 for 15 minutes until the crust feels crisp when squeezed. Spoon the melon and juice into six small glass bowls and garnish each with a small sprig of mint. Serve with the hot garlic bread.

* **145 calories per serving**
* **Fairly high fibre**

Poor Man's Caviare

SERVES 4

1 large aubergine (eggplant)
1 shallot, finely chopped
1 small garlic clove, crushed
2 ripe tomatoes, skinned and chopped
15 ml/1 tbsp olive oil
Lemon juice
Salt and freshly ground black pepper
15 ml/1 tbsp chopped parsley, to garnish
Wholemeal toast, to serve

Grill (broil) the aubergine, turning occasionally, until the skin is blackened and the aubergine feels soft when squeezed. Cool slightly, then cut in half, scoop out the flesh, chop finely, and place in a bowl. Add the shallot, garlic and tomatoes and mix well. Beat in the oil, a drop at a time, until the mixture is glistening. Add lemon juice and seasoning to taste. Spoon into small pots, sprinkle with chopped parsley and serve with wholemeal toast.

* **50 calories per serving**
* **Medium fibre**

Tunis Tapenade

SERVES 6

450 g/1 lb carrots, sliced
1 large parsnip, sliced
Salt
1 small garlic clove, crushed
5 ml/1 tsp ground cumin
5 ml/1 tsp ground cinnamon
2.5 ml/¹/₂ tsp grated fresh root ginger
10 ml/2 tsp paprika
15 ml/1 tbsp olive oil
Lemon juice, to taste
5 ml/1 tsp poppy seeds
Sesame seed pitta breads, to serve

Cook the carrots and parsnip in boiling, lightly salted water until tender. Drain. Place in a blender or food processor with the remaining ingredients except the lemon juice and poppy seeds. Purée until smooth. Stir in lemon juice to taste. Spoon into small bowls and sprinkle with poppy seeds. Chill until ready to serve with sesame seed pitta breads, cut into fingers.

* **60 calories per serving**
* **Fairly high fibre**

Stuffed Tomatoes with Cucumber Ribbons

SERVES 6

6 large tomatoes
1 onion, finely chopped
15 g/¹/₂ oz/1 tbsp low-fat sunflower or olive oil spread
50 g/2 oz/¹/₄ cup brown long-grain rice
150 ml/¹/₄ pt/²/₃ cup vegetable stock, made with ¹/₂ stock cube
Salt and freshly ground black pepper
30 ml/2 tbsp pine nuts
30 ml/2 tbsp currants
A sprig of rosemary
¹/₂ cucumber
Low-fat French Dressing (page 380)

Cut a slice off the rounded end of each tomato and reserve. Scoop out the seedy pulp into a bowl. Fry (sauté) the onion in the low-fat spread gently for 2 minutes, stirring. Add the rice and stir for 1 minute. Add the stock and a little salt and pepper, cover and simmer for 30 minutes. Stir in the pine nuts, currants and rosemary and cook for a further 15 minutes. Taste and re-season, if necessary. Discard the rosemary and add the tomato pulp. Leave the mixture to cool, then spoon into the tomatoes and replace the 'lids'. Using a potato peeler, pare long thin ribbons off the cucumber. Put the tomatoes on plates and arrange a pile of cucumber ribbons to one side, spoon a little dressing over the cucumber and serve.

* **115 calories per serving**
* **Fairly high fibre**

Peking Prawns with Beansprouts

SERVES 6

175 g/6 oz/3 cups beansprouts
1 small red (bell) pepper, cut into very
thin strips
1 carrot, shaved into thin strips with a
potato peeler
5 cm/2 in piece of cucumber, shaved
into thin strips with a potato peeler
2 spring onions (scallions), chopped
100 g/4 oz cooked peeled prawns
(shrimp)
15 ml/1 tbsp reduced-salt soy sauce
10 ml/2 tsp white wine vinegar
5 ml/1 tsp caster (superfine) sugar
A pinch of ground ginger
15 ml/1 tbsp sesame or sunflower oil
Lettuce leaves, to serve

Put the prepared vegetables and the prawns in a bowl. Whisk together the remaining ingredients and pour over. Toss and chill for 30 minutes. Arrange the lettuce leaves in small bowls, spoon the vegetable and prawn mixture over and serve.

* **75 calories per serving**
* **Fairly high fibre**

Chinese Crab with Beansprouts

SERVES 6

Prepare as for Peking Prawns with Beansprouts, but substitute chopped crab sticks for the prawns (shrimp).

* **75 calories per serving**
* **Fairly high fibre**

Prawn and Cucumber Serenity

SERVES 6

1 large cucumber, diced
25 g/1 oz/2 tbsp low-fat sunflower or
olive oil spread
175 g/6 oz button mushrooms, thinly
sliced
15 ml/1 tbsp snipped chives
15 ml/1 tbsp plain (all-purpose) flour
150 ml/¹/₄ pt/²/₃ cup chicken stock,
made with ¹/₂ stock cube
15 ml/1 tbsp medium-dry sherry
90 ml/6 tbsp low-fat crème fraîche
175 g/6 oz cooked peeled prawns
(shrimp)
Salt and freshly ground black pepper
Paprika, to garnish
French bread, to serve

Cook the cucumber in boiling water for 3 minutes. Drain, rinse with cold water and drain again. Melt the low-fat spread in a saucepan, add the mushrooms and chives and fry (sauté) for 2 minutes, stirring. Add the cucumber, cover and cook over a gentle heat for 3 minutes. Stir in the flour, remove from the heat and blend in the stock, sherry and crème fraîche. Return to the heat, bring to the boil and cook for 2 minutes, stirring. Add the prawns and cook for a further 2 minutes. Season to taste. Spoon into small warm bowls, sprinkle with paprika and serve with French bread.

* **75 calories per serving**
* **Medium fibre**

Low-fat Garlic Mushrooms

SERVES 4

8 large flat mushrooms
1–2 large garlic cloves, crushed
Salt and freshly ground black pepper
150 ml/¹/₄ pt/²/₃ cup dry white wine
150 ml/¹/₄ pt/²/₃ cup low-fat crème fraîche
30 ml/2 tbsp chopped parsley
Crusty bread, to serve

Peel the mushrooms and remove the stalks. Chop the stalks and scatter over the gills. Place in a non-stick baking tin (pan). Sprinkle over the garlic to taste and season with salt and pepper. Whisk together the wine and crème fraîche and pour around. Cover with foil and bake in a preheated oven at 190°C/375°F/gas mark 5 for 20 minutes. Transfer the mushrooms to warm plates, spoon the juices over, sprinkle with parsley and serve with lots of crusty bread.

* **80 calories per serving**
* **Low fibre**

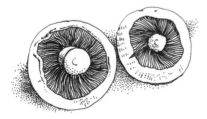

Mushroom and Basil Pâté

Ideally, use a processor to chop the onion and mushrooms.

SERVES 4

15 g/¹/₂ oz/1 tbsp low-fat sunflower or olive oil spread
1 small onion, very finely chopped
350 g/12 oz button mushrooms, very finely chopped
15 ml/1 tbsp lemon juice
225 g/8 oz/1 cup low-fat soft cheese
12 basil leaves, chopped
Salt and freshly ground black pepper
4 small sprigs of basil, to garnish
Hot toast, to serve

Heat the low-fat spread in a saucepan and fry (sauté) the onion for 3 minutes until lightly golden. Add the mushrooms, stir, cover, reduce the heat and cook gently for 5 minutes. Remove the lid, turn up the heat and cook until no liquid remains, stirring all the time. Add the lemon juice, turn into a bowl and leave to cool. Beat in the cheese and chopped basil, then season to taste. Spoon into small pots and chill until ready to serve. Garnish each with a small sprig of basil and serve with hot toast.

* **125 calories per serving**
* **Low fibre**

Warm Chicken Livers with Blueberries

SERVES 4

25 g/1 oz/2 tbsp low-fat sunflower or olive oil spread
450 g/1 lb chicken livers, trimmed
Salt and freshly ground black pepper
175 g/6 oz blueberries
15 ml/1 tbsp port
175 g/6 oz mixed salad leaves
30 ml/2 tbsp raspberry vinegar
15 ml/1 tbsp olive oil
5 ml/1 tsp wholegrain mustard

Heat the low-fat spread in a non-stick frying pan (skillet), add the chicken livers and a little seasoning and toss quickly for 4–5 minutes until just cooked but still soft. Remove from the pan and keep warm. Add the blueberries and port, cover and cook gently for 1 minute. Meanwhile, arrange the salad leaves on plates. Whisk together the vinegar, oil and mustard, season with salt and pepper and spoon over the salad. Top with the chicken livers and spoon over the blueberries and their juices. Serve warm.

* **235 calories per serving**
* **Medium fibre**

Tropical Cheese

SERVES 4

1 small ripe pineapple
225 g/8 oz/1 cup low-fat cottage cheese
5 cm/2 in piece of cucumber, chopped
½ small red (bell) pepper, chopped
Salt and freshly ground black pepper
Lettuce leaves
30 ml/2 tbsp toasted flaked (slivered) almonds

Cut the pineapple in quarters lengthways, leaving the green leaves intact. Cut most of the flesh off the skin, leaving a thin layer of fruit. Chop the flesh, discarding any hard core. Mix with the cottage cheese, cucumber and chopped pepper and season with salt and pepper. Lay the pineapple skins on a bed of lettuce on plates. Pile the cheese mixture on top and sprinkle with the almonds before serving.

* **100 calories per serving**
* **Fairly high fibre**

Honey-glazed Orange and Grapefruit Cocktail

SERVES 4

2 grapefruit
2 oranges
30 ml/2 tbsp medium-dry sherry
30 ml/2 tbsp clear honey

Halve the grapefruit and, using a serrated-edged knife, remove all the flesh in segments and place in a bowl. Discard the membranes and place the grapefruit shells in flameproof dishes. Cut off all the pith and peel from the oranges and separate the fruit into segments, discarding the membranes. Mix with the grapefruit. Stir in the sherry and pile back into the grapefruit shells. Drizzle the honey over and grill (broil) until bubbling and glazed on top. Serve hot.

* **90 calories per serving**
* **Low fibre**

Grilled Pink Grapefruit with Port

SERVES 4

2 pink grapefruit
30 ml/2 tbsp port
30 ml/2 tbsp caster (superfine) sugar

Halve the grapefruit and, using a serrated-edged knife, separate the flesh from the skin all round the edge, then loosen the segments by cutting either side of each membrane. Place in flameproof dishes. Spoon the port over, sprinkle with the sugar and grill (broil) until bubbling and golden on top. Serve straight away.

* **55 calories per serving**
* **Low fibre**

Grilled Liqueur Oranges

SERVES 4

2 large oranges
20 ml/4 tsp light brown sugar
30 ml/2 tbsp orange liqueur
4 maraschino cherries

Halve the oranges and, using a serrated-edged knife, separate the flesh from the skin all round the edge, then loosen the segments by cutting either side of each membrane. Place in flameproof dishes and sprinkle each with 5 ml/1 tsp sugar. Grill (broil) until bubbling, then spoon the liqueur over. Top each with a cherry and serve.

* **75 calories per serving**
* **Low fibre**

Melon Stuffed with Kiwi and Grand Marnier

Choose well-rounded kiwi fruit that will fit nicely in the centre of the melon.

SERVES 4
---

2 small cantaloupe melons
2 kiwi fruit
40 ml/8 tsp Grand Marnier

Halve the melons and scoop out the seeds. Place in individual glass dishes. Peel the kiwi fruit and halve horizontally. Place half a kiwi fruit, cut-sides up, in the melon cavities. Trim the bases, if necessary, so they fit snugly. Spoon the liqueur over and serve.

* **60 calories per serving**
* **Low fibre**

Melon with Gingered Cottage Cheese

SERVES 4
---

2 cantaloupe, ogen or chanterais
*   melons*
225 g/8 oz/1 cup low-fat cottage
*   cheese*
1 piece of stem ginger in syrup, finely
*   chopped*
Freshly ground black pepper

Halve the melons and scoop out the seeds. Place the fruit in bowls. Mix the cottage cheese with the ginger and pile into the centres. Top each with a good grinding of black pepper and chill, if time, before serving.

* **80 calories per serving**
* **Low fibre**

Melon and Cherry Cocktail

SERVES 4 OR 6
---

1 honeydew melon
200 g/7 oz/1 small jar of maraschino
*   cherries*
60 ml/4 tbsp apple juice
Finely grated rind and juice of
*   ¹/₂ lemon*

Halve the melon and scoop out the seeds. Either scoop the flesh into balls with a melon baller or peel and cut into dice. Place in a bowl. Add the contents of the jar of maraschino cherries, the apple juice and lemon rind and juice. Toss gently and chill, if liked, before serving in glass dishes.

* **50 or 35 calories per serving**
* **Low fibre**

Jellied Gazpachio Ring

SERVES 6

150 ml/¹/₄ pt/²/₃ cup water
20 ml/4 tsp powdered gelatine
¹/₂ cucumber, grated
1 litre/1³/₄ pts/4¹/₄ cups tomato juice
Finely grated rind of ¹/₂ lemon
*1 small green (bell) pepper, finely
  chopped*
1 shallot, grated
Watercress, to garnish

Put the water in a small bowl. Sprinkle the gelatine over and leave to soften for 5 minutes. Stand the bowl in a pan of hot water and stir until the gelatine dissolves (or heat in the microwave briefly). Squeeze the cucumber to remove excess liquid. Stir into the gelatine with the remaining ingredients, seasoning with lots of freshly ground black pepper. Pour into a wetted 1.5 litre/2½ pt/6 cup ring mould. Chill until set. Dip the base briefly in hot water and turn out on a serving plate. Fill the centre with watercress to garnish.

* **55 calories per serving**
* **Medium fibre**

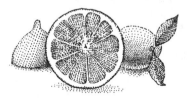

Greek-style Baby Onions

SERVES 4

450 g/1 lb baby (pearl) onions
250 ml/8 fl oz/1 cup dry white wine
30 ml/2 tbsp clear honey
*15 g/¹/₂ oz/1 tbsp low-fat sunflower or
  olive oil spread*
1 bay leaf
Juice of 1 small lime
*225 g/8 oz/1 small can of chopped
  tomatoes*
30 ml/2 tbsp tomato purée (paste)
150 ml/¹/₄ pt/²/₃ cup water
1 bouquet garni sachet
Freshly ground black pepper
*30 ml/2 tbsp chopped parsley, to
  garnish*

Bring a pan of water to the boil. Trim the tops and roots from the onions and drop into the water. Cook for 1 minute, then drain, rinse with cold water and drain again. Peel the onions. Mix together all the remaining ingredients in the saucepan, then add the onions. Bring to the boil, reduce the heat and simmer gently for about 15 minutes or until tender. Lift out the onions with a draining spoon. Bring the liquid to the boil and boil rapidly for about 10 minutes until reduced by half. Return the onions to the pan and leave to cool. Chill thoroughly. Serve in shallow bowls, garnished with the parsley.

* **125 calories per serving**
* **Medium fibre**

Sweet and Sour French Beans

SERVES 6

750 g/1¹/₂ lb thin French (green) beans
15 g/¹/₂ oz/1 tbsp low-fat sunflower or
olive oil spread
100 g/4 oz button mushrooms, sliced
2 spring onions (scallions), chopped
30 ml/2 tbsp Worcestershire sauce
30 ml/2 tbsp reduced-salt soy sauce
15 ml/1 tbsp water
30 ml/2 tbsp light brown sugar
30 ml/2 tbsp white wine vinegar
15 ml/1 tbsp sesame seeds

Top and tail the beans and boil in water for 5 minutes until they are just tender but still have some 'bite'. Drain. Heat the low-fat spread in a large frying pan (skillet). Add the mushrooms and spring onions and fry (sauté) for 3 minutes, stirring. Add the beans and the remaining ingredients except the sesame seeds and toss over a gentle heat for 2 minutes. Pile on to plates, sprinkle with a few sesame seeds and serve hot.

* **70 calories per serving**
* **Fairly high fibre**

Tangy Tofu with Pineapple

These are particularly delicious served with pre-dinner drinks.

SERVES 4 OR 6

225 g/8 oz/1 small can of pineapple
chunks in natural juice
15 ml/1 tbsp sunflower oil
150 ml/¹/₄ pt/²/₃ cup reduced-salt soy
sauce
30 ml/2 tbsp white wine vinegar
1.5 ml/¹/₄ tsp made English mustard
5 ml/1 tsp grated fresh root ginger
1 large garlic clove, crushed
275 g/10 oz firm tofu, drained and
cubed
Lettuce leaves, to garnish

Drain the pineapple juice into a bowl. Whisk in the oil, soy sauce, vinegar, mustard, ginger and garlic. Add the tofu cubes, toss gently and leave in a cool place to marinate for at least 12 and preferably 24 hours. Drain and thread a cube of tofu and a cube of pineapple on to cocktail sticks (toothpicks). Arrange on a bed of lettuce and serve.

* **160 or 110 calories per serving**
* **Medium fibre**

Artichoke, Prawn and Mushroom Cocktail

SERVES 4

425 g/15 oz/1 large can of artichoke
hearts, drained
100 g/4 oz cooked peeled prawns
(shrimp)
50 g/2 oz button mushrooms, thinly
sliced
Low-fat French Dressing (page 380)
60 ml/4 tbsp low-fat crème fraîche
50 g/2 oz/1 small jar of red Danish
lumpfish roe

Dry the artichokes well on kitchen paper (paper towels) then cut into bite-sized pieces. Place in a bowl with the prawns and mushrooms. Add the dressing, toss gently and chill for up to 1 hour to allow the flavours to develop. Spoon into wine goblets. Top each with 15 ml/1 tbsp low-fat crème fraîche, then the lumpfish roe and serve.

* **100 calories per serving**
* **Medium fibre**

Artichoke, Crab and Cucumber Cocktail

SERVES 4

Prepare as for Artichoke, Prawn and Mushroom Cocktail, but substitute chopped crab sticks for the prawns (shrimp) and a 5 cm/2 in piece of cucumber, halved and thinly sliced, for the mushrooms.

* **100 calories per serving**
* **Medium fibre**

Mixed Bean Vinaigrette

SERVES 4

1 garlic clove, crushed
15 ml/1 tbsp olive oil
15 ml/1 tbsp red wine vinegar
15 ml/1 tbsp water
2.5 ml/¹/₂ tsp dried oregano
15 ml/1 tbsp chopped parsley
15 ml/1 tbsp snipped chives
425 g/15 oz/1 large can of mixed
pulses, drained
Salt and freshly ground black pepper
Lollo rosso lettuce leaves

Whisk together the garlic, oil, vinegar, water and herbs in a bowl. Add the beans and toss gently. Season to taste. Chill, if time, before serving on a bed of lollo rosso lettuce.

* **100 calories per serving**
* **High fibre**

Piri Piri Prawns

If you don't like food too hot, halve the amount of chilli powder.

SERVES 4

450 g/1 lb large raw, peeled prawns (jumbo shrimp), with the tails left on
5 ml/1 tsp chilli powder
Finely grated rind and juice of 1 small lemon or lime
Freshly ground black pepper
25 g/1 oz/2 tbsp low-fat sunflower or olive oil spread
Lemon or lime wedges and sprigs of coriander (cilantro), to garnish

Put the prawns in a shallow dish. Sprinkle with the chilli powder, lemon or lime rind and juice and some pepper. Toss gently, cover and leave to marinate for 1 hour. Heat the low-fat spread in a large non-stick frying pan (skillet) and cook the prawns, stirring, for about 3 minutes or until pink all over. Do not overcook. Serve hot, garnished with lemon or lime wedges and sprigs of coriander.

* **160 calories per serving**
* **Low fibre**

Chilli Prawn Wraps

SERVES 6

450 g/1 lb large raw peeled prawns (jumbo shrimp), tails removed
5 ml/1 tsp chilli powder
Finely grated rind and juice of 1 small lemon or lime
Freshly ground black pepper
25 g/1 oz/2 tbsp low-fat sunflower or olive oil spread
6 small flour tortillas
Shredded lettuce
30 ml/2 tbsp low-fat crème fraîche
Lemon or lime wedges and sprigs of coriander (cilantro), to garnish

Put the prawns in a shallow dish. Sprinkle with the chilli powder, lemon or lime rind and juice and some pepper. Toss gently, cover and leave to marinate for 1 hour. Heat the low-fat spread in a large non-stick frying pan (skillet) and cook the prawns, stirring, for about 3 minutes or until pink all over. Do not overcook. Divide the prawns between one half of each tortilla, scatter a little lettuce over and top with 5 ml/1 tsp of the crème fraîche. Fold the tortilla in half over the filling, then in half again to form a wedge-shaped parcel. Serve garnished with lemon or lime wedges and sprigs of coriander.

* **300 calories per serving**
* **Medium fibre**

Crab and Chilli Tomatoes

SERVES 4

4 large tomatoes
175 g/6 oz/³/₄ cup low-fat soft cheese
30 ml/2 tbsp low-fat plain yoghurt
1 small green chilli, seeded and
    chopped
15 ml/1 tbsp tomato ketchup (catsup)
1 shallot, finely chopped
170 g/6 oz/1 small can of crabmeat,
    drained
Lemon juice
Salt and freshly ground black pepper
30–45 ml/2–3 tbsp wholemeal
    breadcrumbs
Lettuce leaves

Cut a slice off the rounded end of each tomato and reserve. Scoop out the seeds. Drain upside down on kitchen paper (paper towels). Mash the cheese with the yoghurt, chilli, ketchup and shallot. Stir in the crabmeat and season to taste with the lemon juice, salt and pepper. Stir in enough of the breadcrumbs to stiffen the mixture slightly. Spoon the mixture into the tomatoes and place on lettuce leaves on plates. Replace the 'lids'. Chill until ready to serve.

* **180 calories per serving**
* **Medium fibre**

Photograph opposite: **Hot Pepper Corns Buns (page 22) and Salmon Kedgeree (page 29)**

Moules Marinière

SERVES 6

2 kg/4¹/₂ lb fresh mussels in their shells
15 g/¹/₂ oz/1 tbsp low-fat sunflower or
    olive oil spread
1 large onion, finely chopped
300 ml/¹/₂ pt/1¹/₄ cups dry white wine
Freshly ground black pepper
30 ml/2 tbsp chopped parsley

Scrub the mussels thoroughly and scrape off any barnacles. Pull off the beards and discard any that are broken, open or don't close completely when sharply tapped. Melt the low-fat spread in a large saucepan. Stir in the onion and 30 ml/2 tbsp water. Cook, stirring, for 3 minutes until softened. Add the mussels, the wine and 150 ml/¹/₄ pt/²/₃ cup water. Season well with pepper. Cover and cook for about 5 minutes, shaking the pan occasionally, until the mussels have opened. Discard any that remain shut. Ladle into warm bowls and sprinkle with the parsley before serving.

* **90 calories per serving**
* **Low fibre**

Mussels in Creamy Parsley Sauce

SERVES 4

Prepare as for Moules Marinière, but after cooking remove the mussels from the pan with a draining spoon. Pull off the tops of the open shells, then place the mussels in their half shells in warm bowls. Stir 60 ml/4 tbsp low-fat crème fraîche into the juices, taste and re-season, if necessary. Heat through, spoon over the mussels and serve.

* **110 calories per serving**
* **Low fibre**

Velvety Chicken Liver Pâté

SERVES 6

1 small onion, finely chopped
1 small garlic clove, crushed (optional)
200 g/7 oz/scant 1 cup chicken livers,
*   trimmed and roughly chopped*
30 ml/2 tbsp water
15 ml/1 tbsp brandy
2.5 ml/½ tsp dried mixed herbs
200 g/7 oz/scant 1 cup low-fat soft
*   cheese*
Salt and freshly ground black pepper
Lemon wedges and parsley sprigs, to
*   garnish*
6 slices of wholemeal bread, freshly
*   toasted, to serve*

Put the onion in a saucepan with the garlic if using, the chicken livers, water, brandy and herbs. Cook, stirring, for 5 minutes or until the chicken livers are just cooked and the onion is softened. Cool slightly, then purée in a blender or food processor. Add the cheese and run the machine again until well blended. Season with a little salt and lots of pepper. Turn into a small container, cover and chill. When ready to serve, divide the pâté between four plates. Garnish with lemon wedges and parsley sprigs and serve with triangles of hot toast.

* **150 calories per serving**
* **Low fibre**

Velvety Turkey Liver Pâté with Port

SERVES 6

Prepare as for Velvety Chicken Liver Pâté, but substitute turkey livers for the chicken livers and port for the brandy. If available, garnish the pâté with small sprigs of redcurrants on the side.

* **150 calories per serving**
* **Low fibre**

Tzatziki

SERVES 4

½ cucumber, finely diced
Salt
1 small garlic clove, crushed
150 ml/¼ pt/⅔ cup low-fat plain
*   yoghurt*
10 ml/2 tsp dried mint
Freshly ground black pepper
Pitta bread, cut into fingers, to serve

Put the cucumber in a colander. Sprinkle with salt, toss and leave to stand for 15 minutes. Squeeze out all the excess moisture. Tip into a bowl and mix with the garlic, yoghurt and mint. Season to taste with pepper. Chill until ready to serve with pitta bread fingers.

* **25 calories per serving**
* **Medium fibre**

Photograph opposite: **Clear Vegetable Strand Soup (page 49)**

Less-rich Taramasalata

SERVES 4

1 slice of white bread
225 g/8 oz smoked cod's roe, skinned
15 g/½ oz/1 tbsp low-fat sunflower or olive oil spread, melted
1 small garlic clove, crushed
15 ml/1 tbsp lemon juice
Freshly ground black pepper
Chopped parsley, to garnish
Pitta bread, cut into fingers, to serve

Break up the bread and place in a food processor or blender. Add enough boiling water to moisten completely and leave to stand for 5 minutes. Add the remaining ingredients and run the machine until smooth, stopping to scrape down the sides from time to time. The mixture will be very stiff. With the machine running, add boiling water, 15 ml/1 tbsp at a time until the mixture forms a soft, spreading consistency. Taste and re-season with pepper and a little more lemon juice, if liked. Leave to cool, then chill. Garnish with chopped parsley and serve with pitta bread fingers.

* **80 calories per serving**
* **Medium fibre**

Oil-free Hummus

SERVES 4

425 g/15 oz/1 large can of chick peas (garbanzos), drained
1 garlic clove, crushed
15 ml/1 tbsp lemon juice
A pinch of cayenne
45 ml/3 tbsp boiling water
Freshly ground black pepper
Pitta bread, cut into fingers, to serve

Put the chick peas in a blender or food processor with the garlic, lemon juice and cayenne. Run the machine until the chick peas are fairly smooth, stopping to scrape down the sides from time to time. Then, with the machine running, add the boiling water, 15 ml/1 tbsp at a time, until the mixture forms a spreadable paste. Season with pepper and a little more lemon juice, if liked. Serve with pitta bread fingers.

* **80 calories per serving**
* **High fibre**

Cheese and Prawn Mousse

SERVES 4

450 g/1 lb/2 cups low-fat cottage
  cheese
150 ml/^{1}/$_4$ pt/^{2}/$_3$ cup low-fat plain
  yoghurt
15 ml/1 tbsp tomato ketchup (catsup)
A few drops of Tabasco sauce
A few drops of Worcestershire sauce
Lemon juice
100 g/4 oz cooked peeled prawns
  (shrimp)
1 egg white
4 slices of cucumber

Sieve (strain) the cottage cheese into a bowl. Stir in the yoghurt and ketchup and flavour to taste with Tabasco and Worcestershire sauces and lemon juice. Reserve four prawns for garnish and chop the remainder. Dry, if necessary, on kitchen paper (paper towels), then fold into the cheese mixture. Whisk the egg white until stiff, then fold into the mixture with a metal spoon. Turn into four small pots. Decorate each with a reserved prawn and a twist of cucumber and chill for at least 1 hour before serving.

* **110 calories per serving**
* **Low fibre**

Cheese and Crab Mousse

SERVES 4

Prepare as for Cheese and Prawn Mousse, but substitute 170 g/ 6 oz/1 small can of crabmeat, drained, for the prawns (shrimp).

* **110 calories per serving**
* **Low fibre**

Salmon-stuffed Lemons

SERVES 6

6 even-sized lemons
185 g/6^1/$_2$ oz/1 small can of pink or red
  salmon, drained
5 ml/1 tsp Dijon mustard
45 ml/3 tbsp low-calorie mayonnaise
45 ml/3 tbsp low-fat fromage frais
A good pinch of cayenne
15 ml/1 tbsp chopped parsley
1 egg white
Lettuce leaves

Cut a slice off the pointed end of each lemon so they will stand up. Cut off the stalk ends and scoop out the flesh into a bowl, discarding all the pips, pith and membranes. Snip the flesh with scissors, if necessary, to chop up. Remove any skin and bones from the fish, then add to the lemon flesh. Stir in the mustard, mayonnaise and fromage frais. Season with cayenne and add the parsley. Whisk the egg white until stiff and fold into the salmon mixture with a metal spoon. Spoon back into the lemon shells and arrange them on a bed of lettuce. Chill until ready to serve.

* **80 calories per serving**
* **Medium fibre**

Tuna-stuffed Lemons

SERVES 6

Prepare as for Salmon-stuffed Lemons, but substitute tuna in brine or water for the salmon and add 1 celery stick, finely chopped, for added 'bite'.

* **75 calories per serving**
* **Medium fibre**

Pâté-stuffed Lemons

SERVES 6

Prepare as for Salmon-stuffed Lemons (page 99), but use 175 g/ 6 oz low-fat liver pâté instead of the salmon. Mash this thoroughly into the lemon flesh before beating in the mayonnaise and cheese.

* 85 calories per serving
* Medium fibre

Crab Rolls with Grapefruit

SERVES 4

170 g/6 oz/1 small can of crabmeat, drained
60 ml/4 tbsp low-calorie mayonnaise
2.5 ml/¹/₂ tsp horseradish sauce
Freshly ground black pepper
4 large or 8 small round lettuce leaves
2 grapefruit, peeled and segmented

Mash the crab with the mayonnaise and horseradish. Season with pepper. Spread on the lettuce leaves, fold in the two sides, then roll up. Wrap in clingfilm (plastic wrap) and chill until ready to serve. Place on plates and surround with grapefruit segments.

* 100 calories per serving
* Medium fibre

Grapefruit with Raisins and Ginger

SERVES 4

2 grapefruit
75 g/3 oz/¹/₂ cup raisins
1 piece of stem ginger in syrup, chopped
30 ml/2 tbsp ginger syrup from the jar
30 ml/2 tbsp ginger wine
A pinch of ground cinnamon

Halve the grapefruit, remove the segments with a serrated-edged knife and place in a bowl with any juice. Remove and discard the membranes and reserve the shells. Add the raisins to the bowl with the ginger, ginger syrup and wine and flavour with cinnamon. Stir gently, then chill. When ready to serve, put the grapefruit shells in four glass dishes. Spoon the fruit mixture and juice into the shells and serve.

* 110 calories per serving
* Medium fibre

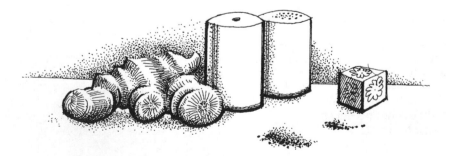

Peperonata

SERVES 4

15 g/½ oz/1 tbsp low-fat sunflower or olive oil spread
2 large red (bell) peppers, cut into thin strips
2 large green peppers, cut into thin strips
1 large onion, thinly sliced and separated into rings
4 beefsteak tomatoes, skinned and chopped
1 garlic clove, crushed
15 ml/1 tbsp tomato purée (paste)
30 ml/2 tbsp water
A pinch of salt
Freshly ground black pepper

Melt the low-fat spread in a fairly large non-stick saucepan. Add the peppers and onion and fry (sauté) for 3 minutes, stirring, until slightly softened. Add the remaining ingredients and stir well. Cover with a lid and simmer gently for 30 minutes until soft and bathed in a tomato sauce. Season with more pepper, if liked, and serve hot or chilled.

* **50 calories per serving**
* **Medium fibre**

Cheese and Onion Rings

SERVES 6

1 green (bell) pepper
1 yellow pepper
1 red pepper
450 g/1 lb/2 cups low-fat cottage cheese
225 g/8 oz/1 cup low-fat soft cheese
2 spring onions (scallions), finely chopped
30 ml/2 tbsp chopped parsley
10 ml/2 tsp chopped sage
Salt and freshly ground black pepper
Parsley sprigs and paprika, to garnish

Cut the top stalk ends off the peppers and remove the seeds and cores. Sieve (strain) the cottage cheese and mix with the remaining ingredients, seasoning to taste with salt and pepper. Spoon into the peppers and press down well. Wrap in clingfilm (plastic wrap) and chill for at least 3 hours but preferably overnight. To serve, slice each pepper into six rounds. Arrange one of each colour, slightly overlapping, on plates, put a sprig of parsley in the centre and dust the slices with paprika.

* **125 calories per serving**
* **Medium fibre**

Mushroom Quichette

This is like a quiche without the pastry!

SERVES 4

*15 g/¹/₂ oz/1 tbsp low-fat sunflower or
  olive oil spread*
1 onion, finely chopped
225 g/8 oz button mushrooms, sliced
2.5 ml/¹/₂ tsp dried oregano
Freshly ground black pepper
*50 g/2 oz/¹/₂ cup low-fat Cheddar
  cheese, grated*
2 eggs
300 ml/¹/₂ pt/1¹/₄ cups skimmed milk
15 ml/1 tbsp chopped parsley

Melt the low-fat spread in a saucepan. Use a little to grease four individual gratin or other shallow ovenproof dishes. Add the onion to the remaining melted spread and fry (sauté) for 2 minutes, stirring. Add the mushrooms and cook for a further 2 minutes. Season well with the oregano and pepper. Spoon into the prepared dishes and sprinkle with the cheese. Beat together the eggs and milk and pour over the cheese. Bake in a preheated oven at 190°C/375°F/gas mark 5 for about 30 minutes until golden and set. Serve hot, sprinkled with the chopped parsley.

* **120 calories per serving**
* **Fairly low fibre**

Courgette Quichette

SERVES 4

Prepare as for Mushroom Quichette, but substitute 2 thinly sliced courgettes (zucchini) for the mushrooms and add to the pan with the onion.

* **100 calories per serving**
* **Fairly low fibre**

Green Beans with Fromage Frais Herb Dressing

SERVES 6

450 g/1 lb dwarf French (green) beans
175 g/6 oz/³/₄ cup low-fat fromage frais
5 ml/1 tsp lemon juice
1 small garlic clove, crushed
15 ml/1 tbsp chopped parsley
*15 ml/1 tbsp chopped marjoram or
  oregano*
15 ml/1 tbsp chopped thyme
*2.5 ml/¹/₂ tsp ground coriander
  (cilantro)*
Freshly ground black pepper
45 ml/3 tbsp skimmed milk

Top and tail the beans. Boil in lightly salted water for 4–5 minutes until just tender. Drain, rinse with cold water and drain again. Meanwhile, mix together the fromage frais, lemon juice, garlic, herbs, coriander and lots of pepper. Thin with the milk. Chill. To serve, lay the cold beans on individual plates and spoon the dressing in a line across the centre.

* **40 calories per serving**
* **Medium fibre**

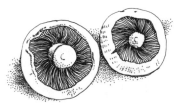

Seafood Main Meals

Fish is highly nutritious and naturally lower in fat than meat. Oily fish like herring or mackerel have more than the white varieties, but fish oil is much better for you than saturated animal fat. The wonderful thing about oily fish, too, is that you can grill (broil) it without any added fat and it will still be moist and delicious.

Crab and Spinach Oat Tart

SERVES 6

100 g/4 oz/1 cup rolled oats
50 g/2 oz/½ cup wholemeal flour
A pinch of salt
5 ml/1 tsp baking powder
75 g/3 oz/⅓ cup low-fat sunflower or
    olive oil spread
For the filling:
15 g/½ oz/1 tbsp low-fat sunflower or
    olive oil spread
1 small onion, finely chopped
225 g/8 oz frozen leaf spinach, thawed
170 g/6 oz/1 small can of crabmeat,
    drained and flaked
Finely grated rind of 1 small lemon
40 g/1½ oz/⅓ cup Parmesan cheese,
    grated
Freshly ground black pepper
1 whole egg
2 egg whites
150 ml/¼ pt/⅔ cup skimmed milk
Fragrant Tomato and Onion Salad
    (page 278), to serve

Mix the oats and flour in a bowl with the salt and baking powder. Add the low-fat spread and rub in with the fingertips. Mix with enough cold water to form a firm dough. Wrap in clingfilm (plastic wrap) and chill for 30 minutes. Knead gently on a lightly floured surface. Roll out and use to line a 23 cm/9 in flan dish (pie pan). Prick the base with a fork. Line with crumpled foil and bake in a preheated oven at 220°C/425°F/ gas mark 7 for 10 minutes. Remove the foil and bake for a further 5 minutes to dry out.

To make the filling, melt the low-fat spread in a saucepan. Add the onion and fry (sauté) for 3 minutes, stirring. Squeeze the spinach to remove excess moisture and add to the onion. Cook, stirring, for 3 minutes. Snip with scissors to chop up. Turn into the flan case (pie shell) and spread out. Top with the crabmeat, sprinkle with the lemon rind, then the cheese, and add a good grinding of pepper. Whisk together the egg, egg whites and milk and pour into the flan. Bake in the oven at 190°C/375°F/gas mark 5 for 35 minutes until set and golden. Serve warm with Fragrant Tomato and Onion Salad.

* **290 calories per serving**
* **High fibre**

Crab and Camembert Heaven

SERVES 4

5 ml/1 tsp low-fat sunflower or olive
oil spread
6 slices of white bread, crusts removed
50 g/2 oz ripe Camembert cheese,
thinly sliced
170 g/6 oz/1 small can of crabmeat,
drained and flaked
30 ml/2 tbsp chopped parsley
2 eggs
250 ml/8 fl oz/1 cup skimmed milk
Salt and freshly ground black pepper
Sprigs of parsley, to garnish
Cucumber and Spring Onion Salad
(page 279), to serve

Grease a 1.2 litre/2 pt/5 cup shallow ovenproof dish with the low-fat spread. Put three of the slices of bread in the base. Cover with the cheese, then the crabmeat and sprinkle with the parsley. Top with the remaining bread. Beat the eggs with a little of the milk, then whisk in the remainder. Season well. Pour over the bread and leave to soak for 30 minutes. Bake in a preheated oven at 180°C/350°F/gas mark 4 for about 30 minutes until puffy and golden brown. Garnish with sprigs of parsley and serve straight away with Cucumber and Spring Onion Salad.

* **270 calories per serving**
* **Medium fibre**

Jansen's Temptation

SERVES 4

50 g/2 oz/¹/₄ cup low-fat sunflower or
olive oil spread, melted
4 potatoes, thinly sliced
2 onions, thinly sliced
50 g/2 oz/1 small can of anchovies,
drained and chopped
Freshly ground black pepper
150 ml/¹/₄ pt/²/₃ cup skimmed milk
40 g/1¹/₂ oz/³/₄ cup breadcrumbs
50 g/2 oz/¹/₂ cup low-fat Emmental
(Swiss) cheese, grated
Chopped parsley, to garnish
Green Bean with Tomato Salsa Salad
(page 279), to serve

Grease a 1.2 litre/2 pt/5 cup ovenproof dish with some of the low-fat spread. Layer the potatoes, onions and anchovies in the dish, sprinkling with black pepper as you go and finishing with a layer of potatoes. Pour the milk over. Cover with foil and bake in a preheated oven at 180°C/ 350°F/gas mark 4 for 40 minutes. Mix the remaining low-fat spread with the breadcrumbs and cheese. Remove the foil, cover with the breadcrumb mixture and return to the oven, uncovered, for a further 30 minutes or until golden brown and the potatoes and onions are tender. Sprinkle with chopped parsley before serving with Green Bean with Tomato Salsa Salad.

* **265 calories per serving**
* **Fairly high fibre**

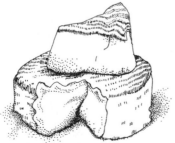

Prawn Omelette

SERVES 1

1 egg
1 egg white
15 ml/1 tbsp skimmed milk
Salt and freshly ground black pepper
5 ml/1 tsp low-fat sunflower or olive
*   oil spread*
25 g/1 oz peeled prawns (shrimp)
15 ml/1 tbsp chopped parsley
5 ml/1 tsp tomato ketchup (catsup)
A few drops of Worcestershire sauce

Beat the egg, egg white and milk with a little salt and pepper. Melt the low-fat spread in a small omelette pan. Add the egg mixture and cook, lifting and stirring gently, until the base is golden and the egg mixture is almost set. Mix the prawns with the parsley, ketchup, and Worcestershire sauce. Spoon over half the omelette. Heat through for a few minutes. Fold the omelette over the filling, slide on to a warm plate and serve.

* 160 calories
* Low fibre

Chilli Prawn Scramble

SERVES 4

Prepare as for Chilli Steak Scramble (page 195), but substitute raw peeled tiger prawns (jumbo shrimp) for the steak.

* 245 calories per serving
* Low fibre

Plaice Mornay

SERVES 4

4 plaice fillets, all dark skin removed,
*   cut into wide strips*
300 ml/¹/₂ pt/1¹/₄ cups skimmed milk
30 ml/2 tbsp cornflour (cornstarch)
50 g/2 oz/¹/₂ cup strong low-fat
*   Cheddar cheese, grated*
5 ml/1 tsp Dijon mustard
Salt and freshly ground black pepper
Extra-fluffed Mashed Potatoes (page
*   260) and Crunchy Spinach*
*   (page 270), to serve*

Put the fish in a saucepan and add all but 30 ml/2 tbsp of the milk. Bring to the boil, reduce the heat and simmer gently for 5 minutes or until the fish is tender. Carefully remove from the pan and place in a shallow flameproof dish. Blend the cornflour with the remaining milk and add to the pan. Bring to the boil and cook for 1 minute, stirring. Stir in three-quarters of the cheese, the mustard and seasoning to taste. Pour over the fish. Sprinkle with the remaining cheese and brown under a hot grill (broiler). Serve with Extra-fluffed Mashed Potatoes and Crunchy Spinach.

* 240 calories per serving
* Very low fibre

Smoked Haddock Mornay

SERVES 4

Prepare as for Plaice Mornay, but substitute undyed smoked haddock for the plaice.

* 240 calories per serving
* Very low fibre

Sizzling Seafood Pizza

SERVES 4

278 g/10 oz/1 packet of pizza base mix
60 ml/4 tbsp tomato purée (paste)
100 g/4 oz/1 cup low-fat Mozzarella cheese, grated
175 g/6 oz seafood cocktail, thawed and drained on kitchen paper (paper towels), if frozen
2.5 ml/¹/₂ tsp dried oregano
A squeeze of lemon juice
1 black olive, to garnish

Make up the pizza mix according to the packet directions. Knead gently on a lightly floured surface. Roll out to a thin round and place on a non-stick baking (cookie) sheet. Blend the tomato purée with a little water to form a smooth sauce. Spread over the pizza base to within 1 cm/¹/₂ in of the edge all round. Sprinkle with half the cheese, then the seafood, then the remaining cheese and the oregano. Sprinkle with a squeeze of lemon juice. Put the olive in the centre and bake in a preheated oven at 200°C/ 400°F/gas mark 6 for about 20 minutes until sizzling and the base is brown round the edge. Serve hot.

* 275 calories per serving
* Medium fibre

Pizza with Tomatoes and Anchovies

SERVES 4

Prepare as for Sizzling Seafood Pizza, but substitute 50 g/2 oz/ 1 small can of anchovies, drained, for the seafood. Arrange them in a starburst pattern on top of all the cheese and lay tomato slices all round the edge before adding the olive in the centre.

* 260 calories per serving
* Medium fibre

Sizzling Sild Pizza

SERVES 4

Prepare as for Sizzling Seafood Pizza, but substitute 410 g/4¹/₂ oz/ 1 small can of sild (small sardines), drained, for the seafood cocktail. Arrange them in a starburst pattern over half the cheese, top with the remaining cheese and sprinkle with 5 ml/1 tsp chopped capers instead of the oregano.

* 280 calories per serving
* Medium fibre

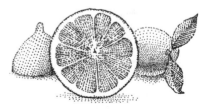

Blushing Tuna Pizza

SERVES 4

Prepare as for Sizzling Seafood Pizza (page 107), but substitute 185 g/6½ oz/1 small can of tuna in brine or water, drained, for the seafood, and scatter two diced baby beetroot (red beets) over before topping with the remaining cheese.

* 275 calories per serving
* Medium fibre

Tuna and Vegetable Mornay

SERVES 4

Prepare as for Chicken and Vegetable Mornay (page 145), but substitute 185 g/6½ oz/1 small can of tuna in brine or water, drained, for the chicken.

* 180 calories per serving
* Medium fibre

Tuna, Sweetcorn and Tomato Pasta

SERVES 4

225 g/8 oz pasta shapes
185 g/6½ oz/1 small can of tuna in brine or water, drained
200 g/7 oz/1 small can of naturally sweet sweetcorn (corn), drained
450 ml/¾ pt/2 cups passata (sieved tomatoes)
5 ml/1 tsp dried oregano
A pinch of salt
Freshly ground black pepper
50 g/2 oz/½ cup strong low-fat Cheddar cheese, grated
2 tomatoes, sliced
Mixed Leaf Salad, (page 278), to serve

Cook the pasta in boiling, lightly salted water according to the packet directions. Drain and return to the saucepan. Add the tuna, sweetcorn, passata, oregano, salt and lots of pepper and heat through, stirring gently. Turn into a flameproof serving dish. Top with the cheese and arrange the tomato slices round the edge. Place under a hot grill (broiler) until the cheese melts and bubbles. Serve hot with Mixed Leaf Salad.

* 350 calories per serving
* Fairly high fibre

Spaghetti with Clams

SERVES 4

350 g/12 oz spaghetti
1 large onion, finely chopped
1 large garlic clove, crushed
15 g/½ oz/1 tbsp low-fat sunflower or olive oil spread
400 g/14 oz/1 large can of chopped tomatoes
15 ml/1 tbsp tomato purée (paste)
2 x 300 g/2 x 11 oz/2 medium cans of baby clams, drained
Salt and freshly ground black pepper
15 ml/1 tbsp chopped parsley
Dressed Green Salad (page 275), to serve

Cook the spaghetti according to the packet directions. Drain and return to the pan. Meanwhile, fry (sauté) the onion and garlic in the low-fat spread for 2 minutes, stirring, until softened but not browned. Add the tomatoes and tomato purée. Bring to the boil, reduce the heat and boil rapidly for 5 minutes until pulpy. Stir in the clams and season with salt and pepper. Heat for 2 minutes. Add to the spaghetti and toss well. Pile on to warm plates and sprinkle with the parsley before serving with Dressed Green Salad.

* **375 calories per serving**

* **Medium fibre**

Grilled Mackerel with Sweet Mustard Sauce

SERVES 4

4 even-sized mackerel, cleaned
Salt and freshly ground black pepper
Ultra-smooth White Sauce (page 376), using only 250 ml/8 fl oz/1 cup milk
15 ml/1 tbsp white wine vinegar
5 ml/1 tsp made English mustard
15 ml/1 tbsp light brown sugar
10 ml/2 tsp black mustard seeds, to garnish
Plain boiled potatoes and broccoli, to serve

Make several slashes in the mackerel on either side and season with salt and pepper. Place on foil on a grill (broiler) rack. Grill (broil) for about 5 minutes on each side until cooked through and golden brown. Meanwhile, make up the Ultra-smooth White Sauce. Stir in the vinegar, mustard and sugar and cook for 1 minute, stirring. Transfer the mackerel to warm plates, spoon the sauce over and sprinkle with the mustard seeds. Serve with plain boiled potatoes and broccoli.

* **395 calories per serving**

* **Low fibre**

Grilled Mackerel with Tomatoes and Horseradish Mayo

SERVES 4

4 even-sized mackerel, cleaned
Salt and freshly ground black pepper
4 tomatoes
30 ml/2 tbsp low-calorie mayonnaise
30 ml/2 tbsp low-fat fromage frais
10 ml/2 tsp horseradish sauce
Pan Scalloped Potatoes (page 258)
* and French (green) beans, to serve*

Make several slashes in the mackerel on either side and season with salt and pepper. Place on foil on a grill (broiler) rack. Grill (broil) for about 5 minutes on each side until cooked through and golden brown. Meanwhile, cut a cross in the rounded end of each tomato and add to the grill pan for the last 4 minutes of cooking. Mix together the remaining ingredients and season to taste with salt and pepper. Transfer the mackerel and tomatoes to warm plates. Put a spoonful of the horseradish mayonnaise to the side of each and serve with Pan Scalloped Potatoes and French beans.

* **360 calories per serving**
* **Medium fibre**

Mackerel with Chick Peas

SERVES 4

4 even-sized mackerel, cleaned
Salt and freshly ground black pepper
425 g/15 oz/1 large can of chick peas
* (garbanzos), drained*
60 ml/4 tbsp passata (sieved
* tomatoes)*
15 ml/1 tbsp tomato purée (paste)
1 garlic clove, crushed
5 ml/1 tsp dried thyme
15 ml/1 tbsp chopped parsley
Lemon wedges, to garnish
Crusty French bread, to serve

Make several slashes in the mackerel on either side and season with salt and pepper. Place on foil on a grill (broiler) rack. Grill (broil) for about 5 minutes on each side until cooked through and golden brown. Meanwhile, put the chick peas in a saucepan with the remaining ingredients. Bring to the boil and cook for about 3 minutes until the chick peas are bathed in sauce. Season to taste. Spoon on to warm plates and top with the mackerel. Garnish with lemon wedges and serve with lots of crusty French bread.

* **420 calories per serving**
* **High fibre**

Tuna and Mushroom Gnocchi

SERVES 4

600 ml/1 pt/2½ cups skimmed milk
5 ml/1 tsp salt
Freshly ground black pepper
1 bay leaf
1.5 ml/¼ tsp ground mace
150 g/5 oz/scant 1 cup semolina
    (cream of wheat)
1 egg
2 egg whites
100 g/4 oz/1 cup low-fat Cheddar
    cheese, grated
185 g/6 oz/1 small can of tuna in brine
    or water, drained
100 g/4 oz button mushrooms, sliced
295 g/10½ oz/1 medium can of low-
    fat condensed mushroom soup
10 g/¼ oz/2 tsp low-fat sunflower or
    olive oil spread
15 ml/1 tbsp chopped parsley, to
    garnish
Mixed Green Salad (page 279), to
    serve

Put the milk, the salt and some pepper, the bay leaf and mace in a saucepan. Stir in the semolina. Bring to the boil and cook for 10 minutes, stirring all the time, until really thick. Discard the bay leaf. Beat together the egg and egg whites and stir into the semolina with three-quarters of the cheese. Turn into a dampened baking tin (pan) lined with non-stick baking parchment and spread the mixture out with a wet palette knife to a square about 2 cm/¾ in thick. Leave to cool, then chill for at least 1 hour. Meanwhile, put the tuna in a 1.2 litre/ 2 pt/5 cup ovenproof serving dish. Add the mushrooms and soup and mix gently. Cut the gnocchi into 4 cm/1½ in squares and arrange around the top of the dish. Brush with the melted low-fat spread and sprinkle with the remaining cheese. Bake in a preheated oven at 200°C/400°F/ gas mark 6 for 30 minutes until golden and bubbling. Sprinkle with the parsley and serve hot with Mixed Green Salad.

* **375 calories per serving**
* **Medium fibre**

Salmon and Celery Gnocchi

SERVES 4

Prepare as for Tuna and Mushroom Gnocchi, but substitute canned salmon, skin and bones removed, for the tuna and low-fat celery soup for the mushroom soup. Add 2 celery sticks, very finely chopped and boiled for 2 minutes in water, then drained, and omit the mushrooms.

* **365 calories per serving**
* **Medium fibre**

Tasty Tuna Pancakes

SERVES 4

Everyday Pancakes (page 353)
100 g/4 oz button mushrooms, sliced
60 ml/4 tbsp water
2 tomatoes, finely chopped
185 g/6½ oz/1 small can of tuna in
brine or water, drained
60 ml/4 tbsp low-fat plain yoghurt
Salt and freshly ground black pepper
Low-fat White Sauce (page 376)
7.5 cm/3 in piece of cucumber, very
finely diced
5 ml/1 tsp dried dill (dill weed)
45 ml/3 tbsp crushed branflakes
Mixed Leaf Salad (page 278), to serve

Make the pancakes. Cook the mushrooms in the water in a covered pan for 4 minutes. Remove the lid and boil rapidly, if necessary, to evaporate any liquid. Add the tomatoes, tuna, yoghurt and a little salt and pepper and mix well. Divide between the pancakes and roll up. Place in an ovenproof dish. Make up the white sauce and stir in the cucumber and dill. Pour over the pancakes and sprinkle with the branflakes. Bake in a preheated oven at 180°C/ 350°F/gas mark 4 for about 20 minutes until piping hot. Serve with Mixed Leaf Salad.

* **265 calories per serving**
* **Medium fibre**

Lemon-Tabasco Whiting

SERVES 4

4 whiting fillets
5 ml/1 tsp Tabasco sauce
Finely grated rind and juice of 1 lemon
15 g/½ oz/1 tbsp low-fat sunflower or
olive oil spread
Salt and freshly ground black pepper
12 spring onion (scallions), trimmed
but left whole
Almond Wild Rice (page 265), to serve

Lay the fish in a shallow dish. Sprinkle with the Tabasco sauce and the lemon rind and juice. Leave to marinate for at least 30 minutes. Place on foil on a grill (broiler) rack, dot with half the low-fat spread and season to taste. Add the spring onions to the grill and dot with the remaining spread. Grill (broil) for about 6 minutes until the fish is cooked and the onions are browning. Turn the onions over half-way through cooking. Serve hot with Almond Wild Rice.

* **150 calories per serving**
* **Low fibre**

Lemon-barbecue Whiting

SERVES 4

4 whiting fillets
Finely grated rind of ¹/₂ lemon
30 ml/2 tbsp bottled barbecue sauce
¹/₄ cucumber
10 g/¹/₄ oz/2 tsp low-fat sunflower or olive oil spread
Savoury Potato Cake (page 258) and baby sweetcorn (corn), to serve

L ay the fish in a shallow dish and sprinkle with the lemon rind. Brush with half the sauce and leave to marinate for at least 30 minutes. Place on foil on a grill (broiler) rack and brush with the remaining sauce. Cut the cucumber lengthways into quarters. Place on the grill rack and dot with the low-fat spread. Grill (broil) for about 6 minutes until the fish is cooked. Transfer the fish and cucumber to warm plates and serve with Savoury Potato Cake and baby sweetcorn.

* **180 calories per serving**
* **Low fibre**

Easy Prawn Supper

SERVES 4

225 g/8 oz cooked peeled prawns (shrimp)
295 g/10¹/₂ oz/1 medium can of low-fat condensed mushroom soup
15 ml/1 tbsp tomato ketchup (catsup)
5 ml/1 tsp Worcestershire sauce
15 ml/1 tbsp chopped parsley
50 g/2 oz/1 cup wholemeal breadcrumbs
100 g/4 oz/1 cup low-fat Cheddar cheese, grated
1 tomato, sliced and 6 slices of cucumber, to garnish
Crusty bread and Mixed Leaf Salad (page 278), to serve

M ix the prawns with the soup, ketchup, Worcestershire sauce, parsley, half the breadcrumbs and half the cheese. Turn into an ovenproof serving dish. Mix together the remaining breadcrumbs and cheese and sprinkle over. Bake in a preheated oven at 200°C/400°F/gas mark 6 for 25 minutes until bubbling and golden. Arrange the tomato and cucumber slices attractively on top and serve with Mixed Leaf Salad.

* **220 calories per serving**
* **Medium fibre**

Easy Crab Supper

SERVES 4

Prepare as for Easy Prawn Supper (page 113), but substitute chopped crabsticks for the prawns (shrimp) and spike with a dash of lemon juice.

* 240 calories per serving
* Medium fibre

Light Salmon Mousse

SERVES 6 OR 8

Prepare as for Light Tuna Mousse, but substitute canned salmon, all skin and bones removed, for the tuna.

* 200 or 150 calories per serving
* Low fibre

Light Tuna Mousse

SERVES 6 OR 8

15 ml/1 tbsp powdered gelatine
30 ml/2 tbsp water
425 g/15 oz/1 large can of tuna in brine or water, drained
45 ml/3 tbsp low-calorie mayonnaise
15 ml/1 tbsp tomato purée (paste)
30 ml/2 tbsp lemon juice
Salt and freshly ground black pepper
300 ml/¹/₂ pt/1¹/₄ cups low-fat whipping cream, whipped
Lettuce leaves and lemon twists, to garnish
New potatoes and English Mixed Salad (page 276), to serve

Sprinkle the gelatine over the water in a small bowl and leave to soften for 5 minutes, then stand the bowl in a pan of hot water and stir until the gelatine dissolves completely (or dissolve briefly in the microwave). Mash the tuna thoroughly in a large bowl. Stir in the mayonnaise, tomato purée, lemon juice and salt and pepper to taste. Mix in the gelatine. Fold in the whipped cream. Turn into an attractive serving dish and chill until set. Spoon on to lettuce leaves, garnish with lemon twists and serve with new potatoes and English Mixed Salad.

* 210 or 155 calories per serving
* Low fibre

Warm Grilled Salmon Salad

SERVES 4

4 small salmon tail fillets, about
*   150 g/5 oz each*
Juice of 1 lime
15 ml/1 tbsp chopped dill (dill weed)
Freshly ground black pepper
225 g/8 oz mixed salad leaves
100 g/4 oz cherry tomatoes, halved
5 cm/2 in piece of cucumber,
*   quartered and sliced*
1 small red onion, thinly sliced and
*   separated into rings*
45 ml/3 tbsp Worcestershire sauce
45 ml/3 tbsp white wine vinegar
15 ml/1 tbsp clear honey
45 ml/3 tbsp water
Lime wedges, to garnish
New potatoes, to serve

Place the salmon fillets on foil on a grill (broiler) rack and brush with the lime juice. Sprinkle with dill and season with pepper. Grill (broil) for 6–8 minutes until cooked through and golden. Meanwhile, arrange the salad leaves, tomatoes, cucumber and onion rings on plates. Mix together the remaining ingredients in a small saucepan. When the fish is cooked, carefully transfer to the piles of salad. Strain the juices into the ingredients in the saucepan and heat through, stirring. Spoon over the fish, garnish with lime wedges and serve straight away with new potatoes.

* **225 calories per serving**
* **Fairly high fibre**

Warm Grilled Red Mullet and Grapefruit Salad

SERVES 4

Prepare as for Warm Grilled Salmon Salad, but substitute red mullet fillets for the salmon and add a segmented grapefruit to the salad ingredients.

* **225 calories per serving**
* **Fairly fibre**

Baked Salmon and Mushroom Parcels

SERVES 6

25 g/1 oz/2 tbsp low-fat sunflower or
olive oil spread
6 salmon fillets, about 175 g/6 oz
each, skinned
Finely grated rind and juice of 1 small
lemon
A pinch of salt
Freshly ground black pepper
175 g/6 oz button mushrooms, sliced
1 bunch of spring onions (scallions),
chopped
30 ml/2 tbsp capers
30 ml/2 tbsp chopped parsley
5 ml/1 tsp dried marjoram
New potatoes and Mixed Green Salad
(page 279), to serve

Grease six sheets of foil with half the low-fat spread. Lay a salmon fillet on each. Sprinkle each with the lemon rind and juice, seasoning, the mushrooms, onions, capers, parsley and marjoram. Dot with the remaining spread, fold the foil over the ingredients and roll the edges together to seal tightly. Place on a baking (cookie) sheet. Cook in a preheated oven at 200°C/400°F/gas mark 6 for 15 minutes or until the fish is cooked through. Open the foil on plates and serve with new potatoes and Mixed Green Salad.

* **350 calories per serving**
* **Medium fibre**

Baked Cod, Olive and Gherkin Parcels

SERVES 6

Prepare as for Baked Salmon and Mushroom Parcels, but substitute cod fillets for the salmon and 15 ml/1 tbsp chopped gherkins (cornichons) and 15 ml/1 tbsp chopped stoned (pitted) black olives for the capers.

* **180 calories per serving**
* **Medium fibre**

Baked Smoked Haddock Parcels

SERVES 6

Prepare as for Baked Salmon and Mushroom Parcels, but substitute smoked haddock fillets for the salmon fillets and omit the marjoram.

* **200 calories per serving**
* **Medium fibre**

Fresh Salmon Wraps

SERVES 4

4 sheets of filo pastry (paste)
15 ml/1 tbsp low-fat sunflower or olive
oil spread, melted
4 small salmon steaks, about 150 g/
5 oz each, skinned
4 mushrooms, finely chopped
2 tomatoes, finely chopped
Salt and freshly ground black pepper
30 ml/2 tbsp chopped basil
300 ml/¹/₂ pt/1¹/₄ cups passata (sieved
tomatoes)
Lemon wedges and basil sprigs, to
garnish
Baby new potatoes and mangetout
(snow peas), to serve

Lay the pastry sheets on a work surface. Brush very lightly with a little of the low-fat spread, then fold into halves. Place a salmon steak on each piece of pastry and top with the chopped mushrooms and tomatoes. Sprinkle with salt and pepper to taste and add about half the chopped basil.

Wrap up the fish in the pastry and lay sealed-sides down on a non-stick baking (cookie) sheet. Brush with the remaining spread. Bake in a preheated oven at 200°C/400°F/ gas mark 6 for 10–15 minutes until golden brown and the fish is cooked through.

Meanwhile, heat the passata in a saucepan with the remaining basil and a little salt and pepper. Spoon on to warm plates. Top each with a salmon parcel, garnish with lemon wedges and sprigs of basil and serve with baby new potatoes and mangetout.

* **440 calories per serving**
* **Medium fibre**

Anyday Salmon Wraps

SERVES 4

Prepare as for Fresh Salmon Wraps, but substitute 400 g/14 oz/1 large can of salmon for the fresh salmon. Divide it into four portions and remove the skin and any bones, if liked.

* **325 calories per serving**
* **Medium fibre**

Grilled Salmon with Dill

SERVES 4

45 ml/3 tbsp chopped dill (dill weed)
40 g/1¹/₂ oz/3 tbsp light brown sugar
Salt and freshly ground black pepper
4 salmon steaks, about 175 g/6 oz
  each
45 ml/3 tbsp cider vinegar
15 g/¹/₂ oz/1 tbsp low-fat sunflower or
  olive oil spread, melted
Mixed lettuce leaves and lemon
  wedges, to garnish
Cucumber and Dill Salsa (page 383)
  and Warm Potato Salad (page
  279), to serve

Mix the dill with the sugar and some salt and pepper. Rub all over the salmon and leave to marinate for 2 hours. Place on foil on a grill (broiler) rack. Mix together the vinegar and low-fat spread and brush all over the salmon. Grill (broil) for about 6–8 minutes, brushing frequently with the vinegar mixture, until golden and cooked through. Transfer to warm plates, garnish with mixed lettuce leaves and lemon wedges and serve with Cucumber and Dill Salsa and Warm Potato Salad.

* **380 calories per serving**
* **Low fibre**

Salmon with Pesto and Wine Sauce

SERVES 4

4 salmon steaks, about 175 g/6 oz
  each
Simple Pesto (page 379)
150 ml/¹/₄ pt/²/₃ cup white wine
Perfect Brown Rice (page 265) and
  Jewel Salad (page 278), to serve

Place the salmon in a shallow dish. Mix together the Simple Pesto and wine and spoon over the salmon. Leave to marinate for 1 hour. Lift out of the dish and place on foil on a grill (broiler) rack. Grill (broil) for about 6–8 minutes or until tender. Meanwhile, heat the remaining marinade until bubbling. When the fish is cooked, transfer to warm plates and spoon the remaining sauce over. Serve with Perfect Brown Rice and Jewel Salad.

* **435 calories per serving**
* **Medium fibre**

Red Almond Pesto Mullet

SERVES 4

Prepare as for Salmon with Pesto and Wine Sauce, but substitute red mullet fillets for the salmon steaks, Red Almond Pesto (page 379) for the Simple Pesto and use red wine instead of white.

* **435 calories per serving**
* **Medium fibre**

Trout with Pernod, Fennel and Mushrooms

SERVES 4

1 fennel bulb
4 trout fillets
25 g/1 oz/2 tbsp low-fat sunflower or
    olive oil spread
175 g/6 oz button mushrooms, sliced
1 garlic clove, crushed
45 ml/3 tbsp Pernod
120 ml/4 fl oz/¹/₂ cup low-fat crème
    fraîche
Salt and freshly ground black pepper
Plain boiled potatoes, to serve

Trim off the feathery fronds from the fennel and reserve. Slice the bulb. Boil in lightly salted water for about 8 minutes until just tender. Drain and reserve.

Wipe the fish. Melt half the low-fat spread in a large non-stick frying pan (skillet). Add the fish, skin-sides up, and brown for 2 minutes. Turn the fish over and cook for a further 3 minutes until tender. Carefully lift out of the pan and keep warm.

Heat the remaining spread in the pan. Add the mushrooms and stir for 2 minutes. Add the fennel, garlic and Pernod, cover with foil or a lid and cook gently for 4 minutes. Stir in the crème fraîche and season to taste. Bring to the boil and boil, stirring, for 2 minutes.

Transfer the trout to warm plates. Spoon the sauce over. Garnish with the reserved fronds and serve with plain boiled potatoes.

* **340 calories per serving**
* **Medium fibre**

Sweet and Sour Monkfish

SERVES 4

¹/₄ cucumber, chopped
2 spring onions (scallions), chopped
225 g/8 oz/1 small can of pineapple
    chunks
225 g/8 oz/1 small can of chopped
    tomatoes
450 g/1 lb monkfish, cubed
20 ml/1¹/₂ tbsp cornflour (cornstarch)
30 ml/2 tbsp reduced-salt soy sauce
Caster (superfine) sugar (optional)
Plain boiled rice, to serve

Put the cucumber, spring onions, the contents of the can of pineapple and the chopped tomatoes in a saucepan. Bring to the boil and simmer for 3 minutes. Add the monkfish and simmer for a further 6 minutes until the fish is tender. Blend the cornflour with the soy sauce and stir into the mixture. Bring to the boil and cook for 2 minutes, stirring gently. Taste and add a little caster sugar, if liked. Spoon on to a bed of boiled rice and serve.

* **145 calories per serving**
* **Fairly low fibre**

Sweet and Sour Scallops

SERVES 4

Prepare as for Sweet and Sour Monkfish, but substitute queen scallops for the monkfish and serve on a bed of Fried Rice (page 265) instead of plain boiled rice.

* **140 calories per serving**
* **Medium fibre**

Baked Cod with Olives and Potatoes

SERVES 4

4 potatoes, scrubbed and cut into eighths
30 ml/2 tbsp olive oil
4 cod fillets, about 175 g/6 oz each, skinned
10 ml/2 tsp chopped oregano
10 ml/2 tsp chopped parsley
Finely grated rind and juice of ¹/₂ lemon
A pinch of salt
Freshly ground black pepper
1 red onion, chopped
2 ripe beefsteak tomatoes, skinned and chopped
1 garlic clove, crushed
16 stoned (pitted) green olives, halved
Dressed Green Salad (page 275), to serve

Boil the potatoes in lightly salted water for 4 minutes until almost tender. Drain. Pour half the oil in a roasting tin (pan) and add the potatoes. Toss gently, then cook on the top shelf of the oven preheated to 200°C/400°F/gas mark 6 for 10 minutes. Lay the fish in a separate baking dish in a single layer. Sprinkle with the herbs, lemon, salt and some pepper. Cover with foil and place on the shelf just below the middle of the oven, under the potatoes. Cook for about 30 minutes until the potatoes are turning golden and the fish is tender. Meanwhile, heat the remaining oil in a small pan. Add the onion and fry (sauté), stirring, for 3 minutes. Add the tomatoes, garlic, olives and a good grinding of pepper. Simmer, stirring occasionally, for about 5 minutes or until pulpy. When the potatoes and fish are cooked, pour off any juices from the fish into the tomato mixture. Arrange the fish and potatoes on warm plates and spoon the tomato sauce over the fish. Serve straight away with Dressed Green Salad.

* **350 calories per serving**
* **Fairly high fibre**

Fresh Tuna, Lime and Coriander Kebabs

SERVES 4

450 g/1 lb tuna steaks, cubed
Finely grated rind and juice of 1 lime
30 ml/2 tbsp chopped coriander (cilantro)
15 g/¹/₂ oz/1 tbsp low-fat sunflower or olive oil spread, melted
15 ml/1 tbsp clear honey
Salt and freshly ground black pepper
Savoury Potato Cake (page 258) and Mixed Leaf Salad (page 278), to serve

Put the tuna in a shallow dish. Whisk together the remaining ingredients and pour over. Toss and leave to marinate for 2 hours. Thread on to soaked wooden skewers. Grill (broil) for about 6 minutes, turning and basting occasionally, until cooked through. Serve with Savoury Potato Cake and Mixed Leaf Salad.

* **160 calories per serving**
* **Low fibre**

Smoked Haddock Rosti

SERVES 4

25 g/1 oz/2 tbsp low-fat sunflower or
    olive oil spread
450 g/1 lb potatoes, grated
Salt and freshly ground black pepper
450 g/1 lb undyed smoked haddock
    fillet, skinned and cut into small
    pieces
Grated rind of ½ lemon
15 ml/1 tbsp chopped parsley
300 ml/½ pt/1¼ cups passata (sieved
    tomatoes)
5 ml/1 tsp chopped basil
Lemon wedges, to garnish
Crunchy Spinach (page 270), to serve

Melt the low-fat spread in a non-stick frying pan (skillet). Add half the potatoes and press down well. Season with salt and pepper. Add the fish in an even layer and sprinkle with the lemon rind, parsley and a little seasoning. Top with the remaining potatoes, press down well again and season lightly. Cover with foil or a lid and cook gently for 30 minutes or until cooked through. Meanwhile, heat the passata with the basil in a small saucepan. Turn the fish cake out on to a warmed serving dish. Garnish with lemon wedges and serve cut into quarters with the tomato sauce and Crunchy Spinach.

* **235 calories per serving**
* **Medium fibre**

Cod Rosti

SERVES 4

Prepare as for Smoked Haddock Rosti, but substitute cod fillet for the smoked haddock and flavour the passata (sieved tomatoes) with dried mixed herbs instead of basil.

* **215 calories per serving**
* **Medium fibre**

Citrus Seafood Kebabs

SERVES 4

8 large shelled scallops
1 orange, ends removed, cut into
    8 slices
8 shelled raw king prawns (jumbo
    shrimp)
1 lemon, ends removed, cut into
    8 slices
175 g/6 oz monkfish, cut into 8 cubes
15 g/½ oz/1 tbsp low-fat sunflower or
    olive oil spread, melted
15 ml/1 tbsp balsamic vinegar
15 ml/1 tbsp finely chopped stoned
    (pitted) black olives
1 small onion, finely chopped
15 ml/1 tbsp chopped parsley
Lower-fat Garlic Bread (page 350) and
    Melon, Cucumber and Tomato
    Salad (page 283), to serve

Thread a scallop on each of four soaked wooden skewers, then add a slice of orange to each. Slide on a prawn, then a slice of lemon then a cube of monkfish. Repeat the threading. Mix together the melted spread and balsamic vinegar and brush over the kebabs. Grill (broil) for 4–6 minutes until cooked through, lightly golden and the prawns are pink, brushing with the baste during cooking. Mix together the olives, onion and parsley. Transfer the kebabs to plates and sprinkle with the olive mixture before serving with Lower-fat Garlic Bread and Melon, Cucumber and Tomato Salad.

* **225 calories per serving**
* **Low fibre**

Tuscan Beans

SERVES 4

100 g/4 oz conchiglie pasta shapes
2 x 425 g/2 x 15 oz/2 large cans of
cannellini beans, drained, rinsed
and drained again
185 g/6½ oz/1 small can of tuna in
water or brine, drained
1 onion, thinly sliced and separated
into rings
1 green (bell) pepper, diced
50 g/2 oz stoned (pitted) black olives
30 ml/2 tbsp lemon juice
15 ml/1 tbsp olive oil
15 ml/1 tbsp water
1 garlic clove, crushed
15 ml/1 tbsp chopped parsley
Salt and freshly ground black pepper
Lettuce leaves

Cook the pasta according to the packet directions. Drain, rinse with cold water and drain again. Place in a bowl and add the beans, tuna, onion, pepper and olives. Whisk together the lemon juice, oil, water, garlic, parsley and some salt and pepper and pour over. Toss gently. Pile on to a bed of lettuce on four plates and serve cold.

* **325 calories per serving**
* **High fibre**

Sharp Prawn and Scallop Kebabs

SERVES 4

15 ml/1 tbsp cumin seeds
Finely grated rind and juice of 1 lemon
1 small onion, grated
15 ml/1 tbsp chopped coriander
(cilantro)
15 ml/1 tbsp chopped parsley
5 ml/1 tsp caster (superfine) sugar
25 g/1 oz/2 tbsp low-fat sunflower or
olive oil spread, melted
Salt and freshly ground black pepper
225 g/8 oz raw, peeled tiger prawns
(jumbo shrimp)
225 g/8 oz shelled scallops
Thai Fragrant Rice Salad (page 280), to
serve

Toss the cumin seeds in a frying pan (skillet) until lightly browned. Tip into a bowl and lightly crush with a pestle or the end of a rolling pin. Mix with the lemon rind and juice, onion, herbs, sugar, low-fat spread and a little salt and pepper. Add the seafood and toss well to coat completely. Leave to marinate for 2 hours. Thread on to soaked wooden skewers. Grill (broil) for about 5 minutes, turning occasionally, until cooked through. Serve with Thai Fragrant Rice Salad.

* **160 calories per serving**
* **Low fibre**

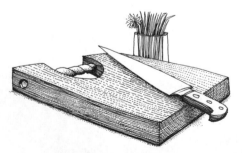

Prawn Pilau

SERVES 4

175 g/6 oz/³/₄ cup long-grain rice
Salt
25 g/1 oz/¹/₄ cup flaked (slivered)
  almonds
15 g/¹/₂ oz/1 tbsp low-fat sunflower or
  olive oil spread
2 onions, thinly sliced
1 large tomato, chopped
1 green (bell) pepper, chopped
50 g/2 oz/¹/₃ cup sultanas (golden
  raisins)
2.5 ml/¹/₂ tsp curry powder
A good a pinch of turmeric
225 g/8 oz cooked, peeled prawns
  (shrimp)
Freshly ground black pepper

Cook the rice in plenty of boiling, lightly salted water for 10 minutes until just tender. Drain, rinse with boiling water and drain again. Brown the almonds in a large non-stick frying pan (skillet), stirring all the time. Remove from the pan and reserve. Heat the low-fat spread in the pan and fry (sauté) the onions for 3 minutes until lightly golden. Add the tomato, pepper, sultanas and spices and fry for 1 minute. Stir in the rice and prawns and toss over a gentle heat for 5 minutes. Season with pepper and serve very hot.

* **310 calories per serving**
* **Fairly high fibre**

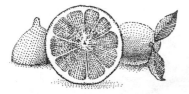

Monkfish and Mushroom Pilau

SERVES 4

Prepare as for Prawn Pilau, but substitute 175 g/6 oz monkfish and 100 g/4 oz button mushrooms, quartered, for the prawns (shrimp) and add them with the tomato and spices.

* **290 calories per serving**
* **Fairly high fibre**

Tarragon Lemon Trout

SERVES 4

4 trout, cleaned
15 g/¹/₂ oz/1 tbsp low-fat sunflower or
  olive oil spread, melted
Salt and freshly ground black pepper
2 lemons, thinly sliced
60 ml/4 tbsp chopped tarragon
25 g/1 oz/2 tbsp caster (superfine)
  sugar
Baked Scalloped Potatoes (page 259)
  and peas, to serve

Brush the fish inside and out with the low-fat spread and season with salt and pepper. Put four large squares of foil on the work surface. Lay two slices of lemon on each sheet of foil and sprinkle with half the tarragon and sugar. Put a fish on top of each. Sprinkle with the remaining tarragon and sugar. Wrap up securely and place on a baking (cookie) sheet. Bake in a preheated oven at 190°C/375°F/ gas mark 5 for 30 minutes. Carefully open the parcels and transfer to warm plates. Serve straight away with Baked Scalloped Potatoes and peas.

* **260 calories per serving**
* **Low fibre**

Warm Summer Seafood

SERVES 4

*450 g/1 lb baby squid, cleaned and
 sliced into rings*
*225 g/8 oz raw peeled tiger prawns
 (jumbo shrimp)*
100 g/4 oz shelled queen scallops
15 ml/1 tbsp olive oil
*15 g/½ oz/1 tbsp low-fat sunflower or
 olive oil spread*
1 garlic clove, crushed
5 ml/1 tsp chopped dill (dill weed)
15 ml/1 tbsp chopped parsley
15 ml/1 tbsp lemon juice
Salt and freshly ground black pepper
1 lollo rosso lettuce, torn into pieces
*½ cucumber, peeled, seeded and cut
 into matchsticks*
8 cherry tomatoes, halved
*A few sprigs of dill, 4 green olives and
 lemon wedges, to garnish*

Put the squid, prawns and scallops
in a frying pan (skillet) with the oil,
low-fat spread and the garlic and cook
gently, stirring, for about 5 minutes
until pink and tender. Stir in the herbs,
lemon juice and some salt and pepper.
Turn into a large salad bowl and add
the remaining ingredients. Toss and
re-season, if necessary. Serve straight
away, garnished with dill sprigs, olives
and lemon wedges.

* **220 calories per serving**
* **Medium fibre**

Miami Cod

SERVES 4

*15 g/½ oz/1 tbsp low-fat sunflower or
 olive oil spread, melted*
1 orange
1 grapefruit
4 cod fillets, about 175 g/6 oz each
*1 onion, thinly sliced and separated
 into rings*
A pinch of ground cinnamon
Salt and freshly ground black pepper
Watercress, to garnish
*New potatoes and sugar snap peas, to
 serve*

Brush four sheets of foil with a little
of the low-fat spread. Finely grate
the rind from the orange and
grapefruit and scatter half over the foil.
Cut off all the pith and peel from the
fruit and separate into segments.
Reserve for garnish. Lay the fish on the
foil and brush with the remaining
spread. Scatter the onion rings over,
then the remaining fruit rind and a
very fine dusting of cinnamon. Season
with salt and pepper. Close the foil
parcels and seal the edges firmly. Place
on a baking (cookie) sheet. Bake in a
preheated oven at 180°C/350°F/ gas
mark 4 for 25 minutes until the fish is
tender. Unwrap on to warm plates.
Garnish with watercress and the fruit
segments and serve with new potatoes
and sugar snap peas.

* **195 calories per serving**
* **Medium fibre**

Speciality Trout With Almonds

SERVES 4

15 g/¹/₂ oz/1 tbsp low-fat sunflower or olive oil spread
4 rainbow trout, cleaned and heads removed, if preferred
120 ml/4 fl oz/¹/₂ cup medium cider
30 ml/2 tbsp toasted flaked (slivered) almonds
15 ml/1 tbsp chopped parsley
15 ml/1 tbsp snipped chives
A pinch of salt
Freshly ground black pepper
New potatoes, boiled in their skins, and French (green) beans, to serve

Melt the low-fat spread in a large non-stick frying pan (skillet). Add the trout and fry (sauté) for 5 minutes on each side until cooked through. Lift out of the pan with a fish slice and transfer to warm serving plates. Keep warm. Add the cider to the juices in the pan and boil, stirring, until reduced by half. Add the nuts and herbs, the salt and a good grinding of pepper. Stir well, then spoon over the trout. Serve straight away with new potatoes in their skins and French beans.

* **265 calories per serving**
* **Fairly high fibre**

Cod and Broccoli Crumble

SERVES 4

225 g/8 oz broccoli, cut into very small florets
75 g/3 oz/³/₄ cup plain (all-purpose) flour
10 ml/2 tsp paprika
40 g/1¹/₂ oz/3 tbsp low-fat sunflower or olive oil spread
50 g/2 oz/¹/₂ cup Edam cheese, grated
450 g/1 lb cod fillet, skinned and cubed
295 g/10¹/₂ oz/1 medium can of low-fat condensed celery soup
2.5 ml/¹/₂ tsp dried thyme
15 ml/1 tbsp snipped chives
Baked Tomatoes with Herbs (page 274), to serve

Cook the broccoli in boiling, lightly salted water for 3 minutes only. Drain. Put the flour in a bowl with the paprika. Add the low-fat spread and rub in with the fingertips or a fork until the mixture resembles breadcrumbs. Stir in the cheese. Put the fish and broccoli in an ovenproof dish and add the soup, thyme and chives. Spoon the crumble mixture over and press down lightly. Bake in a preheated oven at 200°C/400°F/ gas mark 6 for about 30 minutes until golden brown and cooked through. Serve with Baked Tomatoes with Herbs.

* **270 calories per serving**
* **Fairly high fibre**

Smoked Haddock and Cauliflower and Tomato Crumble

SERVES 4

Prepare as for Cod and Broccoli Crumble (page 125), but substitute undyed smoked haddock for the cod, and cauliflower for the broccoli. Use low-fat condensed tomato soup instead of the celery soup and dried basil instead of thyme.

* **290 calories per serving**
* **Fairly high fibre**

Thai Grilled Sole

SERVES 4

4 lemon sole fillets
Coarse sea salt
Juice of 2 limes
1 stem of lemon grass, bruised
3 basil leaves, torn
60 ml/4 tbsp light brown sugar
Lime wedges, to garnish
Yellow Rice with Bay (page 264) and Mixed Green Salad (page 279), to serve

Lay the fish fillets in a shallow dish and sprinkle with coarse sea salt. Sprinkle the lime juice over and add the lemon grass and basil. Leave to marinate for 1 hour. Remove the basil and lemon grass. Lay the fillets on foil on a grill (broiler) rack and sprinkle the sugar over. Grill (broil) for about 5 minutes until tender and the sugar has caramelised. Garnish with lime wedges and serve with Yellow Rice with Bay and a Mixed Green Salad.

* **225 calories per serving**
* **Low fibre**

Mushroom-stuffed Plaice

SERVES 4

100 g/4 oz button mushrooms, finely chopped
25 g/1 oz/2 tbsp low-fat sunflower or olive oil spread
50 g/2 oz/1 cup fresh breadcrumbs
15 ml/1 tbsp chopped parsley
10 ml/2 tsp chopped thyme
Salt and freshly ground black pepper
4 plaice fillets, all dark skin removed
150 ml/¹/₄ pt/²/₃ cup low-fat crème fraîche
4 small sprigs of parsley, to garnish
Plain boiled potatoes and Baked Tomatoes with Herbs (page 274), to serve

Cook the mushrooms in the low-fat spread for 2 minutes, stirring. Add the breadcrumbs, parsley and thyme and season with a little salt and pepper. Halve the plaice fillets lengthways. Divide the stuffing between the centres of the fillets and fold the two ends over to form parcels. Transfer to individual ovenproof dishes and spoon the crème fraîche over. Season very lightly again with pepper and bake in a preheated oven at 180°C/350°F/gas mark 4 for 20 minutes until cooked through. Garnish each with a small sprig of parsley and serve with plain boiled potatoes and Baked Tomatoes with Herbs.

* **300 calories per serving**
* **Medium fibre**

Crusted Cod with Poached Leeks

SERVES 4

10 g/¹/₄ oz/2 tsp low-fat sunflower or olive oil spread
4 pieces of cod fillet, about 175 g/6 oz each
100 g/4 oz/2 cups wholemeal breadcrumbs
5 ml/1 tsp grated fresh root ginger
30 ml/2 tbsp chopped parsley
30 ml/2 tbsp snipped chives
Salt and freshly ground black pepper
Finely grated rind and juice of 1 small lemon
8 baby leeks
150 ml/¹/₄ pt/²/₃ cup chicken stock, made with ¹/₂ stock cube
2.5 ml/¹/₂ tsp ground cumin

Grease a shallow baking dish, large enough to take the fish in a single layer, with the low-fat spread. Lay the fish in the dish. Mix together the breadcrumbs, ginger, parsley, chives, some salt and pepper and the lemon rind, then moisten with the lemon juice. Press the mixture on top of each fish fillet. Bake in a hot oven at 220°C/425°F/gas mark 7 for 20 minutes until the fish is cooked and the crumb mixture is crisp and browning. Meanwhile, trim the leeks and wash thoroughly. Place in a frying pan (skillet) with the stock and cumin. Add a a pinch of salt and a good grinding of pepper. Bring to the boil, cover with a lid or foil, reduce the heat and simmer for 10 minutes or until the leeks are just tender but still holding their shape. Transfer the fish to warm plates. Lay the leeks to the side and serve hot.

* **250 calories per serving**
* **Fairly high fibre**

Jack Daniels Swordfish

SERVES 4

175 ml/6 fl oz/³/₄ cup bourbon
175 ml/6 fl oz/³/₄ cup fish or chicken stock, made with ¹/₂ stock cube
25 g/1 oz/2 tbsp low-fat sunflower or olive oil spread, melted
1 large garlic clove, crushed
Salt and freshly ground black pepper
4 swordfish steaks
30 ml/2 tbsp chopped parsley
Savoury Potato Cake (page 258) and Mixed Leaf Salad (page 278), to serve

Mix together the bourbon and stock with the low-fat spread, garlic and a little salt and pepper. Add the fish, turn to coat completely and leave to marinate for 2 hours. Lift out of the marinade and place on the grill (broiler) rack. Grill (broil) for about 10–15 minutes, turning once, until browned and cooked through. Meanwhile, boil the remaining marinade until reduced and thickened. Stir in the parsley. Transfer the steaks to warmed plates. Spoon the sauce over and serve with Savoury Potato Cake and Mixed Leaf Salad.

* **320 calories per serving**
* **Low fibre**

Plaice with Grapes

SERVES 4

4 plaice fillets, halved lengthways
150 ml/¼ pt/⅔ cups chicken stock,
    made with ½ stock cube
150 ml/¼ pt/⅔ cup dry white wine
1 small bay leaf
1 small piece of cinnamon stick
150 ml/¼ pt/⅔ cup cultured
    buttermilk or low-fat crème fraîche
50 g/2 oz seedless green grapes,
    halved
30 ml/2 tbsp chopped parsley
A pinch of salt
White pepper
Extra-fluffed Mashed Potatoes (page
    260) and Warm Courgette and
    Carrot Salad (page 277), to serve

Remove any dark skin from the fillets, leave it on if it is white. Roll up, skin-sides in, and place in a single layer in a large, shallow, flameproof dish. Pour over the stock and wine and add the bay leaf and cinnamon. Cover with foil and bake in a preheated oven at 190°C/375°F/gas mark 5 for 15–20 minutes until the fish is cooked through. Carefully lift out the plaice rolls and keep warm. Boil the cooking liquid on top of the stove until it has reduced by half. Discard the bay leaf and cinnamon stick. Add the buttermilk or crème fraîche, grapes and parsley, season to taste with the salt and some pepper and heat through. Carefully transfer the fish to warm plates and spoon the sauce over. Serve hot with Extra-fluffed Mashed Potatoes and Warm Courgette and Carrot Salad.

* **220 calories per serving**
* **Medium fibre**

Photograph opposite: Nectarine and Serrano Ham Crostini (page 75)

French-style Cod

SERVES 4

1 onion, finely chopped
1 garlic clove, crushed
10 g/¼ oz/2 tsp low-fat sunflower or
    olive oil spread
1 green (bell) pepper, chopped
400 g/14 oz/1 large can of chopped
    tomatoes
15 ml/1 tbsp tomato purée (paste)
A pinch of salt
Freshly ground black pepper
6 stoned (pitted) black olives, sliced
4 pieces of cod fillet, about 175 g/6 oz
    each, skinned
Plain boiled rice and Mixed Leaf Salad
    (page 278), to serve

Fry (sauté) the onion and garlic in the low-fat spread for 2 minutes, stirring, in a large frying pan (skillet). Add the chopped pepper, tomatoes, tomato purée, salt and lots of pepper and simmer for 5 minutes. Add the olives and fish, cover with a lid or foil and simmer for about 8 minutes until the fish is cooked. Serve on a bed of rice with Mixed Leaf Salad.

* **190 calories per serving**
* **Medium fibre**

Tandoori Fish with Red Rice

SERVES 4

450 g/1 lb cod fillet, skinned
150 ml/¹/₄ pt/²/₃ cup low-fat plain yoghurt
15 ml/1 tbsp lemon juice
5 ml/1 tsp ground coriander (cilantro)
5 ml/1 tsp ground cumin
2.5 ml/¹/₂ tsp turmeric
A pinch of salt
Freshly ground black pepper
175 g/6 oz/³/₄ cup brown long-grain rice
400 g/14 oz/1 large can of chopped tomatoes
300 ml/¹/₂ pt/1¹/₄ cups water
1 vegetable stock cube, crumbled
6 green cardamom pods, split (optional)
2 spring onions (scallions), chopped, to garnish

Cut the fish into four equal pieces. Place in a shallow ovenproof dish in a single layer. Mix together the yoghurt, lemon juice, spices, salt and pepper. Spoon over the fish and turn gently to coat completely. Cover and leave in a cool place to marinate for 1 hour. Remove the cover and bake in a preheated oven at 180°C/ 350°F/gas mark 4 for 20 minutes, basting occasionally. Meanwhile, wash the rice and place in a pan with the remaining ingredients. Bring to the boil, reduce the heat and simmer for 35 minutes, adding a little extra water, if necessary, until the rice is tender but nutty and has absorbed all the liquid. Pile the rice on to warm plates, top with the fish and garnish with the chopped spring onion.

* **285 calories per serving**
* **High fibre**

Smoked Haddock-stuffed Pancakes

SERVES 4

Oat Bran and Wholemeal Pancakes (page 000)
For the filling:
225 g/8 oz undyed smoked haddock fillet, skinned
100 g/4 oz button mushrooms, sliced
350 ml/12 fl oz/1¹/₃ cups skimmed milk
45 ml/3 tbsp plain (all-purpose) flour
5 ml/1 tsp lemon juice
30 ml/2 tbsp chopped parsley
Freshly ground black pepper
Lemon wedges and parsley sprigs, to garnish
Mangetout (snow peas) and baby carrots, to serve

Prepare and cook the pancakes and keep warm over a pan of hot water. To make the filling, poach the fish and mushrooms in 300 ml/¹/₂ pt/1¹/₄ cups of the milk for 6 minutes or until the fish flakes easily with a fork. Lift the fish out of the milk and reserve. Blend the flour with the remaining milk. Stir into the fish milk, bring to the boil and cook for 2 minutes, stirring until thickened. Add the lemon juice, parsley and pepper to taste. Flake the fish and fold in gently. Heat through, stirring lightly, until piping hot. Divide the mixture between the pancakes, roll up and arrange on warm plates. Garnish with lemon wedges and parsley sprigs and serve straight away with mangetout and baby carrots.

* **225 calories per serving**
* **High fibre**

Photograph opposite: Chilli Prawn Wraps (page 95)

Spiced Monkfish and Mango Kebabs with Curried Yoghurt Dressing

If you prefer your vegetables less crunchy, blanch the courgettes (zucchini) and onion in boiling water for 3 minutes before threading them on to the skewers.

SERVES 4

5 ml/1 tsp ground cumin
5 ml/1 tsp ground coriander (cilantro)
5 ml/1 tsp turmeric
30 ml/2 tbsp lemon juice
350 g/12 oz monkfish, cubed
1 mango
2 courgettes (zucchini), cut into chunks
1 small red onion, quartered and
    separated into layers
8 cherry tomatoes
For the dressing:
150 ml/¼ pt/⅔ cup low-fat plain yoghurt
15 ml/1 tbsp curry powder
2.5 cm/1 in piece of cucumber, very
    finely chopped
Plain boiled rice, to serve
Lemon wedges, to garnish

Mix the spices with the lemon juice in a shallow dish. Add the monkfish and toss gently to coat. Leave to marinate for 1 hour. Peel the mango and cut the flesh away from the stone (pit) in large cubes. Thread the fish, mango, courgettes and onion on eight soaked kebab skewers and push a cherry tomato on the end of each. Grill (broil) for 10 minutes, turning occasionally, until cooked through, brushing with any juices left in the fish dish. To make the dressing, mix the yoghurt with the curry powder and cucumber. Serve on a bed of boiled rice, garnished with lemon wedges, with the dressing handed separately.

* **130 calories per serving**
* **Medium fibre**

Mediterranean Cod

SERVES 4

4 cod fillets, about 175 g/6 oz each
25 g/1 oz/2 tbsp low-fat sunflower or
    olive oil spread
1 onion, finely chopped
1 garlic clove, crushed
4 ripe tomatoes, skinned and chopped
Salt and freshly ground black pepper
6 stoned (pitted) black olives, sliced
30 ml/2 tbsp chopped parsley
Sesame Seed Noodles (page 267), to
    serve

Wipe the fish. Heat half the low-fat spread in a large non-stick frying pan (skillet). Add the fish, skin-side up, and fry (sauté) for 3 minutes. Carefully turn the fish over and cook for a further 3 minutes until tender and cooked through. Carefully lift out of the pan and keep warm. Heat the remaining spread in the pan. Add the onion and fry for 2 minutes, stirring. Add the garlic, tomatoes and a little salt and pepper. Cook, stirring, until pulpy. Stir in the olives and parsley. Transfer the fish to warm plates. Spoon the tomato mixture over and serve hot with Sesame Seed Noodles.

* **305 calories per serving**
* **Medium fibre**

Grilled Mackerel with Tarragon Sauce

SERVES 4

4 mackerel, cleaned
4 sprigs of tarragon
Freshly ground black pepper
30 ml/2 tbsp plain (all-purpose) flour
200 ml/7 fl oz/scant 1 cup skimmed milk
5 ml/1 tsp low-fat sunflower or olive oil spread
15 ml/1 tbsp clear honey
15 ml/1 tbsp chopped tarragon
Lemon juice
Salt
Tarragon sprigs, to garnish
Plain boiled potatoes and peas, to serve

Slash the mackerel in several places along either side. Remove the heads, if preferred, and place a sprig of tarragon in the body cavity of each. Season with pepper. Grill (broil) for about 5 minutes on each side until golden and cooked through. Meanwhile, put the flour in a saucepan and whisk in a little of the milk until smooth. Mix in the remainder and add the low-fat spread. Bring to the boil and cook for 2 minutes, stirring, until thick and smooth. Stir in the honey and tarragon and lemon juice, salt and pepper to taste. Transfer the mackerel to warm plates. Garnish each with a sprig of tarragon and spoon a little of the sauce over the centre of each fish. Serve with potatoes, peas and the remaining sauce.

* **375 calories per serving**
* **Very low fibre**

Honey Soused Mackerel

SERVES 4

4 small mackerel, cleaned
Freshly ground black pepper
1 small onion, thinly sliced and separated into rings
30 ml/2 tbsp chopped coriander (cilantro)
300 ml/¹/₂ pt/1¹/₄ cups malt vinegar
300 ml/¹/₂ pt/1¹/₄ cups water
A pinch of salt
15 ml/1 tbsp clear honey
1 bay leaf
New potatoes and English Mixed Salad (page 276), to serve

Cut the heads off the fish, then open out the fish and place skin-side up on a board. Run the thumb firmly down the backbone several times. Turn the mackerel over and remove the backbone and any other bones. Cut off the fins and tails. Season the flesh with pepper and sprinkle with the onion and coriander. Roll up, starting from the head end, and place in a shallow ovenproof dish. Mix the vinegar with the water, salt and honey and pour over. Add the bay leaf. Cover with foil or a lid and cook in a preheated oven at 180°C/350°F/gas mark 4 for about 45 minutes until cooked through. Leave to cool in the liquid, then chill before serving with new potatoes and English Mixed Salad.

* **340 calories per serving**
* **Very low fibre**

Family Fish Pie

SERVES 4

750 g/1½ lb potatoes, cut into bite-
  sized pieces
325 ml/11 fl oz/scant 1⅓ cups milk
50 g/2 oz/½ cup strong low-fat
  Cheddar cheese, grated
100 g/4 oz button mushrooms, sliced
225 g/8 oz frozen mixed vegetables
1 bay leaf
450 g/1 lb white fish fillet
Salt and freshly ground black pepper
45 ml/3 tbsp plain (all-purpose) flour
30 ml/2 tbsp chopped parsley

Cook the potatoes in boiling, lightly salted water until really tender. Drain and mash with 25 ml/1½ tbsp of the milk and half the cheese. Meanwhile, put the mushrooms in a saucepan with the vegetables, bay leaf, fish and 300 ml/½ pt/1¼ cups of the remaining milk. Season with pepper. Bring to the boil, reduce the heat, part-cover and simmer gently for 8–10 minutes until the fish and vegetables are cooked. Carefully lift the fish out of the saucepan. Remove any skin and bones and roughly flake the flesh. Blend the flour with the remaining milk until smooth. Stir into the saucepan with the parsley, bring to the boil and cook for 2 minutes, stirring, until thickened. Discard the bay leaf and season with more salt and pepper, if liked. Stir the fish into the sauce. Turn the mixture into a flameproof serving dish. Top with the cheesy potato and sprinkle with the remaining cheese. Grill (broil) for about 5 minutes until golden and piping hot. Serve straight away.

* **350 calories per serving**
* **Medium fibre**

Fireside Fish Pot

SERVES 4

1 onion, sliced
1 carrot, thinly sliced
2 large potatoes, diced
¼ small cabbage, shredded
25 g/1 oz/2 tbsp low-fat sunflower or
  olive oil spread
400 g/14 oz/1 large can of chopped
  tomatoes
300 ml/½ pt/1¼ cups chicken or fish
  stock, made with 1 stock cube
225 g/8 oz white fish fillet, skinned
  and cubed
225 g/8 oz smoked haddock fillet,
  skinned and cubed
Salt and freshly ground black pepper
Snipped chives, to garnish

Place all the prepared vegetables in a very large saucepan with the low-fat spread. Cook, stirring, for 5 minutes. Add the tomatoes and stock. Bring to the boil, reduce the heat, cover and simmer gently for 15 minutes. Add the fish, re-cover and simmer for a further 5 minutes until the fish and vegetables are tender. Season to taste. Ladle into warm bowls and serve sprinkled with snipped chives.

* **250 calories per serving**
* **Medium fibre**

Plaice with Orange and Vegetables

SERVES 4

4 plaice fillets, skinned
1 carrot, grated
1 turnip, grated
5 ml/1 tsp paprika
5 ml/1 tsp ground coriander (cilantro)
Finely grated rind and juice of 1 orange
A pinch of salt
Freshly ground black pepper
Orange slices and chopped parsley, to garnish
Baked Scalloped Potatoes (page 259) and mangetout (snow peas), to serve

Wipe the fish and fold each fillet into three. Place in a flameproof casserole dish (Dutch oven). Scatter the carrot and turnip over and sprinkle with the paprika and coriander. Make the orange rind and juice up to 150 ml/ ¼ pt/⅔ cup with water and pour over the fish. Add the salt and a good grinding of pepper. Cover and bake in a preheated oven at 180°C/ 350°F/gas mark 4 for 40 minutes until cooked through. Carefully transfer the fish to a warm serving dish, using a fish slice. Boil the juices rapidly for 5 minutes until reduced by half. Spoon over the fish, garnish with orange slices and chopped parsley and serve with Baked Scalloped Potatoes and mangetout.

* **185 calories per serving**
* **Medium fibre**

Summer Waters Swordfish Steaks

SERVES 4

4 swordfish steaks
15 ml/1 tbsp Chinese five spice powder
30 ml/2 tbsp sesame oil
30 ml/2 tbsp lemon juice
100 g/4 oz/2 cups beansprouts
1 red (bell) pepper, finely shredded
2 spring onions (scallions), finely sliced
30 ml/2 tbsp reduced-salt soy sauce
Jacket-baked Potatoes with Yoghurt and Chives (page 260), to serve

Wipe the fish with kitchen paper (paper towels) and remove the skin. Mix the five spice powder with half the oil and half the lemon juice. Brush all over the fish and leave to marinate for 2 hours. Mix the beansprouts with the pepper and spring onions. Whisk together the soy sauce with the remaining oil and lemon juice. Grill (broil) the fish for 3–4 minutes on each side until cooked through, turning once and brushing with any remaining marinade. Add the soy dressing to the beansprout mixture. Toss gently. Spoon on to plates. Transfer the swordfish to the plates and serve with Jacket-baked Potatoes with Yoghurt and Chives.

* **305 calories per serving**
* **Fairly high fibre**

Simple Pan Swordfish

SERVES 4

4 swordfish steaks
Salt and freshly ground black pepper
25 g/1 oz/2 tbsp low-fat sunflower or
 olive oil spread
30 ml/2 tbsp chopped parsley
Lemon wedges and parsley sprigs, to
 garnish
Baby new potatoes and French (green)
 beans, to serve

Cut the skin off the swordfish. Season lightly. Heat the low-fat spread in a frying pan (skillet), add the fish and fry (sauté) for 3–4 minutes on each side until cooked through and golden. Sprinkle with the parsley, then transfer with the juices to warm plates. Garnish with lemon wedges and parsley sprigs and serve with baby new potatoes and French beans.

* 230 calories per serving
* Low fibre

Simple Pan Tuna

SERVES 4

Prepare as for Simple Pan Swordfish, but substitute tuna steaks for the swordfish. Sprinkle with a mixture of chopped coriander (cilantro) and parsley instead of all parsley and add the finely grated rind of ½ lemon.

* 235 calories per serving
* Low fibre

Haddock Creole

SERVES 4

4 small haddock fillets, about 150g/
 5 oz each, skinned
30 ml/2 tbsp plain (all-purpose) flour
Salt and freshly ground black pepper
1 small green chilli, seeded and finely
 chopped
25 g/1 oz/2 tbsp low-fat sunflower or
 olive oil spread
2 green bananas, thickly sliced
10 ml/2 tsp lime juice
Lime wedges and coriander (cilantro)
 sprigs, to garnish
Almond Wild Rice (page 265) and
 Orange and Mango Salsa (page
 385), to serve

Wipe the fish. Season the flour with salt and pepper, add the chilli and use to coat the fish. Heat half the low-fat spread in a non-stick frying pan (skillet), add the fish and fry (sauté) for 3 minutes. Turn over, add the remaining spread and fry the other sides for 3 minutes until cooked through. Carefully slide out of the pan and keep warm. Add the banana slices to the pan with the lime juice and toss over a fairly high heat until softening slightly. Transfer the fish to warm plates and spoon the banana on top. Garnish with lime wedges and coriander sprigs and serve with Almond Wild Rice and Orange and Mango Salsa.

* 215 calories per serving
* Medium fibre

Mixed Seafood Pot

SERVES 4

1 kg/2¼ lb fresh mussels in their shells
1 large onion, halved and thinly sliced
1 large garlic clove, crushed
*10 g/¼ oz/2 tsp low-fat sunflower or
olive oil spread*
30 ml/2 tbsp white wine vinegar
10 ml/2 tsp clear honey
300 ml/½ pt/1¼ cups dry white wine
300 ml/½ pt/1¼ cups water
*400 g/14 oz/1 large can of chopped
tomatoes*
*1 aubergine (eggplant), quartered and
sliced*
1 courgette (zucchini), sliced
1 green (bell) pepper, sliced
*2.5 ml/½ tsp dried mixed
Mediterranean herbs*
*450 g/1 lb white fish fillet, skinned
and cut into large cubes*
*225 g/8 oz baby squid, cleaned and
cut into rings*
Freshly ground black pepper
*Chopped parsley and lemon wedges,
to garnish*

Scrub the mussels thoroughly, scrape off any barnacles and remove the beards. Discard any that are broken or open and do not close immediately when tapped. In a large saucepan, fry (sauté) the onion and garlic in the low-fat spread for 2 minutes, stirring. Add the vinegar, honey, wine, water, tomatoes, prepared vegetables and herbs and simmer for 5 minutes. Add the mussels, white fish and squid, cover and simmer for a further 5 minutes. Season with lots of pepper and stir gently. Serve straight from the pan, sprinkled with chopped parsley and garnished with lemon wedges.

* **315 calories per serving**
* **Medium fibre**

Truite au Bleu

You must use the freshest trout you can buy for this recipe.

SERVES 4

2 litres/3½ pts/8½ cups water
75 ml/5 tbsp white wine vinegar
15 ml/1 tbsp coarse sea salt
*4 fresh rainbow trout, cleaned but not
washed*
*Horseradish Crème (page 386) and
parsley sprigs. to garnish*
*Plain boiled potatoes and mangetout
(snow peas), to serve*

Put the water in a large, shallow pan and add the vinegar and salt. Bring to the boil. Carefully add the trout, cover, reduce the heat and cook gently for 7 minutes or until just cooked. Carefully lift out with a fish slice and drain on kitchen paper (paper towels). The fish will turn a beautiful blue colour if very fresh. Transfer to warm plates. Put a spoonful of Horseradish Crème and a sprig of parsley to one side and serve with plain boiled potatoes and mangetout.

* **210 calories per serving**
* **Very low fibre**

Vitality Fish and Chips

SERVES 4

450 g/1 lb potatoes, scrubbed and cut
    into chips (fries)
15 ml/1 tbsp melted low-fat sunflower
    or olive oil spread
100 g/4 oz/2 cups fresh wholemeal
    breadcrumbs
1 egg white
4 white fish fillets, about 175 g/6 oz
    each
Parsley sprigs and lemon wedges, to
    garnish
Peas, to serve

Boil the potato chips in water for
3 minutes. Drain and dry on
kitchen paper (paper towels). Brush a
baking (cookie) sheet with half the low-
fat spread. Spread the potato chips on
the sheet and brush with the
remaining low-fat spread. Meanwhile,
dry-fry the breadcrumbs or bake in a
hot oven at 200°C/400°F/gas mark 6
until golden brown. Dip the fish in the
egg white, then coat in the toasted
breadcrumbs. Lay them on a second
baking sheet. Place the chips on the
top shelf and the fish just below in the
preheated oven to 200°C/400°F/gas
mark 6 and bake for 30 minutes until
golden and cooked through. Garnish
with parsley sprigs and lemon wedges
and serve with peas.

* **340 calories per serving**
* **Fairly high fibre**

Ceviche

SERVES 4

750 g/1½ lb turbot, skinned and
    boned
1 red (bell) pepper, diced
1 green pepper, diced
1 small green chilli, seeded and
    chopped
Juice of 1 large lemon
Salt and freshly ground black pepper
Lettuce leaves
8 tomatoes, thinly sliced
1 red onion, thinly sliced and
    separated into rings
10 ml/2 tsp olive oil
Warm French bread, to serve

Cut the turbot into thin slices with a
sharp knife, then cut the slices into
narrow strips. Place in a bowl with the
peppers, chilli, lemon juice, a
sprinkling of salt and a good grinding
of pepper. Toss gently and chill for
1–2 hours until the fish is opaque.
Arrange lettuce leaves on four plates.
Put tomato slices and onion rings
alternately in a ring round the edge
and spoon the fish mixture in the
centre. Add a few drops of olive oil to
each and serve with warm French
bread.

* **210 calories per serving**
* **Medium fibre**

Salmon Ceviche

SERVES 4

Prepare as for Ceviche, but
substitute fresh salmon for the
turbot and lime for the lemon.

* **385 calories per serving**
* **Medium fibre**

Normandy Seafood

SERVES 4

900 g/2 lb fresh mussels in their
shells, scrubbed and beards
removed
150 ml/¹/₄ pt/²/₃ cup water
1 large onion, finely chopped
15 g/¹/₂ oz/1 tbsp low-fat sunflower or
olive oil spread
450 g/1 lb cod fillet, skinned and
cubed
225 g/8 oz monkfish fillet, skinned
and cubed
225 g/8 oz shelled scallops, quartered
300 ml/¹/₂ pt/1¹/₄ cups dry cider
1 bay leaf
Salt and freshly ground black pepper
25 g/1 oz/¹/₄ cup plain (all-purpose)
flour
60 ml/4 tbsp skimmed milk
30 ml/2 tbsp chopped parsley
100 g/4 oz cooked peeled prawns
(shrimp)
Lemon juice
Warm French bread, to serve

Discard any mussels that are broken, open or don't close when sharply tapped. Place in a large saucepan with the water. Cover with a lid and cook over a high heat for 5 minutes, shaking the pan occasionally until the mussels have opened. Strain the liquid into a bowl. When cool enough to handle, remove the mussels from their shells and reserve.

Cook the onion in the low-fat spread in the mussel saucepan for 2 minutes, stirring, until softened but not browned. Add the cod, monkfish and scallops. Pour on the mussel cooking liquid and the cider and add the bay leaf, a little salt and a good grinding of pepper. Bring to the boil, cover with a lid, reduce the heat and cook for about 5 minutes until the fish is just cooked.

Blend the flour with the milk until smooth and stir into the pot. Bring to the boil and cook for 2 minutes, stirring very gently until thickened, taking care not to break up the fish. Remove the bay leaf. Add the parsley, mussels and prawns and season to taste with a little lemon juice, salt and pepper. Heat through. Ladle into warm bowls and serve with lots of warm French bread.

* **340 calories per serving**
* **Low fibre**

Baked Red Mullet Parcels

SERVES 4

*20 ml/4 tsp low-fat sunflower or olive
    oil spread*
2 tomatoes, thinly sliced
1 courgette (zucchini), thinly sliced
2 shallots, finely chopped
4 red mullet, cleaned and scaled
1 large garlic clove, cut into thin slivers
1 lemon, sliced
4 sprigs of parsley
4 sprigs of thyme
Salt and freshly ground black pepper
*New potatoes and baby carrots, to
    serve*

Grease four large squares of double
thickness greaseproof (waxed)
paper with the low-fat spread. Lay the
tomato and courgette slices in a thin
layer on the centre of each sheet and
sprinkle with the shallots. Lay a red
mullet on top of each. Make three
slashes in each fish and push a sliver of
garlic into each slash. Push a slice of
lemon, a sprig of parsley and a sprig of
thyme in the body cavity of each. Add
15 ml/1 tbsp water to each pile and
season with salt and pepper. Draw up
opposite sides of the paper and pleat
over the top of the fish, then fold in the
sides to seal completely. Put the
parcels on a baking (cookie) sheet.
Bake in a preheated oven at
180°C/350°F/ gas mark 4 for
30 minutes until the fish is cooked
through and the vegetables are tender.
Transfer to plates, open at the table to
enjoy the fragrant aromas and serve
with new potatoes and baby carrots.

* **335 calories per serving**
* **Medium fibre**

Baked Salmon Parcels

SERVES 4

Prepare as for Baked Red Mullet
Parcels, but substitute salmon
steaks for the red mullet and tarragon
for the thyme, pushing the lemon and
herbs into the centre cavity of each fish
steak.

* **340 calories per serving**
* **Medium fibre**

Whole Poached Salmon

If you have a fish kettle you won't need to use the foil as the fish can lay straight on the trivet.

SERVES 6 OR 8

1 salmon, about 1.5 kg/3 lb, cleaned
1 onion, sliced
6 peppercorns
1 bouquet garni sachet
300 ml/½ pt/1¼ cups dry white wine
Parsley sprigs and either lemon
    wedges or cucumber slices, to
    garnish
Extra-light Mayonnaise (page 385),
    new potatoes and peas or English
    Mixed Salad (page 276), to serve

Lay the fish on a large, wide strip of double thickness foil, long enough to provide tabs to lift the fish in and out of the poaching liquid. Put the onion, peppercorns, bouquet garni and wine in a large shallow pan in which the fish will fit. Add the fish and just enough water to cover it. Cover with a lid or foil and bring slowly to a gentle simmer; don't let the liquid boil rapidly. Simmer for 10 minutes, then turn off the heat and leave the fish to stand for at least 10 minutes. To serve hot, lift out of the pan and transfer the fish to a serving dish. Peel off the skin and garnish with parsley and lemon wedges. To serve cold, leave in the cooking liquid until cold, then transfer to a serving plate, peel off the skin and decorate with cucumber slices. Serve hot or cold with Extra-light Mayonnaise, new potatoes and peas (if hot) or English Mixed Salad (if cold).

* **290 or 220 calories per serving**
* **Low fibre**

Storecupboard Paella

SERVES 4

1 packet of savoury vegetable rice
450 ml/¾ pt/2 cups boiling water
175 g/6 oz/1½ cups cooked chicken,
    diced
250 g/9 oz/1 small can of mussels in
    brine, drained
100 g/4 oz cooked peeled prawns
    (shrimp)
15 ml/1 tbsp chopped parsley
Lower-fat Garlic Bread (page 350) and
    Dressed Green Salad (page 275), to
    serve

Put the rice in a pan with the boiling water. Stir, cover and simmer for 12 minutes. Add the remaining ingredients and cook for a further 8 minutes until all the liquid has been absorbed and the rice is tender. Spoon on to warm plates and sprinkle with chopped parsley. Serve with Lower-fat Garlic Bread and Mixed Green Salad.

* **220 calories per serving**
* **Medium fibre**

Dressed Crab

SERVES 4

1 large cooked crab, about 1.5 kg/3 lb
10 ml/2 tsp fresh breadcrumbs
15 ml/1 tbsp chopped parsley
5 ml/1 tsp Dijon mustard
Cayenne
Salt and freshly ground black pepper
Lettuce leaves, lemon wedges and a
*   bunch of spring onions (scallions),*
*   trimmed, to garnish*
Brown bread, lightly spread with low-
*   fat sunflower or olive oil spread*
*   and Dressed Green Salad (page*
*   275), to serve*

Pull the body away from the back shell of the crab. Pull off the small legs and remove the big claws. Discard the 'dead men's fingers' in the body. Scoop all the dark meat into a small bowl and pick all the white meat out of the shell, small legs and claws and put in a second bowl. Mix the breadcrumbs into the dark meat with half the parsley, the mustard and a good a pinch of cayenne and salt and pepper to taste. Wash out the shell. Spoon the white meat either side and the dark meat down the centre. Garnish with a line of the remaining chopped parsley on both sides of the dark meat where it meets the white. Place on a bed of lettuce. Garnish the dish with lemon wedges and spring onions and serve with brown bread and 'butter' and Dressed Green Salad.

* **90 calories per serving**
* **Medium fibre**

Smoked Salmon, Prawn and Broccoli Pappardelle

SERVES 4

250 g/9 oz pappardelle (wide ribbon
*   noodles)*
175 g/6 oz broccoli, cut into tiny florets
100 g/4 oz smoked salmon pieces, cut
*   up if necessary*
100 g/4 oz cooked peeled prawns
*   (shrimp)*
150 ml/¹/₄ pt/²/₃ cup low-fat crème
*   fraîche*
1 egg
60 ml/4 tbsp skimmed milk
Salt and freshly ground black pepper
A squeeze of lemon juice
20 ml/4 tsp grated Parmesan cheese

Cook the pasta according to the packet directions, adding the broccoli for the last 5 minutes' cooking time. Drain and return to the saucepan. Add the salmon, prawns and crème fraîche. Toss gently. Beat together the egg and milk and add to the pan with some salt and pepper. Toss over a gentle heat until creamy but not totally scrambled. Taste and add lemon juice and a little more seasoning to taste. Pile on to warm plates and sprinkle with the Parmesan cheese.

* **390 calories per serving**
* **Medium fibre**

Thai-style Prawn and Cucumber Curry

SERVES 4

*1 cucumber, quartered lengthways
  and cut into bite-sized chunks*
Salt
*15 g/¹/₂ oz/1 tbsp low-fat sunflower or
  olive oil spread*
2 garlic cloves, finely chopped
15 ml/1 tbsp grated fresh root ginger
1 stem of lemon grass, finely chopped
*1 bunch of spring onions (scallions),
  finely chopped*
5 ml/1 tsp turmeric
10 ml/2 tsp garam masala
1.5 ml/¹/₄ tsp ground cloves
2.5 ml/¹/₂ tsp ground cinnamon
2 green chillies, seeded and chopped
5 ml/1 tsp caster (superfine) sugar
30 ml/2 tbsp plain (all-purpose) flour
300 ml/¹/₂ pt/1¹/₄ cups coconut milk
*300 ml/¹/₂ pt/1¹/₄ cups stock, made
  with 1 fish or chicken stock cube*
*225 g/8 oz raw peeled king prawns
  (jumbo shrimp), split into halves
  lengthways*
Plain boiled Thai fragrant rice, to serve

Put the cucumber in a pan with enough water to just cover. Add a good pinch of salt. Bring to the boil, reduce the heat and cook for 5 minutes. Drain. Heat the low-fat spread in the saucepan and fry (sauté) the garlic, ginger, lemon grass, spring onions, turmeric, garam masala, cloves and cinnamon, stirring, for 1 minute. Stir in the chillies, sugar and flour and cook for a further minute. Remove from the heat and blend in the coconut milk and half the stock. Return to the heat, bring to the boil and cook for 2 minutes, stirring. Add the prawns and cucumber and simmer for 5 minutes. Thin with a little more stock, if necessary. Serve on a bed of Thai fragrant rice.

* **120 calories per serving**
* **Medium fibre**

Thai-style Monkfish and Courgette Curry

SERVES 4

Prepare as for Thai-style Prawn and Cucumber Curry, but substitute 3 courgettes (zucchini) for the cucumber and cubed monkfish for the prawns (shrimp).

* **110 calories per serving**
* **Medium fibre**

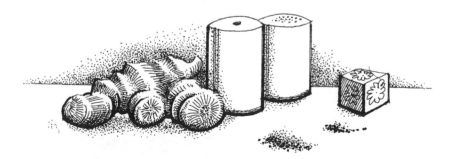

Creamy Squid Risotto

SERVES 4

450 g/1 lb baby squid, cleaned
15 g/¹/₂ oz/1 tbsp low-fat sunflower or
olive oil spread
1 onion, finely chopped
1 leek, finely chopped
1 beefsteak tomato, skinned and finely
chopped
1 large garlic clove, crushed
150 ml/¹/₄ pt/²/₃ cup dry white wine
450 ml/³/₄ pt/2 cups water
175 g/6 oz/³/₄ cup arborio or other
risotto rice
5 ml/1 tsp tomato purée (paste)
Salt and freshly ground black pepper
15 ml/1 tbsp chopped parsley
Celeriac and Carrot Salad (page 280),
to serve

Cut the squid into rings and chop the tentacles. Heat the low-fat spread in a wide, shallow pan. Add the onion and leek and fry (sauté) gently, stirring, for 2 minutes to soften. Add the squid, tomato and garlic and fry gently for 1 minute, stirring. Add the wine and 150 ml/¹/₄ pt/²/₃ cup of the water. Bring to the boil, reduce the heat, cover and simmer gently for 20 minutes. Add the rice and stir in the tomato purée and a little salt and pepper. Simmer, uncovered, until the liquid is absorbed, stirring regularly. Add a little more of the remaining water and simmer again until absorbed. Repeat this process, cooking for about 25 minutes in all until the rice is just tender and creamy, using as much of the water as necessary. Stir in the chopped parsley and serve with Celeriac and Carrot Salad.

* **300 calories per serving**
* **Medium fibre**

Creamy Prawn Risotto

SERVES 4

Prepare as for Creamy Squid Risotto, but substitute raw, peeled tiger prawns (jumbo shrimp) for the squid and add the rice and flavouring as soon as the wine and water are boiling, then continue as before. Serve with Melon, Cucumber and Tomato Salad (page 283) instead of Celeriac and Carrot Salad.

* **325 calories per serving**
* **Medium fibre**

Poultry and Game Main Meals

If you remove all the skin from poultry and game, they are excellent sources of protein and very low in fat. They are also very versatile, as you'll see from this tempting array of recipes. Again, if you're calorie-counting, don't forget to add on those for any side dishes or accompaniments.

Gold-kissed Chicken Grill

SERVES 4

4 skinless chicken breasts, about
175 g/6 oz each
20 g/³/₄ oz/4 tsp low-fat sunflower or
olive oil spread, melted
200g/7 oz/1 small can of naturally
sweet sweetcorn (corn), drained
50 g/2 oz/¹/₂ cup low-fat Emmental
(Swiss) or Cheddar cheese, grated
Sprigs of watercress, to garnish
Mixed Green Salad (page 279), to
serve

Place the chicken breasts one at a time in a plastic bag and beat with a rolling pin or meat mallet to flatten. Brush with the low-fat spread and place on a grill (broiler) rack. Grill (broil) for 3 minutes on each side. Spoon the sweetcorn over and top with the cheese. Grill until the cheese is melted and golden. Garnish with watercress and serve straight away with Mixed Green Salad.

* **365 calories per serving**
* **Fairly high fibre**

Chunky Chicken Loaf

SERVES 4 OR 6

Prepare as for Savoury Chunky Pork Loaf (page 220), but substitute minced (ground) chicken for the pork and chicken livers for the pigs' liver. Flavour with dried thyme instead of sage.

* **245 or 160 calories per serving**
* **Medium fibre**

Curried Chicken and Pasta Salad

SERVES 4

175 g/8 oz pasta shapes
225 g/8 oz/2 cups cooked chicken, all
skin removed and cut into neat
pieces
Curried Mayo (page 385)
1 green (bell) pepper, diced
Lettuce leaves
30 ml/2 tbsp whole almonds
5 ml/1 tsp mixed (apple-pie) spice
Fragrant Tomato and Onion Salad
(page 278), to serve

Cook the pasta according to the packet directions. Drain, rinse with cold water and drain again. Add the chicken, Curried Mayo and pepper. Pile on to lettuce leaves. Dry-fry the almonds in a frying pan (skillet) until golden and toss in the mixed spice. Scatter over the salad and serve with Fragrant Tomato and Onion Salad.

* **360 calories per serving**
* **Fairly high fibre**

Chicken Chéron

SERVES 6

6 skinless chicken breasts
15 g/½ oz/1 tbsp low-fat sunflower or
    olive oil spread
Salt and freshly ground black pepper
425 g/15 oz/1 large can of artichoke
    bottoms
200 g/7 oz/1 small can of sweetcorn
    (corn) with (bell) peppers
1 carrot, grated
90 ml/6 tbsp dry white wine
1.5 ml/¼ tsp caster (superfine) sugar
Pan Scalloped Potatoes (page 258),
    and Dressed Green Salad (page
    275), to serve

Fry (sauté) the chicken in the low-fat spread in a non-stick frying pan (skillet) for 3 minutes on each side to brown. Season with salt and pepper. Cover the pan and cook very gently for 15 minutes until tender and cooked through. Meanwhile, heat the artichokes, drain and keep warm. Heat the sweetcorn with the grated carrot until piping hot. When the chicken is cooked, remove from the pan, transfer to warm plates and keep warm. Add the wine to the pan with the sugar, bring to the boil and boil rapidly until slightly reduced. Spoon over the chicken. Put the artichokes to one side of each chicken breast, spoon the sweetcorn mixture in each and serve with Pan Scalloped Potatoes and Dressed Green Salad.

* **270 calories per serving**
* **Fairly high fibre**

Chicken and Vegetable Mornay

SERVES 4

350 g/12 oz frozen mixed vegetables
30 ml/2 tbsp cornflour (cornstarch)
300 ml/½ pt/1¼ cups skimmed milk
5 ml/1 tsp low-fat sunflower or olive
    oil spread
Salt and freshly ground black pepper
5 ml/1 tsp made English mustard
75 g/3 oz/¾ cup strong low-fat
    Cheddar cheese, grated
175 g/6 oz/1½ cups chopped, cooked
    chicken, all skin removed
1.5 ml/¼ tsp grated nutmeg
Stewed Tomatoes with Herbs (page
    273), to serve

Cook the vegetables according to the packet directions. Drain. Blend the cornflour in a saucepan with a little of the milk, then stir in the remainder. Add the low-fat spread. Bring to the boil and cook for 1 minute, stirring all the time. Stir in a little salt and pepper, the mustard and two-thirds of the cheese. Fold in the vegetables and chicken and season with the nutmeg and a little more salt and pepper, if necessary. Heat through. Turn into a flameproof serving dish, top with the remaining cheese and grill (broil) until golden and bubbling. Serve with Stewed Tomatoes with Herbs.

* **180 calories per serving**
* **Fairly high fibre**

Chicken and Roast Vegetable Fajitas

SERVES 4

4 large skinless chicken breasts
1 large garlic clove, crushed
Finely grated rind and juice of 1 lime
1 red chilli, seeded and finely chopped
15 ml/1 tbsp paprika
5 ml/1 tsp dried oregano
2.5 ml/¹/₂ tsp ground cumin
1.5 ml/¹/₄ tsp ground cinnamon
40 g/1¹/₂ oz/3 tbsp low-fat sunflower
* or olive oil spread, melted*
Salt and freshly ground black pepper
1 red (bell) pepper, cut into 8 thick
* strips*
1 green pepper, cut into 8 thick strips
1 aubergine (eggplant), sliced
1 courgette (zucchini), diagonally
* sliced*
12 flour tortillas
A small bowl of tomato or chilli relish
150 ml/¹/₄ pt/²/₃ cup low-fat crème
* fraîche*
1 onion, finely chopped
Iceberg lettuce leaves, finely shredded

Wipe the chicken and slash in several places with a sharp knife.

Place in a shallow dish. Mix together the garlic, lime, chilli, paprika, oregano, cumin and cinnamon with half the low-fat spread. Season lightly with salt and pepper and pour over the chicken. Turn to coat completely. Cover and leave to marinate for at least 1 hour.

Lay the peppers, aubergine and courgette on a large sheet of foil, shiny side up. Drizzle with the rest of the melted spread and season with salt and pepper. Wrap up the parcel and twist the edges together to seal. Grill (broil) for 10 minutes, then add the chicken breasts and cook for 10–15 minutes, turning occasionally, until the chicken and vegetables are tender and cooked through.

Warm the tortillas in the microwave or between two plates over a pan of boiling water. Carve the chicken breasts into thin slices and place on large plates with the roasted vegetables and the flour tortillas. To serve, spread the tortillas with a little relish, add the vegetables and chicken, top with a little crème fraîche, chopped onion and shredded lettuce and roll up. Eat with the fingers.

* **600 calories per serving**
* **Fairly high fibre**

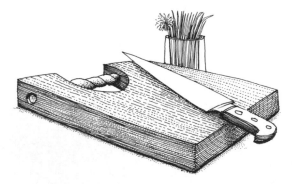

Pimiento Chicken

SERVES 4

2 onions, sliced
25 g/1 oz/2 tbsp low-fat sunflower or
　olive oil spread
4 skinless chicken breasts, about
　175 g/6 oz each
30 ml/2 tbsp paprika
400 g/14 oz/1 large can of chopped
　tomatoes
228 g/8 oz/1 small can of pimientos,
　drained and chopped
Salt and freshly ground black pepper
45 ml/3 tbsp low-fat plain yoghurt
30 ml/2 tbsp chopped coriander
　(cilantro), to garnish
Sesame Seed Noodles (page 267) and
　Mixed Green Salad (page 279), to
　serve

Fry (sauté) the onions in the low-fat spread in a large saucepan for 2 minutes. Add the chicken breasts and fry on each side to brown. Add the remaining ingredients except the yoghurt. Bring to the boil, reduce the heat, part-cover and simmer for 10 minutes. Remove the lid and simmer for a further 10 minutes. Taste and re-season, if necessary. Remove the chicken and transfer to warm plates. Stir the yoghurt into the sauce and heat through but do not boil. Spoon over the chicken, garnish with the coriander and serve with Sesame Seed Noodles and Mixed Green Salad.

* **455 calories per serving**
* **Medium fibre**

Chicken with Lime and Garlic

SERVES 4

4 small skinless chicken breasts
50 g/2 oz/¼ cup low-fat soft cheese
1 large garlic clove, crushed
15 ml/1 tbsp chopped parsley
Grated rind and juice of 1 lime
Salt and freshly ground black pepper
30 ml/2 tbsp toasted desiccated
　(shredded) coconut
Yellow Rice with Bay (page 264) and
　Green Pepper and Onion Salad
　(page 276), to serve

Make a slit in the side of each chicken breast to form a pocket. Mash the low-fat cheese with the garlic, parsley, lime rind and a little salt and pepper. Spoon into the chicken breasts. Place each on a square of foil and sprinkle with lime juice and a little more salt and pepper. Wrap up. Place on a baking (cookie) sheet and bake in a preheated oven at 190°C/375°F/gas mark 5 for 30 minutes. Open up the foil after 20 minutes to allow the chicken to brown. Sprinkle with the toasted desiccated coconut and serve with Yellow Rice with Bay and Green Pepper and Onion Salad.

* **365 calories per serving**
* **Medium fibre**

Indonesian Chicken Rice

SERVES 4

225 g/8 oz/1 cup long-grain rice
50 g/2 oz frozen peas
2 onions, sliced
40 g/1½ oz/3 tbsp low-fat sunflower
or olive oil spread
15 ml/1 tbsp curry powder
2.5 ml/½ tsp ground cinnamon
175 g/6 oz chicken stir-fry meat
Salt and freshly ground black pepper
1 egg
30 ml/2 tbsp water
30 ml/2 tbsp chopped coriander
(cilantro)
Beansprout and Cucumber Salad
(page 285), to serve

Cook the rice according to the packet directions, adding the peas for the last 5 minutes' cooking time. Drain, rinse with cold water and drain again. Meanwhile, fry (sauté) the onions in 25 g/1 oz/2 tbsp of the low-fat spread in a large frying pan (skillet) or wok for 2 minutes until softened but not browned. Add the curry powder, cinnamon and chicken and stir-fry for 5 minutes until the chicken is tender and cooked through. Add the rice and peas and toss over a gentle heat for 4 minutes. Season to taste. Meanwhile, beat the egg and water with a little salt and pepper and stir in the coriander. Melt the remaining low-fat spread in an omelette pan and fry the egg mixture until set underneath. Turn over and cook the other side. Roll up and cut into shreds. Pile the rice mixture on to four warm plates and top with the shredded omelette. Serve with Beansprout and Cucumber Salad.

* **330 calories per serving**
* **Medium fibre**

Chicken Teriyaki Kebabs

SERVES 4

30 ml/2 tbsp reduced-salt soy sauce
30 ml/2 tbsp medium-dry sherry
1 garlic clove, crushed
A good pinch of ground ginger
10 ml/2 tsp clear honey
350 g/12 oz skinless chicken breasts,
cubed
Japanese Salad (page 282), to serve

Mix the soy sauce with the sherry, garlic, ginger and honey. Add the chicken and toss well. Leave in a cool place to marinate for at least 2 hours. Thread on to soaked wooden skewers. Grill (broil) for about 8–10 minutes, turning occasionally, until tender and cooked through, brushing with any remaining marinade. Serve hot with Japanese Salad.

* **140 calories per serving**
* **Low fibre**

Chicken and Red Wine Pasta

SERVES 4

1 large onion, finely sliced
1 garlic clove, crushed
25 g/1 oz/2 tbsp low-fat sunflower or olive oil spread
4 skinless chicken breasts, about 175 g/6 oz each
Salt and freshly ground black pepper
400 g/14 oz/1 large can of chopped tomatoes
90 ml/6 tbsp red wine
30 ml/2 tbsp chopped parsley
A good pinch of caster (superfine) sugar
175 g/6 oz rigatoni pasta
15 ml/1 tbsp chopped basil
Mixed Leaf Salad (page 278), to serve

Fry (sauté) the onion and garlic in half the low-fat spread for 3 minutes, stirring, until softened and lightly golden. Remove from the pan with a draining spoon. Brown the chicken in the remaining low-fat spread in the same pan. Return the onions and garlic to the pan with the remaining ingredients except the pasta and basil. Bring to the boil, reduce the heat and simmer for 15–20 minutes until the chicken is cooked and the sauce is pulpy, stirring occasionally. Meanwhile, cook the pasta according to the packet directions. Drain. When the chicken is cooked, lift out of the pan and transfer to four warm plates. Mix the cooked pasta with the sauce and spoon to one side of the chicken. Sprinkle with the basil and serve with Mixed Leaf Salad.

* **435 calories per serving**
* **Medium fibre**

Quick Italian Chicken

SERVES 4

4 skinless chicken breasts
295 g/10½ oz/1 medium can of low-fat condensed tomato soup
2.5 ml/½ tsp dried basil
Freshly ground black pepper
Broccoli and Sesame Seed Noodles (page 267), to serve

Put the chicken breasts in a non-stick frying pan (skillet) and spoon over the soup. Half-fill the can with water and pour over. Add the basil and lots of pepper. Bring to the boil, reduce the heat, cover and cook gently for 20 minutes, stirring gently occasionally, until the chicken is cooked through and is bathed in a rich tomato sauce. Serve with Broccoli and Sesame Seed Noodles.

* **285 calories per serving**
* **Low fibre**

Chicken Breasts Masala

SERVES 4

Prepare as for Lamb Steaks Masala (page 184) but substitute skinless chicken breasts for the lamb.

* **210 calories per serving**
* **Low fibre**

Chicken Shack Pie

Use minced (ground) turkey instead if you prefer.

SERVES 4

1 onion, finely chopped
350 g/12 oz extra-lean minced
   (ground) chicken
1 large carrot, grated
1 turnip, grated
75 g/3 oz frozen peas
450 ml/³/₄ pt/2 cups chicken stock,
   made with 1 stock cube
2.5 ml/¹/₂ tsp dried mixed herbs
A pinch of salt
Freshly ground black pepper
750 g/1¹/₂ lb potatoes, peeled and cut
   into even-sized pieces
45 ml/3 tbsp skimmed milk
15 g/¹/₂ oz/1 tbsp low-fat sunflower or
   olive oil spread
5 ml/1 tsp Worcestershire sauce
30 ml/2 tbsp plain (all-purpose) flour
45 ml/3 tbsp cold water
2.5 ml/¹/₂ tsp paprika
Caraway Cabbage (page 272), to serve

Put the onion and mince in a large non-stick saucepan. Cook, stirring, for 5 minutes until the meat is no longer pink and all the grains are separate. Spoon off any fat, but not the juices. Add the carrot, turnip, peas and stock. Stir in the herbs, salt and lots of pepper. Bring to the boil, stirring occasionally, then reduce the heat, part-cover and simmer very gently for 20 minutes. Meanwhile, cook the potatoes in boiling, lightly salted water until tender. Drain and mash with the milk, low-fat spread and Worcestershire sauce. Blend the flour with the water and stir into the chicken mixture. Bring to the boil and cook for 2 minutes, stirring, until thickened. Turn into an ovenproof dish. Spoon the potato on top and rough up with a fork.

Dust with paprika. Bake in a preheated oven at 200°C/400°F/ gas mark 6 for 25 minutes until turning golden on top. Serve with Caraway Cabbage.

* **315 calories per serving**
* **Fairly high fibre**

Poached Chicken with Lemon Sauce

SERVES 4

4 skinless chicken breasts
300 ml/¹/₂ pt/1¹/₄ cups chicken stock,
   made with 1 stock cube
Finely grated rind and juice of 1 small
   lemon
30 ml/2 tbsp clear honey
1 bay leaf
Freshly ground black pepper
15 ml/1 tbsp cornflour (cornstarch)
15 ml/1 tbsp cold water
30 ml/2 tbsp low-fat fromage frais
30 ml/2 tbsp chopped parsley
Almond Wild Rice (page 265) and leaf
   spinach, to serve

Put the chicken breasts in a flameproof casserole (Dutch oven). Add the stock, lemon rind and juice, honey, bay leaf and lots of pepper. Bring to the boil, reduce the heat, cover and cook very gently for 15 minutes. Remove the bay leaf, then carefully lift out the chicken breasts. Blend the cornflour with the water and stir into the cooking juices. Bring to the boil and cook for 1 minute, stirring. Stir in the fromage frais. Return the chicken to the sauce and heat through. Sprinkle the parsley over and serve with Almond Wild Rice and leaf spinach.

* **260 calories per serving**
* **Fairly high fibre**

Crunchy-coated Chicken

SERVES 4

8 chicken drumsticks
30 ml/2 tbsp plain (all-purpose) flour
Salt and freshly ground black pepper
1 egg, beaten
85 g/3½ oz/1 small packet of sage
  and onion stuffing mix
40 g/1½ oz/3 tbsp low-fat sunflower
  or olive oil spread
Jacket-baked Potatoes with Yoghurt
  and Chives (page 260) and English
  Mixed Salad (page 276), to serve

Pull all the skin off the chicken legs and discard. Toss the drumsticks in the flour, mixed with a little salt and pepper. Dip in the egg, then in the stuffing mix to coat completely. Melt the low-fat spread in a non-stick baking tin (pan). Add the drumsticks and turn over in the spread. Bake in a preheated oven at 190°C/375°F/gas mark 5 for 20 minutes. Turn the legs over and bake for a further 20 minutes until crisp and golden brown. Drain on kitchen paper (paper towels) and serve hot or cold with Jacket-baked Potatoes with Yoghurt and Chives and English Mixed Salad.

* **260 calories per serving**
* **Medium fibre**

Spicy Chicken Wings

SERVES 4

450 g/1 lb chicken wings, as much
  skin removed as possible
For the marinade:
1 small onion, finely chopped
15 ml/1 tbsp clear honey
30 ml/2 tbsp Worcestershire sauce
15 g/½ oz/1 tbsp low-fat sunflower or
  olive oil spread, melted
15 ml/1 tbsp paprika
5 ml/1 tsp cayenne
5 ml/1 tsp ground cumin
10 ml/2 tsp coarse sea salt
Freshly ground black pepper
Mixed salad leaves and tomato
  wedges, to garnish
Minted Yoghurt and Cucumber (page
  380) and Crispy Potato Skins
  (page 374), to serve

Put the chicken wings in a single layer in a roasting tin (pan). Mix together the marinade ingredients and pour over, rubbing the mixture into the flesh. Leave to marinate for 2 hours. Lift out of the marinade and grill (broil) for 15–20 minutes until cooked through and browned, brushing occasionally with any remaining marinade. Garnish with mixed salad leaves and tomato wedges and serve with Minted Yoghurt and Cucumber and Crispy Potato Skins.

* **125 calories per serving**
* **Low fibre**

Chicken Pan Crumble

SERVES 4

10 g/¼ oz/2 tsp low-fat sunflower or
olive oil spread
4 skinless chicken breasts
200 g/7 oz/1 small can of naturally
sweet sweetcorn (corn)
295 g/10½ oz/1 medium can of low-
fat condensed chicken soup
15 ml/1 tbsp lemon juice
30 ml/2 tbsp water
85 g/3½ oz/1 small packet of parsley
and thyme stuffing mix
1 small red (bell) pepper, cut into thin
strips
Plain boiled potatoes and French
(green) beans, to serve

Heat the low-fat spread in a non-stick frying pan (skillet) and brown the chicken on both sides. Pour off any fat. Mix the contents of the can of sweetcorn with the soup, lemon juice and water and pour over the chicken. Bring to the boil, cover, reduce the heat and simmer for 15–20 minutes until the chicken is tender. Meanwhile, make up the stuffing mix with enough boiling water to form a moist crumble. Scatter over the chicken and arrange the pepper strips in a criss-cross pattern on top. Place under a moderate grill (broiler) for about 10 minutes until golden. Serve hot with plain boiled potatoes and French beans.

* **340 calories per serving**
* **Medium fibre**

Chicken Liver Risotto

SERVES 4

40 g/1½ oz/3 tbsp low-fat sunflower
or olive oil spread
2 onions, chopped
2 garlic cloves, crushed
2 rashers (slices) of rindless, extra-lean
back bacon, diced
2 carrots, chopped
350 g/12 oz chicken livers, trimmed
and cut into bite-sized pieces if
necessary
225 g/8 oz/1 cup long-grain rice
600 ml/1 pt/2½ cups chicken stock,
made with 1 stock cube
2.5 ml/½ tsp dried sage
50 g/2 oz frozen peas
30 ml/2 tbsp chopped parsley, to
garnish
Mixed Green Salad (page 279), to
serve

Melt the low-fat spread in a heavy-based saucepan. Add the onions, garlic, bacon and carrots and fry (sauté), stirring, for 3 minutes. Add the livers and cook for a further 3 minutes or until browned but still very soft. Stir in the rice, then add the stock, sage and a little salt and pepper. Bring to the boil, reduce the heat, cover and simmer very gently for 10 minutes. Add the peas and cook for a further 10 minutes or until the rice is tender and has absorbed the liquid. Spoon on to warm plates and sprinkle with the parsley. Serve hot with Mixed Green Salad.

* **410 calories per serving**
* **Fairly high fibre**

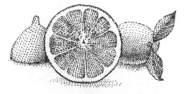

Lasagne Al Forno

SERVES 4

1 large onion, finely chopped
1 garlic clove, crushed
350 g/12 oz extra-lean minced
    (ground) turkey or chicken
1 carrot, finely chopped
75 g/3 oz button mushrooms, sliced
400 g/14 oz/1 large can of chopped
    tomatoes
30 ml/2 tbsp dry white vermouth
    (optional)
15 ml/1 tbsp tomato purée (paste)
2.5 ml/½ tsp dried oregano
A pinch of salt
Freshly ground black pepper
6 sheets no-need-to-precook
    wholewheat lasagne
Cheese Sauce (page 376)
Dressed Green Salad (page 275), to
    serve

Put the onion, garlic, turkey or chicken and carrot in a large non-stick saucepan. Cook, stirring, for 5 minutes until the meat is no longer pink and all the grains are separate. Add the mushrooms, tomatoes, vermouth, if using, the tomato purée, oregano, salt and lots of pepper. Bring to the boil, stirring, then reduce the heat and simmer for 15 minutes until the meat is bathed in a rich sauce, stirring occasionally. Spoon a little of the meat sauce into the base of fairly shallow ovenproof dish. Top with a layer of lasagne, breaking it to fit. Layer the meat and lasagne in the dish, finishing with a layer of lasagne. Spoon the Cheese Sauce over, then bake in a preheated oven at 190°C/375°F/gas mark 5 for 40 minutes until cooked through and golden on top. Serve hot with Dressed Green Salad.

* **350 calories per serving**
* **Fairly high fibre**

Chicken, Ham and Tomato Grill

SERVES 4

4 skinless chicken breasts
20 g/¾ oz/1½ tbsp low-fat sunflower
    or olive oil spread, melted
4 thin slices of lean ham
4 tomatoes, sliced
20 ml/4 tsp finely grated low-fat
    strong Cheddar cheese
New potatoes and broccoli, to serve

Put the chicken breasts one at a time into a plastic bag and beat with a rolling pin or meat mallet to flatten. Brush with a little of the low-fat spread. Place under a hot grill (broiler) and grill (broil) for 3 minutes on each side. Top each with a slice of ham, then with tomato slices. Brush with the remaining spread and sprinkle with cheese. Grill until the cheese, tomatoes and ham are sizzling. Serve straight away with new potatoes and broccoli.

* **300 calories per serving**
* **Low fibre**

Chicken Saag

SERVES 4

Prepare as for Lamb Saag (page 183), but substitute cooked chicken, all skin removed, for the lamb and sprinkle with 15 ml/1 tbsp toasted flaked (slivered) almonds before serving.

* **215 calories per serving**
* **Fairly high fibre**

Mighty Chicken Loaf

SERVES 4

1 onion, quartered
225 g/8 oz/2 cups cooked chicken,
roughly chopped
2 slices of extra-lean cooked ham
25 g/1 oz/2 tbsp low-fat sunflower or
olive oil spread
30 ml/2 tbsp dried breadcrumbs
100 g/4 oz button mushrooms,
chopped
2.5 ml/½ tsp dried mixed herbs
90 ml/6 tbsp oat bran
1 Weetabix, crushed
150 ml/¼ pt/⅔ cup skimmed milk
1 egg, beaten
A pinch of salt
Freshly ground black pepper
300 ml/½ pt/1¼ cups passata (sieved
tomatoes)
2.5 ml/½ tsp dried basil
Seeded Roast Potatoes (page 262) and
Mixed Green Salad (page 279), to
serve

Mince (grind) the onion, chicken and ham or chop, not too finely, in a food processor. Use a little of the low-fat spread to lightly grease a 450 g/1 lb loaf tin (pan). Coat with the breadcrumbs. Melt the remaining spread in a saucepan, add the mushrooms and herbs and fry (sauté) for 2 minutes, stirring. Sprinkle the oat bran over and stir for 1 minute. Add the Weetabix, milk and egg, then stir in the chicken mixture and season with the salt and some pepper. Turn into the prepared tin and smooth the surface. Cover with foil and stand the tin in a roasting tin containing 2.5 cm/1 in boiling water. Bake in a preheated oven at 180°C/350°F/gas mark 4 for 1 hour, then remove the foil and cook for a further 30 minutes until firm and cooked through. Meanwhile, warm the passata with the basil and a good grinding of pepper. Turn the loaf out on to a warm serving dish and serve sliced with the warm passata, Seeded Roast Potatoes and Mixed Green Salad. Alternatively, leave until cold and serve with new potatoes and salad.

* **200 calories per serving**
* **Fairly high fibre**

Fast Food Chicken Chow Mien

SERVES 4

250 g/9 oz/1 packet of quick-cook
Chinese egg noodles
225 g/8 oz/2 cups cooked chicken (no
skin), cut into strips
425 g/15 oz/1 large can of stir-fry
mixed vegetables, drained
1 garlic clove, crushed
30 ml/2 tbsp reduced-salt soy sauce
30 ml/2 tbsp dry sherry
5 ml/1 tsp ground ginger
10 ml/2 tsp light brown sugar

Cook the noodles according to the packet directions. Drain. Put the chicken in a large pan or wok. Rinse the drained vegetables under cold water, drain again and add to the chicken with the remaining ingredients. Heat through, stirring occasionally, until piping hot. Stir in the drained noodles until well coated. Reheat and serve.

* **370 calories per serving**
* **Fairly high fibre**

Chicken with Water Chestnuts

SERVES 4

4 chicken portions, as much skin
   removed as possible
15 ml/1 tbsp sherry
5 ml/1 tsp light brown sugar
25 g/1 oz/2 tbsp low-fat sunflower or
   olive oil spread
1 bunch of spring onions (scallions),
   cut into diagonal pieces
175 g/6 oz button mushrooms,
   quartered
225 g/8 oz/1 small can of water
   chestnuts, quartered
600 ml/1 pt/2½ cups chicken stock,
   made with 1 stock cube
15 ml/1 tbsp reduced-salt soy sauce
30 ml/2 tbsp cornflour (cornstarch)
Plain boiled rice, to serve

Place the chicken in a shallow dish. Add the sherry and sugar. Toss to coat and leave to marinate for 2 hours. Melt the low-fat spread in a flameproof casserole (Dutch oven). Add the chicken and brown on all sides. Remove from the pan with a draining spoon. Add the spring onions and mushrooms and cook, stirring, for 2 minutes. Add the water chestnuts, stock and soy sauce. Return the chicken to the pan and bring to the boil. Cover and transfer to a preheated oven at 180°C/350°F/gas mark 4 for 1½ hours or until really tender. Lift out the chicken on to warm plates and keep warm. Blend the cornflour with a little water and stir into the cooking liquid. Bring to the boil and cook for 2 minutes, stirring. Spoon over the chicken and serve with plain boiled rice.

* **270 calories per serving**
* **Fairly high fibre**

Oriental Chicken with Cashew Nuts and Mushrooms

SERVES 4

25 g/1 oz/2 tbsp low-fat sunflower or
   olive oil spread
225 g/8 oz chicken stir-fry meat
1 bunch of spring onions (scallions),
   cut into short lengths
100 g/4 oz button mushrooms, sliced
225 g/8 oz/4 cups beansprouts
25 g/1 oz/¼ cup raw cashew nuts
300 ml/½ pt/1¼ cups chicken stock,
   made with 1 stock cube
15 ml/1 tbsp cornflour (cornstarch)
15 ml/1 tbsp reduced-salt soy sauce
Plain boiled rice, to serve

Heat the low-fat spread in a large frying pan (skillet) or wok. Add the chicken, onions and mushrooms and stir-fry for 5 minutes. Add the beansprouts and cook, stirring for a further 2 minutes. Add the nuts and stock and bring to the boil. Blend together the cornflour and soy sauce, stir into the pan and cook, stirring, for 2 minutes. Spoon on to a bed of boiled rice and serve.

* **235 calories per serving**
* **Fairly high fibre**

Chicken Biryani

SERVES 4

1 quantity of Yellow Rice with Bay (page 264)
1 onion, sliced
10 ml/2 tsp sunflower oil
225 g/8 oz chicken stir-fry meat
7.5 ml/1 1/2 tsp turmeric
1 garlic clove, crushed
2.5 ml/1/2 tsp ground ginger
2.5 ml/1/2 tsp ground cumin
2.5 ml/1/2 tsp ground coriander (cilantro)
150 ml/1/4 pt/2/3 cup low-fat plain yoghurt
A pinch of salt
Freshly ground black pepper
30 ml/2 tbsp currants
30 ml/2 tbsp flaked (slivered) almonds
Green Pepper and Onion Salad (page 276), to serve

Prepare the Yellow Rice with Bay. While it's cooking, fry (sauté) the onion in the oil in a non-stick saucepan for 3 minutes. Add the chicken and fry for 3 minutes, stirring. Add all the remaining ingredients except the currants and almonds. Bring to the boil, then reduce the heat and simmer for about 20 minutes, stirring occasionally, until almost dry (the mixture will curdle at first). Dry-fry the currants and almonds in a frying pan (skillet) until the nuts are golden, stirring all the time. Rinse the Yellow Rice with Bay to make a fluffy pilau (page 264). Serve the chicken on a bed of the rice with the currants and almonds sprinkled over and Green Pepper and Onion Salad.

* **285 calories per serving**
* **Fairly high fibre**

Pot Roast Paprika Chicken with Rice

SERVES 6

1.5 kg/3 lb oven-ready chicken
15 g/1/2 oz/1 tbsp low-fat sunflower or olive oil spread
1 onion, finely chopped
1 green (bell) pepper, finely chopped
1 celery stick, chopped
225 g/8 oz/1 cup brown long-grain rice
400 g/14 oz/1 large can of chopped tomatoes
450 ml/3/4 pt/2 cups chicken stock, made with 1 stock cube
1 bouquet garni sachet
A pinch of salt
Freshly ground black pepper
15 ml/1 tbsp paprika
200 g/7 oz/1 small can of naturally sweet sweetcorn (corn)

Remove all the skin from the chicken. Pull off any excess fat just inside the rim of the body cavity. Heat the low-fat spread in a large flameproof casserole (Dutch oven) and fry (sauté) the onion, pepper and celery for 2 minutes, stirring. Add the rice and stir for 1 minute. Add the tomatoes, stock, bouquet garni and season with the salt and lots of pepper. Top with the chicken and dust the flesh with the paprika. Bring to the boil, cover and place in a preheated oven at 190°C/375°F/gas mark 5. Cook for 1 1/4 hours. Discard the bouquet garni and stir in the sweetcorn. Re-cover and return to the oven for a further 15 minutes. Carve the chicken and serve hot with the rice.

* **390 calories per serving**
* **High fibre**

Baked Chicken with Orange and Pine Nuts

SERVES 4

1 orange
4 skinless chicken breasts
25 g/1 oz/¹/₄ cup pine nuts
45 ml/3 tbsp medium-dry sherry
15 ml/1 tbsp reduced-salt soy sauce
A pinch of chilli powder
A pinch of ground cinnamon
30 ml/2 tbsp clear honey
10 ml/2 tsp cornflour (cornstarch)
15 ml/1 tbsp water
30 ml/2 tbsp chopped parsley, to garnish
New potatoes, boiled in their skins, and Citrus Chinese Leaf Salad (page 277), to serve

Thinly pare the rind from half the orange. Cut into thin strips and boil in water for 1 minute. Drain and reserve. Finely grate the remaining rind and squeeze out the juice. Make several slashes in each chicken breast and lay them in a flameproof casserole (Dutch oven). Mix together the remaining ingredients except the cornflour and water, and spoon over the chicken. Chill for 1 hour to marinate. Bake in a preheated oven at 200°C/400°F/gas mark 6 for 35 minutes until cooked through. Carefully lift the chicken out of the pan and transfer to warm plates. Blend the cornflour with the water and stir into the juices. Bring to the boil and cook for 1 minute, stirring. Cut the chicken into slices and fan out on the plates. Spoon the sauce over. Garnish with the reserved orange rind and the parsley. Serve with new potatoes in their skins and Citrus Chinese Leaf Salad.

* **265 calories per serving**
* **Fairly high fibre**

Simple Chicken Casserole

SERVES 4

4 chicken portions, as much skin removed as possible
1 onion, finely chopped
1 large carrot, finely chopped
100 g/4 oz button mushrooms
400 g/14 oz/1 large can of chopped tomatoes
30 ml/2 tbsp dry sherry or red or white wine
A pinch of salt
Freshly ground black pepper
1 bouquet garni sachet
Chopped parsley, to garnish
Jacket potatoes and peas, to serve

Put the chicken in a flameproof casserole dish (Dutch oven). Add all the remaining ingredients. Bring to the boil, cover and place in a preheated oven at 180°C/350°F/ gas mark 4 and cook for 1¼ hours or until the chicken is really tender. Discard the bouquet garni sachet and sprinkle with chopped parsley. Serve with jacket potatoes and peas.

* **230 calories per serving**
* **Medium fibre**

Chicken Gumbo

SERVES 4

15 g/½ oz/1 tbsp low-fat sunflower or
olive oil spread
450 g/1 lb skinless chicken meat,
cubed
12 button (pearl) onions, peeled but
left whole
1 extra-lean rasher (slice) of rindless
back bacon, finely diced
5 ml/1 tsp turmeric
5 ml/1 tsp ground coriander (cilantro)
2.5 ml/½ tsp chilli powder
225 g/8 oz okra (ladies' fingers),
trimmed
1 red (bell) pepper, sliced
1 green pepper, sliced
225 g/8 oz/1 small can of chopped
tomatoes
15 ml/1 tbsp tomato purée (paste)
1 large bay leaf
2.5 ml/½ tsp dried oregano
600 ml/1 pt/2½ cups chicken stock,
made with 2 stock cubes
Freshly ground black pepper
15 ml/1 tbsp chopped parsley
Perfect Brown Rice (page 265), to
serve

Heat the low-fat spread in a large
flameproof casserole (Dutch
oven). Add the chicken and brown for
3 minutes, stirring. Add the onions,
bacon and spices and cook, stirring for
a further 1 minute. Add the remaining
ingredients except the parsley. Bring to
the boil, reduce the heat, cover and
simmer very gently for 1 hour. Remove
the bay leaf, sprinkle with the parsley
and serve spooned over the Perfect
Brown Rice in large soup bowls.

* 210 calories per serving
* High fibre

Orange-marinated Chicken

SERVES 4

4 chicken portions, as much skin
removed as possible
Finely grated rind and juice of
1 orange
1 large garlic clove, crushed
A pinch of ground cinnamon
30 ml/2 tbsp clear honey
10 ml/2 tsp coarsely crushed black
peppercorns
Baby New Vegetable Selection (page
273), to serve

Make several slashes in the chicken
right through to the bone and
place in a shallow dish. Mix together
the remaining ingredients and spoon
over the chicken, rubbing well into the
slits. Leave to marinate for at least
2 hours, turning once. Place on foil on
a grill (broiler) rack. Grill (broil) for
about 10 minutes on each side until
cooked through and golden, brushing
with any remaining marinade during
cooking. Serve hot with Baby New
Vegetable Selection.

* 240 calories per serving
* Low fibre

French-style Peasant Chicken

If you can't get chanterelles, use button or chestnut mushrooms instead.

SERVES 4

450 g/1 lb potatoes, peeled and cut into even-sized pieces
15 ml/1 tbsp olive oil
4 chicken portions, skin removed
100 g/4 oz chanterelle mushrooms
A pinch of salt
Freshly ground black pepper
150 ml/¹/₄ pt/²/₃ cup chicken stock, made with ¹/₂ stock cube
1 large garlic clove, finely chopped
30 ml/2 tbsp chopped parsley
Flat Bean Salad (page 275), to serve

Wrap the prepared potatoes in a clean tea towel (dish cloth) to dry while preparing the chicken. Heat the oil in a large non-stick frying pan (skillet) and brown the chicken on all sides. Remove from the pan. Add the potatoes and toss in the pan for about 5 minutes until browning. Add the chanterelles and toss gently. Return the chicken to the pan and sprinkle with the salt and lots of pepper. Add 60 ml/ 4 tbsp of the stock. Cover the pan tightly and turn the heat down low. Cook gently for 45 minutes until everything is tender. Sprinkle the garlic and parsley over and re-cover for a further 5 minutes. Carefully lift the chicken, potatoes and chanterelles out of the pan on to warm plates and keep warm. Add the remaining stock, boil rapidly for 1 minute to reduce slightly, then spoon over. Serve straight away with Flat Bean Salad.

* **190 calories per serving**
* **Medium fibre**

Sticky Glazed Chicken

SERVES 4

4 skinless chicken breasts
25 g/1 oz/2 tbsp low-fat sunflower or olive oil spread
120 ml/4 fl oz/¹/₂ cup dry vermouth
Salt and freshly ground black pepper
Savoury Potato Cake (page 258) and Mixed Leaf Salad (page 278), to serve

Fry (sauté) the chicken in the low-fat spread in a non-stick frying pan (skillet) for 2 minutes on each side. Add the vermouth and a little seasoning, cover and simmer gently for 20 minutes, turning once or twice, until the chicken is cooked through and stickily glazed. Serve with Savoury Potato Cake and Mixed Leaf Salad.

* **270 calories per serving**
* **No fibre**

Chicken, Spinach and Pecan Pies

SERVES 4

2 chicken breasts, cut into small pieces
225 g/8 oz frozen leaf spinach, thawed
100 g/4 oz/¹/₂ cup low-fat cottage
cheese
25 g/1 oz/¹/₄ cup pecan nuts, chopped
A good pinch of grated nutmeg
A pinch of salt
Freshly ground black pepper
4 large sheets of filo pastry (paste)
10 ml/2 tsp melted low-fat sunflower
or olive oil spread
Courgettes à la Provençale (page 272),
to serve

Put the chicken in a bowl. Squeeze out all excess moisture from the spinach, chop, then add to the chicken with the cheese, nuts, nutmeg, the salt and a good grinding of pepper. Mix thoroughly. Lay a sheet of filo on the work surface and brush very lightly with a little of the melted spread. Fold the pastry in half to form a square. Brush with a little more melted spread and fold in half again. Add a quarter of the chicken mixture, then fold the pastry over the filling to form a neat parcel. Transfer to a non-stick baking (cookie) sheet and repeat with the remaining ingredients. Brush each parcel with any remaining spread. Bake in a preheated oven at 190°C/ 375°F/ gas mark 5 for 30 minutes until golden and cooked through. Serve with Courgettes à la Provençale.

* **270 calories per serving**
* **Fairly high fibre**

Photograph opposite: Tandoori Fish with Red Rice (page 129)

Barbecued Chicken Fillets

SERVES 4

Prepare as for Barbecued Turkey Steaks (page 169), but substitute skinless chicken breasts for the turkey steaks.

* **210 calories per serving**
* **No fibre**

Chicken Satay

SERVES 4

Prepare as for Simple Turkey Satay (page 170), but use diced chicken breast instead of the turkey and lemon juice instead of lime.

* **235 calories per serving**
* **Low fibre**

Kentucky Baked Chicken

SERVES 4

Prepare as for Kentucky Baked Turkey (page 171), but use chicken breasts instead of turkey and serve with Hot Pepper Corn Buns (page 22) and Dressed Green Salad (page 275) instead of the potatoes, peas and sweetcorn (corn).

* **280 calories per serving**
* **Medium fibre**

Tandoori Chicken

You can use 5 ml/1 tsp each of tomato purée (paste) and turmeric instead of the food colourings. Simply add them to the yoghurt mixture.

SERVES 4

4 chicken portions, as much skin removed as possible
Juice of 1 small lime
5 ml/1 tsp yellow food colouring
5 ml/1 tsp red food colouring
300 ml/¹/₂ pt/1¹/₄ cups low-fat plain yoghurt
1 small garlic clove, crushed
2.5 ml/¹/₂ tsp ground ginger
15 ml/1 tbsp garam masala
15 ml/1 tbsp paprika
1.5 ml/¹/₄ tsp chilli powder
Shredded lettuce, cucumber and tomato slices and lime wedges, to garnish
Pilau Rice (page 266), to serve

Cut the chicken portions into two pieces and make several deep slashes in the flesh right through to the bone. Place in a large shallow container. Brush all over with the lime juice. Mix together the food colourings and brush all over the surfaces of the meat. Blend together the remaining ingredients and spoon all over the meat, rubbing well into the slits in the chicken. Leave to marinate in the fridge for at least 3 hours, preferably overnight. Remove the chicken from the marinade and place on a baking (cookie) sheet. Bake in a preheated oven at 200°C/400°F/gas mark 6 for 40 minutes or until cooked through, draining off any liquid half-way through cooking. Garnish with shredded lettuce, cucumber and tomato slices and lime wedges and serve with Pilau Rice.

* **290 calories per serving**
* **Low fibre**

Sweet and Sour Chicken

SERVES 4

25 g/1 oz/2 tbsp low-fat sunflower or olive oil spread
225 g/8 oz chicken stir-fry meat
1 carrot, cut into very thin matchsticks
5 cm/2 in piece of cucumber, cut into very thin matchsticks
1 small red (bell) pepper, cut into very thin strips
1 bunch of spring onions (scallions), cut into short lengths
320 g/12 oz/1 medium can of pineapple chunks
30 ml/2 tbsp tomato purée (paste)
45 ml/3 tbsp reduced-salt soy sauce
15 ml/1 tbsp cornflour (cornstarch)
30 ml/2 tbsp water
Plain boiled rice, to serve

Heat the low-fat spread in a large frying pan (skillet), add the chicken and vegetables and stir-fry for 6 minutes until the chicken is tender. Add the pineapple, tomato purée and soy sauce. Bring to the boil. Blend the cornflour with the water and stir into the sauce. Simmer for 2 minutes, stirring. Spoon on to boiled rice and serve.

* **150 calories per serving**
* **Medium fibre**

Photograph opposite: **Baked Chicken with Orange and Pine Nuts (page 157)**

Herby Glazed Chicken Nests

SERVES 4

*450 g/1 lb potatoes, peeled and cut
into small pieces*
*A walnut-sized knob of low-fat
sunflower or olive oil spread*
4 skinless chicken breasts
*120 ml/4 fl oz/¹/₂ cup German
medium-dry white wine*
A pinch of salt
Freshly ground black pepper
15 ml/1 tbsp chopped parsley
15 ml/1 tbsp chopped thyme
15 ml/1 tbsp snipped chives
15 ml/1 tbsp skimmed milk
15 ml/1 tbsp paprika
Broccoli, to serve

Cook the potatoes in boiling, lightly salted water until tender. Drain and mash thoroughly with the skimmed milk and half the low-fat spread. Keep warm. Meanwhile, melt the remaining low-fat spread in a large non-stick frying pan (skillet). Add the chicken and cook for 2 minutes on each side. Add the wine, salt, lots of pepper and 10 ml/2 tsp of each of the herbs and cook for 15–20 minutes until cooked through and the meat is glazed in a sticky sauce. Spoon the mashed potato on to four warm plates in a neat pile in the centre. Rough up with a fork and dust with paprika. Top each with a glazed chicken breast and sprinkle with the remaining herbs. Serve with broccoli.

* **330 calories per serving**
* **Low fibre**

Mushroom-stuffed Chicken Parcels

SERVES 4

4 skinless chicken breasts
*100 g/4 oz button mushrooms, finely
chopped*
60 ml/4 tbsp low-fat soft cheese
15 ml/1 tbsp chopped tarragon
A pinch of salt
Freshly ground black pepper
*Baked Scalloped Potatoes (page 259)
and carrots, to serve*

Make a deep slit in the side of each chicken breast to form a pocket. Mash the mushrooms into the cheese with the tarragon, salt and lots of pepper. Use to fill the chicken pockets. Place each on a double thickness square of greaseproof (waxed) paper or foil. Add 30 ml/2 tbsp water to each. Fold over the paper or foil and twist and fold to seal the edges. Transfer to a baking (cookie) sheet. Bake in a preheated oven at 190°C/375°F/gas mark 5 for 30 minutes or until tender and cooked through. Carefully transfer to warm plates and slide out of the paper with the juices. Serve with Baked Scalloped Potatoes and carrots.

* **200 calories per serving**
* **Low fibre**

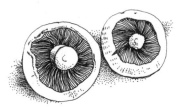

Stuffed Cabbage and Chicken Rolls

SERVES 4

200 g/7 oz/1 small can of naturally sweet sweetcorn (corn)
A pinch of salt
Freshly ground black pepper
4 small chicken breasts
4 large outer cabbage leaves
300 ml/¹/₂ pt/1¹/₄ cups passata (sieved tomatoes)
2.5 ml/¹/₂ tsp dried basil
Green (spinach) tagliatelle, to serve

Purée the corn in a blender or food processor. Season with the salt and some pepper. Place the chicken breasts one at a time in a plastic bag and beat with a rolling pin or meat mallet to flatten. Cut out the thick central base of the stalk on each cabbage leaf in a 'V' shape. Blanch the leaves in boiling water for 3 minutes. Drain, rinse with cold water and drain again. Lay them on a board and place a chicken breast on each. Spread the sweetcorn over the surfaces of the chicken. Fold in the edges of the cabbage leaves, then roll up. Place with the rolled edges underneath in a flameproof casserole dish (Dutch oven). Pour the passata around and sprinkle with the basil. Bring to the boil, cover, then place in a preheated oven at 180°C/350°F/ gas mark 4 for 30 minutes until tender and cooked through. Serve on a bed of green tagliatelle.

* **200 calories per serving**
* **Fairly high fibre**

Chicken Lasagne

SERVES 4

Low-fat White Sauce (page 376)
2 carrots, grated
1 courgette (zucchini), grated
225 g/8 oz/2 cups cooked chicken, all skin removed, chopped
300 ml/¹/₂ pt/1¹/₄ cups passata (sieved tomatoes)
5 ml/1 tsp dried oregano
Freshly ground black pepper
6 sheets of no-need-to-precook lasagne
30 ml/2 tbsp grated Parmesan cheese
Mixed Green Salad (page 279), to serve

Make the white sauce and cover with a circle of wetted greaseproof (waxed) paper to prevent a skin forming. Mix the grated vegetables with the chicken, passata and oregano. Add a good grinding of pepper. Spoon a little of the chicken mixture in the base of a fairly shallow ovenproof dish. Top with two sheets of lasagne, breaking it to fit, if necessary. Repeat the layers, finishing with a layer of lasagne. Stir the white sauce, pour over the lasagne and sprinkle with the cheese. Bake in a preheated oven at 190°C/375°F/ gas mark 5 for 40 minutes until golden and the lasagne feels tender when a knife is inserted down through the centre. Serve hot with Mixed Green Salad.

* **380 calories per serving**
* **Medium fibre**

Roast Chicken Dinner

SERVES 6

1.5 kg/3 lb oven-ready chicken
A small bunch of thyme and parsley
4 onions, quartered
Salt and freshly ground black pepper
750 g/1½ lb potatoes, scrubbed
15 g/½ oz/1 tbsp low-fat sunflower or olive oil spread
450 g/1 lb carrots, sliced
30 ml/2 tbsp plain (all-purpose) flour
450 ml/¾ pt/2 cups stock, made with 1 chicken stock cube or the carrot cooking water
A few drops of gravy browning (optional)
A green vegetable, to serve

Pull any excess fat away from round the inner edge of the body cavity of the chicken and discard. Push the herbs into the body cavity. Put the onion quarters in a small roasting tin (pan) and place the chicken on top. Season with pepper. Cut the unpeeled potatoes into even-sized pieces and place in a saucepan. Cover with water, add a pinch of salt, bring to the boil and boil for 3 minutes. Drain. Turn into a second roasting tin and dot with the low-fat spread. Toss gently to coat. Put the carrots in a casserole dish (Dutch oven) that will sit alongside the chicken. Just-cover with boiling water and add a pinch of salt, if liked. Cover with a lid. Place the potatoes on the top shelf with the chicken and the carrots below them in a preheated oven at 190°C/375°F/gas mark 5 and cook for 45 minutes. Pull the onions out from underneath the chicken and arrange around the bird, turn the potatoes and cook the chicken, potatoes and carrots for a further 45 minutes.

Transfer the chicken to a carving dish. Skim off any fat in the roasting tin. Sprinkle the flour over the juices in the pan and the onions and stir well, scraping up any sediment. Gradually blend in the stock or carrot water. Bring to the boil and cook for 2 minutes, stirring all the time. Add a few drops of gravy browning, if liked, and season with salt and pepper. Strain into a gravy boat. Remove all skin from the chicken and carve the meat. Serve with the roasted potatoes, carrots, gravy and a green vegetable.

* **370 calories per serving**
* **Fairly high fibre**

Chicken with White Wine and Grapes

SERVES 4

Prepare as for Turkey with Red Wine and Grapes (page 173), but substitute chicken stir-fry meat for the turkey, a fruity white wine for the red, and green grapes for the red grapes. Omit the tomato purée (paste).

* **170 calories per serving**
* **Medium fibre**

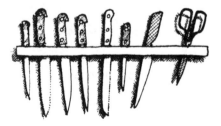

Chicken and Prawn Risotto

SERVES 4

175 g/6 oz chicken stir-fry meat
1 small green (bell) pepper, diced
1 small red pepper, diced
1 onion, finely chopped
25 g/1 oz/2 tbsp low-fat sunflower or olive oil spread
225 g/8 oz/1 cup arborio or other risotto rice
600 ml/1 pt/2½ cups chicken stock, made with 1 stock cube
5 ml/1 tsp saffron powder
100 g/4 oz frozen peas
100 g/4 oz cooked peeled prawns (shrimp)
Salt and freshly ground black pepper
4 stoned (pitted) black olives, sliced
15 ml/1 tbsp chopped parsley, to garnish

Fry (sauté) the chicken and prepared vegetables in the low-fat spread in a large non-stick frying pan (skillet) for 4 minutes, stirring. Add the rice and cook for 1 minute. Add 150 ml/¼ pt/ ⅔ cup of the stock and the saffron. Cook, stirring, until the liquid has been absorbed. Add another 150 ml/¼ pt/ ⅔ cup of the stock and cook again until absorbed. Add the remaining stock, the peas, prawns and some salt and pepper. Cover, reduce the heat and simmer gently for about 10 minutes or until the rice has absorbed the liquid and the mixture is creamy but still has some 'bite'. Stir in the olives, taste and re-season, if necessary. Spoon on to plates and sprinkle with the parsley before serving.

* **350 calories per serving**
* **Medium fibre**

Leftover Chicken Biryani

SERVES 6

100 g/4 oz/½ cup basmati rice
25 g/1 oz/2 tbsp low-fat sunflower or olive oil spread
2 onions, thinly sliced
1 clove
5 cardamom pods, split
2.5 cm/1 in piece of cinnamon stick
10 ml/2 tsp curry paste
15 ml/1 tbsp water
175 g/6 oz/1½ cups cooked chicken, cut into pieces and all skin removed
15 ml/1 tbsp chopped coriander (cilantro)
30 ml/2 tbsp sultanas (golden raisins)
30 ml/2 tbsp toasted flaked (slivered) almonds

Cook the rice in plenty of boiling, lightly salted water for 10 minutes. Drain, rinse with boiling water and drain again. Meanwhile, heat the low-fat spread in a saucepan and fry (sauté) the onions until golden brown, stirring all the time. Add the spices, curry paste and water and cook for 1 minute, stirring. Add the chicken and heat through for 2–3 minutes, stirring gently. Fold in the rice, coriander, sultanas and almonds. Toss gently. Remove the pieces of spice, if preferred, before serving.

* **420 calories per serving**
* **Medium fibre**

Easy Roast Stuffed Chicken Breasts

SERVES 4

4 skinless chicken breasts
85 g/3¹/₂ oz/1 packet of parsley,
thyme and lemon stuffing mix
Salt and freshly ground black pepper
15 g/¹/₂ oz/1 tbsp low-fat sunflower or
olive oil spread
20 ml/1¹/₂ tbsp cornflour (cornstarch)
300 ml/¹/₂ pt/1¹/₄ cups chicken stock,
made with 1 stock cube
30 ml/2 tbsp chopped parsley
Baby Roast Potatoes (page 261) and a
green vegetable, to serve

Make a slit in the side of each chicken breast with a sharp knife to make a pocket. Make up the stuffing according to the packet directions and use to stuff the cavities in the chicken. Lightly grease four large squares of foil, shiny sides up, with the low-fat spread. Put a chicken breast in each, season lightly and wrap up. Place on a baking (cookie) sheet and bake in a preheated oven at 190°C/375°F/gas mark 5 for about 30 minutes until cooked through. Meanwhile, blend the cornflour with a little of the stock in a small saucepan. Stir in the remaining stock and the parsley. Bring to the boil and cook for 2 minutes, stirring until thickened. When the chicken is cooked, open the parcels and pour any juices into the gravy. Put the chicken on warm plates and spoon the gravy over. Serve with Baby Roast Potatoes and a green vegetable.

* **265 calories per serving**
* **Medium fibre**

Chicken Jalfrezi

SERVES 4

2 large or 4 small skinless chicken
breasts, cubed
10 ml/2 tsp garlic powder
5 ml/1 tsp chilli powder
5 ml/1 tsp ground ginger
25 g/1 oz/2 tbsp low-fat sunflower or
olive oil spread
1 onion, very finely chopped
30 ml/2 tbsp curry paste
2 green (bell) peppers, cut into thin
strips
30 ml/2 tbsp water
4 mild green chillies, seeded and
chopped
60 ml/4 tbsp chopped coriander
(cilantro)
Salt and sugar, to taste
Plain boiled basmati rice, to serve

Put the cubed meat in a shallow dish and sprinkle with the garlic and chilli powders and the ginger. Heat the low-fat spread in a large frying pan (skillet). Add the onion and fry, stirring, for 2 minutes. Add the curry paste, chicken and peppers and stir-fry for 6 minutes. Add the water, chillies and coriander and toss for 2 minutes. Season to taste with salt and sugar and serve on a bed of cooked basmati rice.

* **225 calories per serving**
* **Medium fibre**

Chicken with Garlic and Lemon Butter

SERVES 4

4 skinless chicken breasts
40 g/1½ oz/3 tbsp low-fat sunflower
or olive oil spread
30 ml/2 tbsp chopped parsley
1 large garlic clove, crushed
Finely grated rind of ½ lemon
Freshly ground black pepper
Plain boiled rice and Mixed Green
Salad (page 279), to serve

Make a slit in the side of each chicken breast with a sharp knife to make a pocket. Mash the low-fat spread with the parsley, garlic, lemon and a good grinding of pepper. Divide the mixture between the pockets. Secure the openings with cocktail sticks (toothpicks). Wrap in non-stick baking parchment, then foil, shiny side in. Put on a baking (cookie) sheet and bake in a preheated oven at 190°C/ 375°F/gas mark 5 for 30 minutes. Unwrap, remove the cocktail sticks and serve with boiled rice and Mixed Green Salad.

* 245 calories per serving
* Low fibre

Chicken with Garlic and Herb Butter

SERVES 4

Prepare as for Chicken with Garlic and Lemon Butter, but substitute 15 ml/1 tbsp chopped basil for the lemon rind.

* 245 calories per serving
* Low fibre

Chicken Pesto Parcels

SERVES 4

Prepare as for Chicken with Lemon and Garlic Butter, but fill the chicken with Simple Pesto (page 379) and serve with Sesame Seed Noodles (page 267) instead of rice.

* 325 calories per serving
* Medium fibre

Chicken and Red Pesto Parcels

SERVES 4

Prepare as for Chicken with Garlic and Lemon Butter, but fill the chicken with Red Almond Pesto (page 379) and serve on a bed of Almond Wild Rice (page 265).

* 325 calories per serving
* Medium fibre

Lower-fat Chicken Kiev

SERVES 4

Prepare as for Chicken with Garlic and Lemon (or Garlic and Herb) Butter, but do not wrap up. Instead, dip the stuffed chicken in skimmed milk then in 60ml/4 tbsp of plain (all purpose) flour, seasoned with salt and freshly ground black pepper. Chill for 30 minutes, then dip in milk again, then in 50g/2oz/½ cup of toasted breadcrumbs. Brush a non-stick baking tin (pan) with a very little melted low-fat sunflower or olive oil spread. Bake in a pre-heated oven at 190°C/375°F/gas mark 5 for 20 minutes. Carefully turn the chicken over and cook for a further 20 minutes or until well browned and cooked through. Remove the cocktail sticks (toothpicks) and serve with sugar snap peas and hot French bread.

* 305 calories per serving
* Medium fibre

Spiced Chicken and Mushroom Casserole

SERVES 4

1 onion, finely chopped
15 g/^{1}/$_2$ oz/1 tbsp low-fat sunflower or
olive oil spread
75 g/3 oz button mushrooms, sliced
15 ml/1 tbsp curry powder
295 g/10^1/$_2$ oz/1 medium can of low-
fat condensed mushroom soup
8 skinless chicken thighs
Jacket potatoes and Dressed Green
Salad (page 275), to serve

Fry (sauté) the onion in the low-fat spread in a flameproof casserole (Dutch oven) for 2 minutes, stirring. Add the mushrooms, cover, reduce the heat and cook for a further 3 minutes to soften. Add the curry powder and cook for 30 seconds, stirring. Stir in the soup until well blended. Add the skinless chicken thighs and spoon the soup mixture over them. Cover with a lid and cook in a preheated oven at 180°C/350°F/ gas mark 4 for 1¼ hours until tender and bathed in a rich sauce. Serve with jacket potatoes and Dressed Green Salad.

* **245 calories per serving**
* **Low fibre**

Spiced Chicken and Celery Casserole

SERVES 4

Prepare as for Spiced Chicken and Mushroom Casserole, but substitute low-fat celery soup for the mushroom soup and 2 finely chopped celery sticks for the mushrooms.

* **220 calories per serving**
* **Medium fibre**

Barbecued Chicken Drumsticks

SERVES 4

8 chicken drumsticks, skin removed
40 g/1½ oz/3 tbsp low-fat sunflower
or olive oil spread
1 onion, finely chopped
150 ml/¼ pt/⅔ cup passata (sieved
tomatoes)
30 ml/2 tbsp tomato ketchup (catsup)
15 ml/1 tbsp golden (light corn) syrup
60 ml/4 tbsp sweet brown table sauce
5 ml/1 tsp reduced-salt soy sauce
Salt and freshly ground black pepper
Jacket-baked Potatoes with Yoghurt
and Chives (page 260) and Mixed
Green Salad (page 279)

Put the chicken legs in a roasting tin (pan). Melt the low-fat spread in a saucepan and brush half of it over the chicken. Bake in a preheated oven at 190°C/375°F/ gas mark 5 for 15 minutes. Meanwhile, fry (sauté) the onion in the remaining spread in the saucepan for 2 minutes, stirring. Add the remaining ingredients, bring to the boil and simmer for 3 minutes. Spoon over the chicken and cook for a further 10 minutes. Turn over the legs, baste with the sauce and cook for a further 10–15 minutes until cooked through and stickily glazed. Serve hot with Jacket-baked Potatoes with Yoghurt and Chives and Mixed Green Salad.

* **265 calories per serving**
* **Low fibre**

Turkey Temptation

SERVES 4

**4 turkey breast steaks, about 175 g/
6 oz each
Salt and freshly ground black pepper
15 g/½ oz/1 tbsp low-fat sunflower or
olive oil spread
150 ml/¼ pt/⅔ cup ginger wine
10 ml/2 tsp lemon juice
1 piece of stem ginger in syrup,
chopped
45 ml/3 tbsp low-fat crème fraîche
Paprika, for dusting
Savoury Potato Cake (page 000) and
broccoli, to serve**

Season the turkey steaks and fry (sauté) in the low-fat spread for about 6 minutes on each side until golden and cooked through. Remove from the pan and keep warm. Add the ginger wine to the pan. Bring to the boil and boil for 5 minutes. Stir in the lemon juice, ginger and crème fraîche. Bring to the boil and simmer for 2–3 minutes. Taste and re-season, if necessary. Transfer the turkey to warm plates and spoon the sauce over. Dust with paprika and serve straight away with Savoury Potato Cake and broccoli.

* **180 calories per serving**
* **Low fibre**

Turkey Herb Crumble

SERVES 4

Prepare as for Pork Crumble (page 220), but substitute turkey steaks for the pork, low-fat mushroom soup for the celery and use chestnut stuffing mix instead of Sage and Onion.

* **280 calories per serving**
* **Medium fibre**

Barbecued Turkey Steaks

SERVES 4

**10 g/¼ oz/2 tsp low-fat sunflower or
olive oil spread
4 turkey breast steaks
15 ml/1 tbsp lemon juice
15 ml/1 tbsp malt vinegar
30 ml/2 tbsp tomato purée (paste)
15 ml/1 tbsp Worcestershire sauce
30 ml/2 tbsp clear honey
Pan Scalloped Potatoes (page 258)
and French (green) beans, to serve**

Heat the low-fat spread in a large non-stick frying pan (skillet). Add the turkey and brown for 1 minute on each side. Mix together the remaining ingredients and spoon over. Cook over a gentle heat for about 8 minutes, turning occasionally, until cooked through and stickily glazed in the sauce. Serve with Pan Scalloped Potatoes and French beans.

* **195 calories per serving**
* **No fibre**

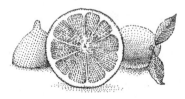

Simple Turkey Satay

SERVES 4

1 shallot, finely chopped
1 large garlic clove, crushed
10 g/¼ oz/2 tsp low-fat sunflower or olive oil spread
30 ml/2 tbsp smooth peanut butter
10 ml/2 tsp lime juice
15 ml/1 tbsp clear honey
15 ml/1 tbsp reduced-salt soy sauce
1.5 ml/¼ tsp chilli powder
120 ml/4 fl oz/½ cup skimmed milk
450 g/1 lb thick turkey breast steaks, diced
175 g/6 oz/¾ cup Thai fragrant rice
Warm Courgette and Carrot Salad (page 277), to serve

Fry (sauté) the shallot and garlic in the low-fat spread for 2 minutes, stirring. Stir in the remaining ingredients except the milk, turkey and rice and bring to the boil, stirring. Blend in 90 ml/6 tbsp of the milk, reduce the heat and simmer for 2 minutes. Thread the turkey on to soaked wooden skewers and brush with a little of the sauce. Grill (broil) for about 8 minutes, turning occasionally, until tender and cooked through. Meanwhile, prepare and cook the rice according to the packet directions. Drain. Reheat the remaining sauce with the remaining milk. Lay the kebabs on a bed of the Thai fragrant rice, spoon the remaining sauce over and serve with Warm Courgette and Carrot Salad.

* **225 calories per serving**
* **Medium fibre**

Turkey Burgers with Cranberry

SERVES 4

350 g/12 oz lean minced (ground) turkey
50 g/2 oz/1 cup wholemeal breadcrumbs
1 small onion, very finely chopped
15 ml/1 tbsp chopped parsley
5 ml/1 tsp dried sage
Freshly ground black pepper
20 ml/4 tsp cranberry sauce
10 g/¼ oz/2 tsp low-fat sunflower or olive oil spread, melted
4 burger buns
Shredded lettuce, tomato and cucumber slices, to garnish
No-fat Chips (page 260), to serve

Put the turkey, breadcrumbs, onion, herbs and lots of pepper in a bowl and mix well with the hands. Shape into eight even-sized flat cakes. Put 5 ml/1 tsp cranberry sauce in the centre of four of the burgers and top with the remaining burgers. Press the edges together well to seal. Place on a grill (broiler) rack and brush with half the melted spread. Grill (broil) under a moderate heat for 8 minutes. Turn over, brush the other sides and grill again for a further 8–10 minutes until golden brown and cooked through. Serve in burger buns, garnished with lettuce, tomato and cucumber slices, with No-fat Chips.

* **400 calories per serving**
* **Medium fibre**

Turkey Stir-fry

SERVES 4

*15 g/¹/₂ oz/1 tbsp low-fat sunflower or
olive oil spread*
175 g/6 oz turkey stir-fry meat
1 onion, thinly sliced
1 large carrot, cut into matchsticks
1 red (bell) pepper, cut into thin strips
*1 courgette (zucchini), cut into
matchsticks*
*100 g/4 oz green cabbage, thinly
shredded*
50 g/2 oz frozen peas
100 g/4 oz/2 cups beansprouts
15 ml/1 tbsp reduced-salt soy sauce
1.5 ml/¹/₄ tsp ground ginger
10 ml/2 tsp clear honey
30 ml/2 tbsp medium-dry sherry
Freshly ground black pepper
*175 g/6 oz wholewheat Chinese egg
noodles*

Heat the low-fat spread in a wok or large frying pan (skillet). Add the turkey and stir-fry for 4 minutes. Add the onion and carrot and stir-fry for 2 minutes. Add all the remaining vegetables and stir-fry for 3 minutes. Add the remaining ingredients except the noodles and toss for 2–3 minutes or until the vegetables are cooked to your liking. Meanwhile, cook the noodles according to the packet directions. Drain. Spoon into bowls and top with the Turkey Stir-fry.

* **280 calories per serving**
* **High fibre**

Kentucky Baked Turkey

SERVES 4

4 turkey breast steaks
*5 ml/1 tsp coarsely ground black
pepper*
5 ml/1 tsp paprika
5 ml/1 tsp dried onion granules
1.5 ml/¹/₄ tsp chilli powder
*15 ml/1 tbsp melted low-fat sunflower
or olive oil spread*
4 small bananas
*Jacket-baked Potatoes with Yoghurt
and Chives (page 260) and mixed
peas and sweetcorn (corn), to serve*

Beat the turkey steaks briefly to flatten slightly and tenderise. Mix together the pepper, paprika, onion granules and chilli powder. Brush the turkey with a little of the melted spread, then dust with the pepper mixture on each side. Brush a non-stick roasting tin (pan) with most of the remaining melted spread and lay the turkey in it. Peel and halve the bananas lengthways. Place flat-sides down in a small roasting tin (pan), brushed with a little of the remaining melted spread. Brush the bananas with the last of the melted spread. Bake towards the top of a preheated oven at 200°C/400°F/gas mark 6 for 20 minutes or until the turkey is tender and cooked through and the bananas have softened slightly. Serve with Jacket-baked Potatoes with Yoghurt and Chives and peas with sweetcorn.

* **280 calories per serving**
* **Medium fibre**

Somerset Orchard Turkey

SERVES 4

4 small turkey steaks
250 ml/8 fl oz/1 cup medium cider
1 bouquet garni sachet
Salt and freshly ground black pepper
1 eating (dessert) apple, cored and cut
    into 4 rings
A pinch of grated nutmeg
30 ml/2 tbsp cornflour (cornstarch)
30 ml/2 tbsp water
30 ml/2 tbsp low-fat crème fraîche
Chopped parsley, to garnish
Baby new potatoes and Braised
    Cabbage with Celery (page 271), to
    serve

Put the turkey steaks one at a time
in a plastic bag and beat lightly
with a rolling pin or meat mallet to
flatten slightly (don't make them too
thin). Place in a large frying pan
(skillet) and add the cider, bouquet
garni and lots of pepper. Top each
turkey steak with an apple slice and
sprinkle with the nutmeg. Bring to the
boil, cover with a lid or foil, reduce the
heat and poach gently for
8–10 minutes or until the turkey is
tender. Carefully lift the turkey topped
with the apple slices on to warm plates
and keep warm. Blend the cornflour
with the water until smooth, then stir
into the cider in the pan. Bring to the
boil and cook for 2 minutes, stirring.
Squeeze the bouquet garni to extract
every bit of flavour, then discard. Stir in
the crème fraîche. Taste and add a little
salt and more pepper if liked. Spoon
over the turkey and sprinkle with
chopped parsley before serving with
baby new potatoes and Braised
Cabbage with Celery.

* **190 calories per serving**
* **Fairly low fibre**

Devilled Turkey Legs

SERVES 4

4 small turkey legs, skin removed
15 g/½ oz/1 tbsp low-fat sunflower or
    olive oil spread, melted
5 ml/1 tsp dried onion granules
15 ml/1 tbsp light brown sugar
30 ml/2 tbsp Worcestershire sauce
15 ml/1 tbsp tomato ketchup (catsup)
5 ml/1 tsp chilli powder
Salt and freshly ground black pepper
Sesame and Garlic Wedges (page 262)
    and Mixed Green Salad (page
    279), to serve

Make a few slashes in the thick part
of the turkey meat. Mix together
the remaining ingredients and rub all
over the turkey, rubbing well into the
slashes. Leave to marinate for 2 hours.
Place in a baking tin (pan), cover
loosely with foil and bake in a
preheated oven at 200°C/400°F/gas
mark 6 for 1½ hours until tender and
cooked through. Serve with Sesame
and Garlic Wedges and Mixed Green
Salad.

* **375 calories per serving**
* **No fibre**

Turkey with Red Wine and Grapes

SERVES 4

150 ml/¹/₄ pt/²/₃ cup chicken stock,
  made with ¹/₂ stock cube
150 ml/¹/₄ pt/²/₃ cup red wine
1 bay leaf
15 ml/1 tbsp tomato purée (paste)
25 g/1 oz/2 tbsp low-fat sunflower or
  olive oil spread
225 g/8 oz turkey stir-fry meat
15 g/¹/₂ oz/2 tbsp plain (all-purpose)
  flour
100 g/4 oz red seedless grapes, halved
Salt and freshly ground black pepper
Caster (superfine) sugar
15 ml/1 tbsp chopped parsley
Extra-fluffed Mashed Potatoes (page
  260) and broccoli, to serve

Put the stock and wine in a saucepan with the bay leaf and tomato purée. Bring to the boil and leave to infuse for 10 minutes, then discard the bay leaf. Meanwhile, heat the low-fat spread in a saucepan. Add the turkey and stir-fry for 5 minutes. Add the flour and cook for 1 minute. Remove from the heat, then gradually blend in the stock and wine mixture. Return to the heat, bring to the boil and cook for 2 minutes, stirring. Add the grapes and season to taste with salt, pepper and sugar. Stir in the parsley. Serve on a pile of Extra-fluffed Mashed Potatoes and broccoli.

* **170 calories per serving**
* **Medium fibre**

Duck with Ginger

SERVES 4

2 large duck breasts
20 g/³/₄ oz/1¹/₂ tbsp low-fat sunflower
  or olive oil spread
Salt and freshly ground black pepper
150 ml/¹/₄ pt/²/₃ cup chicken stock,
  made with ¹/₂ stock cube
30 ml/2 tbsp ginger wine
15 ml/1 tbsp reduced-salt soy sauce
15 ml/1 tbsp cornflour (cornstarch)
Sprigs of parsley, to garnish
Baby potatoes in their skins and
  Braised Cabbage with Celery (page
  271), to serve

Pull all the skin off the duck breasts. Heat the low-fat spread in a non-stick frying pan (skillet). Add the meat, season with salt and pepper and fry (sauté) for 8 minutes. Turn the breasts over, season again and fry for a further 7 minutes or until slightly pink in the centre, or cook a little longer for well-done duck. Remove from the pan and keep warm. Add the stock and ginger wine to the pan and bring to the boil. Blend the soy sauce with the cornflour and stir into the pan. Bring to the boil and cook for 2 minutes, stirring until thickened. Taste and re-season, if necessary. Slice the duck thinly and arrange on four warm plates. Spoon the sauce over, garnish with parsley sprigs and serve with baby potatoes in their skins and Braised Cabbage with Celery.

* **240 calories per serving**
* **Low fibre**

Duck Slivers with Orange

SERVES 4

2 large duck breasts
25 g/1 oz/2 tbsp low-fat sunflower or
olive oil spread
Salt and freshly ground black pepper
15 ml/1 tbsp brandy
150 ml/¹/₄ pt/²/₃ cup chicken stock,
made with ¹/₂ stock cube
5 ml/1 tsp light brown sugar
Finely grated rind and juice of
1 orange
15 ml/1 tbsp cornflour (cornstarch)
Watercress and 1 orange, sliced, to
garnish
New potatoes and mangetout (snow
peas), to serve

Pull all the skin off the duck and discard. Heat the low-fat spread in a non-stick frying pan (skillet). Add the duck, sprinkle with salt and pepper and fry (sauté) for 8 minutes. Turn the breasts over, season again and fry for a further 7 minutes or until just pink in the centre, or cook a little longer for well-done duck. Remove from the pan and keep warm. Add the brandy to the pan and ignite. Shake the pan until the flames subside, then add the stock and sugar. Blend the orange rind and juice with the cornflour and stir into the pan. Cook, stirring, for 2 minutes until thickened and clear. Taste and re-season, if necessary. Slice the duck very thinly and arrange on four plates. Spoon the sauce over and garnish with watercress and orange slices. Serve with new potatoes and mangetout.

* **225 calories per serving**
* **Low fibre**

Duck Slivers with Grapefruit

SERVES 4

Prepare as for Duck Slivers with Orange, but substitute the finely grated rind and juice of 1 pink grapefruit for the orange and use orange liqueur instead of the brandy for sweetness.

* **215 calories per serving**
* **Low fibre**

Blackcurrant Duck

SERVES 4

Prepare as for Duck with Port and Redcurrants, but substitute blackcurrant jelly (clear conserve) for the redcurrant jelly and crème de cassis for the port. Garnish with small bunches of blackcurrants or whitecurrants, if liked.

* **240 calories per serving**
* **Very low fibre**

Duck Brochettes

SERVES 4

Prepare as for Pork Brochettes (page 225), but substitute duck breasts, cut into 16 cubes, for the pork tenderloin.

* **240 calories per serving**
* **Very low fibre**

Duck with Port and Redcurrant

SERVES 4

2 large duck breasts
Salt and freshly ground black pepper
20 g/³/₄ oz/1¹/₂ tbsp low-fat sunflower
or olive oil spread
150 ml/¹/₄ pt/²/₃ cup chicken stock,
made with ¹/₂ stock cube
45 ml/3 tbsp port
15 ml/1 tbsp redcurrant jelly (clear
conserve)
15 ml/1 tbsp cornflour (cornstarch)
15 ml/1 tbsp water
Sprigs of parsley and 4 small bunches
of redcurrants (optional), to garnish
New potatoes and French (green)
beans, to serve

Pull all the skin off the duck. Heat the low-fat spread in a non-stick frying pan (skillet), add the duck, season with salt and pepper and fry (sauté) for 8 minutes. Turn the breasts over, season again and fry for a further 7 minutes or until just pink in the centre, or cook a little longer for well-done duck. Remove from the pan and keep warm. Add the stock, port and redcurrant jelly. Heat, stirring, until the jelly dissolves. Blend the cornflour with the water and stir in. Bring to the boil and cook for 2 minutes, stirring. Taste and re-season, if necessary. Slice the duck thinly and arrange on four plates. Spoon the sauce over. Garnish with parsley sprigs and small bunches of redcurrants, if using, and serve with new potatoes and French beans.

* **240 calories per serving**
* **Very low fibre**

Peppered Duck

SERVES 4

2 large duck breasts
30 ml/2 tbsp coarsely crushed black
peppercorns
Salt
25 g/1 oz/2 tbsp low-fat sunflower or
olive oil spread
30 ml/2 tbsp brandy
150 ml/¹/₄ pt/²/₃ cup chicken stock,
made with ¹/₂ stock cube
10 ml/2 tsp cornflour (cornstarch)
15 ml/1 tbsp water
150 ml/¹/₄ pt/²/₃ cup low-fat crème
fraîche
15 ml/1 tbsp chopped parsley
Broccoli and Sesame Seed Noodles
(page 267), to serve

Pull all the skin off the duck and coat the breasts in the peppercorns. Season with a little salt. Heat the low-fat spread in a non-stick frying pan (skillet) and fry (sauté) the duck for 7 minutes on each side until just cooked through but slightly pink in the centre or a little longer if you like it well done. Remove from the pan and keep warm. Add the brandy to the pan and ignite. Shake the pan until the flames subside, then add the stock and bring to the boil. Blend the cornflour with the water and stir in with the crème fraîche. Bring to the boil and cook for 2 minutes, stirring. Stir in the parsley. Slice the duck thinly and arrange on four warm plates. Spoon the sauce over and serve with broccoli and Sesame Seed Noodles.

* **265 calories per serving**
* **Very low fibre**

Pheasant with Cider and Pears

SERVES 4

1 pheasant, quartered and as much skin removed as possible
40 g/1½ oz/3 tbsp low-fat sunflower or olive oil spread
2 large cooking pears, thinly sliced
Salt and freshly ground black pepper
15 ml/1 tbsp brandy
150 ml/¼ pt/⅔ cup cider
8 baby (pearl) onions, peeled but left whole
30 ml/2 tbsp low-fat crème fraîche
Chopped parsley, to garnish
Extra-fluffed Mashed Potatoes (page 260) and Braised Cabbage with Celery (page 271), to serve

R inse the pheasant under cold running water and dry on kitchen paper (paper towels). Melt half the low-fat spread in a flameproof casserole (Dutch oven) and brown the pheasant all over. Remove with a draining spoon. Put half the pear slices in the base of the casserole and toss in the juices. Lay the pheasant on top and season well. Add the remaining pear slices. Mix together the brandy and cider and pour over. Cover tightly and cook in a preheated oven at 180°C/350°F/ gas mark 4 for 1 hour.

Meanwhile, boil the onions for 5 minutes in water. Drain, dry on kitchen paper and fry (sauté) in the remaining low-fat spread to brown. Arrange around the top of the casserole and return to the oven for 15 minutes. Remove the pheasant, onions and pears and transfer to a warm serving dish. Boil the juices until well reduced and stir in the crème fraîche. Spoon over the pheasant and sprinkle with chopped parsley. Serve with Extra-fluffed Mashed Potatoes and Braised Cabbage with Celery.

* **190 calories per serving**
* **Medium fibre**

Pheasant with White Wine and Apples

SERVES 4

P repare as for Pheasant with Cider and Pears, but substitute eating (dessert) apples for the pears and a fruity white wine for the cider.

* **200 calories per serving**
* **Medium fibre**

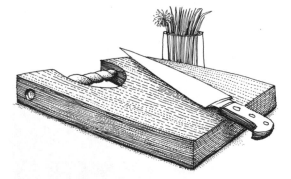

Meat Main Meals

Just because you're now eating a low-fat diet, you don't have to compromise on taste. Here you'll find sensational versions of your everyday favourites like Cottage Pie and Spaghetti Bolognese, but you'll also find some truly mouth-watering and innovative recipes that will make any meal a gourmet experience. If you are counting calories, don't forget to add the serving suggestions to your total.

Lamb Cognac

SERVES 4

1 orange
15 ml/1 tbsp chopped basil
1.5 ml/¼ tsp dried marjoram
Salt and freshly ground black pepper
4 lamb leg steaks, trimmed of any fat
45 ml/3 tbsp cognac
Almond Wild Rice (page 265) and
    Mixed Leaf Salad (page 278), to
    serve

Thinly pare the rind off the orange, cut into thin strips and boil in water for 3 minutes. Drain, rinse with cold water and drain again. Squeeze the orange and mix the juice with the basil, marjoram and a little salt and pepper. Pour over the lamb, turn to coat completely and leave to marinate for 2 hours. Grill (broil) the steaks for about 6 minutes on each side until just cooked through. Transfer to warm plates. Warm the cognac in a soup ladle, ignite and pour over the lamb. Sprinkle with the orange rind and serve hot with Almond Wild Rice and Mixed Leaf Salad.

* **290 calories per serving**
* **Medium fibre**

Crunchy-coated Lamb

SERVES 4

Prepare as for Crunchy Coated Chicken (page 151), but substitute lamb cutlets, trimmed of all fat, for the chicken, and parsley, thyme and lemon stuffing mix for the sage and onion.

* **270 calories per serving**
* **Medium fibre**

Quick Italian Lamb

SERVES 4

Prepare as for Quick Italian Chicken (page 149), but substitute lamb steaks, trimmed of all fat, for the chicken breasts and serve with Cauliflower and Poppy Seed Noodles (page 267).

* **285 calories per serving**
* **No fibre**

Spaghetti with Minted Lamb Meatballs

SERVES 4

Prepare as for Spaghetti with Meatballs, but substitute extra-lean minced (ground) lamb for the beef, add the finely grated rind of ½ lemon to the meat mixture and use dried mint instead of oregano.

* **585 calories per serving**
* **Medium fibre**

Roasted Lamb Slices with Garlic and Rosemary

SERVES 4

12 garlic cloves, peeled, but left whole
2 lamb neck fillets, 275 g/10 oz each,
trimmed
25 g/1 oz/2 tbsp low-fat sunflower or
olive oil spread
2 large sprigs of rosemary
Salt and freshly ground black pepper
150 ml/¹/₄ pt/²/₃ cup lamb or chicken
stock, made with ¹/₂ stock cube
Small sprigs of rosemary, to garnish
Baby Roast Potatoes (page 261) and
French (green) beans, to serve

Put the garlic in a roasting tin (pan) and lay the lamb on top. Spread half the low-fat spread over each fillet. Lay a rosemary sprig on each and season with salt and pepper. Cover with foil and roast in a preheated oven at 200°C/400°F/gas mark 6 for 10 minutes. Remove the foil and cook for a further 15 minutes. Discard the rosemary, transfer the meat and garlic cloves to a carving dish and keep warm. Add the stock to the pan, bring to the boil and boil, stirring, until slightly thickened and reduced. Taste and add more seasoning, if necessary. Slice the lamb thickly. Transfer to warm plates with the garlic. Spoon the sauce over, garnish with small sprigs of rosemary and serve with Baby Roast Potatoes and French beans.

* **360 calories per serving**
* **No fibre**

Minted Lamb and Vegetable Parcels

SERVES 4

10 g/¹/₄ oz/2 tsp low-fat sunflower or
olive oil spread, melted
350 g/12 oz lamb fillet, cut into
16 slices
5 ml/1 tsp dried mint
16 small new potatoes, scrubbed
2 small leeks, sliced
4 carrots, sliced
A pinch of salt
Freshly ground black pepper
¹/₄ chicken or beef stock cube
90 ml/6 tbsp boiling water

Prepare four pieces of foil about 37.5 cm/15 in long and brush with the spread. Lay the slices of lamb fillet in the centre of each and sprinkle each with a little of the mint. Arrange the vegetables around the meat and sprinkle with the salt and some pepper. Dissolve the stock cube in the boiling water and pour over the lamb and vegetables. Draw the opposite sides of the foil up over the ingredients and fold over to seal. Roll in the edges tightly to seal completely. Transfer to a baking (cookie) sheet and bake in a preheated oven at 190°C/375°F/gas mark 5 for 1 hour. Transfer to warm plates and open at the table.

* **340 calories per serving**
* **Fairly high fibre**

Cypriot Lamb Kebabs

SERVES 4

350 g/12 oz lamb neck fillet, trimmed
and cubed
15 ml/1 tbsp red wine
15 g/½ oz/1 tbsp low-fat sunflower or
olive oil spread, melted
5 ml/1 tsp dried oregano
1 garlic clove, crushed
Salt and freshly ground black pepper
100 g/4 oz button mushrooms
1 green (bell) pepper, cut into 8 pieces
4 pitta breads
Shredded lettuce, tomato and
cucumber slices and 1 lemon, cut
into 8 wedges, to serve

Put the meat in a shallow dish.
Whisk together the wine, low-fat
spread, oregano, garlic and a little salt
and pepper and pour over the lamb.
Toss gently and leave to marinate for
2 hours. Meanwhile, blanch the
mushrooms and pepper in boiling
water for 1 minute. Drain, rinse with
cold water and drain again. Thread the
meat, mushrooms and pepper on to
four skewers. Grill (broil) for about
10 minutes, turning occasionally, until
golden and cooked through, brushing
with any remaining marinade during
grilling. Warm the pitta breads, make a
slit along one edge of each and open to
form pockets. Add some shredded
lettuce, tomato and cucumber slices,
then pull a kebab off each skewer and
add to the pocket. Serve with lemon
wedges.

* **405 calories per serving**
* **Medium fibre**

Lemon-glazed Lamb

SERVES 4

350 g/12 oz lamb neck fillet, cut into
12 slices
15 ml/1 tbsp plain (all-purpose) flour
Salt and freshly ground black pepper
25 g/1 oz/2 tbsp low-fat sunflower or
olive oil spread
Finely grated rind and juice of 1 lemon
15 ml/1 tbsp light brown sugar
Watercress, to garnish
Extra-fluffed Mashed Potatoes (page
260) and peas, to serve

Toss the lamb slices in the flour,
seasoned with a little salt and
pepper. Heat the low-fat spread in a
large non-stick frying pan (skillet). Add
the lamb and fry (sauté) for about
6–8 minutes, turning occasionally,
until cooked to your liking. Remove
from the pan and keep warm. Add the
lemon rind and juice and the sugar to
the pan. Bring to the boil, stirring, until
the sugar has dissolved and the
mixture is bubbling. Season to taste.
Spoon over the lamb, garnish with
watercress and serve with Extra-fluffed
Mashed Potatoes and peas.

* **265 calories per serving**
* **Low fibre**

Minted Lemon-glazed Lamb

SERVES 4

Prepare as for Lemon-glazed Lamb, but add 5 ml/1 tsp dried mint to the flour before coating the meat.

* 265 calories per serving
* Low fibre

Lamb and Vegetable Curry

SERVES 4

Prepare as for Beef and Vegetable Curry (page 212), but substitute cubed lamb, all fat removed, for the beef and serve with Minted Yoghurt and Cucumber (page 380) instead of mango chutney.

* 300 calories per serving
* Medium fibre

Lamb Leg Steaks with Caper Sauce

SERVES 4

4 lamb leg steaks, trimmed of all fat
A pinch of salt
Freshly ground black pepper
2.5 ml/¹/₂ tsp dried oregano
1 onion, sliced and separated into rings
30 ml/2 tbsp cornflour (cornstarch)
100 ml/3¹/₂ fl oz/6¹/₂ tbsp skimmed milk
150 ml/¹/₄ pt/²/₃ cup lamb or chicken stock, made with ¹/₂ stock cube
15 ml/1 tbsp chopped parsley
15 ml/1 tbsp capers, chopped
5 ml/1 tsp vinegar from the jar of capers
Sprigs of parsley, to garnish
Plain boiled potatoes in their skins and West Country Carrots (page 268), to serve

Place the meat in a non-stick roasting tin (pan). Add the salt, a good grinding of pepper and the oregano and top with the onion rings. Cook in the top of a preheated oven at 220°C/425°F/gas mark 7 for 30 minutes until cooked through. Meanwhile, blend the cornflour in a saucepan with a little of the milk. Stir in the remaining milk and add the stock. Bring to the boil and cook for 2 minutes, stirring all the time. Stir in the capers and parsley and season to taste with the vinegar and pepper. Transfer the meat to warm plates and spoon any juices over. Garnish with parsley sprigs and serve with the sauce, plain boiled potatoes in their skins and West Country Carrots.

* 265 calories per serving
* Low fibre

Monday Lamb with Aubergine and Capers

SERVES 4

15 g/½ oz/1 tbsp low-fat sunflower or
   olive oil spread, plus extra for
   spreading
2 thick slices of bread
1 aubergine (eggplant), quartered
   lengthways and sliced
15 ml/1 tbsp capers, chopped
10 ml/2 tsp vinegar from the jar of capers
30 ml/2 tbsp chopped parsley
175 g/6 oz/1½ cups diced cooked
   lamb, all fat removed
30 ml/2 tbsp plain (all-purpose) flour
300 ml/½ pt/1¼ cups lamb or chicken
   stock, made with ½ stock cube
1 egg, beaten
Salt and freshly ground black pepper
Shredded Cabbage Salad (page 281),
   to serve

Spread a thin scraping of low-fat
spread on each slice of bread, then
cut into cubes. Reserve. Heat the
measured low-fat spread in a large
non-stick saucepan, add the aubergine
and toss for 2 minutes. Reduce the
heat, cover with a lid and cook gently
for 5 minutes, stirring occasionally.
Add the capers, vinegar, parsley and
lamb, re-cover and cook, stirring
occasionally, for a further 5 minutes.
Sprinkle in the flour and cook, stirring,
for 1 minute. Remove from the heat
and blend in the stock. Return to the
heat, bring to the boil and simmer for
2 minutes, stirring. Stir in the egg, then
season to taste. Turn into four
individual flameproof dishes. Top with
the bread cubes. Place under a
preheated grill (broiler) for a few
minutes until the bread is toasted.
Serve with Shredded Cabbage Salad.

* **180 calories per serving**
* **Medium fibre**

Monday Lamb with Courgettes and Capers

SERVES 4

Prepare as for Monday Lamb with
Aubergine and Capers, but
substitute 2 diced courgettes (zucchini)
for the aubergine (eggplant).

* **180 calories per serving**
* **Medium fibre**

Monday Lamb with Marrow and Gherkins

SERVES 4

Prepare as for Monday Lamb with
Aubergine and Capers, but
substitute 225 g/8 oz diced marrow
(squash) for the aubergine (eggplant)
and chopped sweet-pickled gherkins
(cornichons) for the capers.

* **180 calories per serving**
* **Medium fibre**

Lamb Goulash with Noodles

SERVES 4

1 onion, chopped
2 carrots, diced
15 ml/1 tbsp paprika
15 g/¹/₂ oz/1 tbsp low-fat sunflower or olive oil spread
400g/14 oz/1 large can of chopped tomatoes
15 ml/1 tbsp tomato purée (paste)
150 ml/¹/₄ pt/²/₃ cup lamb or chicken stock, made with ¹/₂ stock cube
225 g/8 oz/2 cups cooked lamb, cut into chunks and all fat removed
Salt and freshly ground black pepper
225 g/8 oz tagliatelle
275 g/10 oz/1 medium can of cut green beans, drained
15 ml/1 tbsp cornflour (cornstarch)
30 ml/2 tbsp water
60 ml/4 tbsp low-fat crème fraîche
10 ml/2 tsp caraway seeds

Fry (sauté) the onion, carrots and paprika in the low-fat spread, stirring, for 2 minutes in a large saucepan. Add the tomatoes, tomato purée, stock and lamb. Season to taste with salt and pepper. Bring to the boil, reduce the heat and simmer gently for 20 minutes. Meanwhile, cook the tagliatelle according to the packet directions and drain. Add the beans to the goulash. Blend the cornflour with the water and stir in. Bring back to the boil and cook for 2 minutes, stirring gently until thickened. Taste and re-season, if necessary. Spoon the pasta on to warm plates and the goulash to one side. Top the goulash with a spoonful of crème fraîche and sprinkle with caraway seeds before serving.

* **380 calories per serving**
* **Fairly high fibre**

Lamb Saag

SERVES 4

2.5 ml/¹/₂ tsp ground cinnamon
2.5 ml/¹/₂ tsp ground cumin
2.5 ml/¹/₂ tsp ground coriander (cilantro)
2.5 ml/¹/₂ tsp chilli powder
1 garlic clove, crushed
30 ml/2 tbsp water
25 g/1 oz/2 tbsp low-fat sunflower or olive oil spread
2 onions, halved and thinly sliced
60 ml/4 tbsp chopped coriander
1 large tomato, finely chopped
Salt
5 ml/1 tsp caster (superfine) sugar
175 g/6 oz frozen leaf spinach, thawed
225 g/8 oz/2 cups lean cooked lamb, diced
Naan bread, to serve

Put the ground spices and the garlic in a small bowl and mix with the water. Heat the low-fat spread and fry (sauté) the onions for 3 minutes, stirring. Add the spices from the cup, the coriander, and tomato and season lightly with salt. Fry for 1 minute. Add the sugar, spinach and meat, stir well, cover and cook gently for 8 minutes. Serve with naan bread.

* **140 calories per serving**
* **Fairly high fibre**

Lamb Steaks Masala

SERVES 4

150 ml/¹/₄ pt/²/₃ cup low-fat plain
  yoghurt
1 garlic clove, crushed
5 ml/1 tsp ground ginger
5 ml/1 tsp chilli powder
5 ml/1 tsp ground cumin
5 ml/1 tsp garam masala
2.5 ml/¹/₂ tsp salt
5 ml/1 tsp black pepper
4 lamb steaks, trimmed of all fat
Lettuce, tomato and cucumber, to
  garnish
Pilau Rice (page 266), to serve

Mix the yoghurt with the garlic,
spices, salt and pepper in a
shallow dish. Add the lamb, turn to
coat completely, cover and chill to
marinate for several hours or
overnight. Place in a baking tin (pan)
and bake in a preheated oven at
190°C/375°F/ gas mark 5 for about
30 minutes until cooked through,
turning once half-way through
cooking. Alternatively, grill (broil) for
about 8 minutes on each side. Garnish
with lettuce, tomato and cucumber
and serve on a bed of Pilau Rice.

* **260 calories per serving**
* **Low fibre**

Kleftico

SERVES 4

1 kg/2¹/₄ lb fillet end half leg of lamb
8 large potatoes, halved
1 large garlic clove, cut into slivers
2.5 ml/¹/₂ tsp dried oregano
Salt and freshly ground black pepper
300 ml/¹/₂ pt/1¹/₄ cups lamb or chicken
  stock, made with 1 stock cube
30 ml/2 tbsp chopped parsley
Village Salad (page 281), to serve

Trim off any fat from the lamb.
Place in a roasting tin (pan) with a
lid and surround with the potatoes.
Scatter the slivers of garlic over the
meat and sprinkle with the oregano
and a little salt and pepper. Pour the
stock around. Cover and cook in a
preheated oven at 160°C/325°F/gas
mark 3 for 3 hours until the lamb is
meltingly tender. Transfer the meat
and potatoes to a carving dish. Spoon
off any fat from the juices (there
should be little or none if you trimmed
the meat well). Boil the juices until
reduced by half. Cut the lamb into
chunky pieces. Transfer to plates with
the potatoes, spoon the juices over and
sprinkle with the parsley. Serve with
Village Salad.

* **545 calories per serving**
* **Medium fibre**

Piquant Peppered Liver

SERVES 4

*30 ml/2 tbsp crushed black
  peppercorns
15 ml/1 tbsp plain (all-purpose) flour
8 thin slices of lambs' liver
40 g/1¹/₂ oz/3 tbsp low-fat sunflower
  or olive oil spread
1 small onion, very finely chopped
15 ml/1 tbsp chopped parsley
45 ml/3 tbsp Worcestershire sauce
Extra-fluffed Mashed Potatoes (page
  260), and peas, to serve*

M ix the peppercorns with the flour and use to coat the slices of liver. Heat 25 g/1 oz/2 tbsp of the low-fat spread in a large non-stick frying pan (skillet), add the liver and fry (sauté) on one side until browned underneath. Turn over and cook just until droplets of juice appear on the surface. Remove from the pan and keep warm. Add the remaining low-fat spread and the onion to the pan and fry for 2 minutes, stirring. Add the parsley and Worcestershire sauce and heat through. Transfer the liver to warm plates and spoon the sauce over. Serve straight away with Extra-fluffed Mashed Potatoes and peas.

* **245 calories per serving**
* **Low fibre**

Peppered Liver with Wine

SERVES 4

P repare as for Piquant Peppered Liver, but substitute 60 ml/4 tbsp red wine for the Worcestershire sauce and add 15 ml/1 tbsp tomato purée (paste) with the parsley. Season to taste with salt and caster (superfine) sugar, then spoon over the liver and serve.

* **250 calories per serving**
* **Low fibre**

Leftover Lamb Biryani

SERVES 4

P repare as for Leftover Chicken Biryani (page 165), but substitute cooked lamb, all fat removed, for the chicken and serve with curried fruit chutney.

* **295 calories per serving**
* **Medium fibre**

Kidneys in Sherry

SERVES 4

*15 g/½ oz/1 tbsp low-fat sunflower or
    olive oil spread*
2 onions, thinly sliced
*8 lambs' kidneys, skinned, quartered
    and cored*
*100 g/4 oz small whole button
    mushrooms*
30 ml/2 tbsp medium-dry sherry
45 ml/3 tbsp low-fat crème fraîche
Salt and freshly ground black pepper
15 ml/1 tbsp chopped parsley
*Plain boiled rice and baby carrots, to
    serve*

Melt the low-fat spread in a non-stick saucepan. Add the onions and fry (sauté) for 2 minutes, stirring. Add the kidneys and toss over a high heat until browned but not hard. Add the mushrooms and sherry, stir, cover with a lid and cook over a gentle heat for 8 minutes, stirring occasionally. Stir in the crème fraîche and season to taste. Allow to bubble for 1 minute, then serve on a bed of plain boiled rice, sprinkled with the chopped parsley, with baby carrots.

* **150 calories per serving**
* **Low fibre**

Welsh-style Braised Lamb

SERVES 6

1.5 kg/3 lb boned shoulder of lamb
2 large onions, quartered
*600 ml/1 pt/2½ cups lamb or chicken
    stock, made with 2 stock cubes*
60 ml/4 tbsp dry sherry
A sprig of thyme
2 large leeks, cut into short lengths
225 g/8 oz baby carrots, scrubbed
450 g/1 lb baby potatoes, scrubbed
Salt and freshly ground black pepper

Remove as much fat from the lamb as possible, then re-tie in a roll, if necessary. Brown on all sides in a flameproof casserole (Dutch oven). Add the onions, stock, sherry and thyme. Bring to the boil, cover and cook in a preheated oven at 180°C/350°F/gas mark 4 for 1 hour. Add the prepared vegetables and some seasoning and return to the oven for a further 1 hour. Skim any fat from the surface, carve the meat and serve with the vegetables and cooking liquid.

* **560 calories per serving**
* **Fairly high fibre**

Provençale Braised Leg of Lamb

SERVES 8

2 kg/4½ lb leg of lamb
2 garlic cloves, cut into slivers
Small sprigs of rosemary
5 ml/1 tsp salt
10 ml/2 tsp ground ginger
Freshly ground black pepper
15 g/½ oz/1 tbsp low-fat sunflower or
    olive oil spread
2 carrots, diced
2 onions, chopped
1 turnip, diced
300 ml/½ pt/1¼ cups red wine
150 ml/¼ pt/⅔ cup lamb or chicken
    stock, made with ½ stock cube
30 ml/2 tbsp redcurrant jelly (clear
    conserve)
Baked Scalloped Potatoes (page 259)
    and Quick-cooked Cabbage (page
    270), to serve

Trim all excess fat from the lamb and discard. Make small slits in the meat all over and push a sliver of garlic and a small sprig of rosemary into each. Mix together the salt and ginger and sprinkle all over the skin. Add a good grinding of pepper. Heat the spread in a large flameproof casserole (Dutch oven) and fry (sauté) the carrots, onions and turnip for 2 minutes, stirring. Put the lamb on top, cover with a lid and bake in a preheated oven at 220°C/425°F/gas mark 7 for 25 minutes. Add the wine and stock, reduce the heat to 180°C/350°F/gas mark 4 and continue cooking for 1½ hours, basting twice. Remove the lamb to a carving dish and keep warm. Spoon off any fat, then strain the juices and return to the casserole. Add the redcurrant jelly, bring to the boil and boil rapidly until reduced by a third. Carve the lamb, spoon a little sauce over and serve with Baked Scalloped Potatoes, Quick-cooked Cabbage and any remaining sauce handed separately.

* **355 calories per serving**
* **Fairly high fibre**

Sharp Soy Lamb

SERVES 6

2 lamb neck fillets, 350 g/12 oz each
15 g/¹/₂ oz/1 tbsp low-fat sunflower or
olive oil spread, melted
Finely grated rind and juice of 1 lime
45 ml/3 tbsp reduced-salt soy sauce
1 garlic clove, crushed
Thai Fragrant Rice Salad (page 280), to
serve

Trim the lamb of all fat and sinews and place in a shallow dish. Mix together the remaining ingredients and spoon over. Leave to marinate for at least 3 hours, preferably overnight. Remove from the marinade and place in a roasting tin (pan). Roast in the oven at 230°C/450°F/gas mark 8 for 20–25 minutes, depending on how well cooked you like your lamb. Remove from the oven and leave to rest for 5 minutes. Carve into thin slices, arrange in fan shapes on plates and serve warm with Thai Fragrant Rice salad.

* **340 calories per serving**
* **Low fibre**

Gaelic Lamb

SERVES 4

350 g/12 oz lamb neck fillet, cut into 8
slices
15 ml/1 tbsp crushed black
peppercorns
25 g/1 oz/2 tbsp low-fat sunflower or
olive oil spread
30 ml/2 tbsp Scotch whisky
5 ml/1 tsp Dijon mustard
60 ml/4 tbsp low-fat crème fraîche
Salt
Extra-fluffed Mashed Potatoes (page
260) and Neeps (page271), to serve

Put the lamb a slice at a time in a plastic bag and beat with a rolling pin or meat mallet to flatten. Sprinkle with the peppercorns. Heat the low-fat spread in a large frying pan (skillet) and fry (sauté) the lamb for 3 minutes on each side or until cooked to your liking. Remove from the pan and keep warm. Add the whisky to the pan and ignite. Shake until the flames subside. Stir in the mustard and crème fraîche and season to taste with salt. Bring to the boil and boil rapidly for 1 minute. Spoon over the lamb and serve with Extra-fluffed Mashed Potatoes and Neeps.

* **225 calories per serving**
* **No fibre**

Minty Roasted Lamb Steaks

SERVES 4

4 lamb leg steaks, all fat removed
30 ml/2 tbsp chopped mint
1 onion, thinly sliced and separated
into rings
30 ml/2 tbsp red wine vinegar
15 ml/1 tbsp clear honey
A pinch of salt
Freshly ground black pepper
Sprigs of mint, to garnish
No-fat Chips (page 260) and peas, to
serve

Put the lamb steaks in a shallow dish. Sprinkle the mint and onion rings over. Mix the vinegar with the honey and drizzle over. Add the salt and a good grinding of pepper. Turn the steaks over in the marinade. Cover and leave in the fridge for 4 hours to marinate, turning once. Lift the meat out of the marinade and place in a single layer in a roasting tin (pan). Roast in a preheated oven at 200°C/400°F/gas mark 6 for 30 minutes until tender and cooked through, basting with any remaining marinade once or twice during cooking. Place on warm plates and spoon any juices over. Garnish with sprigs of mint and serve with No-fat Chips and peas.

* **250 calories per serving**
* **Low fibre**

Lamb and Rosemary Spaghettini

SERVES 4

175 g/6 oz extra-lean minced (ground)
lamb
1 large onion, very finely chopped
1 large garlic clove, crushed
Salt and freshly ground black pepper
15 ml/1 tbsp very finely chopped
rosemary
30 ml/2 tbsp chopped parsley
Finely grated rind of ¹/₂ lemon
150 ml/¹/₄ pt/²/₃ cup lamb or vegetable
stock, made with ¹/₂ stock cube
350 g/12 oz spaghettini
60 ml/4 tbsp grated Parmesan cheese
Green Bean with Tomato Salsa Salad
(page 279), to serve

Put the lamb in a saucepan with the onion, garlic, a little salt and lots of pepper, the herbs and lemon rind. Cook, stirring, until the lamb is no longer pink and all the grains are separate. Spoon off any fat (there shouldn't be any if the lamb is really extra-lean), but leave all the juices. Add the stock, cover and simmer very gently for 15 minutes. Meanwhile, cook the spaghettini in plenty of boiling water for 8 minutes or until just tender. Drain and return to the pan. Add the meat sauce and toss well with half the Parmesan. Pile on to warm plates and sprinkle with the remaining cheese. Serve with Green Bean with Tomato Salsa Salad.

* **420 calories per serving**
* **Medium fibre**

Spiced Roast Lamb Fillet

SERVES 4

10 ml/2 tsp ground coriander (cilantro)
5 ml/1 tsp ground cumin
5 ml/1 tsp paprika
5 ml/1 tsp freshly ground black pepper
2.5 ml/¹/₂ tsp ground ginger
450 g/1 lb lamb neck fillet, trimmed of
    any fat and sinews
10 g/¹/₄ oz/2 tsp low-fat sunflower or
    olive oil spread
2 large carrots, finely chopped
2 celery sticks, finely chopped
1 onion, finely sliced
300 ml/¹/₂ pt/1¹/₄ cups lamb or
    vegetable stock, made with 1 stock
    cube
1 bouquet garni sachet
5 ml/1 tsp tomato purée (paste)
Extra-fluffed Mashed Potatoes (page
    260) and runner beans, to serve

Mix together the spices and rub all over the lamb. Melt the low-fat spread in a flameproof casserole dish (Dutch oven) and brown the meat quickly on all sides. Remove from the dish. Add the prepared vegetables and cook gently, stirring, for 5 minutes. Add the stock, bouquet garni and tomato purée, bring to the boil and simmer for 5 minutes. Replace the lamb and cook in a preheated oven at 230°C/450°F/gas mark 8 for 30 minutes. Carefully lift out the lamb and keep warm. Discard the bouquet garni and purée the juices and vegetables in a blender or food processor. Carve the meat into thick slices. Serve with the puréed vegetable sauce, Extra-fluffed Mashed Potatoes and runner beans.

* **315 calories per serving**
* **Medium fibre**

Scotch Lamb Stew

SERVES 4

900 g/2 lb shoulder of lamb, trimmed
    of all excess fat and skin
1 large onion, quartered
75 g/3 oz/scant ¹/₂ cup pearl barley
1 bouquet garni sachet
2 leeks, sliced
2 large carrots, cut into chunks
2 potatoes, quartered
2 turnips, cut into pieces
Salt and freshly ground black pepper
Chopped parsley, to garnish

Put the lamb in a large saucepan with the onion, barley and bouquet garni sachet. Cover with water. Bring to the boil, reduce the heat, part-cover and simmer very gently for 1¹/₂ hours. Leave to cool in the liquid, then skim the surface of all fat. Lift the lamb out, trim off any remaining fat and cut the meat into large chunks. Return the meat to the pan. Add the prepared vegetables and some salt and pepper. Bring back to the boil, reduce the heat, part-cover and simmer gently for 30 minutes until the vegetables are really tender. Ladle into warm bowls and sprinkle with chopped parsley before serving.

* **400 calories per serving**
* **High fibre**

Rosie's Mustard Lamb

SERVES 4

30 ml/2 tbsp finely chopped rosemary
1 garlic clove, crushed
5 ml/1 tsp dried oregano
A pinch of chilli powder
Salt and freshly ground black pepper
10 ml/2 tsp Dijon mustard
25 g/1 oz/2 tbsp low-fat sunflower or
*   olive oil spread*
4 lamb leg steaks, trimmed of all fat
Pan Scalloped Potatoes (page 258)
*   and mangetout (snow peas), to*
*   serve*

Mash together all the ingredients except the lamb. Spread on both sides of the lamb and leave to stand for 2 hours. Place under a preheated grill (broiler) and grill (broil) for 10 minutes on each side until sizzling and golden. Serve hot with Pan Scalloped Potatoes and mangetout.

* **285 calories per serving**
* **Low fibre**

Succulent Lamb Kebabs

SERVES 4

450 g/1 lb lamb leg meat, all skin and
*   fat removed, cubed*
1 garlic clove, crushed
15 ml/1 tbsp chopped rosemary
45 ml/3 tbsp red wine
A pinch of salt
Freshly ground black pepper
100 g/4 oz button mushrooms
1 green (bell) pepper, diced
Savoury Vegetable Rice (page 264)
*   and Fragrant Tomato and Onion*
*   Salad (page 278), to serve*

Put the lamb in a shallow dish. Mix together the garlic, rosemary, wine, salt and some pepper and pour over. Toss well, then leave in the fridge to marinate for 2–3 hours, turning occasionally. Lift the meat out of the marinade and thread on to eight skewers with the mushrooms and peppers. Place on foil on the grill (broiler) rack. Grill (broil) for about 12–15 minutes, turning once or twice and brushing with any remaining marinade, until cooked through. Transfer to a bed of Savoury Vegetable Rice and serve with Fragrant Tomato and Onion Salad.

* **250 calories per serving**
* **Low fibre**

Grilled Steaks with Mushroom Purée

SERVES 4

350 g/12 oz button mushrooms,
  chopped
30 ml/2 tbsp snipped chives, plus
  extra to garnish
120 ml/4 fl oz/¹/₂ cup water
A pinch of salt
Freshly ground black pepper
100 g/4 oz/¹/₂ cup low-fat fromage
  frais
A little skimmed milk
4 small fillet steaks, trimmed of any
  sinews
A small knob of low-fat sunflower or
  olive oil spread
Pan Scalloped Potatoes (page 258)
  and mangetout (snow peas), to
  serve

Put the mushrooms, chives and water in a pan with the salt and lots of pepper. Bring to the boil, cover, reduce the heat and simmer for 5 minutes until really soft. Purée in a blender or food processor with the fromage frais. Return to the pan. Thin with a little milk, if necessary, then reheat. Meanwhile, put the steaks on a grill (broiler) rack. Dot with half the low-fat spread and add a good grinding of pepper. Grill (broil) until browned on one side. Turn over and dot the other sides with spread. Grill until browned and cooked to your liking. Spoon the mushroom purée on to warm plates. Top each with a steak and sprinkle lightly with chives. Serve hot with Pan Scalloped Potatoes and mangetout.

* **265 calories per serving**
* **Low fibre**

Steaks with Green Peppercorn Sauce

SERVES 4

4 small fillet steaks, about 150 g/5 oz
  each
15 g/¹/₂ oz/1 tbsp low-fat sunflower or
  olive oil spread
15 ml/1 tbsp pickled green
  peppercorns
30 ml/2 tbsp brandy
90 ml/6 tbsp low-fat crème fraîche
Salt and freshly ground black pepper
Mixed Seeded Noodles (page 266) and
  Dressed Green Salad (page 275), to
  serve

Wipe the steaks and trim away any sinews. Heat the low-fat spread in a frying pan (skillet), add the steaks and fry (sauté) for 4–5 minutes on each side or until cooked to your liking. Transfer from the pan to warm plates and keep warm. Add the peppercorns and brandy to the pan. Ignite and shake the pan until the flames subside. Stir in the crème fraîche and allow to bubble. Season to taste. Spoon over the steaks and serve with Mixed Seeded Noodles to one side and Dressed Green Salad.

* **240 calories per serving**
* **Very low fibre**

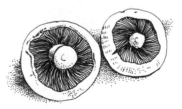

Photograph opposite: Duck with Port and Redcurrant (page 175)

Brittany Steaks and Onions

SERVES 4

4 thin-cut beef steaks, trimmed of all
    fat
25 g/1 oz/2 tbsp low-fat sunflower or
    olive oil spread
8 shallots, finely chopped
150 ml/¼ pt/⅔ cup dry cider
Salt and freshly ground black pepper
425 g/15 oz/1 large can of artichoke
    hearts
15 ml/1 tbsp chopped parsley
Extra-fluffed Mashed Potatoes (page
    260) and baby broad (fava) beans,
    to serve

Put the steaks, one at a time, in a
plastic bag and beat well with a
rolling pin or meat mallet. Heat half
the low-fat spread in a small saucepan.
Add the shallots and cook, stirring, for
1 minute. Add the cider and a little salt
and pepper. Bring to the boil and boil
rapidly until well reduced, stirring
occasionally.

Meanwhile, heat the remaining
low-fat spread in a frying pan (skillet).
Add the steaks and fry for 3–4 minutes
on each side until browned and cooked
through.

Heat the artichokes in a saucepan.
Transfer the steaks to plates. Stir any
juices into the cider and shallots with
the parsley. Taste and re-season, if
necessary. Spoon on to the steaks.
Drain the artichokes and put beside
the steaks. Serve with Extra-fluffed
Mashed Potatoes and baby broad
beans.

* **235 calories per serving**
* **Medium fibre**

American-style Baked Steak

SERVES 4

25 g/1 oz/2 tbsp low-fat sunflower or
    olive oil spread
450 g/1 lb lean rump steak, about
    2.5 cm/1 in thick, all fat removed
1 garlic clove, crushed
30 ml/2 tbsp toasted onion flakes
10 ml/2 tsp coarsely ground black
    pepper
100 g/4 oz button mushrooms, sliced
45 ml/3 tbsp red wine
Salt
Sprigs of parsley, to garnish
Plain boiled rice and broccoli, to serve

Spread half the low-fat spread in the
centre of a large square of double
thickness foil. Sprinkle half the garlic,
onion flakes and pepper on this. Top
with the steak, then the remaining
garlic, onion and pepper. Add the
mushrooms and pour the wine over.
Sprinkle with salt. Wrap securely in the
foil, sealing the edges so the juices
won't run out. Place on a baking
(cookie) sheet and bake in a preheated
oven at 200°C/400°F/ gas mark 6 for
1¼ hours. Leave to rest for 3 minutes,
then slice thickly and pour the juices
over. Garnish with parsley sprigs and
serve with plain boiled rice and
broccoli.

* **175 calories per serving**
* **No fibre**

Photograph opposite: **Provençale
Braised Leg of Lamb (page 187)**

Spaghetti with Meatballs

SERVES 4

450 g/1 lb extra-lean minced (ground)
   beef
1 large onion, finely chopped
50 g/2 oz/1 cup fresh breadcrumbs
7.5 ml/1½ tsp dried mixed herbs
2.5 ml/½ tsp ground cumin
Salt and freshly ground black pepper
1 small egg, beaten
25 g/1 oz/2 tbsp low-fat sunflower or
   olive oil spread
400 g/14 oz/1 large can of chopped
   tomatoes
1 garlic clove, crushed
15 ml/1 tbsp tomato purée (paste)
A pinch of caster (superfine) sugar
350 g/12 oz spaghetti
20 ml/4 tsp grated Parmesan cheese,
   to garnish
Mixed Green Salad (page 279), to
   serve

Mix the beef with half the chopped
onion, the breadcrumbs, 5 ml/1
tsp of the mixed herbs, the cumin and
some salt and pepper. Mix in the egg to
bind. Shape into small balls. Heat the
low-fat spread in a large non-stick
frying pan (skillet) and brown the
meatballs all over. Drain on kitchen
paper (paper towels). Meanwhile, put
the remaining onion in a saucepan
with the tomatoes, garlic, tomato
purée, sugar, the remaining herbs and
a little salt and pepper. Bring to the
boil, stirring. Add the meatballs and
simmer for 12 minutes. Meanwhile,
cook the spaghetti in plenty of boiling,
lightly salted water for 10 minutes.
Drain. Pile on to warm plates and
spoon the meatballs and sauce over.
Sprinkle with the Parmesan and serve
with a Mixed Green Salad.

* **585 calories per serving**
* **Medium fibre**

Steak Chéron

SERVES 6

Prepare as for Chicken Chéron (page
145), but substitute small fillet
steaks for the chicken and add 5 ml/1
tsp Dijon mustard to the wine with the
sugar.

* **290 calories per serving**
* **Medium fibre**

Steak and Vegetable Fajitas

SERVES 4

Prepare as for Chicken and Roast
Vegetable Fajitas (page 146), but
substitute fillet steak for the chicken.

* **610 calories per serving**
* **Fairly high fibre**

Chilli Steak Scramble

SERVES 4

1 large onion, thinly sliced
1 red (bell) pepper, thinly sliced
1 green pepper, thinly sliced
2 tomatoes, skinned and chopped
1 small green chilli, seeded and chopped
225 g/8 oz fillet steak, cut into short thin strips
25 g/1 oz/2 tbsp low-fat sunflower or olive oil spread
15 ml/1 tbsp piccalilli or other mustard pickle, chopped
4 eggs, beaten
30 ml/2 tbsp skimmed milk
Salt and freshly ground black pepper
4 slices of wholemeal toast, cut into triangles
Dressed Green Salad (page 275), to serve

Cook the vegetables and steak in the low-fat spread in a non-stick saucepan, stirring over a moderate heat for about 5 minutes until just tender. Stir in the pickle. Beat the eggs and milk with some salt and pepper. Add to the pan, turn down the heat and cook, stirring gently, until the mixture scrambles. Do not boil. Taste and re-season, if necessary. Pile on to hot plates, garnish with the toast triangles and serve with Dressed Green Salad.

* **265 calories per serving**
* **Medium fibre**

Mighty Beefburgers

SERVES 4

450 g/1 lb extra-lean minced (ground) beef
1 onion, finely chopped
5 ml/1 tsp mustard powder
5 ml/1 tsp tomato purée (paste)
5 ml/1 tsp Worcestershire sauce
Salt and freshly ground black pepper
1 egg, beaten
4 burger baps
2 dill pickles
Tomato ketchup (catsup)
Lettuce, tomato and cucumber, to garnish
No-fat Chips (page 260), to serve

Mix the meat with the onion, mustard, tomato purée, Worcestershire sauce and a little salt and pepper. Add the egg to bind. Shape into four large cakes and chill for 30 minutes. Place under a preheated grill (broiler) and cook for 6 minutes on each side, depending on their thickness, until cooked through. Meanwhile, split open the baps and slice the pickles. Place a burger in each bun and top with dill pickle slices and a little ketchup. Close the buns. Place on plates, garnish with a small side salad of lettuce, tomato and cucumber and serve with No-fat Chips.

* **340 calories per serving**
* **Medium fibre**

Mighty Cheeseburgers

SERVES 4

Prepare as for Mighty Beefburgers (page 195), but top each cooked burger with thin slices of onion and a thin slice of low-fat Cheddar or processed cheese before adding the pickles and ketchup (catsup).

* 380 calories per serving
* Medium fibre

Steak with Mixed Grilled Vegetables

SERVES 4

Prepare as for Steak with Grilled Red Peppers, but substitute 1 small aubergine (eggplant), 1 courgette (zucchini), 1 red (bell) pepper and 1 red onion, thinly sliced, for the peppers. Boil them in water for 1 minute, then drain before mixing with the steak and seasonings.

* 320 calories per serving
* Medium fibre

Steak with Grilled Red Peppers

SERVES 4

350 g/12 oz fillet steak, cut into thin strips
3 red (bell) peppers, each cut into 8 thick strips
1 bunch of spring onions (scallions), cut into short lengths
1 garlic clove, crushed
Salt and freshly ground black pepper
20 g/³/₄ oz/1¹/₂ tbsp low-fat sunflower or olive oil spread, melted
15 ml/1 tbsp chopped parsley
15 ml/1 tbsp chopped basil
Hot French bread and Dressed Green Salad (page 275), to serve

Put the steak, peppers and spring onions in a bowl. Add the garlic, some salt and pepper and the melted spread. Toss well. Spread the mixture out on foil on a grill (broiler) rack and grill (broil) quickly for about 12 minutes, turning occasionally, until lightly browned and the peppers are just tender. Spoon on to plates, sprinkle with the parsley and basil and serve with hot French bread and Dressed Green Salad.

* 270 calories per serving
* Medium fibre

Oriental Beef

SERVES 4

*100 g/4 oz quick-cook Chinese egg
noodles*
*225 g/8 oz fillet steak, cut into thin
strips*
*15 g/¹/₂ oz/1 tbsp low-fat sunflower or
olive oil spread*
*1 bunch of spring onions (scallions),
cut into short lengths*
1 carrot, cut into thin matchsticks
*1 courgette (zucchini), cut into thin
matchsticks*
*1 green (bell) pepper, cut into thin
strips*
3 tomatoes, cut into wedges
100 g/4 oz button mushrooms, sliced
30 ml/2 tbsp dry sherry
2.5 ml/¹/₂ tsp ground ginger
45 ml/3 tbsp reduced-salt soy sauce
15 ml/1 tbsp clear honey

Cook the noodles according to the packet directions and drain. Stir-fry the steak in the low-fat spread in a wok or large non-stick frying pan (skillet) for 2 minutes. Add the onions, carrot and courgette and stir-fry for a further 3 minutes. Add the remaining ingredients and cook, stirring, for 5 minutes. Stir in the noodles and cook for 1 minute. Serve very hot.

* **265 calories per serving**
* **Fairly high fibre**

Spiced Steak Kebabs

SERVES 4

*450 g/1 lb rump steak, all fat removed,
cubed*
15 ml/1 tbsp red wine vinegar
30 ml/2 tbsp low-fat plain yoghurt
1 garlic clove, crushed
5 ml/1 tsp ground coriander (cilantro)
5 ml/1 tsp ground cumin
5 ml/1 tsp turmeric
5 ml/1 tsp ground cardamom
Salt and freshly ground black pepper
*Shredded lettuce, tomato and
cucumber slices, to garnish*
*Mango chutney and naan bread, to
serve*

Put the steak in a shallow dish. Whisk together the vinegar, yoghurt, garlic, spices and a little salt and pepper. Pour over the steak, toss gently and leave to marinate in the fridge for at least 2 hours, or preferably overnight. Thread on to soaked wooden skewers and grill (broil) for about 10 minutes, turning occasionally and brushing with any remaining marinade. Arrange on a bed of shredded lettuce, tomato and cucumber slices and serve with mango chutney and lots of naan bread.

* **200 calories per serving**
* **No fibre**

Athenian Beef Casserole

SERVES 4

**750 g/1½ lb lean braising steak,
cubed**
**25 g/1 oz/2 tbsp low-fat sunflower or
olive oil spread**
Salt and freshly ground black pepper
1.5 ml/¼ tsp cumin seeds
5 cm/2 in piece of cinnamon stick
30 ml/2 tbsp tomato purée (paste)
15 ml/1 tbsp red wine vinegar
**600 ml/1 pt/2½ cups beef stock,
made with 2 stock cubes**
5 ml/1 tsp dried thyme
**225 g/8 oz baby (pearl) onions, peeled
but left whole**
45 ml/3 tbsp plain (all-purpose) flour
45 ml/3 tbsp cold water
**Plain boiled rice and Village Salad
(page 281), to serve**

Fry (sauté) the meat in the low-fat spread in a non-stick frying pan (skillet) until browned all over. Remove from the pan with a draining spoon and transfer to a flameproof casserole dish (Dutch oven). Season with salt and pepper and add the cumin and cinnamon. Blend the tomato purée with the vinegar and stock and stir in. Add the thyme. Bring to the boil, then transfer to a preheated oven at 160°C/325°F/gas mark 3 and cook for 2½ hours. Meanwhile, boil the onions in water for 1 minute. Drain. Blend the flour with the water and stir into the casserole with the onions. Return to the oven and cook for a further 40 minutes until the meat is really tender. Taste and re-season, if necessary. Remove the cinnamon stick before serving with plain boiled rice and Village Salad.

* **275 calories per serving**
* **Medium fibre**

Steak Toss

SERVES 4

**350 g/12 oz fillet steak, cut into thin
strips**
2 onions, thinly sliced
3 celery sticks, thinly sliced
**25 g/1 oz/2 tbsp low-fat sunflower or
olive oil spread**
3 tomatoes, skinned and chopped
**150 ml/¼ pt/⅔ cup beef stock, made
with ½ stock cube**
Salt and freshly ground black pepper
Plain boiled rice, to serve

Cook the steak, onions, and celery in the low-fat spread, stirring, for 5 minutes. Add the tomatoes and stock and simmer for 3–4 minutes until slightly thickened. Season to taste. Serve on a bed of plain boiled rice.

* **145 calories per serving**
* **Medium fibre**

Beef Valpolicella

SERVES 4

25 g/1 oz/2 tbsp low-fat sunflower or
olive oil spread
450 g/1 lb lean rump steak, cubed
1 onion, thinly sliced
100 g/4 oz button mushrooms, sliced
2 thin slices of Parma ham, cut into
small pieces
1 carrot, finely diced
2.5 ml/½ tsp dried oregano
15 ml/1 tbsp brandy
150 ml/¼ pt/⅔ cup Valpolicella
20 ml/1½ tbsp cornflour (cornstarch)
150 ml/¼ pt/⅔ cup beef stock, made
with ½ stock cube
Salt and freshly ground black pepper
Savoury Potato Cake (page 258) and
Dressed Green Salad (page 275), to
serve

Heat half the low-fat spread in a large non-stick frying pan (skillet) and fry (sauté) the steak quickly on all sides to brown. Remove from the pan. Heat the remaining spread in the pan, add the onion, mushrooms, ham and carrot and cook for 2 minutes, stirring. Add the oregano, cover with a lid or foil, reduce the heat and cook gently for 6 minutes. Return the steak to the pan, cover and cook for a further 4 minutes. Add the brandy and ignite. Shake the pan until the flames subside. Blend the wine with the cornflour and stir in with the beef stock. Bring to the boil and cook for 2 minutes, stirring until thickened. Season to taste and serve with Savoury Potato Cake and Dressed Green Salad.

* **280 calories per serving**
* **Low fibre**

Luxury Giant Spring Rolls

SERVES 4

175 g/6 oz fillet steak, cut into very
thin strips
15 ml/1 tbsp cornflour (cornstarch)
20 g/¾ oz/1½ tbsp low-fat sunflower
or olive oil spread, melted
1 garlic clove, crushed
4 spring onions (scallions), chopped
4 mushrooms, thinly sliced
100 g/4 oz/2 cups beansprouts
1 carrot, coarsely grated
25 g/1 oz frozen peas
30 ml/2 tbsp reduced-salt soy sauce
1.5 ml/¼ tsp ground ginger
4 sheets of filo pastry (paste)
Citrus Chinese Leaf Salad (page 271),
to serve

Dust the beef with the cornflour. Heat half the low-fat spread in a large non-stick frying pan (skillet) or wok and stir-fry the meat for 1 minute. Add the garlic and all the vegetables and cook for 3 minutes, stirring. Stir in the soy sauce and ginger. Leave to cool. Lay the pastry sheets on a work surface and fold in half. Divide the meat mixture between the sheets, placing it in the centre of one edge. Fold in the sides, then roll up. Melt the remaining low-fat spread and use to brush a non-stick baking (cookie) sheet. Lay the rolls on the sheet and brush with the remaining melted spread. Bake the rolls on the shelf above the centre in a preheated oven at 190°C/ 375°F/gas mark 5 for 20 minutes until golden brown. Serve hot with Citrus Chinese Leaf Salad.

* **225 calories per serving**
* **Fairly high fibre**

Saturday Night Pasta

SERVES 4

225 g/8 oz pasta shapes
225 g/8 oz extra-lean minced (ground)
  steak
1 onion, finely chopped
30 ml/2 tbsp plain (all-purpose) flour
200 ml/7 fl oz/scant 1 cup beef stock,
  made with 1 stock cube
2.5 ml/½ tsp dried mixed herbs
Salt and freshly ground black pepper
50 g/2 oz/½ cup low-fat Cheddar
  cheese, grated
2 tomatoes, sliced

Cook the pasta according to the packet directions. Drain. Meanwhile, cook the mince and onion in a non-stick saucepan, stirring, until the meat is no longer pink and all the grains are separate. Spoon off any fat (there shouldn't be any if it really is extra-lean) but leave the juices. Stir in the flour and cook for 1 minute, stirring. Remove from the heat and blend in the stock, herbs and a little salt and pepper. Return to the heat and bring to the boil, stirring. Reduce the heat and simmer for 10 minutes. Add the cooked pasta to the meat and toss well. Turn into a flameproof serving dish, sprinkle with the cheese and arrange the tomatoes round the edge. Place under a hot grill (broiler) until the cheese melts and bubbles. Serve hot.

* **485 calories per serving**
* **Medium fibre**

Mediterranean Pasta Grill

SERVES 4

Prepare as for Saturday Night Pasta, but substitute 400 g/14 oz/1 large can of chopped tomatoes for the stock and omit the flour. Season with dried basil instead of mixed herbs and use low-fat Mozzarella cheese instead of Cheddar, if liked.

* **495 calories per serving**
* **Medium fibre**

Sesame Beef Skewers with Chinese Vegetables

SERVES 4

30 ml/2 tbsp sesame seeds
2 garlic cloves, crushed
90 ml/6 tbsp dry white wine or rice wine
90 ml/6 tbsp reduced-salt soy sauce
15 ml/1 tbsp white wine vinegar
10 ml/2 tsp sesame oil
450 g/1 lb lean rump steak, all fat removed, cubed
15 g/¹/₂ oz/1 tbsp low-fat sunflower or olive oil spread
1 red (bell) pepper, cut into strips
1 green pepper, cut into strips
1 bunch of spring onions (scallions), cut into short lengths
2 celery sticks, cut into matchsticks
2 carrots, cut into matchsticks
A pinch of Chinese five spice powder

Brown the sesame seeds in a frying pan (skillet), then tip into a shallow dish and mix with the garlic, wine, half the soy sauce, the vinegar and sesame oil. Add the steak, toss well to coat and leave to marinate for 2 hours. Thread the meat on to four soaked wooden skewers and grill (broil) for 4–6 minutes, turning occasionally and brushing with any remaining marinade. Meanwhile, heat the low-fat spread in a non-stick frying pan or wok. Add the vegetables and toss over a high heat for 5 minutes. Add the remaining soy sauce and the five spice powder and toss again. Pile on to plates and top with the steak.

* **280 calories per serving**
* **Fairly high fibre**

Light Stroganoff

SERVES 4

350 g/12 oz fillet steak
25 g/1 oz/2 tbsp low-fat sunflower or olive oil spread
2 onions, thinly sliced
100 g/4 oz button mushrooms, sliced
30 ml/2 tbsp brandy
150 ml/¹/₄ pt/²/₃ cup low-fat crème fraîche
Salt and freshly ground black pepper
Plain boiled rice and Mixed Leaf Salad (page 278), to serve

Cut the steak into finger-length strips. Heat half the low-fat spread in a non-stick frying pan (skillet) and fry (sauté) the onions and mushrooms for 5 minutes, stirring, until lightly golden. Add the steak and toss for a further 3 minutes until just cooked. Add the brandy and ignite. Shake the pan until the flames subside, then stir in the crème fraîche and season to taste. Stir until the mixture is thickened and bubbling. Spoon on to a bed of boiled rice and serve with Mixed Leaf Salad.

* **210 calories per serving**
* **Very low fibre**

Carpaccio con Salsa Verdi

SERVES 4

350 g/12 oz piece of fillet steak
30 ml/2 tbsp reduced-salt soy sauce
50 g/2 oz/¼ cup low-fat sunflower or
   olive oil spread
2 canned anchovies, drained and
   finely chopped
1 large garlic clove, crushed
5 ml/1 tsp balsamic vinegar
15 ml/1 tbsp capers, finely chopped
2 large sprigs of parsley, finely
   chopped
Freshly ground black pepper
Ciabatta bread and Celeriac and Carrot
   Salad (page 280), to serve

Part-freeze the steak until it can be
sliced as thinly as possible. Place in
a plastic bag and beat until almost
transparent. Lay the beef on two
baking (cookie) sheets and sprinkle
with the soy sauce. Melt the low-fat
spread in a saucepan and add the
anchovies and garlic. Cook, stirring,
until the anchovies 'melt'. Stir in the
vinegar, capers, parsley and a good
grinding of pepper. Place the beef in a
preheated oven at 240°C/475°F/gas
mark 9 for 1–2 minutes until
browning. Transfer to warm plates,
spoon the salsa over and serve with
ciabatta bread and Celeriac and Carrot
Salad.

* **280 calories per serving**
* **Low fibre**

Easy Meatloaf

SERVES 4

750 g/1½ lb extra-lean minced
   (ground) beef
1 onion, finely chopped
30 ml/2 tbsp chopped parsley
A pinch of chilli powder
75 g/3 oz/1½ cups fresh breadcrumbs
1 large egg, beaten
30 ml/2 tbsp skimmed milk
10 ml/2 tsp Dijon mustard
30 ml/2 tbsp plain (all-purpose) flour
100 g/4 oz/1 cup low-fat Cheddar
   cheese, grated
Salt and freshly ground black pepper
Jacket potatoes and Blushing Leaf
   Salad (page 276), to serve

Mix the beef with all the remaining
ingredients, adding a little salt
and lots of pepper. Lay a sheet of non-
stick baking parchment on a sheet of
foil, shiny side up. Shape the meat
mixture into a roll on the parchment.
Wrap securely in the parchment and
foil. Place on a baking (cookie) sheet
and bake in a preheated oven at
180°C/350°F/gas mark 4 for 1 hour.
Leave to cool for 5 minutes, then slice
and serve hot or cold with jacket
potatoes and Blushing Leaf Salad.

* **300 calories per serving**
* **Medium fibre**

Cottage Pie

SERVES 4

1 onion, finely chopped
350 g/12 oz extra-lean minced
(ground) beef
2 large carrots, finely chopped
75 g/3 oz frozen peas
1 beef or vegetable stock cube
A few drops of gravy browning
Salt and freshly ground black pepper
5 ml/1 tsp Worcestershire sauce
2.5 ml/¹/₂ tsp dried mixed herbs
750 g/1¹/₂ lb potatoes
30 ml/2 tbsp skimmed milk
10 g/¹/₄ oz/2 tsp low-fat sunflower or
olive oil spread
30 ml/2 tbsp plain (all-purpose) flour
A green vegetable, to serve

Put the onion, mince and carrots in a saucepan. Cook, stirring, for about 5 minutes until all the grains of meat are brown and separate. Spoon off any fat but leave the juices. Add the peas and just enough water to cover the ingredients. Crumble in the stock cube. Bring to the boil. Stir in the gravy browning, a good grinding of pepper, the Worcestershire sauce and herbs. Part-cover and simmer very gently for 45 minutes until tender and well-flavoured. Meanwhile, cut the potatoes into fairly small pieces and boil in a saucepan of lightly salted water until tender. Drain and mash well with the milk and low-fat spread. Blend the flour with a little water and stir into the meat mixture. Bring back to the boil and cook for 2 minutes, stirring, until thickened. Turn into a flameproof serving dish. Top with the potato and fluff up with a fork. Brown under a preheated grill (broiler). Serve piping hot with a green vegetable.

* **360 calories per serving**
* **Medium fibre**

Beef Stir-fry

SERVES 4

Prepare as for Turkey Stir-fry (page 171), but substitute fillet steak for the turkey and omit the noodles. Serve instead on a bed of Special Fried Rice (page 265).

* **280 calories per serving**
* **Medium fibre**

Spaghetti Bolognese

SERVES 4

350 g/12 oz extra-lean minced (ground) beef
1 large onion, finely chopped
1 carrot, finely chopped
1 garlic clove, crushed
400 g/14 oz/1 large can of chopped tomatoes
30 ml/2 tbsp tomato purée (paste)
45 ml/3 tbsp red wine
A pinch of salt
Freshly ground black pepper
2.5 ml/½ tsp dried oregano
1 lemon slice
1 bay leaf
350 g/12 oz spaghetti
30 ml/2 tbsp grated Parmesan cheese
Mixed Green Salad (page 279), to serve

Put the beef, onion, carrot and garlic in a saucepan and cook over a moderate heat, stirring, for about 5 minutes until the meat is no longer pink and all the grains are separate. Spoon off any fat, but leave the juices. Add the tomatoes, tomato purée, wine, salt, lots of pepper, the oregano, lemon and bay leaf. Bring to the boil, stirring. Part-cover, reduce the heat and simmer gently for 30 minutes until tender and the meat is bathed in a rich sauce. Remove the lemon slice and bay leaf. Meanwhile, cook the spaghetti according to the packet directions. Drain. Pile the spaghetti on warm plates. Top with the Bolognese sauce and sprinkle with the Parmesan before serving with Mixed Green Salad.

* **490 calories per serving**
* **Medium fibre**

Family Lasagne

SERVES 4

Prepare the Bolognese mixture as for Spaghetti Bolognese, but layer the sauce with sheets of no-need-to-precook lasagne in a shallow baking dish. Top with Cheese Sauce (page 376) and bake in a preheated oven at 190°C/ 375°F/gas mark 5 for about 35 minutes until bubbling, browned on top and the lasagne feels tender when a knife is inserted down through the middle.

* **380 calories per serving**
* **Medium fibre**

Cannelloni al Forno

SERVES 4

Prepare the Bolognese mixture as for Spaghetti Bolognese, but use it to fill 8 no-need-to-precook cannelloni tubes. Lay the filled tubes in a shallow baking dish. Cover with Cheese Sauce (page 376) and bake as for Family Lasagne.

* **400 calories per serving**
* **Medium fibre**

Cornish Strudels

SERVES 4

100 g/4 oz extra-lean minced (ground)
beef or lamb
1 large potato, finely diced
½ small swede (rutabaga), finely diced
1 large carrot, finely diced
1 onion, finely chopped
Salt and freshly ground black pepper
2.5 ml/½ tsp dried mixed herbs
4 sheets of filo pastry (paste)
15 g/½ oz/1 tbsp low-fat sunflower or
olive oil spread, melted
Baked beans, to serve

Mix the meat with the prepared vegetables in a bowl. Season with salt, pepper and the herbs and toss well. Lay the sheets of pastry on a work surface. Brush with a very little low-fat spread and fold in half. Divide the meat and vegetable mixture between the sheets, spooning it along the centre of one edge. Add 15 ml/ 1 tbsp water to each. Fold in the two sides, then roll up to form strudel-type rolls. Place on a non-stick baking (cookie) sheet and brush with the remaining spread. Bake in a preheated oven at 190°C/375°F/ gas mark 5 for 30 minutes until golden brown and cooked through. Cover loosely with foil if overbrowning. Serve hot with baked beans.

* **305 calories per serving**
* **Medium fibre**

Beef and Rainbow Pepper Curry

SERVES 4

750 g/1½ lb extra-lean minced
(ground) beef
1 red (bell) pepper, thinly sliced
1 green pepper, thinly sliced
1 yellow pepper, thinly sliced
1 large onion, thinly sliced
5 ml/1 tsp ground cumin
5 ml/1 tsp chilli powder
2.5 ml/½ tsp ground coriander
(cilantro)
5 ml/1 tsp turmeric
15 ml/1 tbsp garam masala
Salt and freshly ground black pepper
150 ml/¼ pt/⅔ cup beef stock, made
with ½ stock cube
Plain boiled rice and mango chutney,
to serve

Put the beef, peppers and onion in a non-stick saucepan. Fry (sauté), stirring, for 5 minutes or until the meat is no longer pink and all the grains are separate. Add the spices and a little salt and pepper and fry for a further 1 minute. Add the stock, cover with a lid, turn the heat down very low and simmer gently for 15 minutes. Taste and re-season, if necessary. The mixture should be fairly dry and crumbly. Spoon on to a bed of boiled rice and serve with mango chutney.

* **280 calories per serving**
* **Medium fibre**

Chilli con Carne

Use a 450 g/15 oz/large can of red kidney beans if you prefer.

SERVES 4

100 g/4 oz/²/₃ cup dried red kidney beans, soaked in cold water for several hours or overnight
1 onion, finely chopped
225 g/8 oz extra-lean minced (ground) beef
1 garlic clove, crushed
2.5 ml/¹/₂ tsp chilli powder
5 ml/1 tsp ground cumin
5 ml/1 tsp dried oregano
400 g/14 oz/1 large can of chopped tomatoes
15 ml/1 tbsp tomato purée (paste)
A pinch of salt
Freshly ground black pepper
Plain boiled rice and Mixed Leaf Salad (page 278), to serve

D rain the beans and place in a saucepan. Cover with water, bring to the boil and boil rapidly for 10 minutes to remove any toxins. Reduce the heat, part-cover and simmer gently for about 1 hour or until tender. Drain, reserving the cooking liquid. Meanwhile, put the onion, meat and garlic in a saucepan. Fry (sauté), stirring, for 5 minutes until the meat is no longer pink and all the grains of meat are separate. Spoon off any fat but leave the juices. Stir in the spices and oregano and fry for 1 minute. Add the tomatoes, tomato purée, salt and pepper and simmer for 30 minutes. Add the drained beans and cook for a further 15 minutes, adding a little of the bean cooking liquid, if necessary, so the meat and beans are bathed in a rich sauce. Serve on a bed of rice with Mixed Leaf Salad.

* **175 calories per serving**
* **High fibre**

Steak Savoury

SERVES 4

4 tenderised minute or top-rump steaks, about 150 g/5 oz each
10 ml/2 tsp lemon juice
10 g/¹/₄ oz/2 tsp low-fat sunflower or olive oil spread
1 onion, very finely chopped or grated
30 ml/2 tbsp chopped parsley
30 ml/2 tbsp Worcestershire sauce
5 ml/1 tsp pickled green peppercorns
Extra-fluffed Mashed Potatoes (page 260) and French (green) beans, to serve

R ub the steaks with the lemon juice. Melt the low-fat spread in a non-stick frying pan (skillet) and brown the steaks for 2–3 minutes on each side. Remove from the pan and keep warm. Add the remaining ingredients to the pan and cook, stirring, for 1 minute. Spoon over the steaks and serve with Extra-fluffed Mashed Potatoes and French beans.

* **215 calories per serving**
* **Low fibre**

Vitality Moussaka

SERVES 4

2 potatoes, sliced
1 aubergine (eggplant), sliced
2 courgettes (zucchini), sliced
350 g/12 oz extra-lean minced
    (ground) beef
1 onion, chopped
1 garlic clove, crushed
5 ml/1 tsp ground cinnamon
2.5 ml/¹/₂ tsp dried marjoram
120 ml/4 fl oz/¹/₂ cup passata (sieved
    tomatoes)
30 ml/2 tbsp tomato purée (paste)
30 ml/2 tbsp chopped parsley
A pinch of salt
Freshly ground black pepper
1 egg
150 ml/¹/₄ pt/²/₃ cup low-fat plain
    yoghurt
30 ml/2 tbsp grated strong low-fat
    Cheddar cheese

Boil the potatoes in a fairly large pan of water for 3 minutes. Add the aubergine and courgettes and continue to boil for about 3 minutes until all the vegetables are tender but still hold their shape. Drain. Put the beef, onion and garlic in a pan and fry (sauté) until the meat is no longer pink and all the grains are separate. Spoon off any fat, but leave the juices. Stir in the cinnamon and marjoram, the passata and tomato purée. Bring to the boil, reduce the heat and simmer for 30 minutes. Stir in the parsley, salt and a good grinding of pepper. Layer the vegetables and meat in an ovenproof dish, finishing with a layer of vegetables. Beat together the egg and yoghurt with a good grinding of pepper and pour over. Sprinkle with the cheese. Bake in a preheated oven at 190°C/375°F/ gas mark 5 for about 40 minutes until the top is set and golden brown.

* **350 calories per serving**
* **Medium fibre**

Dutch Monday Bake

SERVES 4

450 g/1 lb potatoes, sliced
40 g/1½ oz/3 tbsp low-fat sunflower
or olive oil spread
2 large onions, thinly sliced
225 g/8 oz/2 cups cooked beef, pork
or lamb, all fat removed, then
minced (ground)
300 ml/½ pt/1¼ cups beef or chicken
stock, made with 1 stock cube
A good pinch of ground cloves
2.5 ml/½ tsp dried mixed herbs
1 cooking (tart) apple, chopped
Salt and freshly ground black pepper
50 g/2 oz/1 cup fresh breadcrumbs
Fragrant Tomato and Onion Salad
(page 278), to serve

Cook the potatoes in boiling, lightly salted water for 3 minutes until almost tender. Drain. Heat 25 g/1 oz/ 2 tbsp of the low-fat spread in a flameproof casserole (Dutch oven), add the onions and fry (sauté) for 3 minutes, stirring. Add the meat, stock, cloves, herbs, apple and a little salt and pepper and simmer for 10 minutes. Add the potato, stir and cook for a further 20 minutes. Sprinkle with the breadcrumbs and dot with the remaining low-fat spread. Transfer to the oven preheated to 230°C/450°F/ gas mark 8 for 10 minutes until crisp and golden on top. Serve with Fragrant Tomato and Onion Salad.

* **300 calories per serving**
* **Medium fibre**

Chilli Meatballs

SERVES 4

350 g/12 oz extra-lean minced
(ground) beef
10 ml/2 tsp dried onion granules
2.5 ml/½ tsp chilli powder
5 ml/1 tsp ground cumin
15 ml/1 tbsp finely chopped coriander
(cilantro)
Salt and freshly ground black pepper
15 g/½ oz/1 tbsp low-fat sunflower or
olive oil spread, melted
15 ml/1 tbsp tomato ketchup (catsup)
10 ml/2 tsp white wine vinegar
5 ml/1 tsp clear honey
Pasta Salad with Bite (page 281), to
serve

Mix the beef with the onion granules and chilli powder, the cumin and coriander. Season with salt and pepper. Shape into 16 small balls. Thread on to four soaked wooden skewers, squeezing the meat firmly round the skewers. Whisk together the remaining ingredients for a baste. Grill (broil) the meatballs for about 12 minutes, brushing liberally with the baste and turning occasionally, until cooked through and golden. Serve with Pasta Salad with Bite.

* **195 calories per serving**
* **No fibre**

Keema Curry

SERVES 4

1 onion, finely chopped
1 garlic clove, crushed
450 g/1 lb extra-lean minced (ground)
    beef
5 ml/1 tsp ground ginger
5 ml/1 tsp chilli powder
5 ml/1 tsp ground cumin
5 ml/1 tsp turmeric
225 g/8 oz/1 small can of chopped
    tomatoes
30 ml/2 tbsp tomato purée (paste)
150 ml/¹/₄ pt/²/₃ cup beef stock, made
    with ¹/₂ stock cube
150 ml/¹/₄ pt/²/₃ cup low-fat plain
    yoghurt
Salt and freshly ground black pepper
15 ml/1 tbsp garam masala
Pilau Rice (page 266) and Asian
    Banana Salad (page 275), to serve

Put the onion, garlic and beef in a
large non-stick saucepan. Cook,
stirring, for about 5 minutes until the
meat is no longer pink and all the
grains are separate. Spoon off any fat
(there shouldn't be any if the meat was
extra-lean), but leave the juices. Stir in
the spices and cook for a further
1 minute. Add the remaining
ingredients except the garam masala.
Bring to the boil, stirring. Reduce the
heat, part-cover and simmer gently for
40 minutes. Remove the cover for the
last 10 minutes' cooking time to
evaporate the liquid. Stir in the garam
masala. Spoon on to a bed of Pilau
Rice and serve with Asian Banana
Salad.

* **245 calories per serving**
* **Low fibre**

Steak, Potato and Onion Kebabs

SERVES 4

16 baby potatoes, scrubbed but left
    whole
225 g/8 oz button (pearl) onions,
    peeled but left whole
450 g/1 lb rump steak, fat removed,
    cubed
25 g/1 oz/2 tbsp low-fat sunflower or
    olive oil spread, melted
Salt and freshly ground black pepper
5 ml/1 tsp dried mint
Cheesy Tomato and Spring Onion
    Salad (page 277), to serve

Cook the potatoes in boiling water
for about 2 minutes. Add the
onions and cook for 4 minutes until
the potatoes are just tender. Drain,
rinse with cold water and drain again.
Thread the steak, onions and potatoes
on soaked wooden skewers. Lay them
on a grill (broiler) rack and brush them
with the low-fat spread. Sprinkle with
salt, pepper and the mint. Grill (broil)
for about 10 minutes until golden and
cooked through, brushing with any
remaining spread during cooking.
Serve with Cheesy Tomato and Spring
Onion Salad.

* **340 calories per serving**
* **Fairly high fibre**

Beef and Mushroom Patties with Spiced Tomato Sauce

SERVES 4

1 onion, finely chopped
225 g/8 oz button mushrooms, finely chopped
45 ml/3 tbsp water
450 g/1 lb extra-lean minced (ground) beef
2.5 ml/½ tsp dried thyme
Salt and freshly ground black pepper
300 ml/½ pt/1¼ cups passata (sieved tomatoes)
2.5 ml/½ tsp chilli powder
2.5 ml/½ tsp caster (superfine) sugar
Worcestershire sauce, to taste
Extra-fluffed Mashed Potatoes (page 260) and peas, to serve.

Put the onion, mushrooms and water in a saucepan. Bring to the boil, cover, reduce the heat and simmer for 5 minutes. Remove the lid and boil rapidly, if necessary, to evaporate any remaining liquid, stirring all the time. Add the meat, thyme and some salt and pepper. Mix well and shape with the hands into eight patties. Place on foil under a preheated grill (broiler) and cook for 4 minutes on each side until brown and cooked through. Meanwhile, heat the passata in a saucepan with the chilli powder, sugar and Worcestershire sauce. Spoon the sauce on to four warmed plates. Top with the patties and serve with Extra-fluffed Mashed Potatoes and peas.

* **235 calories per serving**
* **Low fibre**

South American Steak

SERVES 4

1 green (bell) pepper, sliced into thin strips
1 red pepper, sliced into thin strips
1 onion, halved and sliced
8 stoned (pitted) black olives, halved
1 red chilli, seeded and chopped
60 ml/4 tbsp water
15 ml/1 tbsp tomato purée (paste)
Salt and freshly ground black pepper
10 g/¼ oz/2 tsp low-fat sunflower or olive oil spread
4 thin-cut sirloin steaks, trimmed of all fat
Sesame Seed Noodles (page 267) and Mixed Leaf Salad (page 278), to serve

Put the peppers, onion, olives and chilli in a saucepan with the water. Cover and cook gently for 15 minutes until soft. Stir in the tomato purée and season with a little salt and lots of pepper. Meanwhile, melt the low-fat spread in a non-stick frying pan (skillet) and fry (sauté) the steaks until cooked to your liking. Transfer to warm plates and spoon the pepper mixture on top. Serve hot with Sesame Seed Noodles and Mixed Leaf Salad.

* **275 calories per serving**
* **Medium fibre**

Country-style Fillet Steak

SERVES 4

4 large flat field mushrooms
60 ml/4 tbsp water
2 carrots
10 g/¼ oz/2 tsp low-fat sunflower or
olive oil spread
4 small fillet steaks, about 100 g/4 oz
each
Salt and freshly ground black pepper
60 ml/4 tbsp red wine
15 ml/1 tbsp tomato purée (paste)
A good pinch of caster (superfine) sugar
Parsley sprigs, to garnish
New potatoes and mangetout (snow
peas), to serve

Peel the mushrooms and remove the stalks. Place the caps in a frying pan (skillet) with the water, cover and simmer for 5 minutes or until tender. Pare the carrots into thin strips with a potato peeler. Cook in a little boiling, lightly salted water for 2 minutes until just tender. Drain and keep warm. Melt the low-fat spread in a non-stick frying pan and swirl round the base to coat. Add the steaks and a good grinding of pepper and fry (sauté) until golden brown on both sides and cooked to your liking – about 4 minutes for medium-rare, 6 minutes for well-done. Place the mushrooms on four warm plates. Top with the carrot shreds and put a steak on top of each. Keep warm. Pour any remaining mushroom liquid into the steak pan. Stir in the wine and tomato purée. Season with the sugar and a little salt and pepper. Bring to the boil, stirring until thickened. Spoon over the steaks and add a sprig of parsley to garnish. Serve with new potatoes and mangetout.

* **180 calories per serving**
* **Medium fibre**

Alpine Braised Steak

SERVES 4

1 red onion, thinly sliced
150 ml/¼ pt/⅔ cup water
1 garlic clove, crushed
450 g/1 lb lean braising steak,
trimmed of all fat, cubed
225 g/8 oz button mushrooms
400 g/14 oz/1 large can of chopped
tomatoes
30 ml/2 tbsp tomato purée (paste)
90 ml/6 tbsp water
Salt and freshly ground black pepper
Herby Jacket Bakes (page 261) and
broccoli, to serve

Simmer the onion in the water in a flameproof casserole dish (Dutch oven) for 5 minutes. Add the remaining ingredients and stir well. Bring to the boil, cover and place in a preheated oven at 160°C/325°F/gas mark 3 for 2–2½ hours until really tender. Serve with Herby Jacket Bakes and broccoli.

* **280 calories per serving**
* **Low fibre**

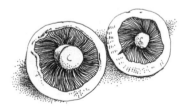

Beef and Vegetable Curry

SERVES 4

450 g/1 lb lean braising steak,
    trimmed of all fat, cubed
30 ml/2 tbsp plain (all-purpose) flour
30 ml/2 tbsp curry powder
Salt and freshly ground black pepper
30 ml/2 tbsp tomato purée (paste)
450 ml/³/₄ pt/2 cups beef or vegetable
    stock, made with 1 stock cube
1 onion, chopped
2 carrots, thinly sliced
100 g/4 oz French (green) beans, cut
    into thirds
2 potatoes, cut into chunks
¹/₂ small cauliflower, cut into florets
Lemon wedges and a little chopped
    coriander (cilantro), to garnish
Plain boiled rice and mango chutney,
    to serve

Toss the meat in the flour and curry powder. Place in a flameproof casserole dish (Dutch oven). Sprinkle with a little salt and pepper and add the tomato purée and stock. Bring to the boil, stirring. Cover, place in a preheated oven at 160°C/325°F/ gas mark 3 and cook for 2 hours. Add the vegetables and stir well. Return to the oven and cook for a further 1 hour until really tender. Spoon on to warm plates, garnish with lemon wedges and chopped coriander and serve with plain boiled rice and mango chutney.

* **230 calories per serving**
* **Fairly high fibre**

Chinese Beef Bowl

SERVES 4

100 g/4 oz Chinese thread noodles
15 g/¹/₂ oz/1 tbsp low-fat sunflower or
    olive oil spread
225 g/8 oz beef stir-fry meat
1 bunch of spring onions (scallions),
    cut into short lengths
1 red (bell) pepper, cut into thin strips
2 carrots, cut into thin matchsticks
5 cm/2 in piece of cucumber, cut into
    matchsticks
175 g/6 oz/3 cups beansprouts
1 garlic clove, crushed
5 ml/1 tsp grated fresh root ginger
15 ml/1 tbsp reduced-salt soy sauce
30 ml/2 tbsp dry sherry
10 ml/2 tsp clear honey

Cook the noodles according to the packet directions. Drain. Melt the low-fat spread in a large frying pan (skillet) or wok. Add the beef and stir-fry for 3 minutes. Add the onions, pepper strips and carrots and stir-fry for a further 3 minutes. Add the cucumber, beansprouts and garlic and stir-fry for 1 minute. Add the noodles and the remaining ingredients. Toss well, cover and cook for 2–3 minutes. Spoon into bowls and serve piping hot.

* **300 calories per serving**
* **Fairly high fibre**

Beef in Red Wine

SERVES 4

750 g/1¹/₂ lb lean braising steak,
    trimmed of all fat, cubed
30 ml/2 tbsp plain (all-purpose) flour
Salt and freshly ground black pepper
25 g/1 oz/2 tbsp low-fat sunflower or
    olive oil spread
1 large carrot, finely diced
12 button (pearl) onions, peeled but
    left whole
300 ml/¹/₂ pt/1¹/₄ cups red wine
300 ml/¹/₂ pt/1¹/₄ cups beef stock,
    made with 1 stock cube
15 ml/1 tbsp tomato purée (paste)
5 ml/1 tsp caster (superfine) sugar
1 bouquet garni sachet
100 g/4 oz small button mushrooms
Jacket-baked Potatoes with Yoghurt
    and Chives (page 260) and
    broccoli, to serve

Put the meat in a plastic bag with
the flour and a good sprinkling of
salt and pepper. Hold the bag shut and
shake it well. Heat the low-fat spread in
a flameproof casserole (Dutch oven).
Add the carrots and onions and fry
(sauté), stirring, for 2 minutes. Remove
from the pan. Add the beef and cook,
stirring, for about 3 minutes until
browned. Add the wine and stock and
bring to the boil, stirring. Stir in the
tomato purée and sugar, add the
bouquet garni and a little more salt
and pepper. Return the carrot and
onions to the pan and add the
mushrooms. Cover and transfer to the
oven, preheated to 160°C/325°F/gas
mark 3. Cook for 2½ hours until the
beef is tender and bathed in a rich
sauce. Stir well, remove the bouquet
garni, taste and adjust the seasoning.
Serve with Jacket-baked Potatoes with
Yoghurt and Chives and broccoli.

* **420 calories per serving**
* **Medium fibre**

Stir-fried Floret Beef

SERVES 4

225 g/8 oz fillet or lean rump steak,
    cut into very thin strips
2.5 ml/¹/₂ tsp salt
10 ml/2 tsp dry sherry
15 ml/1 tbsp cornflour (cornstarch)
2.5 ml/¹/₂ tsp ground ginger
25 g/1 oz/2 tbsp low-fat sunflower or
    olive oil spread
1 bunch of spring onions (scallions),
    cut into short lengths
¹/₂ small cauliflower, cut into tiny florets
175 g/8 oz broccoli, cut into tiny florets
30 ml/2 tbsp reduced-salt soy sauce
Chinese egg noodles, to serve

Put the beef in a shallow dish.
Sprinkle with salt, sherry, cornflour
and ginger. Toss well and leave to stand
for 30 minutes. Heat the low-fat spread
in a large frying pan (skillet) or wok.
Add the spring onions, cauliflower and
broccoli and stir-fry for 4 minutes. Add
the meat and cook, stirring, for a
further 4–5 minutes. Add the soy
sauce, toss well and serve with Chinese
egg noodles.

* **175 calories per serving**
* **Fairly high fibre**

Sharp Soy Pork

SERVES 4

Prepare as for Sharp Soy Lamb (page 188), but substitute pork tenderloin for the lamb and add 225 g/8 oz button mushrooms to the marinade. Put the mushrooms underneath the pork when roasting. Cook for 40 minutes until thoroughly cooked through.

* 320 calories per serving
* Low fibre

Greek Pork Casserole

SERVES 4

Prepare as for Athenian Beef Casserole (page 198), but substitute cubed pork for the beef and use dry white wine instead of red.

* 215 calories per serving
* Low fibre

Pork Stroganoff

SERVES 4

1 onion, thinly sliced
10 g/¹/₄ oz/2 tsp low-fat sunflower or olive oil spread
450 g/1 lb pork tenderloin, trimmed and cut into thin strips
100 g/4 oz button mushrooms, sliced
Freshly ground black pepper
30 ml/2 tbsp brandy
150 ml/¹/₄ pt/²/₃ cup low-fat crème fraîche
A pinch of salt
30 ml/2 tbsp chopped parsley
Plain boiled rice and Mixed Green Salad (page 279), to serve

Fry (sauté) the onion in the low-fat spread in a frying pan (skillet), stirring, for 3 minutes. Add the pork and continue to fry for 5 minutes, stirring, until the pork is tender and almost cooked through. Add the mushrooms, lots of pepper and the brandy. Ignite and shake the pan until the flames subside. Cover with a lid and cook gently for 5 minutes, stirring occasionally. Stir in the crème fraîche, salt and parsley and cook, stirring, for 2 minutes. Serve on a bed of rice with Mixed Green Salad.

* 280 calories per serving
* Low fibre

Pork with Prunes, Onions and Mushrooms

SERVES 4

12 button (pearl) onions, peeled but
    left whole
350 g/12 oz pork tenderloin, trimmed
    of any sinews and fat
10 g/¼ oz/2 tsp low-fat sunflower or
    olive oil spread
100 g/4 oz/⅔ cup ready-to-eat
    prunes, stoned (pitted)
100 g/4 oz button mushrooms
15 ml/1 tbsp dry sherry
200 ml/7 fl oz/scant 1 cup pork or
    vegetable stock, made with
    ½ stock cube
5 ml/1 tsp chopped sage
A pinch of salt
Freshly ground black pepper
10 ml/2 tsp cornflour (cornstarch)
15 ml/1 tbsp water
Sprigs of sage, to garnish
Plain boiled wild rice mix and Braised
    Cabbage with Celery (page 271), to
    serve

Boil the onions in enough water to cover for 4 minutes to soften. Drain. Cut the meat into 1 cm/½ in thick slices. Melt the low-fat spread in a non-stick frying pan (skillet) and brown the pork on both sides for 3 minutes. Remove from the pan with a draining spoon. Add the onions and brown all over. Add the prunes, mushrooms, sherry, stock and sage. Season with the salt and lots of pepper. Bring to the boil, cover the pan with a lid or foil and cook gently for 5 minutes. Return the pork to the pan and continue to simmer, uncovered, for a further 5 minutes. Remove the meat, prunes, onions and mushrooms with a draining spoon. Blend the cornflour with the water and stir into the juices in the pan. Bring to the boil and cook for 2 minutes, stirring. Return everything to the pan and toss gently to glaze. Spoon on to warm plates and garnish with sprigs of sage before serving with plain boiled wild rice mix and Braised Cabbage with Celery.

* **265 calories per serving**
* **Fairly high fibre**

Spiced Pork Kebabs

SERVES 4

Prepare as for Spiced Steak Kebabs (page 197), but substitute pork fillet for the steak and serve with Hot Chilli Salsa (page 383).

* **180 calories per serving**
* **Low fibre**

Pork Gumbo

SERVES 4

Prepare as for Chicken Gumbo (page 158), but substitute pork tenderloin for the chicken and add 200 g/7 oz/ 1 small can of naturally sweet sweetcorn (corn) to the mixture.

* **330 calories per serving**
* **Fairly high fibre**

Farmer's Beans

SERVES 4

225 g/8 oz/2 cups dried haricot (navy)
beans, soaked overnight in cold
water
450 ml/³/₄ pt/2 cups water
1 chicken stock cube
10 g/¹/₄ oz/2 tsp low-fat sunflower or
olive oil spread
225 g/8 oz lean shoulder pork, cubed
2 onions, thinly sliced
1 carrot, diced
1 turnip, diced
3 tomatoes, skinned and chopped
15 ml/1 tbsp black treacle (molasses)
2.5 ml/¹/₂ tsp dried thyme
Freshly ground black pepper
A pinch of salt
15 ml/1 tbsp chopped parsley, to
garnish

Drain the beans and place in a large flameproof casserole (Dutch oven). Cover with the water. Bring to the boil and boil rapidly for 10 minutes. Stir in the stock cube. Meanwhile, heat the low-fat spread in a non-stick frying pan (skillet). Fry (sauté) the meat and onions, stirring, for 3 minutes. Remove from the pan with a draining spoon. Add the meat and onions to the beans with all the remaining ingredients and bring back to the boil. Cover and place in a preheated oven at 150°C/300°F/gas mark 2 for 4 hours or until the beans are really tender and are bathed in a rich sauce. Sprinkle with the parsley and serve hot.

* 300 calories per serving
* High fibre

Larnaca Pork Kebabs

SERVES 4

Prepare as for Cypriot Lamb Kebabs (page 180), but substitute pork fillet for the lamb and thread a stoned (pitted) black olive on to the skewers after each piece of meat.

* 360 calories per serving
* Medium fibre

Barbecued Pork Steaks

SERVES 4

Prepare as for Barbecued Turkey Steaks (page 169), but substitute pork steaks for the turkey.

* 335 calories per serving
* No fibre

Pork, Apple and Vegetable Parcels

SERVES 4

Prepare as for Minted Lamb and Vegetable Parcels (page 179), but substitute pork tenderloin for the lamb fillet, add two sliced eating (dessert) apples, and use dried sage instead of the mint.

* 360 calories per serving
* Medium fibre

Pork Medallions with Juniper and Port

SERVES 4

Finely grated rind and juice of ½ lemon
12 juniper berries, crushed
5 ml/1 tsp coarsely ground black
    peppercorns
350 g/12 oz pork fillet, cut into
    12 slices
15 g/½ oz/1 tbsp low-fat sunflower or
    olive oil spread
1 shallot, finely chopped
10 ml/2 tsp chopped sage
100 ml/3½ fl oz/scant ½ cup port
75 ml/5 tbsp water
½ chicken stock cube, crumbled
Small sprigs of sage, to garnish
Savoury Potato Cake (page 258) and
    broccoli, to serve

Mix the lemon rind and juice with the juniper berries and peppercorns. Put the pork slices in a plastic bag and beat with a rolling pin or meat mallet to flatten slightly. Coat with the juniper mixture. Heat the low-fat spread in a large non-stick frying pan (skillet), and fry (sauté) the pork for 2–3 minutes on each side until cooked through. Transfer with a draining spoon to a warm serving dish. Add the shallot and sage to the pan and fry for 1 minute. Add the port, water and stock cube and cook, stirring, until slightly thickened. Spoon over the pork and garnish with small sprigs of sage. Serve with Savoury Potato Cake and broccoli.

* **300 calories per serving**
* **Low fibre**

Barbecued Pork with Chilli and Cumin

SERVES 4

10 ml/2 tsp cumin seeds, coarsely
    crushed
15 ml/1 tbsp olive oil
15 ml/1 tbsp balsamic vinegar
30 ml/2 tbsp reduced-salt soy sauce
90 ml/6 tbsp dry white wine
1 small red chilli, seeded and finely
    chopped
450 g/1 lb pork tenderloin, trimmed of
    any fat or sinews
Curly endive (frisée lettuce) and Low-
    fat French Dressing (page 380), to
    garnish
Warm Potato Salad (page 279), to
    serve

Whisk together the cumin, oil, vinegar, soy sauce, wine and chilli in a shallow dish. Add the pork and turn to coat completely. Cover and chill overnight, turning occasionally. Remove from the marinade and grill (broil), turning occasionally, for about 25 minutes until golden and the meat gives easily when a skewer is inserted into the thickest part. Wrap in foil and leave to rest for 5 minutes. Slice thickly, lay on warm plates and garnish with curly endive, dressed with a little Low-fat French Dressing. Serve with Warm Potato Salad.

* **325 calories per serving**
* **Low fibre**

Liver and Onion Hotpot

SERVES 4

*450 g/1 lb pigs' liver, cut into bite-
  sized pieces*
30 ml/2 tbsp skimmed milk
*25 g/1 oz/2 tbsp low-fat sunflower or
  olive oil spread*
2 large onions, thinly sliced
1 large carrot, coarsely grated
1 cooking (tart) apple, sliced
30 ml/2 tbsp plain (all-purpose) flour
*300 ml/¹/₂ pt/1¹/₄ cups pork or chicken
  stock, made with 1 stock cube*
*150 ml/¹/₄ pt/²/₃ cup cider or apple
  juice*
5 ml/1 tsp dried sage
Salt and freshly ground black pepper
450 g/1 lb potatoes, thinly sliced
*Quick-cooked Cabbage (page 270), to
  serve*

Put the liver in a shallow dish and
add the milk. Toss and leave to
soak for 15 minutes, then drain.
Meanwhile, heat 20 g/³/₄ oz/1¹/₂ tbsp of
the low-fat spread in a flameproof
casserole dish (Dutch oven). Add the
onions and carrot and fry (sauté) for
3 minutes, stirring. Add the liver and
continue to fry quickly until browned
all over. Stir in the apple and flour.
Remove from the heat and blend in the
stock and cider or apple juice. Return
to the heat and bring to the boil,
stirring. Sprinkle in the sage and a little
salt and pepper to taste. Layer the
potato slices over the top and dot with
the remaining low-fat spread. Cover
with a lid or foil and bake in a
preheated oven at 190°C/375°F/gas
mark 5 for 30 minutes. Remove the lid
or foil and return to the oven for a
further 30 minutes until the potatoes
are turning golden. Serve with Quick-
cooked Cabbage.

* **395 calories per serving**
* **Medium fibre**

Pork Liver and Sage Risotto

SERVES 4

Prepare as for Chicken Liver Risotto
(page 152), but substitute pigs'
liver, cut into very small pieces, for the
chicken livers and use sage instead of
parsley. Garnish with a sliced red
eating (dessert) apple.

* **400 calories per serving**
* **Medium fibre**

Pork Teriyaki Kebabs

SERVES 4

Prepare as for Chicken Teriyaki
Kebabs (page 148), but substitute
pork fillet, cubed, for the chicken.

* **200 calories per serving**
* **Low fibre**

Peachy Pork Casserole

SERVES 4

1 onion, finely chopped
1 large leek, chopped
25 g/1 oz/2 tbsp low-fat sunflower or
olive oil spread
750 g/1½ lb stewing pork, trimmed of
all fat and cubed
30 ml/2 tbsp plain (all-purpose) flour
Salt and freshly ground black pepper
300 ml/½ pt/1¼ cups dry white wine
1 chicken or pork stock cube
75 g/3 oz/½ cup dried peaches,
chopped
1 bouquet garni sachet
Herby Jacket Bakes (page 261) and
broccoli, to serve

Fry (sauté) the onion and leek in the low-fat spread in a flameproof casserole dish (Dutch oven) for 3 minutes, stirring. Add the pork and fry for a further 2 minutes, stirring. Sprinkle in the flour and some salt and pepper. Remove from the heat and blend in the wine. Crumble in the stock cube. Return to the heat and bring to the boil, stirring. Scatter in the peaches and add the bouquet garni sachet. Cover and cook in a preheated oven at 160°C/325°F/ gas mark 3 for 2 hours or until really tender. Taste and re-season, if necessary. Remove the bouquet garni and serve with Herby Jacket Bakes and broccoli.

* **405 calories per serving**
* **Medium fibre**

Pork with Plenty

SERVES 4

750 g/1½ lb stewing pork, trimmed of
all fat, cubed
15 g/½ oz/1 tbsp low-fat sunflower or
olive oil spread
1 Spanish onion, thinly sliced
1 large garlic clove, crushed
1 green (bell) pepper, sliced
400 g/14 oz/1 large can of chick peas
(garbanzos), drained
400 g/14 oz/1 large can of chopped
tomatoes
300 ml/½ pt/1¼ cups red wine
5 ml/1 tsp dried oregano
5 ml/1 tsp dried thyme
Salt and freshly ground black pepper
4 large courgettes (zucchini), sliced
Crusty bread, to serve

Fry (sauté) the pork in the low-fat spread with the onion in a large saucepan for 3 minutes, stirring. Add the remaining ingredients except the courgettes. Bring to the boil, reduce the heat, cover and cook over a very low heat for 2 hours, stirring occasionally. Meanwhile, cook the courgettes in boiling water for 2 minutes. Drain, rinse with cold water and drain again. Add to the saucepan and cook for a further 5 minutes. Serve hot with crusty bread.

* **475 calories per serving**
* **High fibre**

Savoury Chunky Pork Loaf

SERVES 6

450 g/1 lb pigs' liver, cut into small cubes
225 g/8 oz lean minced (ground) pork
2 onions, finely chopped
5 ml/1 tsp dried sage
Salt and freshly ground black pepper
175 g/6 oz/3 cups fresh breadcrumbs
1 egg, beaten
Brown Onion Salsa (page 386), Jacket-baked Potatoes with Yoghurt and Chives (page 260) and peas, to serve

Mix together all the ingredients and turn into a non-stick 900 g/2 lb loaf tin (pan), base-lined with non-stick baking parchment. Cover with foil and bake in a preheated oven at 190°C/375°F/ gas mark 5 for 1½ hours. Cool for 5 minutes, then turn out, remove the paper and serve sliced with Brown Onion Salsa, Jacket-baked Potatoes with Yoghurt and Chives and peas.

* **260 calories per serving**
* **Medium fibre**

Orange Glazed Pork

SERVES 4

Prepare as for Lemon-glazed Lamb (page 181), but substitute pork fillet for the lamb, the finely grated rind and juice of 1 small orange for the lemon, and sharpen with 5 ml/1 tsp lemon juice before seasoning the sauce.

* **265 calories per serving**
* **Low fibre**

Pork Crumble

SERVES 4

4 thin pork steaks, all fat removed
295 g/10½ oz/1 medium can of low-fat condensed celery soup
15 ml/1 tbsp lemon juice
30 ml/2 tbsp water
Freshly ground black pepper
85 g/3½ oz/1 small packet of sage and onion stuffing mix
2 tomatoes, sliced
Shredded Cabbage Salad (page 281), to serve

Put the pork steaks one at a time in a plastic bag and beat with a rolling pin or meat mallet to flatten slightly. Quickly brown on both sides in a non-stick frying pan (skillet). Mix the soup with the lemon juice and water and pour over the pork. Add a good grinding of pepper. Cover with a lid and simmer gently for 15 minutes until the pork is tender and cooked through. Meanwhile, make up the stuffing mix with enough boiling water to form a moist crumble and scatter over the surface. Arrange the tomato slices round the edge. Place the pan under a preheated moderate grill (broiler) and cook for about 10 minutes until crisp and golden. Serve with Shredded Cabbage Salad.

* **280 calories per serving**
* **Medium fibre**

Sweet Spiced Pork with Mint

SERVES 4

25 g/1 oz/2 tbsp low-fat sunflower or olive oil spread
45 ml/3 tbsp chopped mint
2.5 ml/¹/₂ tsp ground cinnamon
2.5 ml/¹/₂ tsp grated nutmeg
15 ml/1 tbsp lemon juice
10 ml/2 tsp caster (superfine) sugar
4 lean loin pork chops, trimmed of any fat
1 lemon, sliced and sprigs of parsley, to garnish
Perfect Brown Rice (page 265) and English Mixed Salad (page 276), to serve

Mash the low-fat spread with the mint, spices, lemon juice and sugar. Spread all over the pork. Place on foil on a grill (broiler) rack and grill (broil) for 6 minutes on each side or until golden brown and cooked through. Garnish with lemon slices and sprigs of parsley and serve with Perfect Brown Rice and English Mixed Salad.

* **255 calories per serving**
* **Low fibre**

Sweet and Sour Pork

SERVES 4

Prepare as for Sweet and Sour Chicken (page 161), but substitute thin strips of pork tenderloin for the chicken and serve on a bed of Fried Rice (page 265).

* **400 calories per serving**
* **Medium fibre**

Tyrolean Pork

SERVES 4

4 lean pork steaks, trimmed of all fat
15 g/¹/₂ oz/1 tbsp low-fat sunflower or olive oil spread
1 onion, finely chopped
1 garlic clove, crushed
1 small white cabbage, finely shredded
15 ml/1 tbsp caraway seeds
Salt and freshly ground black pepper
300 ml/¹/₂ pt/1¹/₄ cups pork or chicken stock, made with 1 stock cube
2 large potatoes, thinly sliced

Brown the pork in the low-fat spread in a flameproof casserole dish (Dutch oven). Remove from the pan. Add the onion and garlic and fry (sauté), stirring, for 1 minute. Add the garlic and cabbage and cook, stirring, for 2 minutes until the cabbage begins to soften slightly. Sprinkle with the caraway seeds and a little salt and pepper. Return the pork to the pan and top with the potato slices. Pour over the stock and season lightly again with salt and pepper. Cover with a lid or foil and bake in a preheated oven at 160°C/325°F/gas mark 3 for 1½ hours. Remove the lid, turn up the heat to 190°C/375°F/gas mark 5 and cook for a further 30 minutes until the potatoes are browning. Serve hot.

* **370 calories per serving**
* **Fairly high fibre**

Yan-ton Fried Rice

SERVES 4

100 g/4 oz/½ cup long-grain rice
2 carrots, diced
25 g/1 oz/2 tbsp low-fat sunflower or
  olive oil spread
100 g/4 oz peeled prawns (shrimp)
225 g/8 oz/2 cups lean cooked pork,
  diced
225 g/8 oz/1 small can of bamboo
  shoots, drained and diced
100 g/4 oz frozen peas
60 ml/4 tbsp boiling water
¼ vegetable stock cube
30 ml/2 tbsp dry sherry
15 ml/1 tbsp reduced-salt soy sauce
Salt and freshly ground black pepper
1 egg

Cook the rice and carrots in plenty of boiling, salted water for about 10–12 minutes until the rice is just tender. Drain, rinse with cold water and drain again. Meanwhile, heat the low-fat spread in a frying pan (skillet). Add the rice, carrots, prawns, pork, bamboo shoots and peas and cook, tossing and stirring, for 5 minutes until piping hot. Mix together the water and stock cube until dissolved. Add to the pan with the sherry, soy sauce and a little salt and pepper. Push the mixture to one side of the pan. Beat the egg and pour in. Cook, stirring, until scrambled, then toss into the rice. Pile on to warm plates and serve piping hot.

* **225 calories per serving**
* **Fairly high fibre**

Sweet Barbecued Pork

SERVES 4

15 ml/1 tbsp lemon juice
15 ml/1 tbsp red wine vinegar
30 ml/2 tbsp tomato purée (paste)
15 ml/1 tbsp Worcestershire sauce
30 ml/2 tbsp clear honey
Freshly ground black pepper
4 lean pork chops, all fat removed
Savoury Vegetable Rice (page 264), to
  serve

Mix together the lemon juice, vinegar, tomato purée, Worcestershire sauce, honey and a good grinding of pepper. Lay the pork on foil on a grill (broiler) rack and brush liberally on both sides with the barbecue sauce. Grill (broil) for about 15 minutes, turning and brushing occasionally with the sauce, until cooked through and stickily glazed. Serve with Savoury Vegetable Rice.

* **260 calories per serving**
* **Low fibre**

Pork and Artichoke Stroganoff

SERVES 4

225 g/8 oz ribbon noodles
2 onions, thinly sliced
25 g/1 oz/2 tbsp low-fat sunflower or
  olive oil spread
350 g/12 oz pork fillet, cut into thin
  strips
425 g/15 oz/1 large can of artichoke
  bottoms, drained and sliced
30 ml/2 tbsp brandy
150 ml/¼ pt/⅔ cup low-fat crème
  fraîche
30 ml/2 tbsp chopped parsley
Salt and freshly ground black pepper
Flat Bean Salad (page 275), to serve

Cook the noodles according to the packet directions. Drain. Meanwhile, fry (sauté) the onions in the low-fat spread for 2 minutes to soften. Add the pork and continue cooking for 6–8 minutes until tender and cooked through. Add the artichokes and toss for 1 minute. Pour in the brandy, ignite and shake the pan until the flames subside. Stir in the crème fraîche and parsley and season to taste. Let the mixture bubble for 1 minute, then spoon over the noodles and serve with Flat Bean Salad.

* **380 calories per serving**
* **Medium fibre**

Creamy Ham and Pea Ribbons

SERVES 4

250 g/9 oz pappardelle (wide ribbon
  noodles)
1 onion, finely chopped
25 g/1 oz/2 tbsp low-fat sunflower or
  olive oil spread
100 g/4 oz/1 cup lean sweet-cured
  ham, finely diced
100 g/4 oz frozen peas
5 ml/1 tsp dried mint
150 ml/¼ pt/⅔ cup low-fat crème
  fraîche
Freshly ground black pepper
Mixed Green Salad (page 279), to
  serve

Cook the pasta in boiling, salted water according to the packet directions. Drain and return to the saucepan. Meanwhile, cook the onion in the low-fat spread in a small saucepan for 2 minutes, stirring. Add the ham, peas and mint. Cover and cook very gently for 8 minutes, stirring occasionally. Add to the cooked noodles with the crème fraîche and a good grinding of pepper. Toss over a low heat, then serve with Mixed Green Salad.

* **340 calories per serving**
* **Fairly high fibre**

Pork Steaks Carbonnade

SERVES 4

4 pork steaks, trimmed of any fat
2 large onions, thinly sliced
1 bay leaf
300 ml/¹/₂ pt/1¹/₄ cups light ale
Salt and freshly ground black pepper
45 ml/3 tbsp black treacle (molasses)
10 ml/2 tsp lemon juice
15 g/¹/₂ oz/1 tbsp low-fat sunflower or
olive oil spread
4 slices of French bread
20 ml/4 tsp wholegrain mustard
Sprigs of parsley, to garnish
Plain boiled potatoes and baby carrots,
to serve

Put the pork in a shallow dish, cover with the onion slices and add the bay leaf. Mix the ale with a little salt and pepper, the treacle and lemon juice. Pour over the pork and leave to marinate for at least 3 hours. Lift the pork out of the marinade and place on a grill (broiler) rack. Dot with half the low-fat spread. Grill (broil) for 6–8 minutes on each side until golden brown and cooked through. Meanwhile, pour the marinade, including the onions and bay leaf, into a saucepan. Bring to the boil and boil rapidly until thickened and the onions are soft. Taste and re-season, if necessary. Discard the bay leaf. Toast the bread slices in a toaster or under the grill with the pork. Mash the remaining low-fat spread with the mustard and spread on the toasted bread. Transfer the pork to warm plates, spoon the hot onion marinade over and top with the mustard bread. Garnish with sprigs of parsley and serve with plain boiled potatoes and baby carrots.

* **250 calories per serving**
* **Medium fibre**

Parma Ham and Pea Strands

SERVES 4

Prepare as for Creamy Ham and Pea Ribbons (page 223), but substitute vermicelli for the pappardelle and Parma ham, all fat removed, for the sweet-cured ham.

* **360 calories per serving**
* **Fairly high fibre**

Pork Satay

SERVES 4

Prepare as for Simple Turkey Satay (page 170), but substitute pork fillet for the turkey and add 2.5 ml/¹/₂ tsp ground cardamom to the marinade.

* **335 calories per serving**
* **Low fibre**

Photograph opposite: Pork
Medallions with Juniper and Port
(page 217)

Sausage and Barley Supper

SERVES 4

8 extra-lean pork sausages, cut into
    bite-sized pieces
1 onion, sliced
4 large carrots, sliced
2 large leeks, sliced
1 parsnip, finely chopped
100 g/4 oz/generous ½ cup pearl
    barley
Salt and freshly ground black pepper
450 ml/¾ pt/2 cups chicken stock,
    made with 1 stock cube
5 ml/1 tsp dried thyme
1 bay leaf
Crusty bread, to serve

Brown the sausages in a non-stick frying pan (skillet). Remove from the pan with a draining spoon and drain on kitchen paper (paper towels). Add the onion to the pan and fry (sauté) for 2 minutes, stirring. Remove from the pan with a draining spoon and drain on kitchen paper. Put all the ingredients, including the sausages and onion, in a flameproof casserole dish (Dutch oven). Bring to the boil, cover and cook in a preheated oven at 160°C/325°F/gas mark 3 for 2½ hours. Taste and re-season, if necessary. Discard the bay leaf and serve hot with crusty bread.

* **390 calories per serving**
* **High fibre**

Pork Brochettes

SERVES 4

60 ml/4 tbsp medium-dry sherry
60 ml/4 tbsp reduced-salt soy sauce
45 ml/3 tbsp clear honey
5 ml/1 tsp grated fresh root ginger
100 ml/3½ fl oz/scant ½ cup pure
    orange juice
350 g/12 oz pork tenderloin, cut into
    16 cubes
1 green (bell) pepper, cut into large
    dice
1 red pepper, cut into large dice
Wild Rice Salad (page 283), to serve

Put the sherry, soy sauce, honey, ginger and orange juice in a shallow dish and whisk well. Add the pork cubes, turn to coat completely, then cover and chill for several hours or overnight. Thread on to skewers with the peppers. Grill (broil), turning frequently and basting with the marinade, for about 10 minutes or until cooked through and golden. Serve with Wild Rice Salad.

* **205 calories per serving**
* **Medium fibre**

Photograph opposite: Mixed
Vegetable Curry (page 254)

Pork Chops in Red Wine

SERVES 4

25 g/1 oz/2 tbsp low-fat sunflower or
  olive oil spread
2 onions, thinly sliced
2 large carrots, thinly sliced
2 courgettes (zucchini), thinly sliced
4 loin pork chops, trimmed of all fat
150 ml/¼ pt/⅔ cup red wine
150 ml/¼ pt/⅔ cup pork or chicken
  stock, made with ½ stock cube
Salt and freshly ground black pepper
1 bouquet garni sachet
15 ml/1 tbsp redcurrant jelly (clear
  conserve)
15 ml/1 tbsp cornflour (cornstarch)
15 ml/1 tbsp water
Chopped parsley, to garnish
New potatoes and Cauliflower Cheese
  (page 235), to serve

Melt the low-fat spread in a flameproof casserole (Dutch oven). Add the onions, carrots and courgettes and fry (sauté) for 2 minutes, stirring. Remove from the pan with a draining spoon. Add the chops to the pan and brown on both sides. Return the vegetables on top of the pork. Pour in the wine, stock, a little salt and pepper and the bouquet garni sachet. Bring to the boil, cover and transfer to a preheated oven at 200°C/400°F/gas mark 6 for about 40 minutes or until the pork and vegetables are tender. Lift the pork and vegetables out of the casserole with a draining spoon and keep warm. Discard the bouquet garni. Stir in the redcurrant jelly until dissolved. Blend the cornflour with the water and a little of the cooking liquid. Return to the pan, bring to the boil and cook for 1 minute, stirring, until thickened. Taste and re-season, if necessary. Return the chops and vegetables to the casserole. Garnish with parsley and serve with new potatoes and Cauliflower Cheese.

* 310 calories per serving
* Medium fibre

Glazed Nutty Pork

SERVES 4

4 lean pork chops, trimmed of any fat
10 ml/2 tsp made English mustard
15 ml/1 tbsp clear honey
15 ml/1 tbsp raw peanuts, chopped
5 ml/1 tsp Worcestershire sauce
2.5 ml/½ tsp salt
Freshly ground black pepper
5 ml/1 tsp melted low-fat sunflower or
  olive oil spread
Braised Cabbage with Celery (page
  271) and baby new potatoes, to
  serve

Grill (broil) the chops for 5 minutes on each side until nearly cooked. Mix together the remaining ingredients and spread over the chops. Grill until golden brown and bubbling. Transfer to warm plates and serve with Braised Cabbage with Celery and baby new potatoes.

* 220 calories per serving
* Low fibre

Vegetable-based Main Meals

All the vegetable dishes in this section are suitable for vegetarians. But if you are usually a meat-eater don't think you should avoid them – they are tempting, filling and delicious for everyone.

Golden Cheese and Chive Bake

SERVES 4

15 g/½ oz/1 tbsp low-fat sunflower or
  olive oil spread
2 eggs, separated
300 ml/½ pt/1¼ cups skimmed milk
75 g/3 oz/1½ cups fresh breadcrumbs
100 g/4 oz/1 cup low-fat Cheddar
  cheese, grated
30 ml/2 tbsp snipped chives
Salt and freshly ground black pepper
Blushing Leaf Salad (page 276), to
  serve

Grease a 1.2 litre/2 pt/5 cup ovenproof dish with the low-fat spread. Beat the egg yolks with the milk and stir in the breadcrumbs, cheese, chives and a little salt and pepper. Whisk the egg whites until stiff, then fold into the cheese mixture with a metal spoon. Turn into the prepared dish. Bake in a preheated oven at 200°C/400°F/ gas mark 6 for about 35 minutes until risen and a rich golden brown. Serve straight away with Blushing Leaf Salad.

* 220 calories per serving
* Medium fibre

Blue Cheese and Celery Bake

SERVES 4

Prepare as for Golden Cheese and Chive Bake, but substitute crumbled low-fat blue cheese for the Cheddar, omit the chives and add a finely chopped celery stick to the mixture before folding in the egg whites.

* 220 calories per serving
* Medium fibre

Tomato, Chick Pea and Potato Bake

SERVES 4

450 g/1 lb potatoes, cut into chunks
425 g/15 oz/1 large can of chick peas
  (garbanzos), drained
400 g/14 oz/1 large can of chopped
  tomatoes
2.5 ml/½ tsp dried basil
25 g/1 oz/½ cup fresh breadcrumbs
50 g/2 oz/½ cup low-fat Cheddar
  cheese, grated
Neapolitan Salad (page 286), to serve

Cook the potatoes in boiling, salted water for about 10 minutes until tender. Drain and arrange in an ovenproof dish. Add the chick peas and tomatoes and sprinkle with the basil. Mix together the breadcrumbs and cheese and sprinkle over. Bake in a preheated oven at 190°C/375°F /gas mark 5 for 25 minutes until golden and bubbling. Serve with Neapolitan Salad.

* 310 calories per serving
* High fibre

Potato Gnocchi with Tomato and Basil Sauce

SERVES 4

450 g/1 lb potatoes, cut into small
  pieces
Salt and freshly ground black pepper
1.5 ml/¹/₄ tsp grated nutmeg
100 g/4 oz/1 cup plain (all-purpose)
  flour
1 egg, beaten
10 g/¹/₄ oz/2 tsp low-fat sunflower or
  olive oil spread, melted
300 ml/¹/₂ pt/1¹/₄ cups passata (sieved
  tomatoes)
15 ml/1 tbsp chopped basil
Garlic salt
30 ml/2 tbsp finely grated low-fat
  Cheddar cheese
Dressed Green Salad (page 275), to
  serve

Boil the potatoes in lightly salted water for 10 minutes or until tender. Drain thoroughly, mash, then pass through a coarse sieve (strainer) into a bowl. Add a little salt and pepper, the nutmeg, and flour. Mix well. Add the beaten egg and mix to form a firm dough. Turn out on to a lightly floured surface and knead gently. Shape into 24 balls. Brush a shallow serving dish with a little of the low-fat spread. Bring a large pan of water to the boil. Add the gnocchi a few at a time and cook for 5 minutes. They will rise to the surface when cooked. Remove from the pan with a draining spoon and place in the dish. Keep warm while cooking the remainder. Meanwhile, heat the passata with the basil and season to taste with garlic salt and pepper. When all the gnocchi are cooked and in the dish, drizzle with the remaining low-fat spread. Pour the warm passata over and sprinkle with the cheese. Serve straight away with Dressed Green Salad.

* **265 calories per serving**
* **Medium fibre**

Tortilla

SERVES 2

1 large potato, thinly sliced
1 small onion, grated
15 g/¹/₂ oz/1 tbsp low-fat sunflower or
  olive oil spread
4 eggs, beaten
Salt and freshly ground black pepper
Parsley, to garnish
Dressed Green Salad (page 275), to
  serve

Put the potato and onion in a frying pan (skillet) with the low-fat spread. Cook gently, stirring, for 5 minutes until the potato is cooked but not brown. Beat the eggs with a little salt and pepper and add to the pan. Cook gently, lifting and stirring, until the egg is almost set. Place under a hot grill (broiler) to brown and set the top. Serve hot or cold, cut into wedges.

* **300 calories per serving**
* **Medium fibre**

Cottage Cheese and Chive Soufflé Omelette

SERVES 2

2 eggs, separated
30 ml/2 tbsp water
Salt and freshly ground black pepper
100 g/4 oz/½ cup low-fat cottage
  cheese with chives
4 egg whites
10 ml/2 tsp low-fat sunflower or olive
  oil spread
A few chives, to garnish (optional)
English Mixed Salad (page 276), to
  serve

Beat the egg yolks with the water and a little salt and pepper. Stir in the cottage cheese. Whisk all the egg whites until stiff and fold into the cheese mixture with a metal spoon. Melt the low-fat spread in an omelette pan. Add the egg mixture and cook until the base is golden and the mixture is almost set. Place the pan under a hot grill (broiler) and cook until the omelette is fluffy and golden. Cut in half, then slide out on to warm plates. Garnish with a few chives, if liked, and serve with English Mixed Salad.

* **180 calories per serving**
* **Low fibre**

Crunchy Cottage Cheese and Vegetable Omelette

SERVES 2

2 eggs, separated
30 ml/2 tbsp water
Salt and freshly ground black pepper
100 g/4 oz/½ cup low-fat cottage
  cheese with chives
1 small red (bell) pepper, finely
  chopped
1 celery stick, finely chopped
4 egg whites
10 ml/2 tsp low-fat sunflower or olive
  oil spread
Chopped parsley, to garnish
Dressed Green Salad (page 275), to
  serve

Beat the egg yolks with the water and a little salt and pepper. Stir in the cheese, half the chopped pepper and all the celery. Whisk all the egg whites until stiff and fold into the cheese mixture with a metal spoon. Melt the low-fat spread in an omelette pan. Add the egg mixture and cook until golden underneath and almost set. Place the pan under a hot grill (broiler) until risen and golden. Cut in half, then slide out on to warm plates. Scatter the remaining red pepper over with the parsley and serve with Dressed Green Salad.

* **170 calories per serving**
* **Medium fibre**

Pan Haggerty

SERVES 4

25 g/1 oz/2 tbsp low-fat sunflower or olive oil spread
450 g/1 lb potatoes, very thinly sliced
2 onions, thinly sliced
100 g/4 oz/1 cup low-fat Cheddar cheese, grated
Salt and freshly ground black pepper
Fragrant Tomato and Onion Salad (page 278), to serve

Melt the low-fat spread in a frying pan (skillet). Add a layer of half the potatoes and onions, then half the cheese. Season well. Repeat the layers. Cover the pan with foil or a lid and cook over a gentle heat for about 30 minutes or until the potatoes and onions are tender. Remove the foil or lid, then place the pan under a hot grill (broiler) until the cheese is golden and bubbling. Serve cut into wedges with a Fragrant Tomato and Onion Salad.

* **215 calories per serving**
* **Medium fibre**

Ritzy Stuffed Peppers

SERVES 4

100 g/4 oz/½ cup long-grain rice
50 g/2 oz frozen peas
4 large green (bell) peppers
2.5 ml/½ tsp made English mustard
150 ml/¼ pt/⅔ cup low-fat crème fraîche
Salt and freshly ground black pepper
75 g/3 oz/¾ cup strong low-fat Cheddar cheese, grated
60 ml/4 tbsp water
Baked Tomatoes with Herbs (page 274), to serve

Boil the rice in plenty of lightly salted water for about 10 minutes or until just tender, adding the peas after 5 minutes. Drain, rinse with cold water and drain again. Meanwhile, cut the tops off the peppers. Remove the cores and seeds. Trim the bases, if necessary, so they will stand upright, but take care not to make a hole. Boil in lightly salted water for 2 minutes. Drain well on kitchen paper (paper towels). Mix the rice with the mustard, crème fraîche, a little salt and pepper and the cheese. Pack into the peppers. Stand the peppers in a roasting tin (pan), add the water and cover with foil. Bake in a preheated oven at 180°C/350°F/gas mark 4 for 15 minutes. Remove the foil and cook for a further 5 minutes to lightly brown the tops. Serve hot with Baked Tomatoes with Herbs.

* **265 calories per serving**
* **Fairly high fibre**

Corn and Potato Pudding

SERVES 4

A small knob of low-fat sunflower or
olive oil spread, for greasing
320 g/12 oz/1 medium can of
sweetcorn (corn) with (bell)
peppers, drained
750 g/1½ lb potatoes, peeled and
grated
1 egg, beaten
Salt and freshly ground black pepper
30 ml/2 tbsp chopped parsley
1 green (bell) pepper, thinly sliced into
rings
1 red pepper, thinly sliced into rings
Dressed Green Salad (page 275), to
serve

Grease an ovenproof dish with the
spread. Empty the corn into the
dish. Mix together the potatoes, egg,
some salt and pepper and the parsley.
Spoon over the sweetcorn and arrange
the pepper rings attractively on top.
Bake in a preheated oven at
180°C/350°F/ gas mark 4 for 1 hour
until cooked through and golden on
the top. Serve with Dressed Green
Salad.

* **250 calories per serving**
* **Fairly high fibre**

Pappardelle with Mixed Mushrooms, Garlic and Herbs

SERVES 4

250 g/9 oz pappardelle
100 g/4 oz button mushrooms, sliced
100 g/4 oz oyster mushrooms, sliced
45 ml/3 tbsp water
50 g/2 oz/¼ cup low-fat sunflower or
olive oil spread
1 garlic clove, crushed
15 ml/1 tbsp chopped parsley
15 ml/1 tbsp snipped chives
Salt and freshly ground black pepper
45 ml/3 tbsp finely grated low-fat
Cheddar cheese

Cook the pasta according to the
packet directions. Drain. Cook the
mushrooms in the water in a covered
pan for 4 minutes. Remove the lid and
boil until the liquid has evaporated,
stirring all the time. Add the low-fat
spread and garlic and cook, stirring,
for 1 minute. Add the pasta, herbs, a
little salt and lots of pepper and toss
together well. Pile on to plates and
sprinkle each portion with a little of the
cheese.

* **305 calories per serving**
* **Medium fibre**

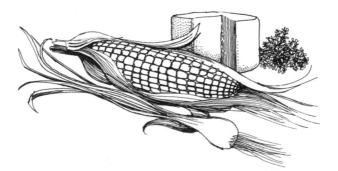

Oven Omelette Wedges

SERVES 4

A small knob of low-fat sunflower or
  olive oil spread
4 eggs, beaten
250 g/9 oz/generous 1 cup low-fat
  cottage cheese
150 ml/¹/₄ pt/²/₃ cup skimmed milk
Salt and freshly ground black pepper
100 g/4 oz button mushrooms, sliced
2 spring onions (scallions), finely
  chopped
A pinch of dried thyme
2 tomatoes, sliced, and sprigs of
  parsley, to garnish

Lightly grease a shallow baking dish
with the low-fat spread. Mix
together all the remaining ingredients
in a bowl and pour into the dish. Bake
in a preheated oven at 200°C/400°F/
gas mark 6 for 20 minutes until golden
brown and firm to the touch. Serve cut
into wedges, garnished with the
tomato slices and sprigs of parsley.

* 160 calories per serving
* Low fibre

Spicy Potato Cakes

SERVES 2

225 g/8 oz potatoes, grated
1 small onion, grated
2.5 ml/¹/₂ tsp garam masala
1.5 ml/¹/₄ tsp chilli powder
1 egg, beaten
5 ml/1 tsp plain (all-purpose) flour
Salt and freshly ground black pepper
25 g/1 oz/2 tbsp low-fat sunflower or
  olive oil spread
Green Pepper and Onion Salad (page
  276), to serve

Mix all the ingredients except the
low-fat spread in a bowl. Melt the
low-fat spread in a frying pan (skillet)
and fry 15 ml/1 tbsp amounts of the
mixture until golden-brown underneath. Turn over and cook the other
sides – about 5 minutes in all. Drain on
kitchen paper (paper towels) and serve
hot with Green Pepper and Onion
Salad.

* 215 calories per serving
* Medium fibre

Spinach Omelette

SERVES 1

100 g/4 oz spinach
1 egg
1 egg white
15 ml/1 tbsp skimmed milk
Salt and freshly ground black pepper
A pinch of grated nutmeg
A small knob of low-fat sunflower or
  olive oil spread

Wash the spinach well and discard
any thick stalks. Tear into pieces
and place in a saucepan. Cover and
cook for 5 minutes, shaking the pan
occasionally, until the spinach is
cooked. Chop well with scissors. Beat
the whole egg and egg white with the
milk and a little salt and pepper. Stir in
the spinach and any juices. Season
lightly and add the nutmeg. Melt the
low-fat spread in a small omelette pan.
Add the egg mixture and cook gently,
lifting and stirring, until the omelette is
golden underneath and just set. Fold
the omelette in half and continue
cooking for a few minutes. Slide out on
to a warm plate and serve.

* 150 calories
* Fairly high fibre

Garlic Spaghetti and Herbs

SERVES 4

225 g/8 oz spaghetti
50 g/2 oz/¼ cup low-fat sunflower or
olive oil spread
1 garlic clove, crushed
15 ml/1 tbsp chopped parsley
15 ml/1 tbsp chopped basil
Salt and freshly ground black pepper
30 ml/2 tbsp grated low-fat Cheddar
cheese
30 ml/2 tbsp grated low-fat Mozzarella
cheese

Cook the spaghetti according to the packet directions. Drain. Melt the low-fat spread in the spaghetti saucepan and add the remaining ingredients. Return the spaghetti to the pan and toss gently until well coated. Spoon on to plates and serve.

* **275 calories per serving**
* **Medium fibre**

Pasta with Tomato and Basil Sauce

SERVES 4

225 g/8 oz pasta shapes
450 ml/¾ pt/2 cups passata (sieved
tomatoes)
Salt and freshly ground black pepper
15 ml/1 tbsp chopped basil
50 g/2 oz/½ cup low-fat Cheddar
cheese, grated
2 tomatoes, sliced

Cook the pasta according to the packet directions. Drain and return to the pan. Add the passata, a little salt, lots of pepper and the basil. Heat through, stirring gently. Turn into a flameproof serving dish. Top with the cheese and garnish with the tomato slices. Grill (broil) until the cheese melts and bubbles.

* **265 calories per serving**
* **Medium fibre**

Macaroni Cheese

SERVES 4

175 g/6 oz quick-cook macaroni
20 g/¾ oz/3 tbsp plain (all-purpose)
flour
300 ml/½ pt/1¼ cups skimmed milk
5 ml/1 tsp made English mustard
A small knob of low-fat sunflower or
olive oil spread
75 g/3 oz/¾ cup strong low-fat
Cheddar cheese, grated
Salt and freshly ground black pepper
2 tomatoes, sliced

Cook the macaroni according to the packet directions. Drain. Whisk together the flour and milk in a saucepan. Add the mustard and low-fat spread and bring to the boil, whisking all the time, until thickened and smooth. Stir in nearly all the cheese and season to taste. Mix in the macaroni. Turn in to a flameproof dish. Sprinkle with the remaining cheese and arrange the sliced tomatoes around the edge. Grill (broil) until golden and bubbling.

* **260 calories per serving**
* **Medium fibre**

Macaroni and Spinach Cheese

SERVES 4

Prepare as for Macaroni Cheese, but spoon half the macaroni mixture into the dish, then add a layer of 225 g/8 oz thawed frozen chopped spinach, then the remaining macaroni, and finish as before.

* 275 calories per serving
* Fairly high fibre

Mediterranean Macaroni Cheese

SERVES 4

Prepare as for Macaroni Cheese, but simmer 1 chopped red (bell) pepper and 1 chopped green pepper in a little water for 4 minutes until tender. Drain and add to the macaroni mixture with 6 stuffed green olives, sliced, then continue as before.

* 280 calories per serving
* Medium fibre

Cauliflower Cheese

SERVES 4

1 cauliflower, cut into florets
15 g/¹/₂ oz/2 tbsp cornflour (cornstarch)
300 ml/¹/₂ pt/1¹/₄ cups skimmed milk
A small knob of low-fat sunflower or
    olive oil spread
Salt and white pepper
75 g/3 oz/³/₄ cup low-fat Cheddar
    cheese, grated
5 ml/1 tsp made English mustard
A pinch of cayenne
30 ml/2 tbsp cornflakes, crushed
2 tomatoes, sliced

Cook the cauliflower in boiling salted water for about 5 minutes until just tender. Drain and place in a flameproof dish. Meanwhile, blend the cornflour with a little of the milk in a saucepan. Add the remaining milk and the low-fat spread. Bring to the boil and cook for 1 minute, stirring all the time. Season to taste and stir in 50 g/ 2 oz/¹/₂ cup of the cheese, the mustard and cayenne. Pour over the cauliflower and sprinkle with the cornflakes and remaining cheese. Arrange the tomatoes round the edge and grill (broil) until golden and bubbling.

* 150 calories per serving
* Fairly high fibre

Cauliflower and Mushroom Cheese

SERVES 4

Prepare as for Cauliflower Cheese, but add 175 g/6 oz sliced button mushrooms, stewed for 3 minutes in 30 ml/2 tbsp water, over the cooked cauliflower before adding the cheese sauce, then continue as before.

* 155 calories per serving
* Fairly high fibre

Broccoli Blue Cheese

SERVES 4

Prepare as for Cauliflower Cheese, but substitute 450 g/1 lb broccoli for the cauliflower and use low-fat blue cheese instead of Cheddar.

* 150 calories per serving
* Fairly high fibre

Melting Sunshine Rice

SERVES 4

175 g/6 oz/³/₄ cup long-grain rice
1 vegetable stock cube
5 ml/1 tsp turmeric
320 g/12 oz/1 medium can of
naturally sweet sweetcorn (corn)
1 yellow (bell) pepper, finely diced
2 spring onions (scallions), finely
chopped
100 g/4 oz Edam cheese, finely diced
Salt and freshly ground black pepper
15 ml/1 tbsp chopped parsley, to
garnish

Cook the rice in plenty of boiling water to which the stock cube and turmeric have been added for about 10 minutes or until just tender. Drain and return to the pan. Add the remaining ingredients. Toss. Cover with a lid and leave to stand for 5 minutes. Fluff up and serve garnished with parsley.

* **330 calories per serving**
* **High fibre**

Soya-stuffed Onions

SERVES 4

4 large onions, peeled but left whole
425 g/15 oz/1 large can of soya beans,
drained and mashed
50 g/2 oz/1 cup white breadcrumbs
45 ml/3 tbsp low-fat plain yoghurt
5 ml/1 tsp chopped sage
Salt and freshly ground black pepper
20 g/³/₄ oz/1¹/₂ tbsp low-fat sunflower
or olive oil spread
4 small sprigs of sage

Boil the onions in lightly salted water for 30 minutes. Drain, reserving the cooking water and rinse in cold water. Cut a slice off the top of each onion and scoop out the centres leaving a wall about 1 cm/¹/₂ in thick. Chop the scooped-out onion and place in a bowl. Add the soya beans and breadcrumbs and mix with the yoghurt. Season with the sage, salt and pepper. Pack into the onion shells and stand the onions in a shallow baking tin (pan). Pour in enough of the onion cooking water to come to about 1 cm/¹/₂ in up the sides of the pan. Dot with the low-fat spread. Bake in a preheated oven at 190°C/375°F/gas mark 5 for about 40 minutes until tender and golden, spooning the cooking liquid over the onions once or twice during cooking. Garnish each with a small sprig of fresh sage before serving.

* **255 calories per serving**
* **High fibre**

Sweetcorn, Cheese and Herb-stuffed Onions

SERVES 4

4 large onions
200 g/7 oz/1 small can of naturally
  sweet sweetcorn (corn)
50 g/2 oz/1 cup white breadcrumbs
50 g/2 oz/½ cup strong low-fat
  Cheddar cheese, grated
30 ml/2 tbsp chopped parsley
10 ml/2 tsp chopped sage
Salt and freshly ground black pepper
15 ml/1 tbsp skimmed milk
15 g/½ oz/1 tbsp low-fat sunflower or
  olive oil spread
Parsley, to garnish
Hot French bread, to serve

Boil the onions in lightly salted water for 30 minutes. Drain, reserving the cooking water, and rinse in cold water. Cut a slice off the top of each onion and scoop out the centres leaving a wall about 1 cm/½ in thick. Chop the scooped-out onion finely and place in a bowl with the contents of the can of sweetcorn, the breadcrumbs, cheese, herbs and a little salt and pepper. Moisten with the milk. Pack into the onion shells and stand the onions in a shallow baking tin (pan). Pour in enough of the onion cooking water to come about 1 cm/½ in up the sides of the pan. Dot with the low-fat spread. Bake in a preheated oven at 190°C/375°F/gas mark 5 for about 40 minutes or until tender and golden, spooning the cooking liquid over the onions occasionally during cooking. Garnish with parsley and serve with hot French bread.

* **170 calories per serving**
* **High fibre**

Quick Ratatouille Rice Supper

SERVES 4

175 g/6 oz/¾ cup long-grain rice
425 g/15 oz/1 large can of ratatouille
50 g/2 oz/½ cup low-fat Cheddar
  cheese, grated
Dressed Green Salad (page 275), to
  serve

Cook the rice according to the packet directions. Drain, rinse with boiling water, drain again and return to the saucepan. Stir in the can of ratatouille and heat through, stirring. Turn into a flameproof serving dish, sprinkle with the cheese and place under a hot grill (broiler) until the cheese melts and bubbles. Serve hot with Dressed Green Salad.

* **240 calories per serving**
* **Fairly high fibre**

Mushrooms and Tomatoes in the Hole

SERVES 4

8 button mushrooms
4 tomatoes, halved
30 ml/2 tbsp sunflower oil
100 g/4 oz/1 cup plain (all-purpose)
  flour
A pinch of salt
2.5 ml/½ tsp dried basil
2 eggs
150 ml/¼ pt/⅔ cup skimmed milk
150 ml/¼ pt/⅔ cup water
Quick-cooked Cabbage (page 270), to
  serve

Arrange the mushrooms and tomatoes in a small non-stick baking tin (pan). Add the oil and place in a preheated oven at 220°C/425°F/gas mark 7 for 5 minutes. Meanwhile, put the flour and salt in a bowl with the basil. Add the eggs and half the milk and water. Beat well until smooth. Stir in the remaining milk and water. Pour into the baking tin and return to the oven on the shelf towards the top for about 30 minutes until well risen, crisp and golden. Serve straight away with Quick-cooked Cabbage.

* **235 calories per serving**
* **Medium fibre**

Spinach and Cottage Cheese in the Hole

SERVES 4

100 g/4 oz/1 cup plain (all-purpose)
  flour
2.5 ml/½ tsp grated nutmeg
A good pinch of salt
Freshly ground black pepper
2 eggs
150 ml/¼ pt/⅔ cup skimmed milk
150 ml/¼ pt/⅔ cup water
30 ml/2 tbsp sunflower oil
225 g/8 oz frozen chopped spinach,
  thawed
100 g/4 oz/½ cup low-fat cottage
  cheese with chives
Stewed Tomatoes with Herbs (page
  273), to serve

Sift the flour, nutmeg and salt into a bowl and add a good grinding of pepper. Make a well in the centre and add the eggs and half the milk and water. Beat well until smooth, then stir in the remaining milk and water. Pour the oil into a small non-stick, shallow baking tin (pan). Heat in a preheated oven at 220°C/425°F/gas mark 7 for a few minutes until sizzling. Add the spinach and cottage cheese and return to the oven until sizzling again. Pour in the batter, return to the oven on the shelf towards the top, and cook for about 30 minutes until risen and golden. Serve hot with Stewed Tomatoes with Herbs.

* **260 calories per serving**
* **Fairly high fibre**

Rustic-style Cauliflower

SERVES 4

1 large cauliflower, cut into florets
1 onion, chopped
1 garlic clove, crushed
1 small green (bell) pepper, sliced
1 red pepper, sliced
15 g/½ oz/1 tbsp low-fat sunflower or
*   olive oil spread*
400 g/14 oz/1 large can of chopped
*   tomatoes*
425 g/15 oz/1 large can of haricot
*   (navy) beans, drained, rinsed and*
*   drained again*
2.5 ml/½ tsp dried oregano
15 ml/1 tbsp tomato purée (paste)
Salt and freshly ground black pepper
4 black olives
A little chopped parsley
Crusty bread, to serve

Cook the cauliflower in boiling, lightly salted water for about 6 minutes or until just tender. Drain. Meanwhile, fry (sauté) the onion, garlic and peppers in the low-fat spread for 2 minutes, stirring. Add the tomatoes, beans, oregano and tomato purée, bring to the boil and boil rapidly for 5 minutes until reduced and pulpy. Season to taste. Spoon the cauliflower into warm individual bowls and spoon the sauce over. Top each portion with an olive, sprinkle with parsley and serve hot with crusty bread.

* **160 calories per serving**
* **High fibre**

Rustic-style Broccoli

SERVES 4

Prepare as for Rustic-style Cauliflower, but substitute 450 g/ 1 lb broccoli for the cauliflower.

* **160 calories per serving**
* **High fibre**

Rustic-style Aubergine and Mushrooms

SERVES 4

Prepare as for Rustic-style Cauliflower, but substitute 2 large aubergines (eggplants), sliced, and 100 g/4 oz button mushrooms, sliced, for the cauliflower.

* **135 calories per serving**
* **High fibre**

Rustic-style Marrows

SERVES 4

Prepare as for Rustic-style Cauliflower, but substitute 2 small marrows (squashes), halved and the seeds removed, for the cauliflower. Boil them for 10–15 minutes until tender, drain, then fill with the sauce.

* **135 calories per serving**
* **High fibre**

Potato and Courgette Brochettes

SERVES 4

8 bay leaves
16 baby potatoes, scrubbed
16 button (pearl) onions, peeled but
*   left whole*
2 large courgettes (zucchini), each cut
*   into 8 chunks*
15 g/½ oz/1 tbsp low-fat sunflower or
*   olive oil spread, melted*
1 garlic clove, crushed
Chinese Soya Bean Salad (page 282),
*   to serve*

Soak the bay leaves in cold water while preparing the vegetables (this helps prevent them burning during cooking). Cook the potatoes and onions in boiling, lightly salted water for 6 minutes until slightly softened. Add the courgettes half-way through cooking. Drain, rinse with cold water and drain again. Thread the vegetables alternately on eight soaked wooden skewers, adding a bay leaf half-way through the threading. Mix together the melted spread and garlic and brush over the vegetables. Grill (broil) for 10–15 minutes, turning occasionally and brushing with the baste, until golden and cooked through. Serve hot with Chinese Soya Bean Salad.

* **220 calories per serving**
* **Fairly high fibre**

Hot and Tasty Quorn Steaks

SERVES 4

4 Quorn steaks
15 ml/1 tbsp golden (light corn) syrup
30 ml/2 tbsp tomato purée (paste)
A pinch of Chinese five spice powder
15 ml/1 tbsp red wine vinegar
Freshly ground black pepper
Tabasco sauce, to taste
100 g/4 oz/2 cups beansprouts
1 small green (bell) pepper, very thinly
*   sliced*
Broccoli and Sesame Seed Noodles
*   (page 267), to serve*

Lay the Quorn steaks in a shallow dish in a single layer. Mix together the remaining ingredients except the beansprouts and sliced pepper. Spoon over the steaks and leave to marinate for at least 2 hours, turning once or twice. Remove from the marinade and grill (broil) for 8–10 minutes, turning once or twice, until cooked and richly coated in the marinade, brushing with any remaining marinade during cooking. Mix together the beansprouts and pepper. Transfer the steaks to plates, garnish with the beansprout mixture to the side of each and serve with Broccoli and Sesame Seed Noodles.

* **180 calories per serving**
* **Fairly high fibre**

Mixed Bean and Vegetable Stew

SERVES 4

100 g/4 oz/²/₃ cup dried red kidney
  beans
100 g/4 oz/²/₃ cup dried flageolet
  beans
100 g/4 oz/²/₃ cup dried black-eye
  beans
2 leeks, sliced
2 carrots, sliced
1 large red onion, sliced
1 yellow (bell) pepper, sliced
100 g/4 oz okra (ladies' fingers)
400 g/14 oz/1 large can of chopped
  tomatoes
1 bouquet garni sachet
A pinch of salt
Freshly ground black pepper
175 g/6 oz green cabbage, shredded
Warm wholemeal bread, to serve

Soak all the beans in cold water for several hours or overnight. Drain and place in a large saucepan. Cover with fresh cold water, bring to the boil and boil rapidly for 10 minutes, then cover, reduce the heat and simmer for about 1 hour or until all the beans are tender. Add all the remaining ingredients except the cabbage. Bring back to the boil, reduce the heat, part-cover and simmer for 20 minutes. Add the cabbage and continue cooking for 10 minutes until tender but still bright green, topping up with a little water if the mixture is getting too dry. Remove the bouquet garni, taste and season with more pepper, if liked. Ladle into warm bowls and serve with warm wholemeal bread.

* **215 calories per serving**
* **High fibre**

Quorn with Sweet and Sour Cabbage

SERVES 4

450 g/1 lb red cabbage, shredded
1 red onion, thinly sliced
1 cooking (tart) apple, sliced
30 ml/2 tbsp red wine vinegar
30 ml/2 tbsp water
30 ml/2 tbsp clear honey
175 g/6 oz Quorn pieces
15 ml/1 tbsp caraway seeds
60 ml/4 tbsp low-fat quark
15 ml/1 tbsp chopped parsley, to
  garnish
Plain boiled rice, to serve

Put the cabbage, onion and apple in a casserole dish (Dutch oven). Toss well. Mix together the vinegar, water and honey and pour over. Cover and cook in a preheated oven at 160°C/325°F/gas mark 3 for 30 minutes. Add the Quorn and caraway seeds, stir well, re-cover and cook for a further 30 minutes. Spoon on to warm plates, add 15 ml/1 tbsp quark to each portion, sprinkle with chopped parsley and serve with plain boiled rice.

* **190 calories per serving**
* **Fairly high fibre**

Carrot and Orange Flan

SERVES 4

6 slices of wholemeal bread, crusts
    removed
4 carrots, sliced
150 ml/¼ pt/⅔ cup pure orange juice
225 g/8 oz/1 cup low-fat soft cheese
15 ml/1 tbsp chopped parsley
15 ml/1 tbsp snipped chives
Freshly ground black pepper
7.5 ml/1½ tsp arrowroot
10 ml/2 tsp water
1 orange and a sprig of parsley, to
    garnish
New potatoes and Cucumber and
    Spring Onion Salad (page 279), to
    serve

Roll the bread lightly with a rolling pin to flatten slightly. Arrange five slices with the corners pointing up around a 20 cm/8 in flan dish (pie pan) and press gently but firmly into the corners of the base. Press the final slice in the middle of the base to form a bread shell. Bake in a preheated oven at 190°C/375°F/gas mark 5 for about 30 minutes until crisp and golden, covering the tips with foil if they are becoming too brown. Remove from the oven and leave to cool. Meanwhile, gently cook the carrots in the orange juice for about 15 minutes or until tender. Drain, reserving the juice. Mash the cheese with the herbs and a good grinding of pepper. Spread into the bread case and arrange the carrots in overlapping circles over the top. Blend the arrowroot with the water and stir into the reserved orange cooking juice. Bring to the boil, stirring, until thickened and clear. Brush all over the carrots. Cut all the pith and rind off the orange and separate into segments. Arrange in a starburst pattern on top of the carrots and place a sprig of parsley in the centre. Chill until ready to serve with new potatoes and Cucumber and Spring Onion Salad.

* **255 calories per serving**
* **High fibre**

Spaghetti with Cherry Tomatoes and Pesto

SERVES 4

350 g/12 oz wholewheat spaghetti
Simple Pesto (page 379)
100 g/4 oz cherry tomatoes, halved
50 g/2 oz stoned (pitted) black olives,
    halved
60 ml/4 tbsp boiling water

Cook the spaghetti according to the packet directions. Drain and return to the pan. Add the Simple Pesto and toss gently. Add the tomatoes, olives and boiling water and continue tossing over a gentle heat for about 3 minutes until the tomatoes are just softening. Pile on warm plates and serve.

* **535 calories per serving**
* **Fairly high fibre**

Ratatouille Summer Pudding

SERVES 6

1 onion, thinly sliced
1 garlic clove, crushed
10 g/¹/₄ oz/2 tsp low-fat sunflower or
    olive oil spread
1 red (bell) pepper, thinly sliced
1 green pepper, thinly sliced
1 aubergine (eggplant), quartered
    lengthways and thinly sliced
2 courgettes (zucchini), sliced
4 ripe tomatoes, skinned and chopped
2.5 ml/¹/₂ tsp dried mixed herbs
15 ml/1 tbsp tomato purée (paste)
5 ml/1 tsp clear honey
30 ml/2 tbsp red wine
Freshly ground black pepper
8 slices of bread from a medium-sliced
    loaf, crusts removed
Sprig of parsley, to garnish
90 ml/6 tbsp low-fat quark and Mixed
    Green Salad (page 279), to serve

Cook the onion and garlic in the low-fat spread in a large saucepan, stirring, for 3 minutes. Add all the remaining ingredients except the bread. Stir well, bring to the boil, reduce the heat, part-cover and simmer gently for 20 minutes. Meanwhile, line a 1.2 litre/2 pt/5 cup pudding basin with six of the bread slices. Stand the basin on a plate. Spoon the cooked ratatouille into the basin. Cover with the remaining bread, trimming to fit and using the trimmings to fill in any gaps. Cover with a saucer, then a heavy weight or a can of food. Leave until cold, then chill overnight. Turn out on to a serving plate, garnish with a sprig of parsley and serve each portion with a spoonful of quark and Mixed Green Salad.

* **300 calories per serving**
* **Fairly high fibre**

Naan Wraps

SERVES 2

2 naan breads
225 g/8 oz/1 small can of pease
    pudding
10 ml/2 tsp curry paste
30 ml/2 tbsp mango chutney
Lemon juice
Shredded lettuce and cucumber slices
Thin onion slices (optional)

Grill or microwave the naans according to the packet directions. Heat the pease pudding with the curry paste in a saucepan or microwave until piping hot. Spread over the breads. Spread the mango chutney on top and sprinkle with lemon juice. Add shredded lettuce and cucumber slices and onion, if liked. Fold into halves and serve in paper napkins.

* **335 calories per serving**
* **High fibre**

Cabbage-wrapped Lentil and Mushroom Loaf

SERVES 6

175 g/6 oz/1 cup green lentils
1 bunch of spring onions (scallions), finely chopped
10 g/¼ oz/2 tsp low-fat sunflower or olive oil spread
100 g/4 oz mushrooms, chopped
10 ml/2 tsp curry powder
100 g/4 oz/2 cups wholemeal breadcrumbs
30 ml/2 tbsp chopped coriander (cilantro)
Salt and freshly ground black pepper
1 egg, beaten
15 ml/1 tbsp Worcestershire sauce
15 ml/1 tbsp water
6 large green cabbage leaves, thick parts of the stalks removed
450 ml/¾ pt/2 cups passata (sieved tomatoes)
Jacket potatoes and naturally sweet sweetcorn (corn), to serve

Rinse the lentils well in a colander. Drain, place in a saucepan and cover with cold water. Bring to the boil, reduce the heat, cover and simmer gently for 45 minutes until tender. Drain thoroughly. Meanwhile, fry (sauté) the spring onions in the low-fat spread for 3 minutes, stirring. Add the mushrooms and cook, stirring, for a further 2 minutes. Add the curry powder and cook for 1 minute. Remove from the heat. Mix in the cooked lentils, the breadcrumbs, half the coriander, a little salt and pepper. Add the egg, Worcestershire sauce and water and mix thoroughly. Meanwhile, plunge the cabbage leaves into a pan of boiling water and cook for 2 minutes. Drain, rinse with cold water and drain again. Pat dry on kitchen paper (paper towels). Use to line a non-stick 900 g/2 lb loaf tin (pan), letting the leaves hang well over the edges. Pack the lentil mixture into the tin. Wrap the overhanging leaves over the top of the mixture to cover it completely. Cover with foil, twisting and folding under the rim to secure. Bake in a preheated oven at 190°C/375°F /gas mark 5 for 1 hour until it feels firm when lightly pressed. Leave to cool slightly. Meanwhile, warm the passata with the remaining coriander and some pepper. Turn the loaf out on to a warm serving plate, spoon a little passata around and serve sliced with jacket potatoes, sweetcorn and the remaining sauce.

* **260 calories per serving**
* **High fibre**

Garbano

SERVES 4

*225 g/8 oz/1¹/₃ cups dried chick peas
  (garbanzos)*
1 large garlic clove, crushed
1 onion, finely chopped
1 red (bell) pepper, chopped
1 carrot, sliced
1 turnip, diced
*100 g/4 oz French (green) beans, cut
  into thirds*
5 ml/1 tsp ground cumin
15 ml/1 tbsp paprika
Salt and freshly ground black pepper
*400 g/14 oz/1 large can of chopped
  tomatoes*
30 ml/2 tbsp tomato purée (paste)
1 bay leaf
60 ml/4 tbsp low-fat crème fraîche
30 ml/2 tbsp snipped chives
Crusty bread, to serve

Soak the chick peas in cold water overnight. Drain and place in a flameproof casserole dish (Dutch oven). Add the prepared vegetables, the spices, a little salt and pepper, the tomatoes, tomato purée and bay leaf. Just cover with water and bring to the boil. Boil for 10 minutes. Cover and transfer to a preheated oven at 160°C/325°F/gas mark 3 and cook for 3 hours or until the chick peas are really tender and bathed in a rich sauce. Spoon into warm soup bowls. Top each with 15 ml/1 tbsp crème fraîche and sprinkle with the chives. Serve with crusty bread.

* **270 calories per serving**
* **High fibre**

Rice Cheese

SERVES 4

*225 g/8 oz/1 cup brown long-grain
  rice*
Salt
*75 g/3 oz/³/₄ cup strong low-fat
  Cheddar cheese, grated*
2.5 ml/¹/₂ tsp made English mustard
*1 quantity of Low-fat White Sauce
  (page 376)*
Freshly ground black pepper
2 tomatoes, sliced
*Stewed Tomatoes with Herbs (page
  273), to serve*

Cook the rice in boiling, lightly salted water according to the packet directions. Drain. Stir two-thirds of the cheese and the mustard into the Low-fat White Sauce and season to taste. Fold in the rice. Turn into a flameproof serving dish, arrange the tomato slices round the edge and sprinkle with the remaining cheese. Grill (broil) until golden brown and bubbling. Serve hot with Stewed Tomatoes with Herbs.

* **315 calories per serving**
* **High fibre**

Baked Bean Lasagne

SERVES 4

1 garlic clove, crushed
15 ml/1 tbsp dried minced onion
225 g/8 oz button mushrooms, sliced
1 carrot, grated
30 ml/2 tbsp water
15 ml/1 tbsp chopped parsley
400 g/14 oz/1 large can of baked
    beans
30 ml/2 tbsp tomato ketchup (catsup)
30 ml/2 tbsp Worcestershire sauce
1.5 ml/¼ tsp chilli powder
Freshly ground black pepper
6 sheets of no-need-to-precook green
    (spinach) lasagne
75 g/3 oz/¾ cup strong low-fat
    Cheddar cheese, grated
Low-fat White Sauce (page 376)
Mixed Green Salad (page 279), to
    serve

Put the garlic, minced onion, mushrooms, carrot and water in a saucepan. Bring to the boil, cover, reduce the heat and simmer for 5 minutes, stirring occasionally. Add the parsley, beans, ketchup, Worcestershire sauce, chilli powder and lots of pepper and simmer gently for 3 minutes. Put a little of the bean mixture in the base of a fairly shallow ovenproof dish. Top with a layer of lasagne sheets, breaking them to fit, if necessary. Repeat the layers, finishing with a layer of lasagne. Stir two-thirds of the cheese into the Low-fat White Sauce and season with pepper. Spoon the sauce over the lasagne and sprinkle with the remaining cheese. Bake in a preheated oven at 190°C/375°F/gas mark 5 for about 40 minutes until the lasagne feels cooked when a knife is inserted down through the centre and the top is golden brown and bubbling. Serve hot with Mixed Green Salad.

* **450 calories per serving**
* **High fibre**

Curried Bean Lasagne

SERVES 4

Prepare as for Baked Bean Lasagne, but use a can of curried beans instead of beans in tomato sauce, adding curry powder to taste instead of chilli powder. Serve with Green Pepper and Onion Salad (page 276) instead of Mixed Green Salad.

* **450 calories per serving**
* **High fibre**

Pizza Margarita

SERVES 4

225 g/8 oz/2 cups strong plain (bread) flour
5 ml/1 tsp dried oregano
10 ml/2 tsp easy-blend dried yeast
30 ml/2 tbsp tomato purée (paste)
225 g/8 oz/1 small can of chopped tomatoes, drained
100 g/4 oz low-fat Mozzarella cheese, thinly sliced
2 tomatoes, sliced
6 basil leaves, torn
Freshly ground black pepper
A few black olives (optional)
Mixed Green Salad (page 279), to serve

Sift the flour into a bowl and stir in the oregano and yeast. Mix with enough hand-hot water to form a soft but not sticky dough. Knead gently on a lightly floured surface, then return to the bowl, cover with a damp cloth and leave in a warm place to rise for 45 minutes. Re-knead the dough, then roll out thinly to a round about 23 cm/9 in in diameter. Transfer to a non-stick baking (cookie) sheet. Spread the tomato purée thinly over the dough to within 1 cm/½ in of the edge all round. Spread the chopped tomatoes over. Cover with cheese slices and arrange the tomato slices around. Scatter the basil over and add a good grinding of black pepper. Garnish with olives, if using. Bake in a preheated oven at 230°C/450°F/gas mark 8 for 15–20 minutes until golden round the edges and the cheese is bubbling. Serve straight away with Mixed Green Salad.

* **350 calories per serving**
* **Medium fibre**

Spaghetti Napoletana

SERVES 4

1 onion, finely chopped
1 garlic clove, crushed
1 celery stick, finely chopped
1 green (bell) pepper, finely chopped
10 g/¼ oz/2 tsp low-fat sunflower or olive oil spread
450 g/1 lb ripe tomatoes, skinned and chopped
15 ml/1 tbsp tomato purée (paste)
30 ml/2 tbsp dry white wine
A pinch of salt
Freshly ground black pepper
10 ml/2 tsp chopped oregano
350 g/12 oz spaghetti
60 ml/4 tbsp grated Parmesan cheese

Put the onion, garlic, celery and chopped pepper in a non-stick saucepan with the low-fat spread. Cook gently, stirring, for 5 minutes. Add the tomatoes, tomato purée, wine, salt, lots of pepper and the oregano. Simmer for 15 minutes until rich and pulpy. Meanwhile, cook the spaghetti according to the packet directions. Drain and pile on to warm plates. Top with the tomato sauce and sprinkle with the Parmesan before serving.

* **400 calories per serving**
* **Medium fibre**

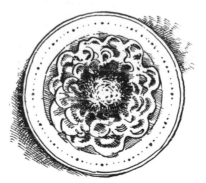

Leek and Corn-stuffed Potatoes

SERVES 4

4 large potatoes, scrubbed
2 leeks, thinly sliced
90 ml/6 tbsp skimmed milk
A pinch of salt
Freshly ground black pepper
15 g/½ oz/1 tbsp low-fat sunflower or olive oil spread
200 g/7 oz/1 small can of naturally sweet sweetcorn (corn), drained
4 small, ripe tomatoes
50 g/2 oz/½ cup low-fat Cheddar cheese, grated
English Mixed Salad (page 276), to serve

Prick the potatoes all over. Bake in a preheated oven at 180°C/350°F/gas mark 4 for 1½ hours or until soft when squeezed. Meanwhile, put the leeks and milk in a saucepan. Bring to the boil, reduce the heat, cover and cook very gently for 10 minutes until the leeks are soft. Cut a slice off the top of each potato and reserve. Scoop out most of the soft flesh into a bowl. Add the leeks and their milk, the salt, a good grinding of pepper and the low-fat spread and mash thoroughly. Stir in the sweetcorn. Spoon half the potato mixture back into the skins and press down well. Add a ripe tomato to each, then a good grinding of pepper. Top with the remaining potato mixture and rough up with a fork. Place on a baking (cookie) sheet and sprinkle with the cheese. Top with the potato lids. Return to the oven for 30 minutes until piping hot and golden brown. Serve hot with English Mixed Salad.

* **330 calories per serving**
* **High fibre**

Wild Rice with Oyster Mushroom Pilau

SERVES 4

175 g/6 oz/¾ cup wild rice mix
100 g/4 oz oyster mushrooms, sliced
1 garlic clove, crushed
40 g/1½ oz/3 tbsp low-fat sunflower or olive oil spread
30 ml/2 tbsp low-fat crème fraîche
Salt and freshly ground black pepper
15 ml/1 tbsp chopped parsley, to garnish
Flat Bean Salad (page 275), to serve

Cook the rice according to the packet directions. Drain and return to the pan. Meanwhile, fry (sauté) the mushrooms and garlic in the low-fat spread for 4 minutes until tender. Stir in the crème fraîche. Add to the rice, toss and season to taste. Garnish with the parsley before serving with Flat Bean Salad.

* **190 calories per serving**
* **High fibre**

Pappardelle with Roast Mediterranean Vegetables

SERVES 4

1 aubergine (eggplant), sliced
1 red (bell) pepper, cut into thick strips
1 green pepper, cut into thick strips
1 yellow or orange pepper, cut into thick strips
1 large courgette (zucchini), cut into chunks
1 red onion, cut into eighths
1 garlic clove, crushed
30 ml/2 tbsp olive oil
Freshly ground black pepper
30 ml/2 tbsp pine nuts
250 g/9 oz pappardelle (wide ribbon noodles)
A few thin shavings of Parmesan cheese

Plunge all the prepared vegetables in boiling water for 3 minutes. Drain and dry on kitchen paper (paper towels). Arrange in a single layer in a non-stick roasting tin (pan). Mix together the garlic and oil and brush all over. Add a good grinding of pepper. Roast towards the top of a preheated oven at 200°C/400°F/gas mark 6 for 40 minutes until tender and colouring slightly round the edges. Meanwhile, dry-fry the pine nuts in a small frying pan (skillet), tossing until golden brown. Cook the pappardelle according to the packet directions. Drain and pile on to four warm plates. Spoon the vegetables over and sprinkle with the pine nuts and Parmesan shavings.

* **355 calories per serving**
* **Fairly high fibre**

Greek-style Broad Beans

SERVES 4

1 large onion, chopped
1 garlic clove, crushed
15 g/¹/₂ oz/1 tbsp low-fat sunflower or olive oil spread
450 g/1 lb fresh, shelled or frozen broad (fava) beans
400 g/14 oz/1 large can of chopped tomatoes
150 ml/¹/₄ pt/²/₃ cup dry white wine
1 bouquet garni sachet
Salt and freshly ground black pepper
Plain boiled rice and Village Salad (page 281), to serve

Fry (sauté) the onion and garlic in the low-fat spread in a saucepan for 2 minutes, stirring. Add the remaining ingredients, cover and simmer gently for 10 minutes or until the beans are tender. Remove the bouquet garni. Spoon on to a bed of boiled rice and serve with Village Salad.

* **150 calories per serving**
* **High fibre**

Lentil and Mushroom Madras

SERVES 4

225 g/8 oz/1¹/₃ cups brown lentils
1 large onion, thinly sliced
15 g/¹/₂ oz/1 tbsp low-fat sunflower or olive oil spread
15 ml/1 tbsp Madras curry powder
175 g/6 oz button mushrooms, halved or quartered
2 large carrots, coarsely grated
30 ml/2 tbsp mango or curried fruit chutney, chopped, if necessary
30 ml/2 tbsp chopped coriander (cilantro)
A pinch of salt
300 ml/¹/₂ pt/1¹/₄ cups vegetable stock, made with 1 stock cube
1 bay leaf
5 ml/1 tsp garam masala
Cucumber slices and a few sprigs of coriander, to garnish
Perfect Brown Rice (page 265), to serve

Soak the lentils in cold water for several hours. Drain and place in a saucepan. Cover with water, bring to the boil and boil for about 45 minutes until really tender. Drain. Fry (sauté) the onion in the low-fat spread in a saucepan for 3 minutes. Stir in the curry powder, mushrooms and carrots and continue cooking for 1 minute, stirring. Add the remaining ingredients except the garam masala and stir in the cooked lentils. Simmer for about 30 minutes, stirring occasionally, until the mixture is thick and well flavoured. Discard the bay leaf and stir in the garam masala. Taste and re-season, if necessary. Serve garnished with cucumber slices and coriander sprigs on a bed of Perfect Brown Rice.

* **200 calories per serving**
* **High fibre**

Spinach and Cottage Cheese Pancakes

SERVES 4

Everyday Pancakes (page 353)
225 g/8 oz frozen chopped spinach, thawed
225 g/8 oz/1 cup low-fat cottage cheese
A good pinch of grated nutmeg
Salt and freshly ground black pepper
150 ml/¹/₄ pt/²/₃ cup passata (sieved tomatoes)
2.5 ml/¹/₂ tsp dried basil
Crispy Crunch Salad (page 284), to serve

Cook the pancakes. Mix the spinach with the cheese, nutmeg and salt and pepper to taste. Use to fill the pancakes. Roll up and place in a shallow baking dish. Cover with foil and heat in a preheated oven at 190°C/375°F/gas mark 5 for 25 minutes until hot through. Meanwhile, heat the passata with the basil. Transfer the pancakes to warm plates, spoon the passata across the middle and serve with Crispy Crunch Salad.

* **215 calories per serving**
* **Fairly high fibre**

Nut Moussaka

SERVES 4

2 aubergines (eggplants), sliced
100 g/4 oz/2 cups wholemeal
    breadcrumbs
1 garlic clove, crushed
90 ml/6 tbsp red wine
60 ml/4 tbsp water
25 g/1 oz/2 tbsp low-fat sunflower or
    olive oil spread
5 ml/1 tsp dried oregano
30 ml/2 tbsp tomato purée (paste)
200 g/7 oz/1¾ cups chopped mixed
    nuts
A pinch of salt
Freshly ground black pepper
Cheese Sauce (page 376)
2.5 ml/½ tsp ground cinnamon
Dressed Green Salad (page 275), to
    serve

Boil the aubergine slices in water for 3 minutes until almost tender. Drain, rinse with cold water and drain again. Meanwhile, mix together the remaining ingredients except the Cheese Sauce and cinnamon seasoning with salt and lots of pepper. Make the Cheese Sauce and flavour with the cinnamon. Layer the aubergine slices and nut mixture in a 1.5 litre/2½ pt/6 cup ovenproof dish and spoon the sauce over. Bake in a preheated oven at 200°C/400°F/gas mark 6 for 35 minutes until the top is golden and bubbling. Serve hot with Dressed Green Salad.

* **580 calories per serving**
* **High fibre**

Dutch Grape Salad

SERVES 4

100 g/4 oz seedless grapes
2 ripe pears, peeled, cored and diced
100 g/4 oz Edam cheese, rinded and
    cubed
45 ml/3 tbsp apple juice
10 ml/2 tsp reduced-salt soy sauce
Lettuce leaves
Warm Potato Salad (page 279), to
    serve

Mix together the fruits and cheese and toss in the apple juice and soy sauce. Pile on to lettuce leaves and serve with Warm Potato Salad.

* **140 calories per serving**
* **Fairly high fibre**

Spinach and Hazelnut Parcels

SERVES 4

450 g/1 lb spinach
1 large red onion, roughly chopped
15 g/½ oz/1 tbsp low-fat sunflower or olive oil spread
175 g/6 oz/1½ cups hazelnuts (filberts)
4 slices of wholemeal bread, torn into pieces
1 egg white
5 ml/1 tsp yeast extract
90 ml/6 tbsp boiling water
2.5 ml/½ tsp dried mixed herbs
A pinch of salt
Freshly ground black pepper
300 ml/½ pt/1¼ cups passata (sieved tomatoes)
30 ml/2 tbsp chopped parsley
1 garlic clove, crushed
5 ml/1 tsp clear honey
60 ml/4 tbsp low-fat plain yoghurt
Perfect Brown Rice (page 265), to serve

Select 12 of the largest spinach leaves and reserve. Discard the thick central stalks from the remainder. Wash the leaves, shake off the excess water, tear up and place in a saucepan. Cover and cook gently for 5 minutes until tender. Drain off any liquid.

Cook the onion gently in the low-fat spread for 3 minutes, stirring, until softened. Turn into a food processor with the cooked spinach, the nuts and the bread pieces. Run the machine briefly to chop, but not too finely. Add the egg white. Dissolve the yeast extract in 30 ml/2 tbsp boiling water. Add to the mixture with the herbs, salt and pepper. Run the machine briefly to mix.

Cut off the thick stalks from the reserved spinach leaves and blanch the leaves briefly in boiling water for 30 seconds. Drain, rinse with cold water and drain again. Open out on a work surface and divide the nut mixture between them. Fold in the sides, then roll up and lay in an ovenproof dish. Add the remaining measured boiling water to the dish. Cover with foil or a lid and bake in a preheated oven at 180°C/350°F/gas mark 4 for about 35 minutes until cooked through.

Meanwhile, blend the passata with half the parsley, the garlic, honey and a little pepper in the spinach cooking saucepan. Heat through, stirring. Spoon the sauce on to warm plates and lay the spinach parcels on top. Spoon the yoghurt over the parcels and serve with Perfect Brown Rice.

* **420 calories per serving**
* **High fibre**

Soya Bean Risotto

SERVES 4 OR 6

1 onion, chopped
25 g/1 oz/2 tbsp low-fat sunflower or
 olive oil spread
1 carrot, chopped
2 celery sticks, chopped
1 red (bell) pepper, diced
100 g/4 oz frozen peas
75 g/3 oz button mushrooms, sliced
225 g/8 oz/1 cup brown long-grain
 rice
600 ml/1 pt/2½ cups vegetable stock,
 made with 2 stock cubes
15 ml/1 tbsp reduced-salt soy sauce
15 ml/1 tbsp tomato purée (paste)
5 ml/1 tsp dried mixed herbs
Freshly ground black pepper
200 g/7 oz/1 small can of naturally
 sweet sweetcorn (corn)
425 g/15 oz/1 large can of soya beans,
 drained and rinsed
30 ml/2 tbsp pumpkin seeds

Fry (sauté) the onion in the low-fat
spread for 2 minutes in a large non-
stick frying pan (skillet). Add the
carrot, celery, red pepper, peas,
mushrooms and rice and cook for
1 minute, stirring. Add the remaining
ingredients except the sweetcorn, soya
beans and pumpkin seeds. Bring to the
boil, reduce the heat, cover and cook
gently for about 30 minutes, stirring
occasionally, until the rice is tender but
nutty and has absorbed the liquid. Add
the contents of the can of sweetcorn,
the beans and pumpkin seeds. Cover
and cook for 5 minutes. Fork through
and serve.

* **500 or 340 calories per serving**
* **High fibre**

Fast Mixed-bean Chilli

SERVES 4

1 onion, finely chopped
1 red (bell) pepper, finely chopped
15 g/½ oz/1 tbsp low-fat sunflower or
 olive oil spread
5 ml/1 tsp ground cumin
5 ml/1 tsp dried oregano
2.5 ml/½ tsp chilli powder (or to taste)
400 g/14 oz/1 large can of chopped
 tomatoes
2 x 425 g/2 x 15 oz/2 large cans of
 mixed pulses, drained
Oat Tortillas (page 354), shredded
 lettuce and chopped cucumber, to
 serve

Fry (sauté) the onion and red pepper
in the low-fat spread, stirring, for
3 minutes. Add the cumin, oregano
and chilli powder and stir for 1 minute.
Add the chopped tomatoes and beans.
Cook, stirring, for 10 minutes until the
beans are bathed in a rich sauce.
Spoon on to Oat Tortillas, top with
some shredded lettuce and chopped
cucumber, roll up and serve. Eat with
the fingers.

* **200 calories per serving**
* **High fibre**

Mixed Vegetable Curry

SERVES 4

1 onion, sliced
30 ml/2 tbsp curry powder
1 small cauliflower, cut into florets
2 carrots, sliced
2 courgettes (zucchini), sliced
1 green (bell) pepper, sliced
1 potato, cut into chunks
50 g/2 oz/¹/₃ cup red lentils, rinsed
150 ml/¹/₄ pt/²/₃ cup coconut milk
150 ml/¹/₄ pt/²/₃ cup vegetable stock,
    made with ¹/₂ stock cube
100 g/4 oz frozen peas
15 ml/1 tbsp mango chutney,
    chopped, if necessary
15 ml/1 tbsp tomato purée (paste)
Salt and freshly ground black pepper
15 ml/1 tbsp chopped coriander
    (cilantro), to garnish
Naan bread, to serve

Put all the ingredients in a saucepan.
Bring to the boil, part-cover and
simmer for 30 minutes until tender
and the sauce is thickened by the
lentils. If the mixture is too runny,
uncover and boil rapidly to reduce the
liquid slightly. Taste and re-season, if
necessary. Garnish with chopped
coriander and serve with naan bread.

* 190 calories per serving
* High fibre

Hot Bulgar Salad

SERVES 4

100 g/4 oz/1 cup bulgar wheat
250 ml/8 fl oz/1 cup boiling water
2.5 ml/¹/₂ tsp salt
15 ml/1 tbsp olive oil
30 ml/2 tbsp lemon juice
1 garlic clove, finely chopped
30 ml/2 tbsp chopped parsley
15 ml/1 tbsp chopped mint
5 ml/1 tsp chopped coriander (cilantro)
3 tomatoes, chopped
5 cm/2 in piece of cucumber, chopped
1 green (bell) pepper, chopped
4 stoned (pitted) black olives, halved
    and a few coriander leaves, torn,
    to garnish

Put the bulgar in a pan and add the
boiling water. Sprinkle with the
salt. Stir and leave to stand for
20 minutes until the wheat has
absorbed all the water. Add the oil,
lemon juice, garlic, herbs, tomatoes,
cucumber and green pepper. Toss over
a gentle heat for 1 minute. Pile on to
plates and garnish with olives and torn
coriander leaves before serving.

* 150 calories per serving
* High fibre

Tabbouleh

SERVES 4

Use the same ingredients as for Hot
Bulgar Salad, but cook the bulgar
wheat, then leave until cold. Stir in the
remaining ingredients and chill until
ready to serve.

* 150 calories per serving
* High fibre

Mexican Rice

SERVES 4

25 g/1 oz/2 tbsp low-fat sunflower or
olive oil spread
1 garlic clove, crushed
1 small red (bell) pepper, diced
1 small green pepper, diced
½ bunch of spring onions (scallions),
chopped
1 carrot, diced
1 green chilli, seeded and finely
chopped
100 g/4 oz/½ cup brown long-grain
rice
2.5 ml/½ tsp chilli powder
375 g/13 fl oz/1½ cups vegetable
stock, made with 1 stock cube
Salt and freshly ground black pepper
425 g/15 oz/1 large can of red kidney
beans, drained, rinsed and drained
again
1 banana, cut into chunks
A sprig of parsley, to garnish

Melt half the low-fat spread in a saucepan. Add the garlic, peppers, spring onions and carrot and fry (sauté) for 2 minutes, stirring. Add the chilli and rice and cook for 1 minute. Add the chilli powder and stock and some salt and pepper. Bring to the boil, cover, reduce the heat and cook very gently for 35 minutes until the rice is just tender and has absorbed the liquid, adding a little water during cooking, if necessary. Add the beans and heat through for 2 minutes. Fry the banana chunks in the remaining low-fat spread for 2 minutes, turning occasionally. Pile the rice on to warm serving dishes, top with the banana and serve garnished with parsley.

* **235 calories per serving**
* **High fibre**

Welsh Hotpot

SERVES 4

450 g/1 lb potatoes, scrubbed and
thinly sliced
2 leeks, halved lengthways and cut
into short lengths
450 g/1 lb Brussels sprouts, trimmed
and halved
150 ml/¼ pt/⅔ cup vegetable stock,
made with ½ stock cube
5 ml/1 tsp made English mustard
5 ml/1 tsp chopped sage
50 g/2 oz/½ cup low-fat Cheddar
cheese, grated
Baked Tomatoes with Herbs (page
274), to serve

Boil the potatoes in lightly salted water for 4 minutes. Drain. Put the leeks and sprouts in a flameproof casserole dish (Dutch oven). Add the stock, bring to the boil, cover and simmer for 3 minutes. Stir in the mustard and sage. Lay the potato slices on top and sprinkle with the cheese. Bake in a preheated oven at 190°C/ 375°F/gas mark 5 for about 45 minutes until all the vegetables are just tender. Serve hot with Baked Tomatoes with Herbs.

* **185 calories per serving**
* **Fairly high fibre**

Caponata

SERVES 6

1 aubergine (eggplant), diced
Salt and freshly ground black pepper
1 red (bell) pepper, halved
25 g/1 oz/2 tbsp low-fat sunflower or
*   olive oil spread*
1 courgette (zucchini), diced
6 okra pods (ladies' fingers), cut into
*   thirds*
1 onion, chopped
1 beefsteak tomato, skinned, seeded
*   and chopped*
150 ml/¼ pt/⅔ cup sweet vermouth
2 garlic cloves, crushed
30 ml/2 tbsp chopped basil
90 ml/6 tbsp crushed cornflakes
45 ml/3 tbsp grated low-fat Cheddar
*   cheese*

Sprinkle the aubergine with salt in a colander and leave to stand for 30 minutes. Meanwhile, put the pepper halves, skin-sides up, on a grill (broiler) rack. Grill (broil) until the skin blisters and blackens. Peel off the skin, then dice the flesh. Rinse the aubergine and pat dry on kitchen paper (paper towels). Heat the low-fat spread in flameproof casserole dish (Dutch oven). Add the aubergine, red pepper, courgette, okra and onion and stir-fry for 4 minutes. Add the tomato, vermouth, garlic and basil. Cook for 15 minutes. Season to taste. Mix the cornflakes with the cheese and sprinkle over. Bake in a preheated oven at 200°C/400°F/gas mark 6 for 15 minutes until the cheese has melted and is turning golden. Serve hot.

* **100 calories per serving**
* **Fairly high fibre**

Photograph opposite: Pappardelle with Roast Mediterranean Vegetables (page 249)

Thunder and Lightning

SERVES 4

225 g/8 oz pasta shapes
1 onion, finely chopped
1 garlic clove, crushed
25 g/1 oz/2 tbsp low-fat sunflower or
*   olive oil spread*
425 g/15 oz/1 large can of chick peas
*   (garbanzos)*
5 ml/1 tsp dried oregano
450 ml/¾ pt/2 cups passata (sieved
*   tomatoes)*
30 ml/2 tbsp tomato purée (paste)
5 ml/1 tsp caster (superfine) sugar
Salt and freshly ground black pepper
15 ml/1 tbsp chopped basil
15 ml/1 tbsp chopped parsley
50 g/2 oz/½ cup low-fat strong
*   Cheddar cheese, finely grated*
4 stoned (pitted) black olives, sliced, to
*   garnish*

Cook the pasta according to the packet directions. Drain. Meanwhile, fry (sauté) the onion and garlic in the low-fat spread for 2 minutes, stirring. Add the remaining ingredients except the cheese and olives and cook for 10 minutes until thick. Stir in the pasta. Pile on to plates and sprinkle with the cheese and olives.

* **390 calories per serving**
* **High fibre**

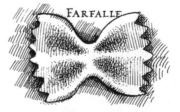

FARFALLE

Side Dishes and Salads

We should all eat far more vegetables, salads and fruit. Apart from being highly nutritious, they are a great way of filling up without piling on the calories. They also add colour and texture to meals and create fabulous flavour combinations to make the taste buds sing. All these dishes make delicious accompaniments to the main courses in the book. They are also a wonderful way of turning a simple grilled (broiled) steak, chicken breast or fish fillet into a special meal.

Photograph opposite: Sesame and Garlic Wedges (page 262) and Baby New Vegetable Selection (page 273)

Savoury Potato Cake

SERVES 4

450 g/1 lb potatoes, scrubbed and
   grated
1 small onion, grated
A pinch of salt
Freshly ground black pepper
15 ml/1 tbsp sunflower oil

Squeeze the potato to remove excess moisture. Mix with the onion and season with the salt and lots of pepper. Heat half the oil in a medium non-stick frying pan (skillet). Add the potato mixture and press down well. Cover with a lid and cook over a moderate heat for 30 minutes until tender and the base is golden brown. Loosen the potato cake with a spatula and turn out on to a plate. Heat the remaining oil in the pan, slide the potato cake back in and cook for a further 5–10 minutes over a fairly high heat until browned on the base. Slide out on to a plate and serve cut into wedges.

* 140 calories per serving
* Fairly high fibre

Smoky Baby Potatoes

SERVES 4

450 g/1 lb baby potatoes, scrubbed
Salt and freshly ground black pepper
15 g/½ oz/1 tbsp low-fat sunflower or
   olive oil spread
30 ml/2 tbsp smoky-flavoured
   barbecue sauce

Boil the potatoes in lightly salted water for 6 minutes until almost tender. Drain. Place on a large sheet of foil, shiny side up. Sprinkle with pepper, dot with the low-fat spread and drizzle with the sauce. Wrap the potatoes tightly in the foil to make a large parcel, taking care to seal the edges well. Bake in a preheated oven at 200°C/400°F/gas mark 6 for about 20 minutes, until cooked through. Alternatively, cook under a hot grill (broiler), turning the parcel once. Serve hot.

* 185 calories per serving
* Fairly high fibre

Pan Scalloped Potatoes

SERVES 4

450 g/1 lb potatoes, thickly sliced
15 g/½ oz/1 tbsp low-fat sunflower or
   olive oil spread
A pinch of salt
Freshly ground black pepper
30 ml/2 tbsp chopped parsley
150 ml/¼ pt/⅔ cup skimmed milk

Boil the potatoes in lightly salted water for 3 minutes. Drain. Grease a flameproof casserole dish (Dutch oven) with the low-fat spread. Lay the potatoes in the casserole, seasoning each layer and sprinkling with parsley. Pour over the milk. Cover with the lid and cook over a very gentle heat for about 40 minutes until cooked through. Serve straight from the pan.

* 120 calories per serving
* Fairly high fibre

Baked Scalloped Potatoes

SERVES 4

10 g/¼ oz/2 tsp low-fat sunflower or olive oil spread, melted
450 g/1 lb potatoes, scrubbed and thinly sliced
Salt and freshly ground black pepper
1.5 ml/¼ tsp ground cumin
120 ml/4 fl oz/½ cup skimmed milk
30 ml/2 tbsp chopped parsley

Brush four large squares of foil lightly with the melted spread. Top with layers of potato, sprinkling each layer with a very little salt, lots of pepper and the cumin. Spoon 30 ml/ 2 tbsp milk over each and sprinkle with the parsley. Carefully draw the foil up over the potatoes and twist and fold the edges to seal securely. Transfer to a baking (cookie) sheet and bake in a preheated oven at 190°C/375°F/gas mark 5 for about 1 hour or until the potatoes are cooked through. Serve straight from the parcels.

* **120 calories per serving**
* **Fairly high fibre**

Sauté Potatoes

SERVES 4

550 g/1¼ lb potatoes, scrubbed and diced
25 g/1 oz/2 tbsp low-fat sunflower or olive oil spread
Salt and freshly ground black pepper
15 ml/1 tbsp chopped parsley

Boil the potatoes in lightly salted water for 3 minutes until almost tender but still holding their shape. Drain thoroughly. Heat the low-fat spread in a large non-stick frying pan (skillet). Add the potatoes and toss to coat with the spread. Fry (sauté), turning occasionally, until golden brown and cooked through. Drain on kitchen paper (paper towels), then sprinkle with salt and pepper and serve garnished with chopped parsley.

* **155 calories per serving**
* **Fairly high fibre**

Sauté Potatoes with Garlic

SERVES 4

Prepare as for Sauté Potatoes, but add 2 garlic cloves, halved, to the potatoes in the frying pan (skillet). Remove the garlic before serving.

* **155 calories per serving**
* **Fairly high fibre**

Extra-fluffed Mashed Potatoes

SERVES 4

450 g/1 lb potatoes, peeled and cut into chunks
10 g/¼ oz/2 tsp low-fat sunflower or olive oil spread
30 ml/2 tbsp skimmed milk
Freshly ground black pepper
A pinch of grated nutmeg
Paprika, to garnish

Boil the potatoes in very lightly salted water until really tender. Drain thoroughly, then add the low-fat spread and milk. Using an electric hand mixer, beat the potatoes until smooth and fluffy. Beat in pepper and nutmeg to taste. Pile on to warm plates and dust with paprika before serving.

* **115 calories per serving**
* **Low fibre**

No-fat Chips

SERVES 4

450 g/1 lb frozen chips suitable for frying (NOT oven chips)
Freshly ground black pepper

Spread out the chips on a non-stick baking (cookie) sheet in a single, even layer. Season lightly with pepper. Bake at the top of a preheated oven at 230°C/450°F/ gas mark 8 for about 30 minutes, turning once, until crisp and brown.

* **100 calories per serving**
* **Low fibre**

Jacket-baked Potatoes with Yoghurt and Chives

You can cook these in a higher or lower oven according to what else you are cooking. Simply adjust the cooking time accordingly. If your main course is not going to take as long as the potatoes, pop them in the oven before starting to prepare the rest of the meal.

SERVES 4

4 fairly large potatoes, scrubbed
Freshly ground black pepper
90 ml/6 tbsp low-fat plain yoghurt
30 ml/2 tbsp snipped chives
A pinch of salt
Paprika, for dusting

Prick the potatoes all over with a fork. Place on a baking (cookie) sheet and bake in a preheated oven at 180°C/350°F/gas mark 4 for about 1½ hours or until really tender when squeezed. Alternatively, bake in the microwave according to the manufacturer's instructions. Meanwhile, mix the yoghurt with the chives and season with the salt and some pepper. Chill until ready to serve. When the potatoes are cooked, cut a cross in the top of each potato and squeeze gently on both sides to open up slightly. Transfer to plates, spoon the yoghurt and chive mixture over and dust with paprika before serving (and don't forget to eat the skins!).

* **200 calories per serving**
* **High fibre**

Herby Jacket Bakes

SERVES 4

4 good-sized potatoes, scrubbed
30 ml/2 tbsp skimmed milk
10 g/¹/₄ oz/2 tsp low-fat sunflower or
olive oil spread
30 ml/2 tbsp chopped mixed herbs,
such as parsley, thyme, sage,
marjoram, tarragon
Freshly ground black pepper

Prick the potatoes all over and either bake in a preheated oven at 160°C/325°F/gas mark 3 for about 2 hours until soft when squeezed, or cook in the microwave for about 4 minutes per potato, depending on the output of your model. Split into halves and scoop the potato out into a bowl. Mash thoroughly with the milk, low-fat spread and herbs and season well with pepper. Pile back into the shells and return to the oven at 230°C/450°F/gas mark 8 or place under a hot grill (broiler) for about 5 minutes to heat through and lightly brown the tops.

* **200 calories per serving**
* **High fibre**

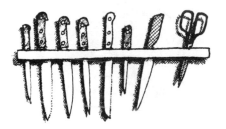

Golden Roast Potatoes

SERVES 4

4 potatoes, scrubbed and quartered
15 g/¹/₂ oz/1 tbsp low-fat sunflower or
olive oil spread
A little paprika (optional)

Dry the potato pieces on kitchen paper. Melt the low-fat spread in a roasting tin (pan). Add the potato pieces and turn to coat completely. Dust with paprika, if liked. Bake towards the top of a preheated oven at 220°C/425°F/gas mark 7 for 45–50 minutes until golden and cooked through.

* **175 calories per serving**
* **Fairly high fibre**

Baby Roast Potatoes

SERVES 4

20 baby potatoes, scrubbed
15 g/¹/₂ oz/1 tbsp low-fat sunflower or
olive oil spread
10 ml/2 tsp coarse sea salt
Freshly ground black pepper

Put the potatoes in a pan and just cover with water. Bring to the boil and cook for 5 minutes. Drain. Melt the low-fat spread in a roasting tin (pan). Add the potatoes and toss to coat. Roast at the top of a preheated oven at 220°C/425°F/ gas mark 7 for about 40 minutes until tender and golden, turning once or twice. Sprinkle with the salt and add a good grinding of pepper. Toss and serve.

* **175 calories per serving**
* **Fairly high fibre**

Seeded Roast Potatoes

SERVES 4

*4 fairly large potatoes, scrubbed and
    quartered*
15 ml/1 tbsp sunflower or olive oil
15 ml/1 tbsp sesame seeds
15 ml/1 tbsp poppy seeds
A pinch of salt
Freshly ground black pepper

Put the potatoes in a small roasting
tin (pan). Add the oil and toss
gently until each piece is coated.
Sprinkle with the seeds and the salt.
Bake towards the top of a preheated
oven at 200°C/400°F/gas mark 6 for
about 1 hour or until golden and
cooked through. Sprinkle with pepper
and serve hot.

* **240 calories per serving**
* **High fibre**

Stock-roast Potatoes

SERVES 4

4 large potatoes, peeled and quartered
*450 ml/³⁄₄ pt/2 cups beef, chicken or
    vegetable stock, made with 2 stock
    cubes*

Boil the potatoes in water for
3 minutes. Drain and place in a
roasting tin (pan). Add the stock. Roast
at the top of a preheated oven at
190°C/375°F/gas mark 5 for about
1½ hours, basting from time to time,
until tender and well browned.

* **200 calories per serving**
* **Low fibre**

Sesame and Garlic Wedges

SERVES 4

*450 g/1 lb even-sized potatoes,
    scrubbed*
*20 g/³⁄₄ oz/1½ tbsp low-fat sunflower
    or olive oil spread*
1 garlic clove, crushed
Salt
15 ml/1 tbsp sesame seeds

Boil the potatoes in their skins or
cook in the microwave until almost
tender but not too soft. Drain, if
necessary. When cool enough to
handle, cut into halves, then cut each
half into fairly small wedges. Melt the
low-fat spread in a roasting tin (pan)
with the garlic. Dip the potatoes in on
one side, then turn over in the low-fat
spread to coat. Sprinkle with salt and
the sesame seeds and bake at the top
of a preheated oven at 200°C/400°F/
gas mark 6 for about 20 minutes or
until golden brown. Drain on kitchen
paper (paper towels) before serving.

* **130 calories per serving**
* **High fibre**

Poppy Seed and Cumin Wedges

SERVES 4

450 g/1 lb even-sized potatoes, scrubbed
20 g/³/₄ oz/1¹/₂ tbsp low-fat sunflower or olive oil spread
Salt
15 ml/1 tbsp poppy seeds
2.5 ml/¹/₂ tsp ground cumin

Cook the potatoes in boiling water or in the microwave until almost tender but not too soft. Drain, if necessary. When cool enough to handle, cut into halves, then cut each half into small wedges. Melt the low-fat spread in a roasting tin (pan). Add the potatoes and turn over in the low-fat spread to coat. Sprinkle with salt, then the poppy seeds, then the cumin. Bake at the top of a preheated oven at 200°C/400°F/ gas mark 6 for about 20 minutes or until golden brown. Drain on kitchen paper (paper towels) before serving.

* **130 calories per serving**
* **High fibre**

Fennel Potatoes

SERVES 4

2 large even-sized potatoes, scrubbed
1 head of fennel, cut into quarters
20 g/³/₄ oz/1¹/₂ tbsp low-fat sunflower or olive oil spread
15 ml/1 tbsp fennel seeds
A pinch of salt

Boil the potatoes and fennel in water for 15 minutes until almost tender. Drain and cut each potato into quarters lengthways. Melt the low-fat spread in a roasting tin (pan). Add the potatoes and fennel and turn in the low-fat spread to coat. Sprinkle with the fennel seeds and salt and bake at the top of a preheated oven at 200°C/400°F/gas mark 6 for about 30 minutes until golden and cooked through. Drain on kitchen paper (paper towels) before serving.

* **150 calories per serving**
* **High fibre**

Yellow Rice with Bay

SERVES 4

75 g/3 oz/¹/₃ cup brown long-grain rice
75 g/3 oz/¹/₃ cup basmati rice
10 ml/2 tsp turmeric
1 vegetable stock cube, crumbled
1 large bay leaf, torn in half
Freshly ground black pepper
1 yellow (bell) pepper, finely chopped

Rinse the brown rice thoroughly, drain well and place in a large non-stick saucepan. Cover with boiling water. Bring back to the boil, cover and cook over a moderate heat for 15 minutes. Meanwhile, rinse the basmati rice and drain well. Add to the brown rice and top up with boiling water again just to cover. Stir in the remaining ingredients, cover and cook for a further 10 minutes or until both types of rice are just tender, topping up with a little more boiling water, if necessary. Then, either remove the lid and boil rapidly, if necessary, to remove any excess liquid and serve hot as a moist risotto or, to make a pilau, turn the cooked rice into a colander, rinse thoroughly with boiling water, drain and fluff up with a fork. Discard the bay leaf before serving.

* **170 calories per serving**
* **High fibre**

Savoury Vegetable Rice

SERVES 4

100 g/4 oz/¹/₂ cup long-grain rice
375 ml/13 fl oz/1¹/₂ cups water
1 bunch of spring onions (scallions), chopped
¹/₂ red (bell) pepper, chopped
1 carrot, finely diced
1 celery stick, chopped
100 g/4 oz button mushrooms, sliced
1 bouquet garni sachet
Freshly ground black pepper

Rinse the rice thoroughly. Drain well and place in a large non-stick saucepan. Add the remaining ingredients and bring to the boil. Cover tightly with a lid (put some foil under it if it does not fit well), reduce the heat to as low as possible and cook for 20 minutes. Remove the lid, discard the bouquet garni and fluff up with a fork. Serve hot or cold.

* **120 calories per serving**
* **Fairly high fibre**

Perfect Brown Rice

SERVES 4 OR 6

225 g/8 oz/1 cup brown long-grain rice
600 ml/1 pt/2½ cups water
A pinch of salt
Freshly ground black pepper
Paprika, to garnish

Rinse the rice thoroughly and drain well. Put the water in a non-stick saucepan and bring to the boil. Add the rice, stir well, reduce the heat, cover and simmer very gently for 30 minutes. Season well with the salt and lots of pepper and fluff up with a fork. Serve sprinkled with a fine dusting of paprika.

* 210 or 140 calories per serving
* High fibre

Almond Wild Rice

SERVES 4

175 g/6 oz/¾ cup wild rice mix
50 g/2 oz frozen peas
45 ml/3 tbsp flaked (slivered) almonds
30 ml/2 tbsp currants
Freshly ground black pepper

Cook the rice according to the packet directions, adding the peas for the last 5 minutes' cooking time. Drain thoroughly. Meanwhile, dry-fry the almonds in a non-stick frying pan (skillet) until golden, stirring all the time to prevent burning. Remove from the pan as soon as they are brown. Add to the rice with the currants and season well with pepper. Toss and serve.

* 215 calories per serving
* High fibre

Fried Rice

SERVES 4

175 g/6 oz/¾ cup long-grain rice
15 g/½ oz/1 tbsp low-fat sunflower or olive oil spread
50 g/2 oz frozen peas, thawed
1 egg, beaten
A dash of reduced-salt soy sauce
A pinch of Chinese five spice powder

Cook the rice according to the packet directions. Drain. Melt the low-fat spread in a non-stick frying pan (skillet). Add the rice and peas and cook, stirring, for 2 minutes. Push to one side. Break the egg into the space in the pan. Cook until almost set, then gradually stir into the rice. Sprinkle with the soy sauce and five spice powder and serve hot.

* 215 calories per serving
* Fairly high fibre

Special Fried Rice

SERVES 4

Prepare as for Fried Rice, but add 50 g/2 oz cooked peeled prawns (shrimp), 2 spring onions (scallions), very finely chopped and 6 button mushrooms, sliced, with the rice and peas.

* 270 calories per serving
* Fairly high fibre

Tomato Rice with Olives

SERVES 4

175 g/6 oz/³/₄ cup long-grain rice
1 onion, chopped
1 green (bell) pepper, chopped
15 g/¹/₂ oz/1 tbsp low-fat sunflower or
   olive oil spread
400 g/14 oz/1 large can of chopped
   tomatoes
Salt and freshly ground black pepper
1 bay leaf
8 stoned (pitted) black olives, sliced

Boil the rice in plenty of lightly salted water for 8 minutes. Drain. Meanwhile, fry (sauté) the onion and green pepper in the low-fat spread in a saucepan for 2 minutes. Add the tomatoes, a little salt and pepper, the bay leaf and rice. Bring to the boil, reduce the heat, cover and cook gently for 15 minutes until the liquid is absorbed and the rice is tender, stirring occasionally to prevent sticking. Discard the bay leaf, stir in the olives and serve.

* **200 calories per serving**
* **Medium fibre**

Pilau Rice

SERVES 4

225 g/8 oz/1 cup basmati rice
600 ml/1pt/2¹/₂ cups water
5 ml/1 tsp turmeric
5 ml/1 tsp garam masala
1 piece of cinnamon stick
6 whole green cardamom pods, split
Salt and freshly ground black pepper
A little chopped coriander (cilantro), to
   garnish

Wash the rice thoroughly and drain well. Place in a non-stick saucepan with the remaining ingredients. Bring to the boil, then cover tightly with a lid (place foil under the lid if it doesn't fit well). Reduce the heat to as low as possible and cook for 20 minutes. Turn off the heat and leave to stand for 5 minutes. Uncover and fluff up with a fork. Discard the cinnamon stick and serve sprinkled with chopped coriander.

* **110 calories per serving**
* **Medium fibre**

Mixed Seeded Noodles

SERVES 4

225 g/8 oz plain or wholewheat
   tagliatelle
10 g/¹/₄ oz/2 tsp low-fat sunflower or
   olive oil spread
5 ml/1 tsp sesame seeds
5 ml/1 tsp poppy seeds
5 ml/1 tsp caraway seeds
Freshly ground black pepper

Break the tagliatelle into small pieces, if preferred. Cook in boiling water according to the packet directions. Drain and return to the pan. Add the low-fat spread and seeds and toss until each strand is coated.

* **210 calories per serving**
* **Fairly high fibre**

Sesame Seed Noodles

SERVES 4

225 g/8 oz wholewheat tagliatelle
45 ml/3 tbsp sesame seeds
15 g/½ oz/1 tbsp low-fat sunflower or
olive oil spread

Cook the tagliatelle according to the packet directions. Drain and return to the saucepan. Meanwhile, dry-fry the sesame seeds in a non-stick frying pan (skillet) until golden. Add to the pasta with the low-fat spread, toss and serve.

* 210 calories per serving
* High fibre

Broccoli and Sesame Seed Noodles

SERVES 4

Prepare as for Sesame Seed Noodles, but add 175 g/6 oz broccoli, cut into tiny florets, to the tagliatelle for the last 4 minutes' cooking time.

* 215 calories per serving
* High fibre

Cauliflower and Poppy Seed Noodles

SERVES 4

Prepare as for Broccoli and Sesame Seed Noodles, but substitute ½ small cauliflower for the broccoli and untoasted poppy seeds for the sesame seeds.

* 215 calories per serving
* High fibre

Herby Tossed Pasta

SERVES 4

225 g/8 oz rigatoni or other tube-
shaped pasta
Salt
10 g/¼ oz/2 tsp low-fat sunflower or
olive oil spread
15 ml/1 tbsp chopped parsley
15 ml/1 tbsp chopped basil
15 ml/1 tbsp snipped chives
Freshly ground black pepper

Cook the pasta in lightly salted, boiling water according to the packet directions. Drain and return to the pan. Add the remaining ingredients and toss over a gentle heat until each piece is coated in fragrant herbs. Serve hot.

* 200 calories per serving
* Medium fibre

Tomato Spaghetti

SERVES 4

225 g/8 oz wholewheat spaghetti
300 ml/¹/₂ pt/1¹/₄ cups passata (sieved
tomatoes)
30 ml/2 tbsp chopped basil
Freshly ground black pepper
A few basil leaves, to garnish

Cook the spaghetti according to the packet directions. Drain and return to the saucepan. Add the passata, chopped basil and some pepper and toss over a gentle heat until hot through. Serve straight away, garnished with a few basil leaves.

* **215 calories per serving**
* **High fibre**

West Country Carrots

SERVES 4

450 g/1 lb carrots, cut into matchsticks
300 ml/¹/₂ pt/1¹/₄ cups medium cider
15 ml/1 tbsp clear honey
A pinch of salt
Freshly ground black pepper

Put the carrots in a saucepan with the cider, honey and salt. Bring to the boil, cover, reduce the heat and simmer gently for 20 minutes until the carrots are just tender and the liquid has evaporated, removing the lid for the last 3 minutes cooking time. Add a good grinding of pepper and serve hot.

* **85 calories per serving**
* **Medium fibre**

Creamed Spinach

SERVES 4

450 g/1 lb spinach
1 garlic clove, crushed
Grated nutmeg
Salt and freshly ground black pepper
75 ml/5 tbsp low-fat crème fraîche

Wash the spinach thoroughly under cold water. Drain, tear off any tough stalks and tear the leaves into pieces. Place in a saucepan with the garlic, lots of nutmeg and a little salt and pepper. Cover and cook gently for 5 minutes until the spinach is tender. Snip with scissors to chop. Drain off any excess liquid. Stir in the crème fraîche until smooth. Taste and re-season, if necessary.

* **50 calories per serving**
* **Fairly high fibre**

Corn with Almonds

SERVES 4

50 g/2 oz/¹/₂ cup flaked (slivered)
almonds
320 g/12 oz/1 medium can of
naturally sweet sweetcorn (corn)

Dry-fry the almonds in a pan until golden, then remove from the pan immediately. Add the contents of the can of sweetcorn and heat through. Drain. Add the almonds, toss and serve.

* **165 calories per serving**
* **High fibre**

Corn with Peppers and Almonds

SERVES 4-6

Prepare as for Corn with Almonds, but finely dice 1 small red and 1 green (bell) pepper and boil in water for 2 minutes. Drain and add to the sweetcorn when heating through.

* 185 calories per serving
* High fibre

Fruity Red Cabbage

The cabbage can be cooked for longer in a slower oven or more quickly in a higher one, depending on what else you are cooking at the same time.

SERVES 4

450 g/1 lb red cabbage, shredded
1 onion, sliced
1 eating (dessert) apple, sliced
50 g/2 oz/¹/₃ cup sultanas (golden raisins)
Salt and freshly ground black pepper
30 ml/2 tbsp red wine vinegar
30 ml/2 tbsp water
30 ml/2 tbsp light brown sugar

Layer the cabbage, onion, apple and sultanas in a casserole dish (Dutch oven), seasoning each layer with a little salt and pepper. Mix together the vinegar, water and sugar and pour over. Cover with a piece of greaseproof (waxed) paper, then the lid. Bake in a preheated oven at 180°C/350°F/gas mark 4 for about 1½ hours until tender. Stir well before serving.

* 90 calories per serving
* High fibre

Baked Spiced Carrots with Orange

SERVES 4

450 g/1 lb carrots, sliced
20 g/³/₄ oz/1¹/₂ tbsp low-fat sunflower or olive oil spread
2 oranges
A pinch of ground ginger
A pinch of grated nutmeg
Salt and freshly ground black pepper
15 ml/1 tbsp chopped parsley

Put the carrots in an ovenproof serving dish and dot with the low-fat spread. Finely grate the rind and squeeze the juice from one orange and add with the ginger, nutmeg and some salt and pepper. Cover tightly with foil and bake in a preheated oven at 190°C/375°F/gas mark 5 for 45 minutes or until just tender. Meanwhile, cut all the peel and pith off the second orange and separate into segments. Toss the cooked carrots well, then scatter the orange segments over with the parsley before serving.

* 50 calories per serving
* Medium fibre

Crunchy Spinach

SERVES 4

450 g/1 lb spinach
Salt and freshly ground black pepper
2 slices of bread, crusts removed
Low-fat sunflower or olive oil spread
2.5 ml/½ tsp garlic salt
1.5 ml/¼ tsp grated nutmeg

Wash the spinach thoroughly and remove any thick stalks. Tear the leaves into pieces, place in a saucepan and sprinkle with a little salt and pepper. Cover and cook over a moderate heat for about 5 minutes until tender. Drain in a colander and snip with scissors. Meanwhile, spread the bread very thinly with low-fat spread. Cut into small dice. Fry (sauté) in a frying pan (skillet), tossing until golden brown. Sprinkle with the garlic salt and nutmeg. Spoon the spinach on to warm plates, scatter the crunchy bread over and serve straight away.

* **50 calories per serving**
* **Fairly high fibre**

Quick-cooked Cabbage

SERVES 4

1 small green cabbage, finely
*   shredded*
A pinch of salt

Put 4 cm/1½ in water in a large saucepan. Add the salt and bring to the boil. Add the cabbage, bring back to the boil, stir well, cover and cook for 3 minutes only. Drain and serve very hot.

* **25 calories per serving**
* **Fairly high fibre**

Tomato Braised Celery

SERVES 4

1 large head of celery
25 g/1 oz/2 tbsp low-fat sunflower or
*   olive oil spread*
1 onion, chopped
225 g/8 oz/1 small can of chopped
*   tomatoes*
300–450 ml/½–¾ pt/1¼–2 cups
*   vegetable stock, made with 1 stock*
*   cube*
Salt and freshly ground black pepper
30 ml/2 tbsp chopped basil

Trim off the celery leaves and reserve for garnish. Remove the thick outer sticks, scrub, peel off any strings, finely chop and reserve. Halve the remaining celery widthways, then cut into thick pieces. Melt the low-fat spread in a flameproof casserole dish (Dutch oven) and fry (sauté) the celery pieces for 3 minutes, turning occasionally. Remove from the pan with a draining spoon. Add the onion and chopped celery and fry, stirring, for 1 minute. Pour on the tomatoes and lay the celery pieces on top. Pour over enough of the stock to just cover the tomatoes. Sprinkle with salt and pepper. Cover and simmer gently for about 45 minutes until the celery is just tender.

Lift out of the pan on to a warm dish and keep warm. Boil the remaining mixture rapidly until well reduced and pulpy. Stir in the basil. Taste and re-season, if necessary. Spoon over the celery and serve garnished with the celery leaves.

* **60 calories per serving**
* **Fairly high fibre**

French-style peas

SERVES 4

¹/₂ round lettuce, shredded
1 bunch of spring onions (scallions),
*   cut into short lengths*
5 ml/1 tsp chopped mint
5 ml/1 tsp chopped parsley
450 g/1 lb frozen peas
150 ml/¹/₄ pt/²/₃ cup vegetable stock,
*   made with ¹/₂ stock cube*
Salt and freshly ground black pepper
A pinch of caster (superfine) sugar
Chopped parsley, to garnish

Put the lettuce in a pan with the spring onions, herbs, peas and stock. Sprinkle with a little salt and pepper and the sugar. Bring to the boil, cover tightly and simmer for 10 minutes. Remove the lid and boil rapidly, if necessary, to evaporate any liquid. Serve garnished with chopped parsley.

* **100 calories per serving**
* **High fibre**

Neeps

SERVES 4

1 small swede (rutabaga)
2 turnips
10 g/¹/₄ oz/2 tsp low-fat sunflower or
*   olive oil spread*
Freshly ground black pepper

Peel the swede and turnips and cut into small pieces. Cook in a little boiling, very lightly salted water until tender. Drain and mash thoroughly with the low-fat spread and lots of black pepper. Serve very hot.

* **50 calories per serving**
* **Medium fibre**

Brussels Sprouts with Almonds

SERVES 4

450 g/1 lb Brussels sprouts
25 g/1 oz/¹/₄ cup flaked (slivered)
*   almonds*
15 g/¹/₂ oz/1 tbsp low-fat sunflower or
*   olive oil spread*
5 ml/1 tsp lemon juice
Freshly ground black pepper

Trim the sprouts and cut a small cross in the base of each. Boil in lightly salted water for 5 minutes or until just tender but still with some bite. Drain and return to the saucepan. Meanwhile, fry (sauté) the almonds in the low-fat spread until golden, then sprinkle the lemon juice over. Add the almonds and their cooking juices to the sprouts and season with pepper. Toss gently and serve.

* **90 calories per serving**
* **Fairly high fibre**

Braised Cabbage With Celery

SERVES 4

3 celery sticks, finely sliced
300 ml/¹/₂ pt/1¹/₄ cups water
1 bay leaf
450 g/1 lb green cabbage, shredded
Freshly ground black pepper

Put the celery, water and bay leaf in a saucepan and bring to the boil. Cover and simmer for 5 minutes. Add the cabbage and some pepper, re-cover and cook for a further 5 minutes until just tender. Drain, if necessary, and discard the bay leaf. Serve hot.

* **35 calories per serving**
* **Fairly high fibre**

Courgettes à la Provençale

SERVES 4

1 onion, finely chopped
1 garlic clove, crushed
15 g/½ oz/1 tbsp low-fat sunflower or olive oil spread
400 g/14 oz/1 large can of chopped tomatoes
4 courgettes (zucchini), sliced
2.5 ml/½ tsp dried mixed herbs
A pinch of salt
Freshly ground black pepper

Fry (sauté) the onion and garlic in the low-fat spread in a saucepan for 2 minutes, stirring. Add the remaining ingredients. Bring to the boil, reduce the heat and simmer for 15 minutes, stirring occasionally, until the courgettes are just tender and bathed in a rich tomato sauce. Taste and re-season, if necessary.

* **80 calories per serving**
* **Medium fibre**

Stir-fried Vegetables

Vary the vegetables according to what you have to hand.

SERVES 4

25 g/1 oz/2 tbsp low-fat sunflower or olive oil spread
1 onion, sliced
1 garlic clove, finely chopped
2 carrots, cut into matchsticks
5 cm/2 in piece of cucumber, cut into matchsticks
¼ green cabbage, shredded
1 red (bell) pepper, cut into thin strips
Reduced-salt soy sauce

Heat the low-fat spread in a large frying pan (skillet) or wok. Add the prepared vegetables and stir-fry for about 5 minutes or until almost tender but still with some bite. Add soy sauce to taste. Toss again and serve. If you don't like your vegetables too crunchy, cover the pan after 3 minutes and cook for a few minutes longer than suggested.

* **55 calories per serving**
* **Fairly high fibre**

Caraway Cabbage

SERVES 4

150 ml/¼ pt/⅔ cup chicken or vegetable stock, made with ½ stock cube
450 g/1 lb green cabbage, very finely shredded
15 ml/1 tbsp caraway seeds
Freshly ground black pepper

Put the stock in a saucepan and bring to the boil. Add the cabbage and stir well. Cover tightly and boil for 5 minutes, shaking the pan occasionally, until the cabbage is still bright green and just tender but still has some bite. Season with the caraway seeds and pepper and serve straight away.

* **45 calories per serving**
* **Fairly high fibre**

Honeyed Baby Carrot and Corn Crunch

SERVES 4

225 g/8 oz baby carrots, scrubbed
100 g/4 oz baby sweetcorn (corn) cobs
25 g/1 oz/¼ cup flaked (slivered)
almonds
5 ml/1 tsp lemon juice
10 ml/2 tsp clear honey
Salt and freshly ground black pepper

Boil the carrots in lightly salted water for about 5 minutes until just tender. Add the sweetcorn for the last 2 minutes. Drain and return to the pan. Meanwhile, dry-fry the almonds in a frying pan (skillet) until lightly toasted. Add to the vegetables with the lemon juice and honey. Toss over a gentle heat and season to taste. Serve hot.

* **70 calories per serving**
* **Fairly high fibre**

Baby New Vegetable Selection

SERVES 4

350 g/12 oz baby new potatoes,
scrubbed
175 g/6 oz baby carrots, scrubbed
100 g/4 oz baby sweetcorn (corn) cobs
100 g/4 oz mangetout (snow peas)
20 g/³⁄₄ oz/1½ tbsp low-fat sunflower
or olive oil spread
15 ml/1 tbsp chopped tarragon
Freshly ground black pepper

Steam or boil the vegetables separately until just tender – the potatoes will take 10–15 minutes, the carrots about 10 minutes and the sweetcorn and mangetout about 4 minutes. Melt the low-fat spread and stir in the tarragon. Arrange the vegetables on a warm flat platter and drizzle the tarragon mixture over. Add a good grinding of pepper and serve.

* **110 calories per portion**
* **High fibre**

Stewed Tomatoes with Herbs

SERVES 4

8 tomatoes
30 ml/2 tbsp water
15 ml/1 tbsp chopped basil
15 ml/1 tbsp chopped parsley
Freshly ground black pepper

Cut a cross in the rounded end of each tomato and place in a saucepan. Add the remaining ingredients. Bring to the boil, cover, reduce the heat and simmer very gently for about 5 minutes until the tomatoes are just cooked but still hold their shape. Do not boil rapidly or they will break up. Serve hot.

* **20 calories per serving**
* **Medium fibre**

Baked Tomatoes with Herbs

SERVES 4

Prepare as for Stewed Tomatoes with Herbs (page 273), but place the ingredients in a casserole dish (Dutch oven) and bake in a preheated oven at 190°C/375°F/ gas mark 5 for 10–15 minutes until cooked through but still holding their shape.

* * 20 calories per serving
* * Medium fibre

Sesame Spring Green Stir-fry

SERVES 4

15 g/¹/₂ oz/1 tbsp low-fat sunflower or olive oil spread
5 ml/1 tsp sesame oil
350 g/12 oz spring (collard) greens, shredded
15 ml/1 tbsp sesame seeds
A squeeze of lemon juice
Salt and freshly ground black pepper

Melt the low-fat spread and oil in a large frying pan (skillet) with a lid. Add the spring greens and toss until coated with the oil mixture. Reduce the heat, cover and cook very gently for 5 minutes until almost tender. Remove the lid, turn up the heat, add the sesame seeds and toss over a high heat for several minutes until sizzling and just tender. Sprinkle with the lemon juice and season to taste. Serve.

* * 60 calories per serving
* * High fibre

Green Apple Salad

SERVES 4

1 garlic clove, halved
¹/₂ lollo biondo lettuce, torn into pieces
1 small bunch of rocket, separated into pieces
30 ml/2 tbsp snipped chives
1 crisp green eating (dessert) apple, sliced
15 ml/1 tbsp lemon juice
15 ml/1 tbsp olive oil
15 ml/1 tbsp apple juice
Salt and freshly ground black pepper
5 ml/1 tsp chopped tarragon
5 ml/1 tsp chopped parsley

Wipe the garlic clove thoroughly round the inside of the salad bowl and discard. Add the lollo biondo and rocket and sprinkle the chives over. Dip the apple slices in some of the lemon juice to prevent browning and add to the bowl. Whisk the remaining lemon juice with the oil, apple juice, some salt and pepper and the herbs. Pour over the salad, toss and serve.

* * 60 calories per serving
* * Fairly high fibre

Dressed Green Salad

SERVES 4

1 little gem lettuce, separated into
    leaves
1 small avocado
Lemon juice
5 cm/2 in piece of cucumber, sliced
1 green (bell) pepper, cut into thin
    strips
4 spring onions (scallions), cut into
    short lengths
A few small sprigs of coriander
    (cilantro), torn into pieces
A few small sprigs of parsley, torn into
    pieces
Low-fat French Dressing (page 380)

Tear the lettuce leaves into pieces
and place in a salad bowl. Halve
the avocado, remove the stone (pit),
peel and slice. Toss the slices gently in
lemon juice to prevent browning and
scatter over the lettuce. Scatter the
remaining salad ingredients over, then
drizzle with the dressing. Toss gently
and serve.

* **150 calories per serving**
* **Fairly high fibre**

Asian Banana Salad

SERVES 4

2 green or under-ripe bananas
Lemon juice
1 green (bell) pepper, finely diced
2 tomatoes, finely diced
5 cm/2 in piece of cucumber, finely
    diced
15 ml/1 tbsp desiccated (shredded)
    coconut
10 ml/2 tsp garam masala

Chop the bananas, place in a bowl
and toss in a little lemon juice. Add
the remaining ingredients, toss again
and chill before serving.

* **70 calories per serving**
* **Fairly high fibre**

Flat Bean Salad

SERVES 4

175 g/6 oz flat beans
A pinch of salt
1 small red onion, very finely chopped
15 ml/1 tbsp olive oil
10 ml/2 tsp red wine vinegar
Freshly ground black pepper
15 ml/1 tbsp chopped parsley

Cut the beans into 2.5 cm/1 in
lengths. Cook in boiling water to
which the salt has been added for
5 minutes until just tender. Drain, rinse
with cold water and drain again. Place
in a shallow dish and sprinkle with the
onion. Drizzle the oil and vinegar over
and add a good grinding of pepper.
Toss gently and chill for at least
30 minutes to allow the flavours to
develop. Sprinkle with the parsley
before serving.

* **50 calories per serving**
* **Fairly high fibre**

Green Pepper and Onion Salad

SERVES 4

2 large green (bell) peppers, sliced into
    rings
1 white onion, sliced and separated
    into rings
1 red onion, sliced and separated into
    rings
5 ml/1 tsp chopped sage
Freshly ground black pepper
Honey Nut Dressing (page 380)
1 small sprig of sage, to garnish

Plunge the pepper rings in boiling
water for 30 seconds. Drain, rinse
with cold water and drain again. Place
in a salad bowl. Add the onion rings
and sprinkle with the sage and lots of
pepper. Drizzle the dressing over, toss
gently and chill for at least
30 minutes to allow the flavours to
develop. Garnish with a small sprig of
sage before serving.

* 110 calories per serving
* Medium fibre

English Mixed Salad

SERVES 4

$^1/_2$ round lettuce, separated into leaves
5 cm/2 in piece of cucumber, sliced
2 tomatoes, cut into small wedges
2 spring onions (scallions), chopped
1 small bunch of radishes, trimmed
    and halved
2 celery sticks, sliced
Gran's Light Dressing (page 380)

Tear the lettuce leaves into bite-
sized pieces and place in a salad
bowl. Scatter the remaining salad
ingredients over. Pour the dressing into
a small glass jug and hand separately.

* 55 calories per serving
* Fairly high fibre

Blushing Leaf Salad

SERVES 4

1 small head of radicchio lettuce
$^1/_2$ lollo rosso lettuce
2 small cooked beetroot (red beets),
    diced
4 cherry tomatoes, halved
8 radishes, sliced
1 red onion, finely chopped
15 ml/1 tbsp red wine vinegar
Freshly ground black pepper
Rosy Dressing (page 385), to serve

Separate the radicchio and lollo
rosso into leaves. Tear into neat
pieces and lay on a flat platter. Arrange
the remaining salad ingredients in neat
piles on the leaves and sprinkle with
the vinegar and pepper. Pour the
dressing into a small glass jug and
hand separately.

* 65 calories per serving
* Fairly high fibre

Citrus Chinese Leaf Salad

SERVES 4

¹/₂ small head of Chinese leaves (stem
    lettuce)
1 pink grapefruit
2 oranges
15 ml/1 tbsp olive or sunflower oil
A few drops of reduced-salt soy sauce
10 ml/2 tsp lemon juice
Freshly ground black pepper
15 ml/1 tbsp snipped chives, to garnish

Cut the Chinese leaves into chunks
and place in a shallow dish.
Holding the fruit over a bowl to catch
the juice, cut off all the skin and pith
from the grapefruit and oranges. Cut
the grapefruit in segments either sides
of each membrane. Lay the fruit over
the Chinese leaves. Squeeze the
membranes over the bowl to catch any
remaining juice. Slice the oranges and
cut the slices in half, if preferred.
Arrange over the leaves. Add the oil,
soy sauce and lemon juice to the juices
in the bowl and whisk well. Season
with pepper. Drizzle over the salad and
sprinkle with the chives before serving.

* **80 calories per serving**
* **Fairly high fibre**

Warm Courgette and Carrot Salad

SERVES 4

2 carrots
2 courgettes (zucchini)
15 ml/1 tbsp sunflower oil
30 ml/2 tbsp black mustard seeds
15 ml/1 tbsp lemon juice
5 ml/1 tsp clear honey

Coarsely grate the carrots and
courgettes into a salad bowl. Mix
well. When ready to serve, heat the oil
in a frying pan (skillet), add the
mustard seeds and cook until they
start to pop. Quickly stir in the lemon
juice and honey and drizzle over the
vegetables. Toss and serve straight
away.

* **120 calories per serving**
* **Fairly high fibre**

Cheesy Tomato and Spring Onion Salad

SERVES 4

2–3 beefsteak tomatoes, halved and
    sliced
6 spring onions (scallions), finely
    chopped
15 ml/1 tbsp cider or wine vinegar
Freshly ground black pepper
Light Cheese Dressing (page 381)

Arrange the tomato slices
attractively in four small salad
bowls. Sprinkle the spring onions over
and drizzle with the vinegar. Season
with pepper. Just before serving, spoon
the Light Cheese Dressing over and
serve.

* **45 calories per serving**
* **Medium fibre**

Mixed Leaf Salad

SERVES 4

½ small iceberg lettuce
1 bunch of watercress
1 small head of radicchio lettuce
2 small sprigs of coriander (cilantro)
1 sprig of basil
2 sprigs of flatleaf parsley
Non-oil Vinaigrette Dressing (page 381)

Separate the layers of iceberg lettuce and tear into small pieces. Place in a salad bowl. Trim the feathery stalks off the watercress, separate into small sprigs and add to the bowl. Separate the radicchio leaves and tear each in half. Add to the bowl. Tear the coriander, basil and parsley leaves into smaller pieces and add to the bowl. Just before serving, drizzle the dressing over and toss gently.

* **25 calories per serving**
* **Fairly high fibre**

Fragrant Tomato and Onion Salad

SERVES 4

6 ripe tomatoes, sliced
1 small red onion, thinly sliced and
separated into rings
Honeyed Basil Dressing (page 382)
Freshly ground black pepper
A sprig of basil, to garnish

Arrange the tomato slices overlapping in a shallow dish. Scatter the onion rings over. Drizzle the dressing over, add a good grinding of pepper and leave to stand for at least 30 minutes to allow the flavours to develop. Garnish with a sprig of basil before serving.

* **30 calories per serving**
* **Medium fibre**

Jewel Salad

SERVES 4

1 small round lettuce
5 cm/2 in piece of cucumber, sliced
2 tomatoes, quartered
50 g/2 oz raw fresh or cooked frozen
peas
2 carrots, grated
2 cooked beetroot (red beets), diced
1 bunch of spring onions (scallions),
white part only, trimmed to
7.5 cm/3 in long
English Dressing (page 383)

Separate the lettuce into leaves, discarding any damaged outer ones. Arrange on a flat serving platter. Put neat piles of all the remaining salad ingredients on the lettuce. Chill until ready to serve. Pour the dressing into a small glass jug and hand separately.

* **40 calories per serving**
* **Fairly high fibre**

Cucumber and Spring Onion Salad

SERVES 4

½ cucumber, diced
1 bunch of spring onions (scallions), chopped
Freshly ground black pepper
Minted Yoghurt Dressing (page 384)
A sprig of mint, to garnish

Put the cucumber and spring onions in a bowl and toss gently. Add a good grinding of pepper and toss again. Pour over the dressing, toss and turn into a serving dish. Garnish with a sprig of mint and chill for 30 minutes before serving.

* **30 calories per serving**
* **Medium fibre**

Mixed Green Salad

SERVES 4

1 little gem lettuce
5 cm/2 in piece of cucumber, sliced
1 green (bell) pepper, sliced into rings
1 bunch of spring onions (scallions), cut into short lengths
Green Herb Dressing (page 384)
½ box of cress

Separate the lettuce into leaves and tear each one in half. Place in a salad bowl. Add the cucumber, green pepper and spring onions and toss gently. Just before serving, add the dressing and toss. Snip the cress with scissors and scatter all over the top of the salad.

* **20 calories per serving**
* **Medium fibre**

Green Bean with Tomato Salsa Salad

SERVES 4

225 g/8 oz French (green) beans
225 g/8 oz/1 small can of tomatoes, drained and finely chopped
1 small onion, finely chopped
15 ml/1 tbsp chopped marjoram
7.5 ml/1½ tsp Worcestershire sauce
Freshly ground black pepper

Cook the beans in boiling water for about 6 minutes until just tender. Drain, rinse with cold water and drain again. Lay in one direction in a shallow serving dish. Mix together the remaining ingredients and spoon across the centre of the beans. Chill until ready to serve.

* **30 calories per serving**
* **Fairly high fibre**

Warm Potato Salad

SERVES 4

450 g/1 lb potatoes, scrubbed and cut into bite-sized pieces
Extra-light Mayonnaise (page 385)
Paprika, for dusting
30 ml/2 tbsp snipped chives

Boil the potatoes in water for about 6 minutes or until just tender. Drain and turn into a bowl. Cool slightly, then add the Extra-light Mayonnaise. Toss gently, turn into a serving dish and sprinkle with paprika and the chives. Serve warm.

* **130 calories per serving**
* **Medium fibre**

Celeriac and Carrot Salad

SERVES 4

1 small celeriac (celery root)
2 large carrots
45 ml/3 tbsp white wine vinegar
30 ml/2 tbsp water
15 ml/1 tbsp olive oil
5 ml/1 tsp caster (superfine) sugar
Salt and freshly ground black pepper
6 stuffed olives, sliced

Peel the celeriac, cut into thin slices, then cut the slices into thin strips. Prepare the carrots in the same way. Mix together in a salad bowl. Whisk the vinegar with the water and oil. Whisk in the sugar and salt and pepper to taste. Pour over the vegetables and toss thoroughly. Scatter the olive slices on top and leave to marinate for at least 30 minutes before serving.

* **75 calories per serving**
* **Fairly high fibre**

Chinese Leaf and Watercress Salad

SERVES 4

¹/₂ small head of Chinese leaves (stem lettuce), cut into chunks
1 bunch of watercress
10 ml/2 tsp sesame oil
15 ml/1 tbsp cider vinegar
15 ml/1 tbsp reduced-salt soy sauce
Freshly ground black pepper
15 ml/1 tbsp sesame seeds, toasted

Put the Chinese leaves in a bowl. Trim off any feathery stalks from the watercress, pull into small sprigs and add to the Chinese leaves. Whisk the sesame oil with the cider vinegar, soy sauce and some pepper. Drizzle over, toss and sprinkle with sesame seeds before serving.

* **60 calories per serving**
* **Fairly high fibre**

Thai Fragrant Rice Salad

SERVES 4

175 g/6 oz/³/₄ cup Thai fragrant rice
1 carrot, finely diced
50 g/2 oz frozen peas
2 spring onions (scallions), chopped
2 tomatoes, finely chopped
2.5 cm/1 in piece of cucumber, finely diced
30 ml/2 tbsp white wine vinegar
10 ml/2 tsp sesame oil
15 ml/1 tbsp water
A pinch of chilli powder
Salt and freshly ground black pepper

Cook the rice according to the packet directions, adding the carrot after 4 minutes of cooking and the peas after 8 minutes. Drain, rinse with cold water and drain again. Add the spring onions, tomatoes and cucumber. Whisk together the remaining ingredients, pour over and toss gently. Chill for at least 30 minutes to allow the flavours to develop.

* **190 calories per serving**
* **Fairly high fibre**

Shredded Cabbage Salad

SERVES 4

1 small white cabbage, about
450 g/1 lb
30 ml/2 tbsp sunflower oil
30 ml/2 tbsp white wine vinegar
15 ml/1 tbsp water
A good pinch of caster (superfine)
sugar
Salt and freshly ground black pepper

Quarter the cabbage, cut out the thick core, then cut the cabbage into very thin shreds. Alternatively, grate it coarsely. Whisk together the oil, vinegar and water and drizzle over. Sprinkle with the sugar and salt and pepper and toss well. Leave to stand for at least 30 minutes to allow the flavours to develop.

* 100 calories per serving
* Fairly high fibre

Village Salad

SERVES 4

¼ small white cabbage
¼ cos (romaine) lettuce, torn into
pieces
2 ripe tomatoes, cut into wedges
5 cm/2 in piece of cucumber, cubed
1 small onion, sliced and separated
into rings
2.5 ml/½ tsp dried oregano
15 ml/1 tbsp diced Feta cheese
4 stoned (pitted) black olives, sliced
15 ml/1 tbsp olive oil
15 ml/1 tbsp red wine vinegar
15 ml/1 tbsp water
Salt and freshly ground black pepper

Quarter the cabbage, cut out the thick core, then shred. Arrange in a shallow bowl with the lettuce over.

Scatter the tomatoes, cucumber and onion over. Sprinkle with the oregano, cheese and olives. Whisk together the oil, vinegar and water and drizzle over. Sprinkle with salt and a good grinding of pepper.

* 70 calories per serving
* Fairly high fibre

Pasta Salad with Bite

SERVES 4

100 g/4 oz multi-coloured conchiglie
pasta
200 g/7 oz/1 small can of naturally
sweet sweetcorn (corn), drained
1 small green (bell) pepper, finely
chopped
1 small red chilli, seeded and chopped
8 stuffed olives, sliced
15 ml/1 tbsp chilli oil
15 ml/1 tbsp water
15 ml/1 tbsp red wine vinegar
Salt and freshly ground black pepper
8 cherry tomatoes
Small sprigs of coriander (cilantro)

Cook the pasta according to the packet directions. Drain, rinse with cold water and drain again. Turn into a salad bowl. Add the corn, green pepper, chilli and olives. Whisk together the chilli oil and water with the wine vinegar and a little salt and pepper. Pour over the salad and toss gently. Make three cross-cuts in the tomatoes from the rounded ends not quite through the stalk end. Gently ease back the flesh around the seeds to resemble flower heads. Arrange around the top of the salad and garnish with small sprigs of coriander.

* 195 calories per serving
* High fibre

Japanese Salad

SERVES 4

50 g/2 oz/1 small can of anchovy fillets, drained
30 ml/2 tbsp skimmed milk
175 g/6 oz/³/₄ cup long-grain rice
75 g/3 oz small button mushrooms, thinly sliced
1 carrot, cut into short, very fine matchsticks
1 celery stick, cut into short, very fine matchsticks
5 cm/2 in piece of cucumber, cut into short, very fine matchsticks
45 ml/3 tbsp reduced-salt soy sauce
30 ml/2 tbsp white wine vinegar
15 ml/1 tbsp sesame oil
15 ml/1 tbsp toasted sesame seeds
15 ml/1 tbsp chopped coriander (cilantro)

Soak the anchovies in the milk. Rinse the rice, drain, then cook in boiling, lightly salted water according to the packet directions until just tender. Drain, rinse with cold water and drain again. Turn into a salad bowl. Add the mushrooms, carrot, celery and cucumber to the rice and toss gently. Whisk together the soy sauce, vinegar and oil and pour over the salad. Toss. Sprinkle with the sesame seeds and coriander. Pat the anchovies dry on kitchen paper (paper towels). Roll up each and arrange attractively over the salad.

* **220 calories per serving**
* **Fairly high fibre**

Chinese Soya Bean Salad

SERVES 4

425g/15 oz/1 large can of soya beans, rinsed and drained
100 g/4 oz/2 cups beansprouts
1 large carrot, grated
300 g/11 oz/1 medium can of mandarin oranges in natural juice, drained, reserving the juice
2 spring onions (scallions), chopped
2.5 cm/1 in piece of cucumber, finely diced
30 ml/2 tbsp reduced-salt soy sauce
15 ml/1 tbsp white wine vinegar

Put the soya beans in a salad bowl with the beansprouts, carrot, oranges, spring onions and cucumber. Whisk the soy sauce and vinegar with 30 ml/2 tbsp of the mandarin orange juice. Pour over the salad, toss, and chill until ready to serve.

* **180 calories per serving**
* **Fairly high fibre**

Wild Rice Salad

SERVES 4

175 g/6 oz/³/₄ cup wild rice mix
50 g/2 oz mangetout (snow peas),
trimmed
100 g/4 oz baby sweetcorn (corn) cobs
50 g/2 oz button mushrooms, thinly
sliced
2.5 cm/1 in piece of cucumber, finely
chopped
15 ml/1 tbsp sunflower oil
30 ml/2 tbsp white wine vinegar
15 ml/1 tbsp apple juice
A few drops of Tabasco sauce
Salt and freshly ground black pepper
30 ml/2 tbsp finely chopped parsley
15 ml/1 tbsp chopped thyme
Thin twists of cucumber, to garnish

Cook the rice according to the packet directions. Add the mangetout and sweetcorn cobs for the last 3 minutes' cooking time. Drain, rinse with cold water and drain again. Add the mushrooms and cucumber and mix in gently. Whisk the oil, vinegar, apple juice and Tabasco with a little salt and pepper to taste and the herbs. Drizzle over the salad and toss gently. Cover and chill until ready to serve, garnished with thin twists of cucumber.

* **200 calories per serving**
* **High fibre**

Melon, Cucumber and Tomato Salad

SERVES 4

1 small honeydew melon, skin
removed, seeded and cubed
1 small cucumber, peeled and diced
8 cherry tomatoes, halved
15 ml/1 tbsp chopped mint
15 ml/1 tbsp chopped parsley
Finely grated rind and juice of ¹/₂ orange
Finely grated rind and juice of 1 lemon
15 ml/1 tbsp olive oil
A pinch of salt
Freshly ground black pepper
1 bunch of watercress
15 ml/1 tbsp toasted pine nuts

Mix the melon with the cucumber and tomatoes in a bowl. Whisk together all the remaining ingredients except the watercress and pine nuts and pour over the salad. Toss gently. Chill until ready to serve. Trim the feathery ends of the stalks from the watercress and separate into sprigs. Arrange in a salad bowl Spoon in the melon mixture and sprinkle with the pine nuts before serving.

* **95 calories per serving**
* **Medium fibre**

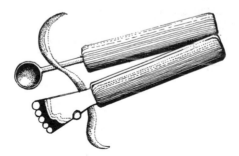

Crispy Crunch Salad

SERVES 4

1 unpeeled red eating (dessert) apple,
    diced
15 ml/1 tbsp lemon juice
1/2 small iceberg lettuce, shredded
1 bunch of radishes, sliced
1 red onion, sliced and separated into
    rings
2 celery sticks, chopped
15 ml/1 tbsp olive oil
15 ml/1 tbsp red wine vinegar
15 ml/1 tbsp apple juice
15 ml/1 tbsp chopped basil
Salt and freshly ground black pepper

Toss the apple in the lemon juice to prevent browning. Put in a salad bowl with the lettuce, radishes, onion and celery. Whisk the oil with the vinegar, apple juice, basil and salt and pepper to taste. When ready to serve, pour over the salad, toss and serve.

* 65 calories per serving
* Fairly high fibre

Warm Carrot and Mustard Salad

SERVES 4

4–6 large carrots
Salt and freshly ground black pepper
15 ml/1 tbsp sunflower oil
30 ml/2 tbsp black mustard seeds
30 ml/2 tbsp lemon juice

Thinly pare the carrots into long ribbons with a potato peeler or grate coarsely. Place in a salad bowl and sprinkle with a little salt and pepper. Heat the oil in a frying pan (skillet). Add the mustard seeds. As soon as they start to pop, add the lemon juice, swirl round and pour over the salad. Toss and serve straight away.

* 85 calories per serving
* Fairly high fibre

Spinach, Cucumber and Kiwi Salad

SERVES 4

100 g/4 oz young spinach leaves,
    trimmed
2 kiwi fruit
1/4 cucumber, peeled and thinly sliced
2 spring onions (scallions), finely
    chopped
15 ml/1 tbsp olive oil
15 ml/1 tbsp white wine vinegar
15 ml/1 tbsp apple juice
15 ml/1 tbsp chopped thyme
15 ml/1 tbsp chopped parsley
Salt and freshly ground black pepper

Rinse the spinach thoroughly and pat dry on kitchen paper (paper towels). Arrange on a flat serving plate. Peel and halve the kiwi fruit and slice thinly. Arrange the cucumber and kiwi slices attractively on the spinach. Whisk together the remaining ingredients and drizzle over. Chill for 30 minutes to allow the flavours to develop.

* 65 calories per serving
* Fairly high fibre

Beansprout and Cucumber Salad

SERVES 4

175 g/6 oz/3 cups beansprouts
¼ cucumber, very thinly sliced
1 green (bell) pepper, very thinly sliced
30m/2 tbsp reduced-salt soy sauce
15 ml/1 tbsp dry sherry

Mix the vegetables together. Stir the soy sauce and sherry together and drizzle over. Toss and leave to stand for 30 minutes to allow the flavours to develop.

* **35 calories per serving**
* **Fairly high fibre**

Grated Winter Salad

SERVES 4

Lettuce leaves
½ celeriac (celery root), coarsely grated
½ small swede (rutabaga), coarsely grated
2 carrots, coarsely grated
Low-fat French Dressing (page 380)
Mustard and cress, to garnish

Put lettuce leaves on four individual plates. Put three separate piles of the grated vegetables on each plate. Spoon a little dressing over each plate and garnish with mustard and cress.

* **65 calories per serving**
* **Fairly high fibre**

English Cucumber Salad

SERVES 4

½ cucumber, peeled and very thinly sliced
30 ml/2 tbsp malt vinegar
Freshly ground black pepper
15 ml/1 tbsp snipped chives

Place the cucumber in a shallow dish and add the vinegar and pepper. Toss thoroughly and leave to stand for at least 15 minutes. Sprinkle with the chives before serving.

* **10 calories per serving**
* **Low fibre**

Chicory, Orange and Poppy Seed Salad

SERVES 4

2 heads of chicory (Belgian endive)
1 orange
Non-oil Vinaigrette Dressing (page 381)
15 ml/1 tbsp poppy seeds

Cut a cone-shaped core out of the base of each head of chicory. Separate into leaves and arrange on four small plates. Cut off all the pith and rind from the orange. Cut into thin slices, then cut each slice into quarters. Arrange on the chicory and pour over any juice. Spoon the dressing over, sprinkle with poppy seeds and serve.

* **40 calories per serving**
* **Medium fibre**

Chinese Leaf and Mango Salad

SERVES 4

1/2 small head of Chinese leaves (stem lettuce), shredded
1 ripe mango
5 cm/2 in piece of cucumber, finely diced
4 spring onions (scallions), diagonally sliced
Light Soy Dressing (page 384)

Put the Chinese leaves in four shallow salad bowls. Peel the mango, cut the flesh away from the stone (pit) and dice. Arrange the mango and cucumber over the Chinese leaves, then sprinkle with the spring onions. Spoon over the dressing and serve.

* **50 calories per serving**
* **Medium fibre**

Sesame Coleslaw

SERVES 4

1/4 white cabbage, finely shredded or coarsely grated
2 carrots, coarsely grated
1 celery stick, thinly sliced
1/2 small onion, grated
30 ml/2 tbsp low-calorie mayonnaise
15 ml/1 tbsp skimmed milk
Salt and freshly ground black pepper
15 ml/1 tbsp toasted sesame seeds

Mix the prepared vegetables thoroughly. Blend the mayonnaise with the milk and pour over. Toss and season to taste. Spoon into a serving bowl and sprinkle with the sesame seeds before serving.

* **55 calories per serving**
* **Fairly high fibre**

Neapolitan Salad

SERVES 4

1/2 curly endive (frisée lettuce)
2 courgettes (zucchini), very thinly sliced
4 cherry tomatoes, thinly sliced
6 stuffed green olives, sliced
1 small red onion, thinly sliced and separated into rings
45 ml/3 tbsp dry white wine
2.5 ml/1/2 tsp Dijon mustard
10 ml/2 tsp olive oil
Salt and freshly ground black pepper
Lemon juice (optional)

Separate the curly endive into small pieces and arrange on four small plates. Scatter the courgettes, tomatoes, olives and onion over. Whisk together the wine, mustard, oil and a little salt and pepper. Add a dash of lemon juice, if liked. Drizzle over the salads and serve.

* **45 calories per serving**
* **Medium fibre**

Snack Attack

When you're feeling peckish and need a quick bite, the temptation is to grab at convenience foods, which are often high in fat and other undesirables like salt and sugar. This chapter is packed with tasty, nutritious, easy snacks, suitable to eat at lunchtime or in the evening. Keep pittas, sliced breads and small part-baked baguettes in the freezer and you'll always have the basis for these tasty treats to hand.

Toasted Pizza Triangles

SERVES 2

Low-fat sunflower or olive oil spread
4 slices of white bread
2 slices of low-fat Cheddar or
　　processed cheese
1 large tomato, sliced
2 good pinches of dried oregano

Thinly scrape low-fat spread on one side of each slice of bread. Sandwich together in pairs, spread-sides out, with the cheese, tomato slices and oregano. Grill (broil) or fry (sauté) in a non-stick frying pan (skillet), pressing down firmly with a fish slice, or use a sandwich toaster to cook the sandwiches until golden brown on both sides. Cut into triangles and serve.

* 210 calories per serving
* Medium fibre

Sage and Onion Toastie

SERVES 1

Low-fat sunflower or olive oil spread
2 slices of granary bread
25 g/1 oz/¼ cup low-fat Cheddar
　　cheese, grated
4 sage leaves, chopped
2 onion slices, separated into rings
Freshly ground black pepper

Thinly scrape low-fat spread on one side of each slice of bread. Cover one half, spread-side down, with the cheese and top with the sage leaves and onion rings. Add a good grinding of pepper, then top with the other slice of bread, spread-side up. Cook as for Toasted Pizza Triangles, pressing down firmly with a fish slice during cooking, unless using a sandwich toaster.

* 265 calories
* High fibre

Curried Bean Toastie

SERVES 2

Low-fat sunflower or olive oil spread
4 slices of wholemeal bread
10 ml/2 tsp curry paste
225 g/8 oz/1 small can of baked
　　beans
10 ml/2 tsp sultanas (golden raisins)

Thinly scrape low-fat spread on one side of each slice of bread. Spread the curry paste on the other side of two of the slices. Top with the beans, then sprinkle with the sultanas. Cover with the other two slices of bread, spread-sides up. Cook as for Toasted Pizza Triangles.

* 250 calories per serving
* High fibre

Ham and Pineapple Perfection

SERVES 1

Low-fat sunflower or olive oil spread
2 slices of white bread
1 thin slice of lean ham, fat removed
1 canned pineapple ring, drained on
　　kitchen paper (paper towels)
1 slice of low-fat Cheddar cheese

Thinly scrape low-fat spread on one side of each slice of bread. Sandwich together, spread-sides out, with the ham, pineapple and cheese. Cook as for Toasted Pizza Triangles, pressing down well with a fish slice during cooking, unless using a sandwich toaster.

* 230 calories
* Medium fibre

Photograph opposite: Village Salad (page 281) and Chinese Leaf and Mango Salad (page 286)

Blue Cheese, Celery and Pickle Cruncher

SERVES 1

Low-fat sunflower or olive oil spread
2 slices of wholemeal bread
10 ml/2 tsp tomato pickle
25 g/1 oz/¼ cup low-fat blue cheese,
*   crumbled*
1 celery stick, finely chopped

Thinly scrape low-fat spread on one side of each slice of bread. Spread the other side of one slice with the pickle. Top with the crumbled cheese and the celery. Press the other slice of bread, spread-side up, firmly on top. Cook as for Toasted Pizza Triangles, pressing down well with a fish slice during cooking, unless using a sandwich toaster.

* 255 calories
* High fibre

Chicken and Mushroom Muncher

SERVES 1

Low-fat sunflower or olive oil spread
2 slices of wholemeal bread
1 slice of cooked chicken breast
2 mushrooms, chopped
A pinch of dried thyme
Freshly ground black pepper
15 ml/1 tbsp low-fat condensed
*   mushroom soup*

Thinly scrape low-fat spread on one side of each slice of bread. Lay the chicken on one slice, spread-side down. Top with the mushrooms, thyme and a good grinding of pepper. Spread the soup on the plain side of the other slice of bread. Lay this on top of the sandwich, spread-side up. Cook as for Toasted Pizza Triangles, pressing down firmly with a fish slice during cooking, unless using a sandwich toaster.

* 185 calories
* High fibre

Minted Pea, Ham and Mozzarella Muncher

SERVE 2

Low-fat sunflower or olive oil spread
4 slices of white bread
200 g/7 oz/1 small can of garden
*   peas, drained*
A good pinch of dried mint
2 thin slices of ham, all fat removed
50 g/2 oz/½ cup low-fat Mozzarella
*   cheese, thinly sliced*
Freshly ground black pepper

Thinly scrape low-fat spread on one side of each slice of bread. Mash the peas with the mint. Spread on two slices of the bread, spread-sides down. Top with a slice of ham, then the Mozzarella. Add a good grinding of pepper. Cover with the remaining slices of bread, spread-sides up. Cook as for Toasted Pizza Triangles, pressing down well with a fish slice during cooking, unless using a sandwich toaster.

* 360 calories per serving
* High fibre

Photograph opposite: **Strawberry Cheese Baskets (page 322)**

Kentucky Fried Chicken Sandwich

SERVES 2

Low-fat sunflower or olive oil spread
4 slices of granary bread
2 slices of cooked chicken breast
1 small banana, sliced
2.5 ml/½ tsp ground cumin
2.5 ml/½ tsp dried onion granules
Salt and freshly ground black pepper
15 ml/1 tbsp chopped parsley

Thinly scrape low-fat spread on one side of each slice of bread. Put the chicken on two of the slices, spread-sides down. Mash the banana and spread over. Mix together the cumin, onion granules, a little salt and pepper and the parsley and sprinkle over. Top with the remaining bread, spread-sides up. Cook as for Toasted Pizza Triangles (page 288), pressing down firmly with a fish slice during cooking, unless using a sandwich toaster.

* 235 calories per serving
* High fibre

Turkey and Cranberry Crispie

SERVES 2

Low-fat sunflower or olive oil spread
4 slices of wholemeal bread
2 slices of cooked turkey breast
15 ml/1 tbsp cranberry sauce
15 ml/1 tbsp low-fat soft cheese
15 ml/1 tbsp chopped parsley
A good pinch of dried thyme
Salt and freshly ground black pepper

Thinly scrape low-fat spread on one side of each slice of bread. Put the turkey on two of the slices, spread-sides down. Mix the cranberry sauce with the cheese, herbs and a little salt and pepper. Spread over the turkey. Top with the remaining bread, spread-sides up. Cook as for Toasted Pizza Triangles (page 288), pressing down firmly with a fish slice during cooking, unless using a sandwich toaster.

* 255 calories per serving
* High fibre

Cheese, Citrus and Pine Nut Bite

SERVES 2

Low-fat sunflower or olive oil spread
4 slices of granary bread
50 g/2 oz/½ cup Edam cheese, grated
1 orange, peeled and chopped
15 ml/1 tbsp pine nuts
A good pinch of dried mixed herbs

Thinly scrape low-fat spread on one side of each slice of bread. Top two slices with the cheese, spread-sides down. Add the orange, pine nuts and herbs. Top with the remaining bread, spread-sides up. Cook as for Toasted Pizza Triangles (page 288), pressing down well with a fish slice during cooking, unless using a sandwich toaster.

* 325 calories per serving
* High fibre

Corn and Tuna Pitta Pockets

SERVES 4

200 g/7 oz/1 small can of naturally sweet sweetcorn (corn), drained
185 g/6¹/₂ oz/1 small can of tuna in brine or water, drained
¹/₂ small red (bell) pepper, chopped
2.5 cm/1 in piece of cucumber, chopped
30 ml/2 tbsp low-calorie mayonnaise
A good pinch of paprika
Salt and freshly ground black pepper
4 wholemeal pitta breads

Mix together all the ingredients except the pitta breads. Warm the pittas either under the grill (broiler) or in the microwave. Cut into halves, then gently open along the cut edges to form pockets. Fill with the tuna mixture and serve two halves per person.

* **300 calories per serving**
* **High fibre**

Greek Village Pittas

SERVES 4

4 pitta breads
1 wedge of iceberg lettuce, shredded
1 small red onion, sliced and separated into rings
2.5 cm/1 in piece of cucumber, thinly sliced
2 tomatoes, thinly sliced
4 stoned (pitted) black olives, sliced
75 g/3 oz/¹/₃ cup Feta cheese, crumbled
15 ml/1 tbsp olive oil
10 ml/2 tsp red wine vinegar
Salt and freshly ground black pepper
1.5 ml/¹/₄ tsp dried oregano

Warm the pittas either under the grill (broiler) or in the microwave. Cut into halves and gently open along the cut edges to form pockets. Pack a little lettuce, onion, cucumber and tomato into each pocket, then add the olive slices and cheese. Whisk together the oil, vinegar, a pinch of salt and pepper and the oregano then drizzle a little over each portion of salad. Serve two halves per person.

* **255 calories per serving**
* **Fairly high fibre**

Curried Chicken and Peach Pittas

SERVES 4

5 ml/1 tsp curry paste
30 ml/2 tbsp low-fat crème fraîche
Salt and freshly ground black pepper
100 g/4 oz/1 cup cooked chicken, all skin removed, finely chopped
220 g/8 oz/1 small can of peach slices, drained and chopped
15 ml/1 tbsp chopped coriander (cilantro)
4 garlic pitta breads
4 crisp lettuce leaves

Mix together the curry paste and crème fraîche with a little salt and pepper. Stir in the chicken, peaches and coriander. Warm the pittas either under the grill (broiler) or in the microwave. Make a slit along one side of each and open up to form a pocket. Line each with a lettuce leaf, then fill with the curried chicken and peach mixture.

* **240 calories per serving**
* **Medium fibre**

Rosy Prawn and Cucumber Pittas

SERVES 4

*100 g/4 oz cooked peeled prawns
   (shrimp), thawed if frozen
30 ml/2 tbsp low-calorie mayonnaise
5 ml/1 tsp tomato ketchup (catsup)
5 ml/1 tsp Worcestershire sauce
Tabasco sauce
4 cm/1½ in piece of cucumber,
   chopped
1 tomato, chopped
4 pitta breads
4 lollo rosso lettuce leaves*

Drain the prawns on kitchen paper (paper towels). Mix the mayonnaise with the ketchup, Worcestershire sauce and Tabasco sauce to taste. Stir in the prawns, cucumber and tomato. Warm the pittas either under the grill (broiler) or in the microwave. Make a slit along one side of each and open up to form a pocket. Line each with a lettuce leaf, then fill with the prawn mixture.

* **235 calories per serving**
* **Medium fibre**

Ploughman Pitta

SERVES 4

*4 wholemeal pitta breads
30 ml/2 tbsp sweet pickle
4 round lettuce leaves
50 g/2 oz/½ cup low-fat Cheddar
   cheese, grated
4 pickled onions, sliced
2 tomatoes, sliced
2.5 cm/1 in piece of cucumber, thinly
   sliced*

Warm the pittas either under the grill (broiler) or in the microwave. Make a slit along one side of each and open up to form a pocket. Spread a little pickle in one side of each pocket and line with a lettuce leaf. Divide the cheese between the pockets, then tuck in the slices of onion, tomato and cucumber and serve.

* **235 calories per serving**
* **High fibre**

Crunchy Carrot Cooler

SERVES 4

*2 large carrots, grated
30 ml/2 tbsp chopped walnuts
30 ml/2 tbsp sultanas (golden raisins)
60 ml/4 tbsp low-fat plain yoghurt
15 ml/1 tbsp snipped chives
Salt and freshly ground black pepper
4 pitta breads*

Mix the carrots with the walnuts and sultanas. Blend the yoghurt with the chives and a little salt and pepper. Warm the pittas either under the grill (broiler) or in the microwave. Cut into halves and gently open along the cut edges to form pockets. Fill the pockets with the carrot mixture, add a spoonful of the yoghurt mixture to each and serve two halves per person.

* **235 calories per serving**
* **High fibre**

Strawberry and Cucumber Delight

SERVES 4

100 g/4 oz strawberries, sliced
5 cm/2 in piece of cucumber, peeled
*   and sliced*
10 ml/2 tsp balsamic vinegar
Freshly ground black pepper
4 sesame pitta breads
60 ml/4 tbsp low-fat fromage frais
4 crisp lettuce leaves

Put the strawberries and cucumber in a shallow dish. Sprinkle the balsamic vinegar over and season with pepper. Leave to stand for 15 minutes. Warm the pittas either under the grill (broiler) or in the microwave. Make a slit along one side of each and open up to form a pocket. Spread the insides with the fromage frais and line each with a lettuce leaf. Spoon in the strawberry and cucumber mixture and serve.

* **200 calories per serving**
* **Fairly high fibre**

Herb, Ham and Melon Pittas

SERVES 4

½ honeydew melon
30 ml/2 tbsp chopped parsley
30 ml/2 tbsp snipped chives
30 ml/2 tbsp chopped basil
Freshly ground black pepper
4 pitta breads
8 wafer-thin slices of Parma (or similar)
*   ham, all fat removed*

Scoop the seeds out of the melon and discard. Cut the skin off the fruit and cut the flesh into thin strips. Mix the herbs together with a good grinding of pepper. Dip the melon strips in the herb mixture until coated. Warm the pittas either under the grill (broiler) or in the microwave. Make a slit along one side of each and open up to form a pocket. Lay a slice of ham in each pitta, then top with the melon strips, then the remaining slices of ham.

* **200 calories per serving**
* **Medium fibre**

Spicy Bean Pittas

SERVES 4

425 g/15 oz/1 large can of red kidney
    beans, drained, rinsed and drained
    again
30 ml/2 tbsp chilli relish
1 green (bell) pepper, chopped
1 small onion, finely chopped
Freshly ground black pepper
A few drops of Tabasco sauce
    (optional)
4 wholemeal pitta breads
4 crisp lettuce leaves
30 ml/2 tbsp low-fat plain yoghurt

Mix the beans with the relish, green pepper and onion. Season with a good grinding of pepper. Add a few drops of Tabasco sauce to spice it up, if liked. Warm the pittas either under the grill (broiler) or in the microwave. Make a slit along one side of each and open up to form a pocket. Line with the lettuce leaves, then fill with the chilli bean mixture. Top each with a dollop of yoghurt and serve.

* **265 calories per serving**
* **High fibre**

Chick Pea, Mozzarella and Tomato Pittas

SERVES 4

425 g/15 oz/1 large can of chick peas
    (garbanzos), drained
10 ml/2 tsp lemon juice
Freshly ground black pepper
1 garlic clove, crushed
4 pitta breads
1 beefsteak tomato, sliced
50 g/2 oz/½ cup low-fat Mozzarella
    cheese, grated
4 stoned (pitted) green olives, sliced
16 basil leaves, torn

Mash the chick peas with the lemon juice, some pepper and the garlic. Thin with water to form a thick but spreadable paste. Warm the pitta breads under the grill (broiler) or in the microwave. Make a slit along one side of each and open up to form a pocket. Halve the tomato slices. Spread the chick pea mixture in the pitta pockets and top with the tomato slices. Add the cheese, olive slices and basil and serve.

* **295 calories per serving**
* **High fibre**

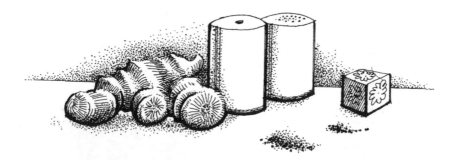

Scandinavian Sticks

SERVES 4

4 small baguettes
4 rollmop herrings, drained on kitchen
  paper (paper towels)
2.5 cm/1 in piece of cucumber, peeled
  and grated
60 ml/4 tbsp low-fat fromage frais
5 ml/1 tsp dried dill (dill weed)
Salt and freshly ground black pepper
2 onions, thinly sliced and separated
  into rings

Make a slit along one side of each baguette. Slice the rollmops, discarding any cocktail sticks (toothpicks). Squeeze the cucumber to remove the moisture, then mix with the fromage frais, dill and some salt and pepper. Spread this mixture in the baguettes, add the fish slices and the onion rings and serve.

* **250 calories per serving**
* **Medium fibre**

Russian Roulette

SERVES 4

50 g/2 oz/1 small can of anchovies,
  drained
30 ml/2 tbsp skimmed milk
295 g/10½ oz/1 medium can of diced
  mixed vegetables
15 ml/1 tbsp low-calorie mayonnaise
15 ml/1 tbsp low-fat crème fraîche
Freshly ground black pepper
4 small baguettes
2 cooked beetroot (red beets), thinly
  sliced
15 ml/1 tbsp snipped chives

Put the anchovies in a small bowl with the milk and leave to soak while preparing the filling. Drain the mixed vegetables and dry on kitchen paper (paper towels). Tip into a bowl and mix in the mayonnaise and crème fraîche. Season to taste with pepper. Drain the anchovies and dry on kitchen paper. Cut along one side of each baguette. Fill with the beetroot, then the vegetable salad, then the anchovies. Sprinkle with the chives and serve.

* **275 calories per serving**
* **Fairly high fibre**

Scrambled Egg and Smoked Salmon Sensation

SERVES 4

10 g/¼ oz/2 tsp low-fat sunflower or olive oil spread
2 eggs
2 egg whites
15 ml/1 tbsp skimmed milk
Salt and freshly ground black pepper
100 g/4 oz smoked salmon pieces
15 ml/1 tbsp chopped parsley
4 small baguettes

Melt the low-fat spread in a saucepan. Whisk together the eggs, egg whites and milk with a little salt and pepper and pour into the pan. Cook over a gentle heat, stirring, until scrambled. Do not allow to boil. Leave to cool slightly, then stir in the salmon and parsley. Cut along one side of each baguette and fill with the salmon and egg mixture. Serve straight away while still warm.

* **335 calories per serving**
* **Medium fibre**

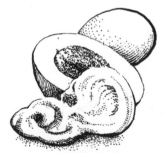

Salmon and Cucumber Special

SERVES 4

5 cm/2 in piece of cucumber, thinly sliced
15 ml/1 tbsp red wine vinegar
5 ml/1 tsp black mustard seeds
185 g/6½ oz/1 small can of pink or red salmon, drained
60 ml/4 tbsp low-fat fromage frais
30 ml/2 tbsp chopped watercress
4 small baguettes

Toss the cucumber slices with the vinegar and mustard seeds in a shallow bowl. Empty the salmon into a dish and discard any black skin. Remove the bones, if liked, but they are very good for you. Mash the fish and stir in the fromage frais and watercress. Cut along one side of each baguette. Spread the fish filling inside and top with the cucumber slices.

* **285 calories per serving**
* **Medium fibre**

Pâté Crunch

SERVES 4

4 small baguettes
100 g/4 oz low-fat smooth liver pâté
15 ml/1 tsp sunflower seeds
1 celery stick, finely chopped
30 ml/2 tbsp low-fat fromage frais
5 cm/2 in piece of cucumber, sliced
2 tomatoes, sliced
Mustard and cress, to garnish

Cut along one side of each baguette. Mash together the liver pâté, sunflower seeds, celery and fromage frais and spread in the baguettes. Fill with slices of cucumber and tomato and garnish with mustard and cress.

* **265 calories per serving**
* **Medium fibre**

Paprika Chicken

SERVES 4

45 ml/3 tbsp low-fat plain yoghurt
15 ml/1 tbsp paprika
5 ml/1 tsp clear honey
200 g/7 oz/1 small can of pimientos,
    drained and chopped
175 g/6 oz/1¹/₂ cups cooked chicken,
    all skin removed, finely chopped
Salt and freshly ground black pepper
4 small baguettes
4 lettuce leaves

Mix the yoghurt with the paprika and honey. Stir in the pimientos and chicken and season with salt and pepper. Cut along one side of each baguette. Line with the lettuce leaves, fill with the chicken mixture and serve.

* **250 calories per serving**
* **Medium fibre**

Light BLT Baguettes

SERVES 4

8 extra-lean rashers (slices) of rindless
    smoked streaky bacon
30 ml/2 tbsp low-calorie mayonnaise
30 ml/2 tbsp low-fat plain yoghurt
15 ml/1 tbsp snipped chives
Freshly ground black pepper
4 small baguettes
3 tomatoes, sliced
6 crisp lettuce leaves, shredded

Grill (broil) the bacon rashers until really crisp. Drain on kitchen paper (paper towels). Mix the mayonnaise with the yoghurt, chives and some pepper. Cut along one side of each baguette. Spread the mayonnaise mixture in each one. Lay the bacon on top, then a line of tomato slices and some shredded lettuce.

* **300 calories per serving**
* **Medium fibre**

Chicken Stir-fry Sticks

Use any vegetables and salad stuffs you like.

SERVES 4

15 g/¹/₂ oz/1 tbsp low-fat sunflower or
    olive oil spread
1 carrot, pared into ribbons with a
    potato peeler
1 celery stick, thinly sliced
5 cm/2 in piece of cucumber, thinly
    sliced
4 mushrooms, thinly sliced
2 tomatoes, chopped
¹/₂ green (bell) pepper, cut into very
    thin strips
1 garlic clove, crushed
30 ml/2 tbsp reduced-salt soy sauce
A pinch of ground ginger
75 g/3 oz/³/₄ cup cooked chicken, all
    skin removed, chopped
4 small baguettes

Melt the low-fat spread in a large frying pan (skillet) or wok. Add the prepared vegetables and stir-fry for 3 minutes. Add the soy sauce, ginger and chicken and toss for 2 minutes until piping hot. Cut along one side of each baguette and fill with the stir-fry. Serve straight away.

* **255 calories per serving**
* **Fairly high fibre**

Tuna and Rainbow Pepper Stir-fry Sticks

SERVES 4

15 g/½ oz/1 tbsp low-fat sunflower or
  olive oil spread
1 small onion, thinly sliced
1 red (bell) pepper, cut into very thin
  strips
1 green pepper, cut into very thin
  strips
1 yellow pepper, cut into very thin
  strips
185 g/6½ oz/1 small can of tuna in
  brine or water, drained
30 ml/2 tbsp reduced-salt soy sauce
4 small baguettes

Melt the low-fat spread in a large frying pan (skillet) or wok. Add the onion and peppers and stir-fry for 4 minutes. Add the tuna and soy sauce and toss for 1 minute. Cut along one side of each baguette, fill with the pepper and tuna mixture and serve hot.

* **300 calories per serving**
* **Fairly high fibre**

Herb Omelette and Salad Baguettes

SERVES 4

2 eggs
2 egg whites
15 ml/1 tbsp skimmed milk
Salt and freshly ground black pepper
15 ml/1 tbsp chopped parsley
2.5 ml/½ tsp dried mixed herbs
15 g/½ oz/1 tbsp low-fat sunflower or
  olive oil spread
4 small baguettes
60 ml/4 tbsp low-fat fromage frais
4 crisp lettuce leaves
2 tomatoes, sliced
2.5 ml/1 in piece of cucumber, thinly
  sliced

Beat together the eggs, egg whites and milk with a little salt and pepper and stir in the parsley and mixed herbs. Heat the low-fat spread in a non-stick frying pan (skillet). Add the egg mixture and cook, lifting and stirring gently, until set. Invert on to a plate, then slide back in the pan and cook for a further minute to cook the other side. Slide out on to the plate again and cut into strips. Cut along one side of each baguette and spread inside with the fromage frais. Line with the lettuce leaves, fill with the egg strips, then the slices of tomato and cucumber. Serve straight away.

* **275 calories per serving**
* **Medium fibre**

Barbecued Beany Micro-jackets

SERVES 4

4 fairly large potatoes, scrubbed
400 g/14 oz/1 large can of baked
*   beans*
10 ml/2 tsp tomato ketchup (catsup)
10 ml/2 tsp brown table sauce
10 ml/2 tsp golden (light corn) syrup
5 ml/1 tsp red wine vinegar
2.5 cm/1 in piece of cucumber, finely
*   chopped*

Prick the potatoes all over with a fork. Wrap each in a piece of kitchen paper (paper towel). Place them in the microwave and cook for about 15 minutes (or according to the manufacturer's instructions) until the potatoes feel tender when squeezed. Leave to stand for 5 minutes. Meanwhile, heat the beans with the ketchup, brown sauce, syrup and vinegar in a saucepan. Cut a cross in the top of each potato and squeeze gently. Place in shallow bowls, spoon the beans over and sprinkle with the cucumber before serving.

* **290 calories per serving**

* **High fibre**

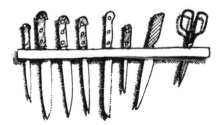

Tzatziki Micro-jackets

SERVES 4

4 fairly large potatoes, scrubbed
Tzatziki (page 97)
5 ml/1 tsp dried mint

Cook the potatoes as for Barbecued Beany Micro-jackets. When cooked, top with Tzatziki and sprinkle with the dried mint.

* **225 calories per serving**

* **High fibre**

Pea and Ham Micro-jackets

SERVES 4

4 fairly large potatoes, scrubbed
Cooling Pea Pâté (page 77)
4 thin slices of lean ham, all fat
*   removed, diced*

Cook the potatoes as for Barbecued Beany Micro-jackets. When cooked, top with Cooling Pea Pâté and sprinkle with the diced ham.

* **270 calories per serving**

* **High fibre**

Hot Chilli Salsa Micro-jackets

SERVES 4

4 fairly large potatoes, scrubbed
Hot Chilli Salsa (page 383)
30 ml/2 tbsp low-fat plain yoghurt
15 ml/1 tbsp snipped chives

Cook the potatoes as for Barbecued Beany Micro-jackets. When cooked, top with Hot Chilli Salsa, then a dollop of low-fat plain yoghurt and sprinkle with the chives.

* **205 calories per serving**

* **High fibre**

Prawn and Pepper Micro-jackets

SERVES 4

4 fairly large potatoes, scrubbed
175 g/6 oz cooked, peeled prawns
(shrimp), thawed if frozen
1 red (bell) pepper, finely chopped
Rosy Dressing (page 385)
Paprika, for dusting

Cook the potatoes as for Barbecued Beany Micro-jackets (page 299). Drain the prawns on kitchen paper (paper towels). Mix the red pepper with the prawns and the dressing. Spoon over the split and squeezed potatoes and dust with paprika before serving.

* 295 calories per serving
* High fibre

Blue Cheese and Broad Bean Micro-jackets

SERVES 4

4 fairly large potatoes, scrubbed
75 g/3 oz/³/₄ cup low-fat blue cheese,
crumbled
45 ml/3 tbsp low-fat plain yoghurt
295 g/10¹/₂ oz/1 medium can of broad
(fava) beans, drained
Freshly ground black pepper
15 ml/1 tbsp chopped parsley

Cook the potatoes as for Barbecued Beany Micro-jackets (page 299). Mash the cheese with the yoghurt and fold in the beans. Season with pepper. Top the cooked potatoes with the bean and cheese mixture and sprinkle with the chopped parsley.

* 270 calories per serving
* High fibre

Cheese and Coleslaw Micro-jackets

SERVES 4

4 fairly large potatoes, scrubbed
175 g/6 oz low-calorie coleslaw
50 g/2 oz/¹/₂ cup strong low-fat
Cheddar cheese, grated
1 tomato, chopped

Cook the potatoes as for Barbecued Beany Micro-jackets (page 299). When cooked, top with the coleslaw, then the cheese, and top each with a little chopped tomato.

* 270 calories per serving
* High fibre

Luscious Asparagus Micro-jackets

SERVES 4

4 fairly large potatoes, scrubbed
295 g/10¹/₂ oz/1 medium can of cut
asparagus spears, drained
225 g/8 oz/1 cup low-fat cottage
cheese
5 ml/1 tsp dried thyme
Salt and freshly ground black pepper

Cook the potatoes as for Barbecued Beany Micro-jackets (page 299). Reserve four head pieces of the asparagus spears for garnish and mix the remainder into the cottage cheese with the thyme. Season with salt and pepper. Top the cooked potatoes with the asparagus cheese mixture and garnish with the reserved asparagus.

* 270 calories per serving
* High fibre

Citrus Cheese Micro-jackets

SERVES 4

4 fairly large potatoes, scrubbed
1 orange
225 g/8 oz/1 cup low-fat cottage cheese
2 spring onions (scallions), finely chopped
1 celery stick, finely chopped
Salt and freshly ground black pepper

Cook the potatoes as for Barbecued Beany Micro-jackets (page 299). Finely grate the rind from the orange. Cut off all the pith, then segment the orange, discarding the membranes. Chop the flesh. Mix the rind and flesh with the cheese. Reserve a little of the green onion tops for garnish and mix the remainder into the cheese with the celery. Season to taste. Top the cooked potatoes with the cheese mixture, then garnish with the reserved green tops.

* **270 calories per serving**
* **High fibre**

Mushroom Micro-jackets

SERVES 4

4 fairly large potatoes, scrubbed
200 g/7 oz/1 small can of sliced mushrooms, drained
1 small garlic clove, crushed
100 g/4 oz/¹/₂ cup low-fat fromage frais
30 ml/2 tbsp chopped parsley
Salt and freshly ground black pepper

Cook the potatoes as for Barbecued Beany Micro-jackets (page 299). Mix the mushrooms with the garlic, fromage frais, half the parsley and salt and pepper to taste. Pile on top of the cooked potatoes and sprinkle with the remaining parsley before serving.

* **220 calories per serving**
* **High fibre**

Mozzarella Citrus Open-top

SERVES 2

2 thick slices of bloomer bread
A scraping of low-fat sunflower or olive oil spread
50 g/2 oz/¹/₂ cup low-fat Mozzarella cheese, grated
1 orange
Freshly ground black pepper
2 small sprigs of basil

Spread the bread with a thin scraping of low-fat spread and top with the cheese. Cut all the rind and pith off the orange and cut into slices. Arrange the orange slices on the cheese, add a good grinding of pepper and garnish each with a small sprig of basil.

* **180 calories per serving**
* **Medium fibre**

Quick Cheese and Tomato Pizza

SERVES 2 OR 4

100 g/4 oz/1 cup self-raising (self-rising) flour
A pinch of salt
40 g/1½ oz/3 tbsp low-fat sunflower or olive oil spread
225 g/8 oz/1 small can of chopped tomatoes, drained
50 g/2 oz/½ cup low-fat Cheddar cheese, grated
1.5 ml/¼ tsp dried basil

Mix the flour and salt in a bowl. Rub in 25 g/1 oz/2 tbsp of the low-fat spread. Mix with enough water to form a soft but not sticky dough. Roll out to a round the size of the base of a medium frying pan (skillet). Heat the remaining low-fat spread in the pan and cook the dough round for about 3 minutes until golden brown. Turn it over. Spread the tomatoes on top and sprinkle with the cheese, then the basil. Cover with a lid or foil and cook over a gentle heat for about 5 minutes until the cheese has melted. Place under a hot grill (broiler) to lightly brown the top. Serve cut into wedges.

* **380 or 190 calories per serving**
* **Medium fibre**

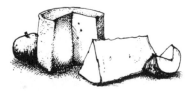

Quick Tomato and Anchovy Pizza

SERVES 2 OR 4

Prepare as for Quick Cheese and Tomato Pizza, but top the cheese with drained canned anchovy fillets and garnish with a few slices of stuffed olive, then continue as before.

* **420 or 210 calories per serving**
* **Medium fibre**

Quick Ham and Mushroom Pizza

SERVES 2 OR 4

Prepare as for Quick Cheese and Tomato Pizza, but add 200 g/7 oz/ 1 small can of sliced mushrooms, drained, and 1 thin slice of lean ham, chopped and any fat discarded, to the pizza before adding the cheese. Sprinkle with dried oregano instead of basil.

* **405 or 205 calories per serving**
* **Medium fibre**

Quick Florentine Pizza

SERVES 2

Prepare as for Quick Cheese and Tomato Pizza, but add 100 g/4 oz frozen chopped spinach, thawed, on top of the tomatoes. Then make two small wells in the centre and break 2 small eggs on top. Sprinkle with 25 g/1 oz/2 tbsp low-fat Mozzarella instead of the Cheddar and use dried oregano instead of basil. Cook until the eggs are cooked to your liking, but don't brown under the grill (broiler). Serve cut in half.

* **405 calories per serving**
* **Fairly high fibre**

Quick Ham and Pineapple Pizza

SERVES 2 OR 4

Prepare as for Quick Cheese and Tomato Pizza (page 302), but scatter 2 chopped canned pineapple rings and 2 slices of lean ham, diced and all fat removed, over the tomatoes before adding the cheese. Flavour with dried oregano instead of basil.

* 405 or 205 calories per serving
* Medium fibre

Quick Corn and Olive Pizza

SERVES 2 OR 4

Prepare as for Quick Cheese and Tomato Pizza (page 302), but add 200 g/7 oz/1 small can of naturally sweet sweetcorn (corn), drained, to the pizza before adding the cheese and scatter 3 sliced stuffed olives over the cheese.

* 410 or 210 calories per serving
* High fibre

Quick Chicken Tikka Pizza

SERVES 2 OR 4

Prepare as for Quick Cheese and Tomato Pizza (page 302), but mix 100 g/4 oz/1 cup diced cooked chicken, all skin removed, with 15 ml/1 tbsp low-fat plain yoghurt and 10 ml/2 tsp curry paste and put on top of the tomato. Sprinkle with 25 g/ 1 oz/2 tbsp grated low-fat Mozzarella cheese instead of the Cheddar.

* 405 or 205 calories per serving
* Medium fibre

Quick Mediterranean Vegetable Pizza

SERVES 2 OR 4

Prepare as for Quick Cheese and Tomato Pizza (page 302), but substitute a small can of ratatouille for the tomatoes, then top with the cheese and basil and finish as before.

* 405 or 205 calories per serving
* Fairly high fibre

Quick Baked Bean Pizza

SERVES 2 OR 4

Prepare as for Quick Cheese and Tomato Pizza (page 302), but substitute 225 g/8 oz/1 small can of baked beans for the tomatoes, then continue as before but sprinkle with dried mixed herbs instead of basil.

* 415 or 210 calories per serving
* High fibre

Quick Courgette and Garlic Pizza

SERVES 2 OR 4

Prepare as for Quick Cheese and Tomato Pizza (page 302), but add a small grated courgette (zucchini) with the tomatoes and scatter with a crushed garlic clove before adding the cheese.

* 385 or 195 calories per serving
* Medium fibre

Oriental Topper

SERVES 2

2 thick slices of sesame seed bloomer
Low-fat sunflower or olive oil spread
1 carrot, grated
50 g/2 oz/1 cup fresh beansprouts
½ green (bell) pepper, grated
5 ml/1 tsp reduced-salt soy sauce
A pinch of dried onion granules
15 ml/1 tbsp toasted sesame seeds

Spread the bread with a thin scraping of low-fat spread. Mix together the carrot, beansprouts and green pepper. Add the soy sauce and onion granules and toss. Pile on to the bread and sprinkle with the sesame seeds.

* 185 calories per serving
* Fairly high fibre

German Giant

SERVES 2

30 ml/2 tbsp low-fat soft cheese
5 ml/1 tsp German mustard
2 slices of pumpernickel
90 ml/6 tbsp sauerkraut
5 ml/1 tsp caraway seeds
1 slice of Westphalian ham, all fat
    removed

Mix the cheese with the mustard and spread on the pumpernickel. Drain the sauerkraut thoroughly on kitchen paper (paper towels) and pile on top of the cheese. Sprinkle with the caraway seeds. Cut the slice of ham in half and roll up each half. Place one roll on top of each pile of sauerkraut and serve.

* 145 calories per serving
* High fibre

Pine Nut Panache

SERVES 2

30 ml/2 tbsp pine nuts
2 thick slices of wholemeal bread
Low-fat sunflower or olive oil spread
2 crisp lettuce leaves
1 kiwi fruit
60 ml/4 tbsp low-fat cottage cheese
    and chives
Freshly ground black pepper

Toss the pine nuts over a moderate heat in a non-stick frying pan (skillet) until brown. Remove from the pan immediately. Spread the bread with a thin scraping of low-fat spread. Top each with a lettuce leaf. Peel the kiwi fruit, cut off two slices for garnish and chop the remainder. Stir into the cottage cheese with the pine nuts and season with pepper. Pile on the lettuce and garnish each with a slice of kiwi fruit.

* 170 calories per serving
* High fibre

Sumptuous Smoked Salmon Treat

SERVES 2

2 thick slices of wholemeal bread
30 ml/2 tbsp low-fat soft cheese
2 thin slices of smoked salmon
Lemon juice
Freshly ground black pepper
6 thin slices of cucumber
6 stoned (pitted) black olives, sliced

Spread the bread with the cheese. Lay a slice of salmon on each. Sprinkle with lemon juice and black pepper. Top each with 3 thin slices of cucumber, slightly overlapping, and surround with olive slices.

* 150 calories per serving
* High fibre

Prawn and Asparagus Pleasure

SERVES 2

60 ml/4 tbsp low-fat soft cheese
75 g/3 oz cooked peeled prawns (shrimp)
A few drops of Tabasco sauce
Salt and freshly ground black pepper
2 thick slices of granary bread
8 canned asparagus spears
2 small lemon twists

Put the cheese in a bowl. Reserve six prawns for garnish, chop the remainder and mix into the cheese with the Tabasco sauce and a little salt and pepper. Spread on to the bread, top with the asparagus spears and garnish with the prawns and a small twist of lemon on each.

* 210 calories per serving
* High fibre

Cheese and Date Delight

SERVES 2

2 thick slices of rye bread
Low-fat sunflower or olive oil spread
4 sprigs of watercress
2 thin slices of low-fat Cheddar cheese
50 g/2 oz/¹/₃ cup chopped stoned (pitted) dates
30 ml/2 tbsp low-fat fromage frais
15 ml/1 tbsp chopped parsley
2 orange slices

Spread the bread with a thin scraping of low-fat spread. Top with the watercress sprigs. Lay a thin slice of Cheddar on each. Mix the dates with the fromage frais and parsley and pile on top. Garnish each with an orange twist.

* 240 calories per serving
* High fibre

Warm Chicken Open Sandwich

SERVES 2

2 very small chicken breast fillets
15 g/¹/₂ oz/1 tsp low-fat sunflower or
  olive oil spread
Salt and freshly ground black pepper
2 thick slices of bloomer bread
30 ml/2 tbsp tomato relish
2 lollo rosso lettuce leaves
1 small tomato, cut into small wedges
2 small sprigs of parsley

Fry (sauté) the chicken in the low-fat spread for 5–6 minutes on each side until cooked through, seasoning with salt and pepper. Meanwhile, spread the bread with the relish and lay a lettuce leaf on top of each. Transfer the chicken fillets to the lettuce, arrange the tomato wedges on top and top each with a sprig of parsley.

* **240 calories per serving**
* **Medium fibre**

Steak Surprise

SERVES 2

2 thin slices of fillet steak
5 ml/1 tsp steak seasoning
10 g/¹/₄ oz/2 tsp low-fat sunflower or
  olive oil spread
30 ml/2 tbsp low-fat soft cheese
5 ml/1 tsp Dijon mustard
1 English muffin (home-made,
  page 25, or use bought), halved
1 small carrot, grated
2 gherkins (cornichons), cut into 'fans'

Sprinkle the steak with the seasoning. Fry (sauté) in the low-fat spread in a non-stick frying pan (skillet) until brown on each side and cooked to your liking. Meanwhile, mix the cheese with the mustard and spread on the muffin halves. Top with the grated carrot. Add the cooked steak and garnish each with a gherkin fan. Serve straight away.

* **180 calories per serving**
* **Fairly high fibre**

Hot Garlic Prawn Bites

SERVES 2

12 raw shelled tiger prawns (jumbo
  shrimp)
15 g/¹/₂ oz/1 tbsp low-fat sunflower or
  olive oil spread
1 garlic clove, crushed
Finely grated rind and juice of ¹/₂ small
  lemon
A few drops of Tabasco sauce
Salt and freshly ground black pepper
2 thick slices of granary bread
30 ml/2 tbsp low-fat soft cheese
2 crisp lettuce leaves
5 ml/1 tsp poppy seeds

Fry (sauté) the prawns and garlic in the low-fat spread for about 3 minutes, stirring occasionally, until the prawns are pink all over. Add the lemon rind and juice, the Tabasco sauce and a little salt and pepper. Toss over a high heat until the liquid has almost evaporated. Meanwhile, spread the bread with the cheese and top each with a lettuce leaf. Arrange the hot prawns on top and sprinkle with poppy seeds. Serve straight away.

* **200 calories per serving**
* **High fibre**

Desserts

For many people, a main meal is not complete without a pudding. Now you are reducing your fat intake, it doesn't mean you have to stop eating desserts. Here is a range of sensational afters, including a rich and delicious chocolate pudding for those who thought they would never be able to eat it again. But if you don't fancy a full-blown dessert, treat yourself to some fabulous fresh fruit, carefully prepared and prettily presented on a plate with a dollop of low-fat crème fraîche, fromage frais or vanilla yoghurt on the side. Don't forget, the calorie counts don't include the serving suggestions.

Flaming Normandy Apples

SERVES 4

100 g/4 oz/¹/₂ cup light brown sugar
300 ml/¹/₂ pt/1¹/₄ cups water
A pinch of ground cloves
4 eating (dessert) apples, peeled and cored but left whole
60 ml/4 tbsp calvados
Low-fat crème fraîche, to serve

Put the sugar and water in a large shallow saucepan with the cloves and heat gently until the sugar has dissolved. Add the apples and bring to the boil. Cover, reduce the heat and simmer gently for about 20 minutes, basting frequently, until the apples are translucent. Carefully lift the fruits out on to dishes. Boil the syrup rapidly until well reduced and syrupy. Pour over the apples. Warm the calvados in a large soup ladle, then ignite and pour over the apples. Serve while still flaming with a little low-fat crème fraîche.

* **190 calories per serving**
* **Medium fibre**

Brandied Cherries

SERVES 6

750 g/1¹/₂ lb red or black cherries, stoned (pitted)
45 ml/3 tbsp brandy
120 ml/4 fl oz/¹/₂ cup apple juice
50–75 g/2–3 oz/¹/₄–¹/₃ cup granulated sugar
10 ml/2 tsp arrowroot
30 ml/2 tbsp water

Put the cherries in a pan with the brandy, apple juice and sugar. Heat gently, stirring, until the sugar dissolves. Bring to the boil, reduce the heat and simmer very gently for 5 minutes. Blend the arrowroot with the water. Stir into the cherries and cook, stirring, until thickened and clear. Leave to cool, then chill before serving.

* **140 calories per serving**
* **Medium fibre**

Minted Melon and Raspberries

SERVES 6

1 honeydew melon
225 g/8 oz raspberries
12 mint leaves
50 g/2 oz/¹/₄ cup granulated sugar
A sprig of mint, to decorate

Halve the melon, remove the seeds, then scoop out the flesh with a melon baller or cut off the rind and dice the flesh. Mix with the raspberries in a glass dish. Put the mint on a board with the sugar and chop finely. Sprinkle over the fruit, toss gently and chill for at least 1 hour. Decorate with a sprig of mint just before serving.

* **65 calories per serving**
* **Medium fibre**

Gooseberry Compôte

SERVES 6

750 g/1¹/₂ lb gooseberries, topped and tailed
100 g/4 oz/¹/₂ cup granulated sugar
300 ml/¹/₂ pt/1¹/₄ cups water
30 ml/2 tbsp redcurrent jelly (clear conserve)
Low-fat Custard (page 387), to serve

Put the gooseberries in a pan, cover with boiling water and bring back to the boil. Cook for 2 minutes. Drain, rinse with cold water and drain again. Put the sugar and water in a saucepan. Heat gently, stirring, until the sugar has dissolved, then boil for 5 minutes. Stir in the recurrant jelly until dissolved, then add the gooseberries. Bring back to the boil, reduce the heat and simmer very gently for 10 minutes until the fruit is really tender but still holds its shape. Remove the fruit with a draining spoon and transfer to a serving dish. Boil the syrup rapidly until reduced by about a third. Pour over and serve with Low-fat Custard.

* **110 calories per serving**
* **Medium fibre**

Caramelised Oranges

SERVES 4

6 oranges
175 g/6 oz/³/₄ cup granulated sugar
100 ml/3¹/₂ fl oz/scant ¹/₂ cup cold water
100 ml/3¹/₂ fl oz/ scant ¹/₂ cup hot water

Thinly pare the rind off one of the oranges and cut into very thin strips. Boil in a little water for 2 minutes, then drain, rinse with cold water and drain again. Cut off all the rind and pith from all the oranges and cut the fruit into thick slices. Place in a shallow glass dish. Place the sugar and cold water in a saucepan and stir well. Heat gently, without stirring or boiling, until the sugar has completely dissolved. Then bring to the boil and boil until the mixture is a rich golden brown. Using oven gloves to protect from spluttering, pour the hot water into the caramel, then return to the heat and stir until the caramel has dissolved. Cool slightly, then pour over the oranges and leave until cold. Sprinkle the orange shreds over and chill until ready to serve.

* **265 calories per serving**
* **Medium fibre**

Caramelised Clementines

SERVES 4

Prepare as for Caramelised Oranges, but substitute clementines for the oranges. Peel the fruit and remove as much white pith as possible. Either leave the fruit whole or segment or slice, as preferred.

* **265 calories per serving**
* **Medium fibre**

Pineapple with Kirsch

SERVES 4 OR 6

1 ripe pineapple
150 ml/¹/₄ pt/²/₃ cup water
60 ml/4 tbsp granulated sugar
45 ml/3 tbsp kirsch
Low-fat crème fraîche, to serve

Remove all the rind from the pineapple, then cut the fruit into six or eight slices. Cut out the hard core. Place with any juice in a shallow heatproof serving dish. Put the water and sugar in a saucepan and heat gently, stirring, until the sugar dissolves. Bring to the boil and boil for 2 minutes. Stir in the kirsch and, while still hot, pour over the pineapple. Leave until cold, then chill. Serve with low-fat crème fraîche.

* 110 or 70 calories per serving
* Medium fibre

Gingered Melon

SERVES 4

1 honeydew melon
15 ml/1 tbsp finely chopped
  crystallised ginger
15 ml/1 tbsp grated fresh root ginger
120 ml/4 fl oz/¹/₂ cup dry white wine
5 ml/1 tsp ground cinnamon
5 ml/1 tsp caster (superfine) sugar
Brandy Snaps (page 368), to serve

Cut the rind off the melon, cut the fruit into eight wedges and discard the seeds. Put the remaining ingredients in a saucepan and bring to the boil. Add the melon and cook for 2 minutes. Remove the melon wedges and place on warm plates. Keep warm. Boil the liquid rapidly until syrupy, then spoon over the melon. Serve with Brandy Snaps.

* 50 calories per serving
* Low fibre

Almost Tiramisu

If you use a crème caramel mix for this recipe, reserve the sachet of caramel to drizzle over fresh fruit and low-fat plain yoghurt for another dessert.

SERVES 6

4 trifle sponges
150 ml/¹/₄ pt/²/₃ cup strong black
  coffee
1 packet of egg custard or crème
  caramel mix
450 ml/³/₄ pt/2 cups skimmed milk
15–30 ml/1–2 tbsp brandy or coffee
  liqueur
150 ml/¹/₄ pt/²/₃ cup low-fat whipping
  cream, whipped
15 ml/1 tbsp drinking (sweetened)
  chocolate powder

Break up the sponges and place in a shallow round dish. Add the coffee and leave to soak. Make up the egg custard or crème caramel with the milk according to the packet directions and leave to cool slightly. Stir in the brandy or liqueur. Gently pour over the sponge, leave until cold, then chill until set. Spread the whipped cream over and dust with drinking chocolate before serving.

* 135 calories per serving
* Low fibre

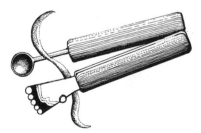

Drunken Peaches

SERVES 4

15 ml/1 tbsp light brown sugar
5 ml/1 tsp lemon juice
300 ml/¹/₂ pt/1¹/₄ cups red wine
4 peaches, peeled, halved and stoned
(pitted)

Put the sugar, lemon juice and wine in a saucepan and heat until the sugar dissolves. Transfer to an ovenproof dish and add the peaches. Cover with foil and bake in a preheated oven at 160°C/ 325°F/gas mark 3 for 30 minutes. Serve hot with the wine spooned over, or cool then chill.

* **100 calories per serving**
* **Low fibre**

Drunken Nectarines

SERVES 4

Prepare as for Drunken Peaches, but substitute nectarines for the peaches and use a fruity white wine for the red.

* **100 calories per serving**
* **Low fibre**

Summer Melon with Strawberries

SERVES 4 OR 6

1 small honeydew melon, balled or
the flesh cubed
175 g/6 oz strawberries, sliced
Grated rind and juice of 1 lime
15 ml/1 tbsp clear honey
Smooth Strawberry Sauce (page 391)

Put the melon and strawberries in a bowl. Mix the lime rind and juice with the honey and spoon over. Toss gently and chill for at least 30 minutes. Spoon on to plates and drizzle the Smooth Strawberry Sauce over before serving.

* **95 or 65 calories per serving**
* **Medium fibre**

Poached Apricots with Passion Fruit Sauce

SERVES 4

8 ripe apricots, halved and stoned
(pitted)
300 ml/¹/₂ pt/1¹/₄ cups sweet white
wine
15 ml/1 tbsp clear honey
2 passion fruit
15 ml/1 tbsp cornflour (cornstarch)
60 ml/4 tbsp water
Lemon juice (optional)
Amaretti Biscuits (page 367), to serve

Put the apricots in a saucepan. Add the wine and honey, bring to the boil, reduce the heat and simmer very gently for about 5 minutes until the apricots are just tender but still hold their shape. Remove the fruit with a draining spoon and place in four dishes. Halve the passion fruit and scoop the flesh into the poaching liquid. Blend together the cornflour and water and add to the pan. Bring to the boil and cook for 2 minutes, stirring. Spike with a dash of lemon juice, if liked. Spoon the sauce over the apricots and either serve warm or leave to cool then chill before serving with Amaretti Biscuits.

* **105 calories per serving**
* **Medium fibre**

Light Christmas Pudding

SERVES 10

Oil, for greasing
100 g/4 oz/1 cup plain (all-purpose)
  flour
5 ml/1 tsp baking powder
100 g/4 oz/¹/₂ cup low-fat sunflower or
  olive oil spread
100 g/4 oz/²/₃ cup raisins
100 g/4 oz/²/₃ cup sultanas (golden
  raisins)
100 g/4 oz/²/₃ cup currants
100 g/4 oz/¹/₂ cup caster (superfine)
  sugar
100 g/4 oz/2 cups fresh breadcrumbs
5 ml/1 tsp mixed (apple-pie) spice
1 egg
150 ml/¹/₄ pt/²/₃ cup milk
30 ml/2 tbsp brandy or rum
Brandy Sauce (page 393), to serve

Grease a 1.2 litre/2 pt/5 cup pudding
basin. Sift the flour and baking
powder into a bowl. Add the low-fat
spread and rub in with the fingertips.
Stir in the fruit, sugar, breadcrumbs
and mixed spice. Mix with the egg,
milk and brandy or rum. Turn into the
basin and level the surface. Cover with
a double thickness of greased
greaseproof (waxed) paper with a pleat
in the middle to allow for rising,
twisting and folding under the rim to
secure. Steam for 3 hours. Leave to
cool, then re-cover with clean paper
and store in the fridge for up to
3 weeks. Re-steam for 1½ hours before
serving with Brandy Sauce.

* **275 calories per serving**
* **High fibre**

Golden Christmas Puddings

SERVES 10 PER PUDDING

450 g/1 lb ready-to-eat dried apricots,
  chopped
450 g/1 lb/2²/₃ cups sultanas (golden
  raisins)
175 g/6 oz/1¹/₂ cups chopped mixed
  (candied) peel
350 g/12 oz/3 cups chopped mixed
  nuts
Finely grated rind and juice of
  2 oranges
Finely grated rind and juice of 1 lemon
225 g/8 oz/1 cup light brown sugar
5 ml/1 tsp ground mace
225 g/8 oz/4 cups white breadcrumbs
50 g/2 oz/¹/₂ cup plain (all-purpose)
  flour
100 g/4 oz/¹/₂ cup low-fat sunflower or
  olive oil spread, plus extra for
  greasing
2 eggs, beaten
2 egg whites
30 ml/2 tbsp apricot or orange liqueur
60 ml/4 tbsp skimmed milk
Sherry Sauce (page 386), to serve

Put all the ingredients in a large bowl
and mix well. Grease two 1.2 litre/
2 pt/5 cup pudding basins and line the
bases with a circle of greased
greaseproof (waxed) paper. Spoon in
the mixture and level the surfaces.
Cover with a double thickness of
greaseproof (waxed) paper, twisting
and folding under the rim to secure.
Steam for 5 hours. Leave to cool, then
re-cover in clean paper and foil. Make
up to two weeks before Christmas.
Steam for a further 3 hours before
serving with Sherry Sauce.

* **280 calories per serving**
* **High fibre**

Alternative Christmas Pudding

SERVES 10

2 oranges
200 g/7 oz/1 good cup chopped cooking dates
2 cooking (tart) apples, quartered
3 carrots
175 g/6 oz/1½ cups plain (all-purpose) flour
175 g/6 oz/3 cups wholemeal breadcrumbs
150g/5 oz/generous ½ cup low-fat sunflower or olive oil spread, plus extra for greasing
100 g/4 oz/½ cup light brown sugar
75 g/3 oz/½ cup currants
75 g/3 oz/½ cup raisins
2.5 ml/½ tsp ground cinnamon
2.5 ml/½ tsp grated nutmeg
1 egg
2 egg whites
Skimmed milk
Fluffy Brandy Cream (page 394), to serve

Finely grate the rind from the oranges. Cut away all the pith and peel and quarter the flesh, discarding any pips. Pass the oranges, dates, apples and carrots through a mincer (grinder) or finely chop in a food processor. Stir in the flour and breadcrumbs and rub in the low-fat spread. Add the remaining dry ingredients. Beat together the egg and egg whites and stir in, adding a little skimmed milk, if necessary, to moisten well. Grease a 1.75 litre/3 pt/7½ cup pudding basin and line the base with a circle of greased greaseproof (waxed) paper. Spoon in the mixture and cover with a double thickness of greaseproof paper, twisting and folding under the rim to secure. Steam for 3 hours. Turn out and serve hot with Fluffy Brandy Cream.

* **290 calories per serving**
* **High fibre**

Cranberry Fluff Bake

SERVES 6

450 g/1 lb fresh cranberries
60 ml/4 tbsp water
Granulated sugar
2 egg whites
100 g/4 oz/½ cup caster (superfine) sugar
2.5 ml/½ tsp vanilla essence (extract)
Low-fat single (light) cream, to serve

Put the cranberries in a pan with the water. Heat gently until the fruit begins to pop. Stir in granulated sugar to taste. Turn into an ovenproof serving dish. Whisk the egg whites until stiff. Whisk in half the caster sugar and the vanilla essence. Fold in the remaining sugar and pile on top of the cranberries. Bake in a preheated oven at 140°C/275°F/ gas mark 1 for 1 hour until crisp and pale straw-coloured. Serve warm with a little low-fat single cream.

* **135 calories per serving**
* **Medium fibre**

Raspberry Hazelnut Yoghurt

SERVES 4

2 egg whites
50 g/2 oz/¼ cup caster (superfine) sugar
150 ml/¼ pt/⅔ cup low-fat hazelnut (filbert) yoghurt
300 g/11 oz/1 small can of raspberries, drained
30 ml/2 tbsp chopped toasted hazelnuts

Whisk the egg whites until stiff. Whisk in the sugar until stiff and glossy. Fold in the hazelnut yoghurt. Layer the yoghurt mixture and raspberries in four glasses, sprinkle with the toasted hazelnuts and chill until ready to serve.

* **180 calories per serving**
* **Medium fibre**

Summer Pudding

SERVES 6

900 g/2 lb soft fruit such as raspberries, blackberries, blackcurrants, strawberries (sliced or quartered if large)
Finely grated rind of ½ orange (optional)
45 ml/3 tbsp water
100–175 g/4–6 oz/½–¾ cup granulated sugar
8 slices of white bread, crusts removed
Light Chantilly Cream (page 394), to serve

Put the fruit in a saucepan with the orange rind, if using, the water and 100 g/4 oz/½ cup of the sugar. Heat gently until the juices run and the fruit is soft but still holding its shape. Taste and add more sugar, if necessary. Line a large pudding basin with some of the bread, cutting the slices to fit. Spoon in the fruit and juice and cover with the remaining bread, again trimming to fit and filling in any gaps. Stand the basin on a small plate and cover with a saucer or small plate. Top with weights or a couple of cans. Chill overnight. The pudding is ready when all the juice has soaked through the bread. Turn out on to a shallow serving dish and serve with Light Chantilly Cream.

* **245 calories per serving**
* **Medium fibre**

Rich Moist Chocolate Pudding

SERVES 4 OR 6

50 g/2 oz/¹/₂ cup self-raising (self-
  rising) flour
45 ml/3 tbsp low-fat drinking
  (sweetened) chocolate powder
5 ml/1 tsp instant coffee powder
50 g/2 oz/1 cup fresh white
  breadcrumbs
40 g/1¹/₂ oz/3 tbsp caster (superfine)
  sugar
50 g/2 oz/¹/₂ cup low-fat sunflower or
  olive oil spread, plus extra for
  greasing
1 egg, beaten
Skimmed milk, to mix
Luscious Mint Custard (page 387), to
  serve

Sift the flour and drinking chocolate into a bowl. Stir in the remaining dry ingredients. Rub in the low-fat spread, then mix with the egg and enough skimmed milk to form a very soft dropping consistency. Grease and flour a 900 ml/1¹/₂ pt/3¾ cup pudding basin. Spoon in the chocolate mixture. Cover with a double thickness of greaseproof (waxed) paper, twisting and folding under the rim to secure. Steam for 2 hours. Turn out and serve with Luscious Mint Custard.

* **260 or 175 calories per serving**
* **Medium fibre**

Extra-light Fruit Pudding

SERVES 6

100 g/4 oz/1 cup self-raising (self-
  rising) flour
2.5 ml/¹/₂ tsp baking powder
A pinch of salt
75 g/3 oz/¹/₃ cup low-fat sunflower or
  olive oil spread, plus extra for
  greasing
100 g/4 oz/2 cups white breadcrumbs
25 g/1 oz/3 tbsp currants
25 g/1 oz/3 tbsp sultanas (golden
  raisins)
25 g/1 oz/3 tbsp raisins
75 g/3 oz/¹/₃ cup caster (superfine)
  sugar
1 egg, beaten
120 ml/4 fl oz/1 cup milk
Apricot Jam Sauce (page 388), to
  serve

Sift the flour, baking powder and salt into a bowl. Add the low-fat spread and rub in with the fingertips until the mixture resembles breadcrumbs. Stir in the fresh breadcrumbs, the fruit and sugar. Add the beaten egg and enough of the milk to form a soft dropping consistency. Turn into a greased 1.2 litre/2 pt/5 cup pudding basin. Cover with a double thickness greaseproof (waxed) paper, twisting and folding under the rim to secure. Steam for 2¹/₂ hours. Turn out on to a warm plate and serve with hot Apricot Jam Sauce.

* **260 calories per serving**
* **High fibre**

Rhubarb Fluff

SERVES 4

*170 g/6 oz/1 small can of low-fat
    evaporated milk*
*450 g/1 lb rhubarb, cut into short
    lengths*
175 g/6 oz/³/₄ cup light brown sugar
150 ml/¹/₄ pt/²/₃ cup pure orange juice
*Almond Shortbread Fingers (page
    364), to serve*

Boil the can of evaporated milk in a saucepan of water for 15 minutes. Drain, leave to cool, then chill for at least 2 hours. Meanwhile, put the rhubarb, sugar and orange juice in a saucepan. Bring to the boil, stirring, then reduce the heat, cover and simmer gently until really tender. Leave until cold. Empty the chilled can of milk into a bowl. Whisk until thick and peaking. Beat the rhubarb until pulpy and fold into the whipped milk. Turn into four glass dishes and serve straight away with Almond Shortbread Fingers.

* **220 calories per serving**
* **Medium fibre**

The Lightest Egg Custard

SERVES 4

1 whole egg
2 egg whites
600 ml/1 pt/2¹/₂ cups skimmed milk
30 ml/2 tbsp caster (superfine) sugar
*Low-fat sunflower or olive oil spread,
    for greasing*
Grated nutmeg, for dusting

Whisk the egg with the egg whites to mix thoroughly. Bring the milk just to the boil, then whisk into the eggs. Stir in the sugar until dissolved. Lightly grease a 900 ml/1¹/₂ pt/3³/₄ cup ovenproof dish. Pour in the custard and dust with a little nutmeg. Stand the dish in a roasting tin (pan) and add enough hot water to come half-way up the sides of the dish. Bake in a preheated oven at 160°C/325°F/gas mark 3 for about 1 hour until set. Serve warm or cold.

* **110 calories per serving**
* **No fibre**

Baked Apples

SERVES 4

4 even-sized cooking (tart) apples
60 ml/4 tbsp dried mixed fruit (fruit
cake mix)
20 ml/4 tsp clear honey
30 ml/2 tbsp water
Low-fat Custard (page 387), to serve

Cut out the core from each apple and slit the skin round the centre with the point of a sharp knife to prevent bursting during cooking. Fill with the dried fruit, packing it in firmly. Stand the fruit in a baking dish, put 5 ml/1 tsp honey over each apple and add the water to the dish. Bake in a preheated oven at 190°C/375°F/gas mark 5 for about 50 minutes until the fruit is tender. Serve hot with Low-fat Custard.

* **100 calories per serving**
* **Fairly high fibre**

Dried Fruit Dome

SERVES 6

225 g/8 oz/2 cups self-raising (self-
rising) flour
5 ml/1 tsp baking powder
75 g/3 oz/¹/₃ cup low-fat sunflower or
olive oil spread, diced, plus extra
for greasing
75 g/3 oz/¹/₃ cup caster (superfine)
sugar
50 g/2 oz/¹/₃ cup ready-to-eat dried
apricots, chopped
50 g/2 oz/¹/₃ cup chopped stoned
(pitted) dates
50 g/2 oz/¹/₃ cup dried pears, chopped
1 egg, beaten
Skimmed milk
45 ml/3 tbsp apricot jam (conserve)
5 ml/1 tsp lemon juice

Grease and line the base of a 900 ml/1½ pt/3¾ cup pudding basin with a circle of greased greaseproof (waxed) paper. Sift the flour and baking powder into a bowl. Add the low-fat spread and rub in with the fingertips until the mixture resembles breadcrumbs. Stir in the sugar and dried fruits, then mix with the egg and enough milk to form a soft dropping consistency. Turn into the prepared basin. Cover with a double thickness of greased greaseproof paper with a pleat in the centre to allow for rising, twisting and folding under the rim to secure. Steam for 1½ hours. Just before serving, warm the jam and lemon juice in a saucepan. Turn the pudding out on to a warm serving dish, spoon the warm jam over and serve.

* **325 calories per serving**
* **High fibre**

Light Bread and Butter Pudding

SERVES 4

Low-fat sunflower or olive oil spread
4–6 thin slices of white bread
25 g/1 oz/2 tbsp granulated sugar
50 g/2 oz/¹/₃ cup raisins or sultanas (golden raisins)
1 egg
600 ml/1 pt/2¹/₂ cups skimmed milk
Grated nutmeg, for dusting

Grease a 1.2 litre/2 pt/5 cup ovenproof dish with a very little low-fat spread. Lightly spread each slice of bread with low-fat spread and cut into triangles. Layer the bread with a sprinkling of sugar and raisins or sultanas between each layer in the dish, finishing with a sprinkling of sugar and fruit. Beat together the egg and milk and strain into the dish. Dust with grated nutmeg. Leave to stand for 30 minutes, if possible, then cover with foil and bake in a preheated oven at 180°C/350°F/gas mark 4 for 1 hour, then remove the foil and continue to cook for about 30 minutes or until set and golden brown.

* **190 calories per serving**
* **Fairly high fibre**

Spotted Dick

SERVES 4

50 g/2 oz/¹/₂ cup self-raising (self-rising) wholemeal flour
50 g/2 oz/¹/₂ cup self-raising white flour
5 ml/1 tsp baking powder
75 g/3 oz/¹/₃ cup low-fat sunflower or olive oil spread, plus extra for greasing
100 g/4 oz/2 cups wholemeal breadcrumbs
1.5 ml/¹/₄ tsp ground cinnamon
50 g/2 oz/¹/₄ cup caster (superfine) sugar
150 g/5 oz/scant 1 cup dried mixed fruit (fruit cake mix) or raisins
2 egg whites, lightly beaten
About 100 ml/3¹/₂ fl oz/scant ¹/₂ cup skimmed milk
Low-fat Custard (page 387), to serve

Mix together the flours and baking powder in a bowl. Rub in the low-fat spread and mix in the breadcrumbs, cinnamon, sugar and fruit. Add the egg whites and mix with enough of the milk to form a soft dropping consistency. Turn into a lightly greased 1.2 litre/2 pt/5 cup pudding basin. Cover with a double thickness of greaseproof (waxed) paper, twisting and folding under the rim to secure. Steam for 2¹/₂ hours. Turn out and serve with Low-fat Custard.

* **265 calories per serving**
* **High fibre**

Profiteroles with Hot Chocolate Caramel Sauce

For a lower-fibre version, use plain (all-purpose) rather than wholemeal flour.

SERVES 4

65 g/2½ oz/good ½ cup wholemeal flour
25 g/1 oz/2 tbsp low-fat sunflower or olive oil spread
150 ml/¼ pt/⅔ cup water
2 egg whites
150 ml/¼ pt/⅔ cup low-fat whipping cream
Finely grated rind of 1 orange (optional)
Hot Chocolate Caramel Sauce (page 388)

Sift the flour into a bowl. Add the bran left in the sieve (strainer). Put the low-fat spread and water in a saucepan and heat until the fat melts. Add the flour in one go and beat with a wooden spoon until the mixture forms a smooth paste and leaves the side of the pan clean. Remove from the heat and cool slightly. Whisk the egg whites until stiff. Beat a little egg white into the paste to soften it, then fold in the remainder with a metal spoon. Put spoonfuls of the mixture well apart on a baking (cookie) sheet lined with non-stick baking parchment. Bake in a preheated oven at 200°C/400°F/gas mark 6 for 15 minutes, turn them over and bake for a further 10 minutes until crisp and golden. Transfer to a wire rack, make a slit in the side of each to allow the steam to escape and leave to cool. Whip the cream until peaking and add the orange rind, if using. Scoop any remaining soft dough out of each profiterole, then fill with the cream. Pile into dishes and spoon the Hot Chocolate Caramel Sauce over.

* **215 calories per serving**
* **High fibre**

Light Brulée

SERVES 4

1 quantity of The Lightest Egg Custard (page 316)
45 ml/3 tbsp caster (superfine) sugar

Prepare the egg custard. When cooked, leave to cool, then chill. Sprinkle the top liberally with the caster sugar to cover completely. Place under a preheated grill (broiler) until the sugar melts and caramelises. Leave until cold, then chill again before serving.

* **150 calories per serving**
* **No fibre**

Rich and Creamy Brown Rice Pudding

SERVES 4

50 g/2 oz/¼ cup brown round-grain rice
450 ml/¾ pt/2 cups water
30 ml/2 tbsp caster (superfine) sugar
420 g/15 oz/1 large can of low-fat evaporated milk
1.5 ml/¼ tsp grated nutmeg

Rinse the rice and place in a saucepan with the water. Bring to the boil, reduce the heat and simmer gently for 20 minutes. Stir in the sugar and evaporated milk. Turn into a fairly shallow ovenproof dish, dust with the nutmeg, then place in a preheated oven at 180°C/350°F/gas mark 4 for about 2–2½ hours or until creamy, golden brown and the rice is tender but nutty. Serve warm.

* **130 calories per serving**
* **High fibre**

Rich and Creamy White Rice Pudding

SERVES 4

Prepare as for Rich and Creamy Brown Rice Pudding, but substitute white round-grain rice for the brown and cook for 1½–2 hours.

* **130 calories per serving**
* **Medium fibre**

Pear and Yoghurt Brulée

SERVES 4

425 g/15 oz/1 large can of pear quarters, drained, reserving the juice
10 ml/2 tsp arrowroot
5 ml/1 tsp lemon juice
150 ml/¼ pt/⅔ cup low-fat vanilla yoghurt
1 large egg
1.5 ml/¼ tsp ground cinnamon
45 ml/3 tbsp granulated sugar

Chop the pears and place in a 900 ml/1½ pt/3¾ cup ovenproof dish. Blend a little of the pear juice with the arrowroot and stir in the remaining juice in a saucepan. Add the lemon juice. Bring to the boil, stirring, until thickened and clear. Pour over the pears. Beat together the yoghurt and egg until smooth, then beat in the cinnamon. Spoon over the pear mixture and bake in a preheated oven at 180°C/350°F/gas mark 4 for about 15–20 minutes until the custard is set. Remove from the oven and sprinkle liberally with the sugar. Place under a hot grill (broiler) until the sugar melts and caramelises. Serve hot.

* **125 calories per serving**
* **Low fibre**

Photograph opposite: **Sun-dried Tomato and Cheese Loaf (page 351) and Savoury Yoghurt Scones (page 355)**

Banana Pudding

SERVES 4

50 g/2 oz/¹/₄ cup low-fat sunflower or
   olive oil spread
45 ml/3 tbsp clear honey
1 egg
30 ml/2 tbsp skimmed milk
30 ml/2 tbsp sultanas (golden raisins)
2 bananas, thickly sliced
75 g/3 oz/³/₄ cup self-raising (self-
   rising) wholemeal flour
5 ml/1 tsp baking powder
2.5 ml/¹/₂ tsp ground cinnamon
Hot Lemon Sauce (page 387), to serve

Beat together the low-fat spread and
honey until fluffy. Beat in the egg,
milk and sultanas and fold in the
bananas. Sift the flour, baking powder
and cinnamon over the surface, then
sprinkle in the bran left in the sieve
(strainer). Fold in lightly with a metal
spoon. Wet a 450 g/1 lb loaf tin (pan)
and line with non-stick baking
parchment. Add the banana mixture
and level the surface. Bake in a
preheated oven at 180°C/350°F/gas
mark 4 for about 40 minutes until
risen and golden and a skewer comes
out clean when inserted in the centre.
Turn out on to a serving dish, remove
the paper and serve sliced with Hot
Lemon Sauce.

* **245 calories per serving**
* **High fibre**

Mulled Claret Jelly

SERVES 6

450 ml/³/₄ pt/2 cups claret or other
   full-bodied red wine
30 ml/2 tbsp clear honey
1 piece of cinnamon stick
3 cloves
2 lemon slices
1 orange
15 ml/1 tbsp powdered gelatine

Put the wine, honey, cinnamon,
cloves and lemon slices in a
saucepan. Squeeze the juice from the
orange into a measuring jug and make
up to 150 ml/¹/₄ pt/²/₃ cup with water.
Add the orange shells to the saucepan.
Sprinkle the gelatine over the orange
juice mixture in the measuring jug and
leave to soften for 5 minutes.
Meanwhile, bring the wine mixture to
the boil, reduce the heat and simmer
gently for 5 minutes. Remove from the
heat. Stir the softened gelatine mixture
into the wine and stir until completely
dissolved. Taste and add more honey, if
liked. Strain into a 600 ml/1 pt/2¹/₂ cup
wetted jelly (jello) mould or an
attractive glass dish. Leave until cold,
then chill until set. Dip the mould, if
using, briefly in hot water, then turn
out on to a serving dish. Serve
completely plain.

* **95 calories per serving**
* **No fibre**

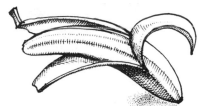

Photograph opposite: Devil's Food
Cake with Marshmallow Frosting
(page 362) and Apricot Cut-and-
come-again Cake (page 371)

Strawberry Cheese Baskets

SERVES 6

3 sheets of filo pastry (paste)
25 g/1 oz/2 tbsp low-fat sunflower or olive oil spread, melted
100 g/4 oz/¹/₂ cup strawberry-flavoured low-fat fromage frais
100 g/4 oz small, ripe strawberries, hulled
30 ml/2 tbsp redcurrant jelly (clear conserve)
15 ml/1 tbsp water

Lay a sheet of pastry on a board and brush very lightly with the melted low-fat spread. Fold in half, then half again and brush again. Cut the oblong into two squares. Repeat with the remaining pastry. Carefully press into six individual flan tins (pie pans) and brush with the remaining spread. Bake in a preheated oven at 190°C/375°F/ gas mark 5 for 15 minutes until crisp and golden. Transfer to a wire rack and leave to cool. Fill with fromage frais and top with the strawberries. Melt the redcurrant jelly with the water. Brush all over the strawberries to glaze. Serve within 1 hour of filling or the pastry will go soft.

* 120 calories per serving
* Medium fibre

Mocha Mousse

SERVES 4

10 ml/2 tsp powdered gelatine
150 ml/¹/₄ pt/²/₃ cup hot black coffee
50 g/2 oz/¹/₂ cup reduced-fat drinking (sweetened) chocolate powder, plus extra for dusting
30 ml/2 tbsp caster (superfine) sugar
420 g/15 oz/1 large can of low-fat evaporated milk, well chilled

Sprinkle the gelatine over the hot coffee. Stir until completely dissolved. Stir in the drinking chocolate and sugar until dissolved. Leave until cold, then chill until the consistency of egg white. Whisk the evaporated milk until really thick and fluffy. Whisk in the coffee and chocolate mixture. Turn into four dishes and chill until set. Dust with a little extra drinking chocolate before serving.

* 145 calories per serving
* No fibre

Luscious Maple Syrup Pancakes

SERVES 4

Everyday Pancakes (page 353)
60 ml/4 tbsp maple syrup
Low-fat Vanilla Ice Dream (page 344) or bought low-fat vanilla ice cream, to serve

Cook the pancakes and fold into quarters. Place on warm plates, drizzle with maple syrup and top each portion with a scoop of Low-fat Vanilla Ice Dream or ice cream.

* 250 calories per serving
* Medium fibre

Apricot-stuffed Pancakes

SERVES 6

*Oat Bran and Wholemeal Pancakes
(page 354)
410 g/14 oz/1 large can of apricot
halves in natural juice
10 ml/2 tsp arrowroot
15 ml/1 tbsp apricot brandy (optional)
100 g/4 oz/¹/₂ cup low-fat plain or
apricot-flavoured fromage frais
30 ml/2 tbsp toasted flaked (slivered)
almonds*

Make the pancakes and leave to cool. Strain the juice from the apricots into a saucepan. Chop the fruit. Blend the arrowroot into the juice and add the brandy, if using. Bring to the boil, stirring until thickened and clear. Remove from the heat and leave to cool. Stir in the chopped fruit. Spread each pancake with a little fromage frais. Fold into quarters to make a cone shape. Place two on each plate. Gently lift up the top flap of each pancake and spoon in the apricot mixture. Scatter the almonds over before serving.

* **240 calories per serving**
* **High fibre**

Honeyed Kiwis and Oranges

SERVES 6

*4 oranges
45 ml/3 tbsp clear honey
45 ml/3 tbsp water
300 ml/¹/₂ pt/1¹/₄ cups apple juice
4 kiwi fruit*

Over a saucepan, to catch any drips, pare off all the rind from the oranges. Put the rind in the saucepan. Slice the fruit and place in a glass bowl. Add the honey and water to the saucepan. Bring to the boil and boil for 2 minutes. Remove from the heat and stir in the apple juice. Leave until cold, then strain over the oranges. Peel and slice the kiwi fruit and add to the oranges. Stir gently, then chill before serving.

* **100 calories per serving**
* **Medium fibre**

Crêpes Suzie

SERVES 4

Everyday Pancakes (page 353)
60 ml/4 tbsp light brown sugar
Finely grated rind and juice of
1 orange
Finely grated rind and juice of 1 lemon
30 ml/2 tbsp brandy
60 ml/4 tbsp low-fat crème fraîche

Cook the pancakes. Put the sugar and fruit rinds and juice in a frying pan (skillet) and heat, stirring, until the sugar dissolves. Fold the pancakes into quarters and add one at a time to the pan, turning in the juice and pushing to one side when coated. Pour the brandy over, ignite and shake the pan gently until the flames subside. Serve straight away with a little low-fat crème fraîche.

* 240 calories per serving
* Medium fibre

Strawberry Crêpes

SERVES 4

Everyday Pancakes (page 353)
60 ml/4 tbsp strawberry jam
  (conserve)
100 g/4 oz strawberries, thinly sliced
1 small carton of low-fat strawberry-
  flavoured yoghurt
4 whole strawberries, to decorate

Make the pancakes. Spread each with a little jam and cover with a few slices of strawberries. Fold or roll up and arrange on plates. Top each serving with a dollop of the yoghurt and decorate with a whole strawberry.

* 210 calories per serving
* Medium fibre

Peach Melba Crêpes

SERVES 4

Prepare as for Strawberry Crêpes but use raspberry jam (conserve), 2 fresh peaches, stoned (pitted), and peach-flavoured yoghurt.

* 225 calories per serving
* Medium fibre

Banana and Carob Crêpes

SERVES 4

Prepare as for Strawberry Crêpes, but use apricot jam (conserve), 2 thinly sliced bananas, tossed in lemon juice, and 30 ml/2 tbsp carob chips for the filling. Top with banana-flavoured yoghurt and sprinkle with a few extra carob chips to decorate.

* 250 calories per serving
* Medium fibre

Raspberry Crêpes

SERVES 4

Prepare as for Strawberry Crêpes (page 324), but use raspberry jam (conserve), fresh raspberries and raspberry-flavoured yoghurt.

* 210 calories per serving
* Medium fibre

Cinnamon Cheese Blintzes

SERVES 4

Everyday Pancakes (see page 353)
350 g/12 oz/1½ cups low-fat cottage
*   cheese*
60 ml/4 tbsp icing (confectioners')
*   sugar*
5 ml/1 tsp vanilla essence (extract)
5 ml/1 tsp ground cinnamon

Cook the pancakes on one side only. Mix the cheese with half the sugar, the vanilla and cinnamon. Divide between the centres of the cooked sides of the pancakes. Fold two sides of the pancake over the filling, then fold the bottom flap up over and the top one down to form an envelope. Heat a non-stick frying pan (skillet) until very hot, then cook the blintzes on both sides until browned and hot through. Dust with the remaining icing sugar and serve.

* **235 calories per serving**
* **Medium fibre**

Cinnamon and Raisin Blintzes

SERVES 4

Prepare as for Cinnamon Cheese Blintzes, but reduce the quantity of cottage cheese to 275 g/10 oz/1¼ cups and add 75 g/3 oz/½ cup raisins to the cheese mixture.

* **245 calories per serving**
* **Fairly high fibre**

Cinnamon and Banana Blintzes

SERVES 4

Prepare as for Cinnamon Cheese Blintzes, but reduce the quantity of cottage cheese to 250 g/9 oz/ generous 1 cup and add 2 ripe mashed bananas and the finely grated rind of ½ lemon to the mixture.

* **225 calories per serving**
* **Medium fibre**

Cinnamon and Orange Blintzes

SERVES 4

Prepare as for Cinnamon Cheese Blintzes, but omit the vanilla essence (extract) and add the finely grated rind of 1 orange to the cheese.

* **245 calories per serving**
* **Medium fibre**

Spiced Strawberry Blintzes

SERVES 4

Prepare as for Cinnamon Cheese Blintzes, but substitute mixed (apple-pie) spice for the cinnamon and spread each pancake with 10 ml/2 tsp strawberry jam (conserve) before adding the cheese. Decorate with a few fresh strawberries, if liked.

* **265 calories per serving**
* **Medium fibre**

Almond Raspberry Blintzes

SERVES 4

Prepare as for Cinnamon Cheese Blintzes (page 325), but flavour with almond essence (extract) instead of vanilla, spread each pancake with 10 ml/2 tsp raspberry jam (conserve) and decorate with a few fresh raspberries, if liked.

* **265 calories per serving**
* **Medium fibre**

Melon with Orange Raspberry Drizzle

SERVES 4

1 honeydew melon
1 small orange
320 g/12 oz/1 medium can of
   raspberries in natural juice
8 small mint sprigs, to decorate

Cut the melon into eight wedges. Scoop out the seeds, then cut off the rind. Cover and chill. Finely grate the rind from the orange. Cut off all the pith and then segment or thinly slice the fruit. Drain off the juice from the raspberries, then purée the fruit in a blender or food processor with the orange rind. Pass the purée through a sieve (strainer) into a measuring jug. Thin with enough of the juice to form a smooth pouring consistency. Chill until ready to serve. Lay the melon on plates. Drizzle the raspberry sauce over the centres of the melon wedges and decorate each with the orange segments or slices and a small sprig of mint.

* **45 calories per serving**
* **Medium fibre**

Poached Pears in Cider

SERVES 4

4 ripe dessert pears
15 ml/1 tbsp chopped mixed nuts
15 ml/1 tbsp wholemeal breadcrumbs
10 ml/2 tsp clear honey
300 ml/¹/₂ pt/1¹/₄ cups medium cider
1 clove
4 angelica 'leaves', to decorate

Peel the pears and cut out a cone-shaped core at the base of each. Mix the nuts with the breadcrumbs and honey and press firmly into the holes. Stand the pears in a casserole dish (Dutch oven) and pour the cider over. Add the clove to the dish. Cover and cook in a preheated oven at 160°C/325°F/gas mark 3 for 45 minutes, basting occasionally. Remove from the oven and leave to cool, then chill until ready to serve. Carefully transfer the fruit to four dishes. Spoon the juice around and press an angelica leaf into the top of each.

* **95 calories per serving**
* **Fairly high fibre**

Spiced Poached Pears with Dates

If you use unripe pears, simply cook for longer until tender.

SERVES 4

4 ripe pears
20 ml/4 tsp chopped stoned (pitted) dates
150 ml/¹/₄ pt/²/₃ cup red wine
150 ml/¹/₄ pt/²/₃ cup apple juice
5 ml/1 tsp lemon juice
1 piece of cinnamon stick
2 cloves

Peel the pears and cut out a cone-shaped core at the base of each. Gently stuff each with 5 ml/1 tsp of the dates. Stand the pears in a casserole dish (Dutch oven). Add the remaining ingredients to the dish. Cover and cook in a preheated oven at 160°C/325°F/ gas mark 3 for 30–40 minutes, basting once or twice during cooking. Remove the spices and serve hot, or leave to cool then chill.

* **100 calories per serving**
* **Fairly high fibre**

Steamed Chocolate Cherry Pudding

SERVES 6

75 g/3 oz/³/₄ cup self-raising (self-rising) flour
25 g/1 oz/¹/₄ cup low-fat drinking (sweetened) chocolate powder
5 ml/1 tsp baking powder
45 ml/3 tbsp clear honey
50 g/2 oz/¹/₄ cup low-fat sunflower or olive oil spread, plus extra for greasing
1 large egg
30 ml/2 tbsp skimmed milk
50 g/2 oz/¹/₄ cup glacé (candied) cherries, quartered
Velvet Chocolate Sauce (page 387), to serve

Sift together the flour, drinking chocolate and baking powder together in a bowl. Add the honey, low-fat spread and egg and beat thoroughly until smooth. Beat in the milk to form a soft dropping consistency. Fold in the cherries. Turn into a lightly greased 1 litre/1¾ pt/4¼ cup pudding basin. Cover with a double thickness of greaseproof (waxed) paper, twisting and folding under the rim to secure. Steam for 1½ hours. Alternatively, leave uncovered and microwave for 4–5 minutes, depending on the output of your oven until risen and the mixture is beginning to shrink away from the side of the basin. (The top may still appear slightly moist in places.) Turn out and serve with Velvet Chocolate Sauce.

* **260 calories per serving**
* **Medium fibre**

Apple Strudel

SERVES 6

4 large sheets of filo pastry (paste)
10 g/¹/₄ oz/2 tsp low-fat sunflower or
olive oil spread, melted
2 soft eating (dessert) apples, chopped
Finely grated rind of ¹/₂ lemon
45 ml/3 tbsp sultanas (golden raisins)
2.5 ml/¹/₂ tsp ground cinnamon
90 ml/6 tbsp low-fat crème fraîche, to
serve

Lay the sheets of pastry on a work surface on top of each other. Brush the surface with half the low-fat spread. Mix the apple with the lemon rind, sultanas and cinnamon. Spoon over the pastry to within 2.5 cm/1 in of the edge. Turn in the short edges, then roll up starting from a long side. Carefully transfer to a non-stick baking (cookie) sheet, gently shaping the roll into a curve. Brush with the remaining melted spread. Bake in a preheated oven at 200°C/400°F/ gas mark 6 for about 25 minutes until the fruit is cooked and the pastry is crisp and golden. Transfer to a serving plate and serve warm or cold with the crème fraîche.

* **200 calories per serving**
* **Fairly high fibre**

Autumn Compôte

SERVES 4

2 clementines or satsumas
100 g/4 oz/²/₃ cup no-need-to-soak
prunes
2 eating (dessert) apples, peeled,
quartered and cored
2 pears, peeled, cored and quartered
150 ml/¹/₄ pt/²/₃ cup cold black tea
150 ml/¹/₄ pt/²/₃ cup cider
30 ml/2 tbsp apricot jam (conserve)
60 ml/4 tbsp low-fat plain yoghurt

Peel the clementines or satsumas and discard as much white pith as possible. Separate into segments. Place in a saucepan with the prunes, apples and pears. Add the tea, cider and jam. Bring to the boil, reduce the heat, part-cover and simmer gently for about 10 minutes until the fruits are tender but still hold their shape. Serve hot, or cool then chill, topped with the yoghurt.

* **150 calories per serving**
* **Fairly high fibre**

Raspberry Roulade

SERVES 6

175 g/6 oz raspberries
60 ml/4 tbsp clear honey
2 eggs
50 g/2 oz/½ cup plain (all-purpose)
flour
15 ml/1 tbsp hot water
45 ml/3 tbsp raspberry jam (conserve)

Purée the raspberries in a blender or food processor with 15 ml/1 tbsp of the honey, then pass through a sieve (strainer) into a saucepan to remove the seeds. Heat through gently. Put the remaining honey and the eggs in a bowl and whisk with an electric beater until thick and pale. Sift the flour over the surface and fold in gently with a metal spoon, adding the hot water. Turn into a Swiss roll tin (jelly roll pan) lined with non-stick baking parchment. Bake in a preheated oven at 200°C/400°F/gas mark 6 for 8–10 minutes until the centre springs back when lightly pressed. Turn out on to a clean sheet of baking parchment and remove the cooking paper. Spread quickly with the jam. Make an indent with the back of a knife about 1 cm/½ in from one short end. Fold this over firmly, then roll up. Cut into slices and serve on plates with the hot sauce spooned to one side.

* **130 calories per serving**
* **Medium fibre**

Cherry Almond Clafoutie

SERVES 4

5 ml/1 tsp sunflower or olive oil
225 g/8 oz fresh cherries, stoned
(pitted)
100 g/4 oz/1 cup plain (all-purpose)
flour
1 egg
300 ml/½ pt/1¼ cups skimmed milk
A few drops of almond essence
(extract)
10 ml/2 tsp flaked (slivered) almonds
15 ml/1 tbsp granulated sugar

Brush a 20 cm/8 in shallow ovenproof serving dish with the oil. Put the cherries in a single layer in the dish. Sift the flour into a bowl. Make a well in the centre of the flour and add the egg and half the milk. Whisk until smooth. Stir in the remaining milk and the almond essence and pour over the cherries. Sprinkle the almonds and sugar over. Bake in a preheated oven at 200°C/400°F/gas mark 6 for about 30 minutes until golden and set. Serve hot.

* **200 calories per serving**
* **Medium fibre**

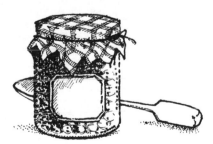

James's Strawberry Whirls

SERVES 6

2 eggs
50 g/2 oz/¼ cup caster (superfine)
  sugar
25 g/1 oz/¼ cup wholemeal flour
25 g/1 oz/¼ cup plain (all-purpose)
  flour
225 g/8 oz strawberries
120 ml/4 fl oz/1½ cup low-fat fromage
  frais
5 ml/1 tsp clear honey

Line a Swiss roll tin (jelly roll pan) with non-stick baking parchment. Whisk together the eggs and sugar in a bowl until thick and pale and the whisk leaves a trail when lifted out of the mixture. Mix the flours together and sprinkle over the egg mixture. Fold in very gently with a metal spoon. Pour the mixture into the prepared tin and spread out. Bake just above the centre of the oven for 7–10 minutes until risen and golden brown and the centre springs back when lightly pressed. Meanwhile, reserve a few strawberries for decoration and purée the remainder in a blender or food processor. Turn the sponge out on to a sheet of baking parchment on a clean tea towel (dish cloth) and remove the cooking paper. Spread some of the strawberry purée on the sponge and trim the edges, if necessary. Roll up, using the paper as a guide. Transfer to a wire rack with the join underneath and leave to cool. Mix a little of the remaining strawberry purée with the fromage frais and sweeten with the honey. Slice the Swiss roll. Put a slice on each plate, cut side up so you canof see the spiral of purée. Place a spoonful of the flavoured fromage frais to the side and decorate with the reserved strawberries.

* **200 calories per serving**
* **Fairly high fibre**

Apricot Floating Islands

SERVES 4

410 g/14½ oz/1 large can of apricot
  halves in natural juice
45 ml/3 tbsp clear honey
2 egg whites
Almond essence (extract)

Purée the contents of the can of fruit in a blender or food processor with 15 ml/1 tbsp of the honey. Turn into a fairly shallow ovenproof dish. Whisk the egg whites until stiff. Whisk in the remaining honey a spoonful at a time until stiff and glossy, adding a few drops of almond essence. Place the mixture in four or eight piles on top of the apricot mixture. Bake in a preheated oven at 150°C/300°F/gas mark 2 for 25 minutes until pale golden on top. Cool, then chill before serving.

* **100 calories per serving**
* **Medium fibre**

Fresh Fruit Salad

SERVES 4

300 ml/¹/₂ pt/1¹/₄ cups apple juice
2 nectarines
1 red eating (dessert) apple
1 green eating apple
1 kiwi fruit
2 clementines
1 pear

Pour the apple juice into a serving dish. Halve the nectarines, discard the stones (pits) and slice the fruit. Add to the juice. Quarter the apples but do not peel. Remove the cores, then cut into small chunks. Add to the juice. Peel and slice the kiwi fruit, then cut each slice in half. Add to the juice. Peel and segment the clementines, discarding as much white pith as possible. Add to the juice. Peel, quarter and core the pear and cut into small chunks. Add to the juice. Stir all together gently. Top up with more apple juice, if liked. Cover with clingfilm (plastic wrap) and chill for at least 1 hour to allow the flavours to develop.

* **105 calories per serving**
* **Fairly high fibre**

Tropical Fruit Salad

SERVES 6

300 ml/¹/₂ pt/1¹/₄ cups apple juice
1 ripe mango
1 passion fruit
1 small pineapple
2 star fruit
2 kiwi fruit
1 pomegranate

Pour the apple juice into a large plastic container with a lid. Peel the mango and mark into small cubes, cutting right through to the stone (pit). Cut the flesh off the stone. Add to the container. Halve the passion fruit and scoop the seeds into the container. Cut off the green top of the pineapple, then cut off all the rind. Slice the pineapple, remove any hard core, and cut the flesh into chunks. Add to the container. Wipe the star fruit and cut into star-shaped slices. Add to the container. Peel and slice the kiwi fruit. Add to the container. Quarter the pomegranate, bend back the skin, then carefully loosen the juicy seeds from the white pith and add to the container. Add more apple juice, if liked. Cover the container and chill for at least 1 hour to allow the flavours to develop. Turn into a glass serving dish and serve very cold.

* **70 calories per serving**
* **Fairly high fibre**

Raspberry Flan with Lemon Fromage Frais

SERVES 6

50 g/2 oz/¹/₂ cup plain (all-purpose) flour
2.5 ml/¹/₂ tsp baking powder
2 eggs
40 g/1¹/₂ oz/3 tbsp caster (superfine) sugar
150 ml/¹/₄ pt/²/₃ cup low-fat fromage frais
Finely grated rind of 1 lemon
15 ml/1 tbsp icing (confectioners') sugar
100 g/4 oz raspberries
15 ml/1 tbsp redcurrant jelly (clear conserve)
15 ml/1 tbsp lemon juice

Sift together the flour and baking powder. Whisk together the eggs and sugar with an electric beater until thick and pale. Fold in the flour lightly with a metal spoon. Line the raised base of a non-stick sponge flan tin (pie pan) with a circle on non-stick baking parchment. Turn the mixture into the sponge tin and level the surface. Bake in a preheated oven at 200°C/400°F/ gas mark 6 for about 15 minutes until risen and golden brown and the centre springs back when lightly pressed. Leave to cool in the tin for 5 minutes, then turn out on to a wire rack, remove the paper and leave to cool completely. Beat the fromage frais with the lemon rind and icing sugar. Place the flan case (pie shell) on a serving plate and spread the fromage frais in the flan. Arrange the raspberries over. Heat the redcurrant jelly with the lemon juice until melted and brush all over the raspberries to glaze. Chill until ready to serve.

* **150 calories per serving**
* **Medium fibre**

Marbled Honey Fruit Fool

SERVES 4

450 g/1 lb any fruit
30 ml/2 tbsp pure pineapple juice
Clear honey
Sweet Vanilla Sauce (page 386), cooled

Prepare the fruit and cut into small pieces. Place in a saucepan with the pineapple juice. Stew gently until soft. Purée in a blender or food processor and sweeten to taste with a little honey. Leave until cold. Fold into the vanilla sauce, just until the mixture forms a marbled effect. Spoon into four glasses and chill until ready to serve.

* **110 calories per serving**
* **Medium fibre**

Bite-sized Meringues

MAKES ABOUT 24

White or Brown Meringue Nests mixture (page 333)

Prepare the meringue mixture and put small spoonfuls on baking parchment on two baking (cookie) sheets. Bake as for the nests until crisp and dry. Cool, then store in an airtight container. Serve with any fruit desserts.

* **30 calories per meringue**
* **No fibre**

Peach Quark Delight

SERVES 4

410 g/14¹/₂ oz/1 large can of peach slices in natural juice, drained, reserving the juice
1 orange-flavoured jelly (jello) tablet
300 ml/¹/₂ pt/1¹/₄ cups low-fat quark
Mint leaves, to decorate

Make up the peach juice to 300 ml/¹/₂ pt/1¹/₄ cups with water, if necessary. Make up the jelly using this liquid. Reserve four peach slices for decoration and purée the remainder in a blender or food processor. Stir into the jelly. Chill until cold and on the point of setting, then fold in the quark. Spoon into four glasses and chill until set. Decorate each with a peach slice and a mint leaf before serving.

* **150 calories per serving**
* **Medium fibre**

White Meringue Nests

You can use bought meringue nests for quick individual desserts but the real things are in a completely different class – sophisticated and sumptuous.

MAKES 8

3 egg whites
175 g/6 oz/³/₄ cup caster (superfine) sugar
A few drops of vanilla essence (extract)

Lay a sheet of baking parchment on a dampened baking (cookie) sheet. Whisk the egg whites until stiff. Add 15 ml/1 tbsp of the sugar and the vanilla essence and whisk again until stiff and glossy. Gradually whisk in half the remaining sugar, then fold in the remainder with a metal spoon. Spoon eight mounds of the mixture a little apart on the baking sheet and hollow out slightly in the centres to form nests. Rough up the mixture slightly round the tops. Bake in a preheated oven at 110°C/225°F/ gas mark ¼ for 2–3 hours or until crisp but still white. Remove from the oven and leave to cool. Carefully lift off the paper and store in an airtight container.

* **95 calories per nest**
* **No fibre**

Brown Meringue Nests

MAKES 8

3 egg whites
A pinch of cream of tartar
175 g/6 oz/³/₄ cup dark brown sugar

Whisk the egg whites with the cream of tartar until stiff. Whisk in the sugar 15 ml/1 tbsp at a time, whisking well between each addition until stiff and glossy. Lay a sheet of baking parchment on a dampened baking (cookie) sheet. Spoon the mixture on to the baking parchment in mounds and hollow out slightly in the centres to form nests. Bake in a preheated oven at 120°C/250°F/gas mark ½ for about 1 hour or until crisp and dry. Turn the oven off and leave the meringue nests until cold in the oven. Carefully lift off the paper and store in an airtight container.

* **95 calories per nest**
* **No fibre**

Fresh Strawberry Nests

MAKES 8

*8 White or Brown Meringue Nests
(page 333)
250 ml/8 fl oz/1 cup low-fat
strawberry or plain fromage frais
15 ml/1 tbsp orange liqueur
175–225 g/6–8 oz strawberries, sliced*

Place the meringue nests on plates. Mix the fromage frais with the orange liqueur. Spoon into the meringues and top with sliced strawberries. Serve straight away.

* **140 calories per nest**
* **Medium fibre**

Fresh Raspberry Nests

MAKES 8

Prepare as for Fresh Strawberry Nests, but use raspberry fromage frais and substitute amaretto liqueur for the orange, and whole raspberries for the strawberries.

* **140 calories per nest**
* **Medium fibre**

Fresh Peach Nests

MAKES 8

Prepare as for Fresh Strawberry Nests, but use peach or apricot fromage frais and substitute peach liqueur or brandy for the orange liqueur, and 4 sliced peaches for the strawberries.

* **150 calories per nest**
* **Medium fibre**

Strawberry Italian Meringue Basket

SERVES 6

*3 large egg whites
175 g/6 oz/1 cup icing (confectioners')
sugar
Light Chantilly Cream (page 394)
350 g/12 oz strawberries, halved
Mint sprigs, to decorate*

Line two baking (cookie) sheets with baking parchment and draw a 23 cm/9 in circle on each. Lightly whisk the egg whites. Sift a little of the icing sugar over the surface and whisk in. Continue like this until all the sugar has been added, whisking all the time. Place the bowl over a pan of hot water and continue whisking for about 5 minutes until the meringue mixture is stiff and glossy. Put about a third of the meringue in a piping (pastry) bag fitted with a large star tube (tip). Pipe a ring round the edge of one of the circles. Fill the bag with the remaining meringue mixture and pipe a ring round the outside of the second circle, then continue piping to fill the circle to make the base. Bake the ring below the disc in a preheated oven at 140°C/275°F/gas mark 1 for 1½ hours, then turn off the oven and leave the meringue in the oven to cool completely. When ready to serve, place the meringue disc on a serving plate. Spread a little of the Chantilly Cream round the top edge and stick the ring on top. Fill the centre with the remaining Chantilly Cream, top with the strawberry halves and decorate with a few mint sprigs.

* **295 calories per serving**
* **Medium fibre**

Pear Italian Meringue Basket

SERVES 6

Prepare as for Strawberry Italian Meringue Basket, but substitute 550 g/1¼ lb/1 very large can of pear quarters, drained, for the strawberries. Drizzle with Hot Chocolate Caramel Sauce (page 388) to decorate just before serving. Omit the mint sprigs.

* 295 calories per serving
* Medium fibre

Apricot Italian Meringue Basket

SERVES 6

Prepare as for Strawberry Italian Meringue Basket, but substitute 550 g/1¼ lb/1 very large can of apricot halves, drained, for the strawberries. Decorate with a few toasted flaked (slivered) almonds instead of the mint sprigs.

* 300 calories per serving
* Medium fibre

Raspberry Italian Meringue Basket

SERVES 6

Prepare as for Strawberry Italian Meringue Basket, but substitute raspberries for the strawberries.

* 295 calories per serving
* Medium fibre

Easy Apple Strudels

SERVES 4

1 cooking (tart) apple, peeled, cored and chopped
40 g/1½ oz/3 tbsp granulated sugar
30 ml/2 tbsp sultanas (golden raisins)
2.5 ml/½ tsp ground cinnamon
4 sheets of filo pastry (paste)
20 g/¾ oz/1½ tbsp low-fat sunflower or olive oil spread, melted

Mix the apple with the sugar, sultanas and cinnamon. Brush the pastry sheets with a little of the low-fat spread. Fold into halves and brush again. Divide the filling between the pastry squares towards the middle of one edge. Fold in the sides, then roll up. Transfer to a lightly greased baking (cookie) sheet and brush with any remaining low-fat spread. Bake in a preheated oven at 190°C/375°F/gas mark 5 for 10–15 minutes until golden and cooked through.

* 125 calories per serving
* Medium fibre

Easy Pear and Ginger Strudels

SERVES 4

Prepare as for Easy Apple Strudels, but substitute 2 ripe pears, chopped, and 2 pieces of stem ginger in syrup, chopped, for the apple and sultanas. Serve with a little warmed syrup from the ginger jar spooned over.

* 135 calories per serving
* Medium fibre

Cloudy Apple Jelly

SERVES 4

*450 g/1 lb cooking (tart) apples,
peeled, cored and sliced
About 120 ml/4 fl oz/¹/₂ cup apple
juice
15 ml/1 tbsp powdered gelatine*

Put the apples in a saucepan with 30 ml/2 tbsp apple juice. Cover and cook very gently until pulpy. Meanwhile, sprinkle the gelatine over 30 ml/2 tbsp apple juice in a small bowl. Leave to soften for 5 minutes, then stir into the stewed apple until completely dissolved. Purée in a blender or food processor. Turn into a measuring jug and make up to 600 ml/1 pt/2½ cups with apple juice. Turn into a wetted 600 ml/ 1 pt/2½ cup jelly (jello) mould and chill until set. Dip the mould briefly in hot water, then turn out on to a serving plate.

* **85 calories per serving**
* **Medium fibre**

Kiwi Pavlova

SERVES 8

*4 egg whites
225 g/8 oz/1 cup caster (superfine)
sugar
15 ml/1 tbsp cornflour (cornstarch)
1.5 ml/¹/₄ tsp vanilla essence (extract)
10 ml/2 tsp vinegar
150 ml/¹/₄ pt/²/₃ cup low-fat whipping
cream, whipped
3–4 kiwi fruit, sliced*

Whisk the egg whites until stiff. Gradually whisk in the sugar, then the cornflour, vanilla essence and vinegar. Spoon in a large circle on baking parchment on a baking (cookie) sheet, making a slight hollow in the centre. Bake in a preheated oven at 150°C/300°F/gas mark 2 for 1½ hours until a pale biscuit colour, crisp on the outside and slightly fluffy in the middle. Leave to cool. Transfer to a serving plate, fill the centre with the low-fat cream and top with the kiwi fruit slices.

* **160 calories per serving**
* **Medium fibre**

Strawberry Pavlova

SERVES 8

Prepare as for Kiwi Pavlova, but substitute 175 g/6 oz small halved strawberries for the kiwi fruit.

* **160 calories per serving**
* **Medium fibre**

Mandarin and Raspberry Pavlova

SERVES 8

Prepare as for Kiwi Pavlova, but substitute 100 g/4 oz raspberries and 300 g/11 oz/1 medium can of mandarins, drained, for the kiwi fruit.

* **170 calories per serving**
* **Medium fibre**

Fresh Orange Jelly

SERVES 4

Finely grated rind and juice of
1 orange
15 ml/1 tbsp powdered gelatine
About 500 ml/17 fl oz/2¼ cups pure
orange juice

Put the orange rind and juice in a measuring jug and sprinkle the gelatine over. Leave to soften for 5 minutes. Stand the jug in a pan of hot water and stir until the gelatine has dissolved (or heat briefly in the microwave). Make up to 600 ml/1 pt/ 2½ cups with orange juice. Turn into a 600 ml/1 pt/2½ cup jelly (jello) mould. Chill until set. Dip briefly in hot water then turn out on to a serving plate and serve cold.

* **70 calories per serving**
* **Very low fibre**

Fresh Lemon Jelly

SERVES 4

Prepare as for Fresh Orange Jelly, but substitute the finely grated rind and juice of 2 lemons for the orange, and make up with pure pineapple juice instead of orange juice.

* **75 calories per serving**
* **Very low fibre**

Raspberry and Apple Jelly

SERVES 4

10 ml/2 tsp powdered gelatine
30 ml/2 tbsp lemon juice
1 raspberry-flavoured jelly (jello) tablet
750 ml/1¼ pts/3 cups medium-sweet
cider or apple juice
1 eating (dessert) apple
100 g/4 oz raspberries

Put the gelatine in a small bowl with the lemon juice and leave to soften for 5 minutes. Stand the bowl in a pan of hot water and stir until dissolved (or heat briefly in the microwave). Break up the jelly and dissolve in 300 ml/ ½ pt/1¼ cups of the cider or apple juice in a saucepan or in the microwave. Peel and core the apple and cut into very thin matchsticks. Add to the dissolved jelly. Stir in the dissolved gelatine and the remaining cider or juice. Divide the raspberries between four glass dishes and pour the jelly and apples over. Leave until completely cold, then chill until set.

* **160 calories per serving**
* **Medium fibre**

Fresh Blackcurrant Jelly

SERVES 6

850 g/1³/₄ lb blackcurrants
45 ml/3 tbsp water
Juice of ¹/₂ lemon
100 g/4 oz/¹/₂ cup caster (superfine)
*   sugar, plus extra for frosting*
20 g/³/₄ oz/1¹/₂ tbsp powdered gelatine
Low-fat fromage frais, to serve

Strip 750 g/1¹/₂ lb of the blackcurrants from their stalks and place in a saucepan with the water. Simmer until the fruit pops and is becoming pulpy. Purée in a blender or food processor, then pass through a sieve (strainer). Return to the saucepan. Make up the lemon juice to 300 ml/ ¹/₂ pt/1¹/₄ cups with water. Add to the pan with the sugar. Heat gently, stirring, until the sugar has dissolved. Tilt the pan and sprinkle on the gelatine. Stir until the gelatine has dissolved completely. Cool slightly. Turn into a glass serving dish and leave until cold, then chill until set. Meanwhile, dip the reserved blackcurrant sprigs in cold water, then sprinkle liberally with caster sugar. Leave to dry. Lay the frosted blackcurrant sprigs on top of the set jelly (jello) before serving with low-fat fromage frais.

* **130 calories per serving**
* **Medium fibre**

Fresh Redcurrant Jelly

SERVES 6

Prepare as for Fresh Blackcurrant Jelly, but substitute redcurrants for the blackcurrants. Try using the juice of an orange instead of a lemon, if liked.

* **130 calories per serving**
* **Medium fibre**

Cranberry and Claret Jelly

SERVES 4

75 g/3 oz/¹/₃ cup caster (superfine)
*   sugar*
30 ml/2 tbsp lemon juice
30 ml/2 tbsp brandy
150 ml/¹/₄ pt/²/₃ cup cranberry juice
15 ml/1 tbsp powdered gelatine
300 ml/¹/₂ pt/1¹/₄ cups claret

Put the sugar, lemon juice, brandy and cranberry juice in a saucepan. Sprinkle over the gelatine and leave to soften for 5 minutes. Heat gently until the gelatine has completely dissolved but do not allow to boil. Stir in the claret. Pour into a jelly (jello) mould, cool, then chill until set. Dip the mould briefly in hot water, then turn out on to a serving plate.

* **185 calories per serving**
* **No fibre**

Port and Claret Jelly

SERVES 6

100 g/4 oz/¹/₂ cup granulated sugar
15 ml/1 tbsp redcurrant jelly (clear conserve)
5 cm/2 in piece of cinnamon stick
1 clove
250 ml/8 fl oz/1 cup water
250 ml/8 fl oz/1 cup claret
15 ml/1 tbsp powdered gelatine
150 ml/¹/₄ pt/²/₃ cup ruby port
15 ml/1 tbsp brandy
Cigarettes Russes (page 368), to serve

Put the sugar, redcurrant jelly, cinnamon stick, clove and water in a saucepan and heat gently, stirring, until the sugar has dissolved completely. Pour a little of the claret in a small bowl. Sprinkle the gelatine over and leave to soften for 5 minutes. Stand the bowl in a pan of hot water and heat, stirring, until the gelatine has completely dissolved (or heat briefly in the microwave). Stir in the remaining claret, then stir into the flavoured water with the port and brandy. Leave until cold, then strain into six wine goblets and chill until set. Serve with Cigarettes Russes.

* **165 calories per serving**
* **No fibre**

Pear Lime Delight

SERVES 6

300 ml/¹/₂ pt/1¹/₄ cups water
60 ml/4 tbsp clear honey
2 limes
4 pears, quartered and cored
16 maraschino cherries, drained thoroughly and halved
1 lime-flavoured jelly (jello) tablet
300 ml/¹/₂ pt/1¹/₄ cups apple juice
Low-fat crème fraîche, to serve

Put the water and honey in a saucepan. Finely grate the rind and squeeze the juice from one of the limes and add to the pan. Add the pear quarters and simmer gently until they are almost transparent and are just tender. Leave until cold. Strain off the liquid and, if necessary, make up to 300 ml/¹/₂ pt/1¹/₄ cups with water. Return the liquid to the saucepan. Add half the jelly tablet and heat until dissolved. Pour this mixture into a round glass serving dish, leave until cold, then chill until set. Arrange the pears in a starburst pattern over the top and decorate in between with halved maraschino cherries. Meanwhile, dissolve the remaining jelly in the apple juice. Leave until cold but not set. Pour gently over the pears and cherries and chill again until set. Serve with crème fraîche.

* **90 calories per serving**
* **Medium fibre**

Apricot Crisp

SERVES 6

100 g/4 oz dried apricots
450 ml/³/₄ pt/2 cups water
15 ml/1 tbsp granulated sugar
1 orange-flavoured jelly (jello) tablet
15 ml/1 tbsp lemon juice
25 g/1 oz/2 tbsp low-fat sunflower or olive oil spread
15 ml/1 tbsp golden (light corn) syrup
50 g/2 oz/1 cup bran flakes
150 ml/¹/₄ pt/²/₃ cup low-fat crème fraîche

Put the apricots in a pan with the water and leave to soak overnight. Stir in the sugar. Bring to the boil, reduce the heat and simmer gently for 10 minutes until the fruit is tender. Remove the fruit with a draining spoon and leave to cool. Dissolve the jelly in the liquid in the saucepan. Stir in the lemon juice. Purée the apricots in a blender or food processor with some of the dissolved jelly. Stir in the remainder and pour into six glasses. Chill until set. Melt the low-fat spread and syrup in a saucepan and stir in the bran flakes. Spread the crème fraîche over the set apricot mixture, top with the bran flake mixture and chill again until firm.

* **205 calories per serving**
* **Fairly high fibre**

Apple Chartreuse

SERVES 6

300 ml/¹/₂ pt/1¹/₄ cups water
45 ml/3 tbsp granulated sugar
Thinly pared rind and juice of 1 lemon
4 cooking (tart) apples, peeled, cored and thickly sliced
15 ml/1 tbsp powdered gelatine
A little apple juice
Light Chantilly Cream (page 394), to serve

Put the water, sugar, lemon rind and juice in a saucepan. Heat gently, stirring, until the sugar has dissolved. Add the apple slices, bring to the boil, reduce the heat and poach gently until they are translucent but still hold their shape. Lift out with a draining spoon and transfer to a 900 ml/1¹/₂ pt/3³/₄ cup jelly (jello) mould. Stir the gelatine into the hot syrup and stir until completely dissolved. Strain into a measuring jug. Make up to 600 ml/1 pt/2¹/₂ cups with apple juice. Leave until cold, then chill until the consistency of egg white. Pour into the mould and chill until set. Dip the base of the mould briefly in hot water, then turn out on to a serving plate and serve with Light Chantilly Cream.

* **85 calories per serving**
* **Medium fibre**

Peach Fruit Dream

SERVES 4

1 lemon-flavoured jelly (jello) tablet
90 ml/6 tbsp boiling water
410 g/14½ oz/1 large can of peaches,
   drained, reserving the juice
Finely grated rind of 1 lemon
150 ml/¼ pt/⅔ cup low-fat peach
   yoghurt
175 g/6 oz green seedless grapes, in
   tiny bunches
175 g/6 oz black seedless grapes, in
   tiny bunches
1 egg white
Caster (superfine) sugar

Break up the jelly and place in a measuring jug. Make up to 150 ml/¼ pt/⅔ cup with boiling water and stir until completely dissolved. Make up to 300 ml/½ pt/1¼ cups with the peach juice. Purée the peaches in a blender or food processor and stir into the jelly with the lemon rind and yoghurt. Mix well, then turn into a 600 ml/1 pt/2½ cup wetted jelly mould. Chill until set. Meanwhile, brush the bunches of grapes with egg white and sprinkle liberally with caster sugar. Place on a sheet of greaseproof (waxed) paper to set. Turn the jelly out on to a serving dish and arrange clusters of fruit on top and round the edge. Serve cold.

* **175 calories per serving**
* **Medium fibre**

Milk Jelly

SERVES 4

1 fruit-flavoured jelly (jello) tablet
150 ml/¼ pt/⅔ cup boiling water
450 ml/¾ pt/2 cups skimmed milk

Dissolve the jelly in the water. Cool slightly and whisk in the milk. Turn into a wetted 600 ml/1 pt/2½ pt jelly mould or glass dish and chill until set. If set in a mould, dip briefly in hot water and turn out before serving.

* **125 calories per serving**
* **No fibre**

Lemon Milk Jelly

SERVES 4

1 lemon
30 ml/2 tbsp water
20 ml/4 tsp powdered gelatine
600 ml/1 pt/2½ cups milk
50 g/2 oz/¼ cup caster (superfine)
   sugar
Yellow food colouring (optional)
Angelica 'leaves', to decorate

Finely grate the rind from the lemon and place in a small bowl. Cut off all the white pith, then cut the fruit into slices, then into quarters. Add the water to the lemon rind and sprinkle with the gelatine. Leave to soften for 5 minutes. Stand the bowl over a pan of hot water and stir until the gelatine has dissolved completely. Warm the milk in a saucepan. Stir in the sugar until dissolved. Mix a little of the milk into the gelatine, then pour back into the remaining milk and stir well. Colour lightly with food colouring, if liked. Pour into wetted 750 ml/1¼ pt/ 3 cup jelly (jello) mould and leave to cool. Chill until set. Turn out and decorate with the quartered lemon slices and angelica 'leaves'.

* **140 calories per serving**
* **No fibre**

Orange Milk Jelly

SERVES 4

Prepare as for Lemon Milk Jelly (page 341), but substitute ½ an orange for the lemon, colour orange instead of yellow, if liked, and decorate with quartered orange slices.

* **140 calories per serving**
* **No fibre**

Lime Milk Jelly

SERVES 4

Prepare as for Lemon Milk Jelly (page 341), but substitute 1 lime for the lemon, colour green instead of yellow, if liked, and decorate with quartered lime slices.

* **130 calories per serving**
* **No fibre**

Coffee Milk Jelly

SERVES 4

Prepare as for Lemon Milk Jelly (page 341), but omit the lemon and dissolve 15 ml/1 tbsp instant coffee powder or granules, in the milk with the sugar. Decorate with chopped walnuts, if liked.

* **135 calories per serving**
* **No fibre**

Chocolate Milk Jelly

SERVES 4

Prepare as for Lemon Milk Jelly (page 341), but omit the lemon and flavour the milk with 45 ml/3 tbsp low-fat drinking (sweetened) chocolate powder and halve the amount of sugar.

* **140 calories per serving**
* **No fibre**

Quark Blackcurrant and Orange Jelly

SERVES 4

1 blackcurrant-flavoured jelly (jello) tablet
100 g/4 oz/½ cup low-fat quark
2 oranges, rinded, sliced and quartered

Break up the jelly and place in a measuring jug. Make up to 150 ml/¼ pt/⅔ cup with boiling water. Stir until completely dissolved, then make up to 450 ml/ ¾ pt/2 cups with cold water. Chill until the consistency of egg white. Stir in the quark and turn into four glasses. Chill until set. Decorate all over the top with the quartered orange slices.

* **140 calories per serving**
* **No fibre**

Flummery

SERVES 4

15 ml/1 tbsp powdered gelatine
45 ml/3 tbsp water
2 eggs, separated
100 g/4 oz/$\frac{1}{2}$ cup caster (superfine)
    sugar
150 ml/$\frac{1}{4}$ pt/$\frac{2}{3}$ cup buttermilk
1 large lemon
Mint sprigs, to decorate

Sprinkle the gelatine over the water in a small bowl and leave to soften for 5 minutes. Stand the bowl in a pan of hot water and stir until the gelatine is completely dissolved (or heat briefly in the microwave). Whisk together the egg yolks and sugar until thick and pale. Whisk in the dissolved gelatine. Stir in the buttermilk. Cut four slices from the lemon and reserve for decoration. Finely grate the rind and squeeze the juice from the remainder. Stir into the buttermilk mixture, then leave until on the point of setting. Whisk the egg whites until stiff and fold in with a metal spoon. Turn into four glasses and chill until set. Decorate each with a twist of lemon and a sprig of mint before serving.

* **200 calories per serving**
* **Very low fibre**

Lychee Bavarois

SERVES 6

1 lemon-flavoured jelly (jello) tablet
15 ml/1 tbsp lemon juice
425 g/15 oz/1 large can of lychees,
    drained, juice reserved
150 ml/$\frac{1}{4}$ pt/$\frac{2}{3}$ cup milk
30 ml/2 tbsp custard powder
30 ml/2 tbsp caster (superfine) sugar
150 ml/$\frac{1}{4}$ pt/$\frac{2}{3}$ cup low-fat whipping
    cream

Break up the jelly and place in a measuring jug. Add the lemon juice and make up to 300 ml/$\frac{1}{2}$ pt/ 1$\frac{1}{4}$ cups with boiling water. Stir until dissolved. Add the lychee syrup and make up to 450 ml/$\frac{3}{4}$ pt/2 cups with water, if necessary. Quarter the lychees. Arrange in the base of a 900 ml/1$\frac{1}{2}$ pt/3$\frac{3}{4}$ cup jelly mould and pour over about half the jelly to cover. Chill until set. Meanwhile, blend a little of the milk with the custard powder and sugar in a saucepan. Add the remaining milk. Bring to the boil and cook for 2 minutes, stirring, to form a thick custard. Stir in the remaining jelly. Leave until cool and on the point of setting. Whip the cream until softly peaking and fold in. Spoon over the lychees and chill until set. When ready to serve, dip the mould briefly in hot water and turn out on to a serving plate. Serve very cold.

* **140 calories per serving**
* **Medium fibre**

Vanilla Ice

SERVES 4

1 egg white
25 g/1 oz/3 tbsp icing (confectioners')
*   sugar*
10 ml/2 tsp vanilla essence (extract)
410 g/14½ oz/1 large can of low-fat
*   evaporated milk, thoroughly chilled*

Whisk the egg white until stiff, then whisk in the icing sugar and vanilla. Whisk the evaporated milk until thick and doubled in volume. Fold in the meringue mixture with a metal spoon. Turn into a freezerproof container, cover and freeze until firm around the edges. Whisk with a fork to break up the ice crystals, then freeze again until firm.

* **100 calories per serving**
* **No fibre**

Fresh Fruit Ice

SERVES 4

5 ml/1 tsp powdered gelatine
15 ml/1 tbsp cold water
450 g/1 lb any sweet, ripe soft-fleshed
*   fruit such as strawberries,*
*   raspberries, stoned (pitted)*
*   peaches, nectarines or apricots,*
*   peeled pineapple or melon*
60 ml/4 tbsp icing (confectioners')
*   sugar*
170 g/6 oz/1 small can of low-fat
*   evaporated milk, chilled*

Sprinkle the gelatine over the water in a small bowl. Leave to soften for 5 minutes, then stand the bowl in a pan of hot water and stir until dissolved (or heat briefly in the microwave). Purée the fruit in a blender or food processor, then pass through a sieve (strainer), if necessary, to remove any pips or skins. Sweeten with the icing sugar and stir in the dissolved gelatine. Whip the evaporated milk until thick and doubled in volume. Fold in the fruit purée gently but thoroughly. Turn into a freezerproof container, cover and freeze until firm around the edges. Whisk with a fork to break up the ice crystals, then freeze until firm.

* **100 calories per serving**
* **Medium fibre**

Low-fat Vanilla Ice Dream

SERVES 6

600 ml/1 pt/2½ cups skimmed milk
30 ml/2 tbsp custard powder
100 g/4 oz/½ cup caster (superfine)
*   sugar*
5 ml/1 tsp vanilla essence (extract)
1 packet of low-calorie Dream Topping
*   mix*

Pour off 150 ml/¼ pt/⅔ cup of the milk and reserve in the fridge for making up the Dream Topping. Blend the custard powder with a little of the remaining milk and the sugar in a saucepan. Add the remaining milk, bring to the boil and cook for 2 minutes, stirring all the time, until thick and smooth. Stir in the vanilla essence. Cover with a circle of wetted greaseproof (waxed) paper to prevent a skin forming and leave until cold. Make up the Dream Topping with the reserved milk as directed on the packet. Fold into the custard. Turn into a freezerproof container and freeze for 1½ hours. Whisk with a fork to break up the ice crystals, then freeze until firm.

* **145 calories per serving**
* **No fibre**

Fresh Strawberry Ice Dream

SERVES 6

Prepare as for Low-fat Vanilla Ice Dream, but blend in 225 g/8 oz strawberries, puréed with 5 ml/1 tsp lemon juice, before folding in the Dream Topping.

* 155 calories per serving
* Medium fibre

Fresh Raspberry Ice Dream

SERVES 6

Prepare as for Low-fat Vanilla Ice Dream, but blend in 225 g/8 oz raspberries, puréed then sieved (strained) to remove the seeds, before folding in the Dream Topping.

* 155 calories per serving
* Medium fibre

Raspberry Ripple Ice Dream

SERVES 6

Prepare as for Low-fat Vanilla Ice Dream, but after the final whisking when half frozen, fold in All Year Raspberry Sauce (page 390) just until it forms a rippled effect, then freeze until firm.

* 205 calories per serving
* Very low fibre

Chocolate Ice Dream

SERVES 6

Prepare as for Low-fat Vanilla Ice Dream, but dissolve 60 ml/4 tbsp low-fat drinking (sweetened) chocolate powder in the milk when making the custard and use only 85 g/3½ oz/scant ½ cup caster (superfine) sugar.

* 155 calories per serving
* No fibre

Coffee Ice Dream

SERVES 6

Prepare as for Low-fat Vanilla Ice Dream, but dissolve 15 ml/1 tbsp instant coffee powder or granules in the milk when making the custard.

* 145 calories per serving
* No fibre

Carob Chip Ice Dream

SERVES 6

Prepare as for Low-fat Vanilla Ice Dream, but add 100 g/4 oz/1 cup carob chips at the last whisking when half frozen, before freezing until firm.

* 240 calories per serving
* Very low fibre

Lemon Sorbet

SERVES 8

600 ml/1 pt/2½ cups water
225 g/8 oz/1 cup granulated sugar
Thinly pared rind and juice of 2 large
lemons
About 350 ml/12 fl oz/1½ cups bottled
lemon juice
2 egg whites

Put the water and sugar in a saucepan. Heat gently, stirring, until the sugar has dissolved. Bring to the boil and boil for 10 minutes until syrupy but not coloured. Add the lemon rind and leave until cold. Make the squeezed lemon juice up to 450 ml/¾ pt/2 cups with bottled lemon juice and stir into the syrup. Strain into a freezerproof container and freeze for about 1½ hours until frozen round the edges. Whisk with a fork to break up the ice crystals. Whisk the egg whites until stiff and fold in with a metal spoon. Return to the freezer and freeze until firm.

* **125 calories per serving**
* **Very low fibre**

Orange Sorbet

SERVES 8

Prepare as for Lemon Sorbet, but substitute the thinly pared rind and juice of 2 oranges for the lemons. Make up with pure orange juice instead of bottled lemon juice, and spike to taste with lemon juice, if liked.

* **150 calories per serving**
* **Very low fibre**

Grapefruit and Vodka Sorbet

SERVES 6

175 g/6 oz/¾ cup granulated sugar
300 ml/½ pt/1¼ cups water
2 grapefruit, all pith and rind removed
and segmented
75 ml/5 tbsp vodka
1 egg white
Cigarettes Russes (page 368), to serve

Put the sugar and water in a saucepan and heat gently until the sugar has dissolved. Bring to the boil and simmer for 5 minutes, without stirring. Leave to cool. Purée the grapefruit flesh in a blender or food processor with the vodka. Stir into the cold syrup, turn into a freezerproof container and freeze until firm round the edges. Whisk thoroughly with a fork to break up the ice crystals. Whisk the egg white until stiff and fold in with a metal spoon. Return to the freezer and freeze until firm. Remove from the freezer about 15 minutes before serving with Cigarettes Russes.

* **165 calories per serving**
* **Very low fibre**

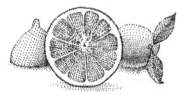

Strawberry Sorbet

SERVES 6

*100 g/4 oz/¹/₂ cup caster (superfine)
sugar
300 ml/¹/₂ pt/1¹/₄ cups water
225 g/8 oz ripe strawberries
Juice of 1 small lemon
1 egg white*

Put the sugar and water in a saucepan. Heat gently until the sugar has dissolved completely. Leave to cool. Purée the strawberries in a blender or food processor. Sieve (strain), if liked, to remove the pips. Stir into the syrup with the lemon juice. Turn into a freezerproof container and freeze until firm round the edges. Whisk with a fork to break up the ice crystals. Whisk the egg white until stiff and fold into the sorbet. Return to the freezer and freeze until firm. Remove from the freezer 10 minutes before serving to soften slightly.

* **90 calories per serving**
* **Medium fibre**

Blackcurrant Sorbet

SERVES 6

*325 ml/11 fl oz/scant 1¹/₃ cups water
225 g/8 oz blackcurrants, stripped
from their stalks
100 g/4 oz/¹/₂ cup caster (superfine)
sugar
5 ml/1 tsp lemon juice
2 egg whites*

Put 30 ml/2 tbsp of the water in a saucepan with the blackcurrants and stew gently for 10 minutes. Meanwhile, place the remaining water and the sugar in a separate saucepan. Heat gently, stirring, until the sugar has dissolved, then bring to the boil and boil for 5 minutes. Purée the blackcurrants and sugar syrup in a blender or food processor. Pass through a sieve (strainer) to remove the seeds. Turn into a freezerproof container, leave until cold, then freeze until firm round the edges. Whisk thoroughly with a fork to break up the ice crystals. Whisk the egg whites until stiff and fold in with a metal spoon. Return to the freezer and freeze until firm.

* **95 calories per serving**
* **Medium fibre**

Cranberry Sorbet

SERVES 6

Prepare as for Blackcurrant Sorbet, but substitute cranberries for the blackcurrants.

* **90 calories per serving**
* **Medium fibre**

Coffee Granita

SERVES 4

600 ml/1 pt/2½ cups boiling water
40 ml/2½ tbsp instant coffee powder
or granules
75 g/3 oz/⅓ cup caster (superfine)
sugar
Amaretti Biscuits (page 367), to serve

Mix together the water, coffee and sugar until completely dissolved. Leave until cold. Pour into a freezerproof container and freeze for about 45–60 minutes or until firm round the edges. Whisk with a fork to break up the ice crystals. Repeat this process a further two or three times until frozen and granular – about 3 hours in all. Spoon into glasses and serve with Amaretti Biscuits.

* **90 calories per serving**
* **No fibre**

Baked Alaska

SERVES 4 OR 6

1 small ready-made sponge flan case
(pie shell)
3 egg whites
175 g/6 oz/¾ cup caster (superfine)
sugar
2.5 ml/½ tsp vanilla essence (extract)
8 scoops of Low-fat Vanilla Ice Dream
(page 344) or bought low-fat
vanilla ice cream

Put the flan case on an ovenproof plate. Whisk the egg whites until stiff. Whisk in half the sugar and the vanilla essence and continue whisking until stiff and glossy. Fold in the remaining sugar. Pile the scoops of vanilla ice in the flan case. Cover completely with the meringue mixture. Bake in a preheated oven at 230°C/450°F/gas mark 8 for 2 minutes until the meringue is just turning golden. Serve straight away.

* **330 or 220 calories per serving**
* **Medium fibre**

Fruity Baked Alaska

SERVES 4 OR 6

Prepare as for Baked Alaska, but add enough soft fresh fruit, sliced if necessary, to cover the base of the flan case (pie shell) before adding the vanilla ice.

* **345 or 230 calories per serving**
* **Medium fibre**

Breads, Biscuits, Cakes and Nibbles

You can buy a variety of low-fat biscuits, cakes and snacks these days, but they tend to be high in sugar and salt – and anyway, there is nothing so satisfying as making your own. There's even a recipe for a lower-fat garlic bread, so you can indulge yourself far more than you ever thought possible!

Lower-fat Garlic Bread

SERVES 6

1 small French stick
25 g/1 oz/2 tbsp low-fat sunflower or
olive oil spread
50 g/2 oz/¼ cup low-fat soft cheese
30 ml/2 tbsp chopped parsley
2 garlic cloves, crushed

Cut the bread into 12 slices, not quite through to the bottom crust. Mash together the remaining ingredients and spread between the cuts. Wrap in foil and bake in a preheated oven at 200°C/400°F/gas mark 6 for 15 minutes until the crust feels crisp when squeezed. Serve hot.

* 75 calories per slice
* Medium fibre

Garlic and Herb Bread

SERVES 6

1 small wholemeal baguette
50 g/2 oz/¼ cup low-fat sunflower or
olive oil spread
1–2 garlic cloves, crushed
15 ml/1 tbsp chopped parsley
15 ml/1 tbsp chopped tarragon

Cut the bread into 12 slices, not quite through to the bottom crust. Mash together the remaining ingredients and spread between the cuts. Spread any remainder over the top. Wrap in foil and bake in a preheated oven at 200°C/ 400°F/gas mark 6 for about 15 minutes until the crust feels crisp and the centre soft when squeezed.

* 65 calories per slice
* High fibre

Fresh Herb Baguette

SERVES 4 OR 6

Prepare as for Garlic and Herb Bread, but omit the garlic and add 15 ml/1 tbsp chopped thyme with the other herbs.

* 65 calories per slice
* High fibre

Sage and Onion Rolls

SERVES 6

Prepare the spread as for Garlic and Herb Bread, but substitute a small, finely chopped onion for the garlic and sage for the tarragon. Use the mixture to spread inside 6 split bread rolls. Wrap in foil and bake as for the bread.

* 170 calories per roll
* Medium fibre

Perfect Poppadums

Instructions usually tell you to brush with oil before cooking, or even to deep-fry. For the low-fat alternative, simply place two at a time under a preheated grill (broiler) and grill (broil), watching all the time, until the surface begins to bubble. Turn over and cook the other side in the same way. Do not allow to brown. Alternatively, cook one at a time in the microwave for about 20 seconds or until beginning to bubble. Turn over and cook the other side until puffy.

* 50 calories per poppadum
* Medium fibre

Walnut and Cheese Loaf

SERVES 4 OR 6

1 small wholemeal baguette
50 g/2 oz/¼ cup low-fat soft cheese
25 g/1 oz/2 tbsp low-fat sunflower or
olive oil spread
15 ml/1 tbsp finely chopped walnuts
15 ml/1 tbsp chopped parsley

Cut the bread into 12 slices, not quite through to the bottom crust. Mash together the remaining ingredients and spread between the cuts. Wrap in foil and bake in a preheated oven at 200°C/400°F/gas mark 6 for about 15 minutes until the crust feels crisp when squeezed.

* **75 calories per slice**
* **High fibre**

Sun-dried Tomato and Cheese Loaf

SERVES 4 OR 6

Prepare as for Walnut and Cheese Loaf, but soak 4 sun-dried tomatoes in hot water for several hours, then drain, chop and add to the cheese instead of the walnuts.

* **70 calories per slice**
* **High fibre**

Melba Toast

SERVES 4

4 thin slices of white bread, crusts
removed

Toast the bread on both sides. Using a sharp knife, cut through the middle of the bread and toast the cut sides until crisp, golden and curling at the edges.

* **60 calories per slice**
* **Medium fibre**

Granary Bread Sticks

MAKES 24

300 ml/½ pt/1¼ cups skimmed milk
15 ml/1 tbsp sunflower or olive oil
450 g/1 lb/4 cups granary flour
A pinch of salt
10 ml/2 tsp easy-blend dried yeast

Warm the milk and oil until hand-hot. Meanwhile, mix together the remaining ingredients in a bowl. Add the hot milk mixture and mix, adding a little hot water, if necessary, to form a soft but not sticky dough. Knead on a lightly floured surface for about 5 minutes until elastic. Return to the bowl, cover with clingfilm (plastic wrap) and leave in a warm place for about 45 minutes until doubled in size. Re-knead and divide into 24 pieces. Roll each piece into a long sausage about 30 cm/12 in long. Place on a non-stick baking (cookie) sheet and leave for 20 minutes to rise again. Bake in a preheated oven at 220°C/425°F/gas mark 7 for about 30 minutes until crisp and brown. Transfer to a wire rack and leave until cold. Store in an airtight container.

* **80 calories per stick**
* **High fibre**

Caraway Bread Sticks

MAKES 24

Prepare as for Granary Bread Sticks (page 351), but substitute plain strong (bread) flour for the granary flour and add 30 ml/2 tbsp caraway seeds to the mixture.

* 80 calories per stick
* High fibre

Banana Bread

MAKES 1 LOAF

2 ripe bananas
5 ml/1 tsp bicarbonate of soda (baking soda)
50 g/2 oz/¼ cup low-fat sunflower or olive oil spread, plus extra for spreading
100 g/4 oz/½ cup caster (superfine) sugar
275 g/10 oz/2½ cups self-raising (self-rising) flour
2.5 ml/½ tsp ground cinnamon or mixed (apple-pie) spice
1 egg

Put the bananas in a food processor and run the machine until smooth. Add the remaining ingredients and run the machine until well blended. Turn into a900 g/2 lb loaf tin (pan), dampened and lined with non-stick baking parchment. Bake in a preheated oven at 180°C/350°F/gas mark 4 for about 50 minutes until risen, golden and a skewer inserted in the centre comes out clean. Remove from the tin, take off the paper and leave to cool on a wire rack. Serve cut into thin slices with a scraping of low-fat spread.

* 160 calories per slice
* Fairly high fibre

Banana and Raisin Bread

MAKES 1 LOAF

Prepare as for Banana Bread, but add 50 g/2 oz/⅓ cup of raisins to the mixture before turning into the tin (pan).

* 165 calories per slice
* High fibre

Banana and Cherry Bread

MAKES 1 LOAF

Prepare as for Banana Bread, but add 50 g/2 oz/¼ cup glacé (candied) cherries, quartered, to the mixture before turning into the tin (pan).

* 165 calories per slice
* Fairly high fibre

Banana and Carob Bread

MAKES 1 LOAF

Prepare as for Banana Bread, but add 50 g/2 oz/½ cup carob chips to the mixture before turning into the tin (pan).

* 165 calories per slice
* High fibre

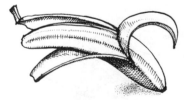

Banana and Apricot Bread

MAKES 1 LOAF

Prepare as for Banana Bread, but add 50 g/2 oz/⅓ cup chopped ready-to-eat dried apricots to the mixture before turning into the tin (pan).

* 165 calories per slice
* High fibre

Cottage Cheese Buns

MAKES 12

100 g/4 oz/½ cup low-fat cottage
    cheese, plus extra to serve
225 g/8 oz/2 cups self-raising (self-
    rising) flour
100 g/4 oz/½ cup caster (superfine)
    sugar
1 egg, beaten
45–60 ml/3–4 tbsp skimmed milk

Mix the cheese with the flour and sugar in a bowl. Stir in the egg and enough of the milk to form a soft but not sticky dough. Shape into 12 rounds and flatten slightly on a non-stick baking (cookie) sheet. Bake in a preheated oven at 220°C/425°F/gas mark 7 for 10–15 minutes until risen and browned. Serve warm, split and topped with a little more cottage cheese.

* 125 calories per bun
* Medium fibre

Cottage Cheese and Chive Buns

MAKES 12

Prepare as for Cottage Cheese Buns, but omit the sugar and add 30 ml/2 tbsp snipped chives, a good grinding of black pepper and a pinch of salt to the mixture.

* 125 calories per bun
* Medium fibre

Everyday Pancakes

MAKES 8

100 g/4 oz/1 cup plain (all-purpose)
    flour
A pinch of salt
300 ml/½ pt/1¼ cups skimmed milk
1 egg
Low-fat sunflower or olive oil spread,
    for shallow-frying

Sift the flour and salt in a bowl. Add half the milk and the egg and beat well until smooth. Stir in the remaining milk and leave to stand for 15 minutes before cooking. Heat a little low-fat spread in a non-stick frying pan (skillet). Pour off the excess. Add enough batter to just cover the base of the pan when swirled around. Fry (sauté) until golden on the underside, then flip over and cook the other side. Slide out of the pan and repeat until all the batter is used. Use as required.

* 65 calories per pancake
* Medium fibre

Oat Bran and Wholemeal Pancakes

Use these as an alternative to the Everyday Pancake mix for the stuffed pancake recipes given in this book, or simply drizzle with warm clear honey and freshly squeezed lemon juice for a delicious pudding.

MAKES 12

25 g/1 oz/¹/₄ cup oat bran
75 g/3 oz/³/₄ cup wholemeal flour
A pinch of salt
1 egg
150 ml/¹/₄ pt/²/₃ cup skimmed milk
175 ml/6 fl oz/³/₄ cup water
30 ml/2 tbsp sunflower oil

Mix the oat bran and flour in a bowl with the salt. Make a well in the centre and add the egg. Add half the milk, half the water and half the oil and whisk thoroughly until smooth. Stir in the remaining milk and water. Leave to stand for 30 minutes if possible. Brush a small non-stick frying pan (skillet) lightly with a little of the remaining oil and heat the pan until your hand feels very hot when held 5 cm/2 in above the pan. Pour 30–45 ml/2–3 tbsp of the batter into the pan and swirl round to coat the base (don't let the pancake be too thick). Cook over a fairly high heat until brown underneath and set on top, then flip over and cook the other side. Slide out on to a plate and keep warm over a pan of hot water. Repeat until all the batter is used.

* **70 calories per pancake**
* **High fibre**

Oat Tortillas

MAKES 12

100 g/4 oz/1 cup medium oatmeal, plus extra for dusting
100 g/4 oz/1 cup plain (all-purpose) flour, plus extra for dusting
A pinch of salt
5 ml/1 tsp baking powder
250 ml/8 fl oz/1 cup hand-hot water

Mix together the oatmeal, flour, salt and baking powder in a bowl. Mix in enough of the hot water to form a soft but not sticky dough. Knead gently on a lightly floured surface. Divide into 12 balls and roll out each one on a surface dusted with a mixture of oatmeal and flour. Heat a heavy non-stick frying pan (skillet) until very hot. Cook each tortilla for 1–2 minutes on each side until just browning in patches. Slide out on to a plate and repeat until all the tortillas are cooked. Either keep warm wrapped in a napkin on a plate over a pan of hot water or reheat briefly in the microwave when ready to serve.

* **70 calories per tortilla**
* **High fibre**

Poppy Seed Scones

MAKES 8

100 g/4 oz/1 cup wholemeal self-
raising (self-rising) flour
100 g/4 oz/1 cup white self-raising flour
5 ml/1 tsp baking powder
50 g/2 oz/¹/₄ cup low-fat sunflower or
olive oil spread, plus extra to serve
15 ml/1 tbsp caster (superfine) sugar
30 ml/2 tbsp poppy seeds
90 ml/6 tbsp skimmed milk, plus extra
to glaze
5 ml/1 tsp lemon juice
Any flavour jam (conserve), to serve

Sift the flours and baking powder
into a bowl. Stir in the bran left in
the sieve (strainer). Rub in the low-fat
spread, then stir in the sugar and
seeds. Mix together the milk and
lemon juice and stir into the mixture to
form a soft but not sticky dough.
Knead gently on a lightly floured
surface. Pat out to about 2 cm/¾ in
thick and cut into rounds using a
4 cm/1½ in fluted cutter. Re-knead the
trimmings and use to make more
scones (biscuits). Place well apart on a
non-stick baking (cookie) sheet. Brush
with a little milk to glaze, then bake in
a preheated oven at 220°C/425°F/gas
mark 7 for about 10–12 minutes until
risen and golden. Split and serve with
a scraping of low-fat sunflower or olive
oil spread and jam.

* **125 calories per scone**
* **Fairly high fibre**

Sesame Seed Scones

MAKES 8

Prepare as for Poppy Seed Scones,
but use all white flour and
substitute toasted sesame seeds for the
poppy seeds.

* **125 calories per scone**
* **Fairly high fibre**

Savoury Yoghurt Scones

MAKES 10

225 g/8 oz/2 cups self-raising (self-
rising) flour
A pinch of salt
A pinch of cayenne
10 ml/2 tsp baking powder
25 g/1 oz/2 tbsp low-fat sunflower or
olive oil spread
15 ml/1 tbsp snipped chives
120 ml/4 fl oz/¹/₂ cup low-fat plain
yoghurt
Low-fat soft cheese, to serve

Sift the flour, salt, cayenne and
baking powder into a bowl. Add the
low-fat spread and rub in with the
fingertips. Mix in the chives and
yoghurt. Add a little water, if necessary,
to form a soft but not sticky dough.
Flatten with the hand to about 2 cm/
¾ in thick. Cut into small scones
(biscuits) using a small biscuit (cookie)
cutter. Place on a non-stick baking
(cookie) sheet and bake in a preheated
oven at 200°C/400°F/gas mark 6 for
about 15 minutes until well risen and
golden and the bases sound hollow
when tapped. Serve warm or cold, split
and spread with a scraping of low-fat
soft cheese.

* **180 calories per scone**
* **Medium fibre**

Fruit and Fibre Scones

MAKES 8

100 g/4 oz/1 cup wholemeal flour
100 g/4 oz/1 cup plain (all-purpose)
flour
15 ml/1 tbsp baking powder
15 ml/1 tbsp wheat bran
A pinch of salt
50 g/2 oz/¼ cup low-fat sunflower or
olive oil spread, plus extra to serve
45 ml/3 tbsp clear honey
45 ml/3 tbsp dried banana slices,
crushed
30 ml/2 tbsp raisins
1 egg
45 ml/3 tbsp low-fat plain yoghurt
Skimmed milk

Mix the flours and baking powder with the bran and salt. Rub in the low-fat spread. Stir in the honey, banana and raisins. Beat together the egg and yoghurt and mix in, adding a little milk, if necessary, to form a soft but not sticky dough. Knead gently on a lightly floured surface and pat out to about 2 cm/¾ in thick. Cut into rounds using a 5 cm/2 in biscuit (cookie) cutter. Transfer to a non-stick baking (cookie) sheet and brush with a little milk to glaze. Bake the scones (biscuits) in a preheated oven at 220°C/425°F/gas mark 7 for about 12 minutes until risen, golden and the bases sound hollow when tapped. Cool on a wire rack. Split and serve with a scraping of low-fat sunflower or olive oil spread.

* **180 calories per scone**
* **High fibre**

Sweet Yoghurt Scones

MAKES 10

225 g/8 oz/2 cups self-raising (self-
rising) flour
10 ml/2 tsp baking powder
A pinch of salt
15 ml/1 tbsp caster (superfine) sugar
25 g/1 oz/2 tbsp low-fat sunflower or
olive oil spread
120 ml/4 fl oz/½ cup low-fat plain
yoghurt
No-sugar Apple and Cinnamon Spread
(page 395), to serve

Sift together the flour, baking powder, salt and sugar in a bowl. Add the low-fat spread and rub in with the fingertips. Mix with the yoghurt and a little water, if necessary, to form a soft but not sticky dough. Pat out to a round about 2 cm/¾ in thick and cut in to rounds using a small biscuit (cookie) cutter. Transfer to a very lightly greased baking (cookie) sheet and bake the scones (biscuits) in a preheated oven at 200°C/400°F/gas mark 6 for about 15 minutes until risen, golden and the bases sound hollow when tapped. Serve warm or cold, split and spread with a very little No-sugar Apple and Cinnamon Spread.

* **100 calories per scone**
* **Medium fibre**

Cottage Griddle Cakes

MAKES 12

*25 g/1 oz/2 tbsp low-fat sunflower or
olive oil spread, melted, plus extra
for cooking*
*100 g/4 oz/½ cup low-fat cottage
cheese with chives*
2 eggs, beaten
50 g/2 oz/½ cup plain (all-purpose) flour
5 ml/1 tsp baking powder
15 ml/1 tbsp skimmed milk

Mix the low-fat spread with the cheese and beat in the remaining ingredients to form a thick batter. Heat a little low-fat spread in a heavy-based frying pan (skillet). Pour off the excess. Drop spoonfuls of the batter into the pan and cook until the undersides are golden. Flip over with a palette knife and cook the other sides until brown. Wrap in a clean napkin while cooking the remainder. They can be reheated very briefly in the microwave or on a plate over a pan of hot water.

* **50 calories per cake**
* **Medium fibre**

Cottage Pineapple Griddle Cakes

MAKES 12

Prepare as for Cottage Griddle Cakes, but substitute low-fat cottage cheese with pineapple for the cottage cheese and chives and add a good pinch of mixed (apple-pie) spice to the mixture.

* **55 calories per cake**
* **Medium fibre**

Oven-fresh Scones

MAKES 8

225 g/8 oz/2 cups self-raising (self-rising) flour
10 ml/2 tsp baking powder
*25 g/1 oz/2 tbsp low-fat sunflower or
olive oil spread*
15 ml/1 tbsp caster (superfine) sugar
Skimmed milk, to mix

Sift the flour and baking powder into a bowl. Rub in the low-fat spread. Stir in the sugar and mix with enough milk to form a soft but not sticky dough. Knead very briefly on a lightly floured surface. Pat out to about 1 cm/½ in thick and cut into eight scones (biscuits), using a 5 cm/2 in biscuit (cookie) cutter. Transfer to a non-stick baking (cookie) sheet and bake immediately in a preheated oven at 230°C/450°F/gas mark 8 for about 10 minutes until risen, golden and the bases sound hollow when tapped. Transfer to a wire rack to cool slightly. Best served warm.

* **80 calories per scone**
* **Medium fibre**

Honeyed Wholemeal Oven-fresh Scones

MAKES 8

Prepare as for Oven-fresh Scones (page 357), but substitute self-raising (self-rising) wholemeal flour for the white flour and clear honey for the sugar.

* 80 calories per scone
* High fibre

Sweet Scotch Pancakes

MAKES 12

100 g/4 oz/1 cup plain (all-purpose) flour
A pinch of salt
15 ml/1 tbsp caster (superfine) sugar
1 egg
150 ml/¹/₄ pt/²/₃ cup skimmed milk
Low-fat sunflower or olive oil spread, for greasing

Sift the flour, salt and sugar into a bowl. Add the egg and beat until smooth. Stir in the milk. Lightly grease a non-stick frying pan (skillet) with low-fat spread. Drop spoonfuls of the mixture into the pan and cook for about 2 minutes until golden brown underneath. Flip over with a palette knife and cook the other sides. Keep warm in a napkin over a pan of hot water while cooking the remainder. Eat warm. They can be reheated briefly in the microwave or on a plate over a pan of hot water.

* 50 calories per pancake
* Medium fibre

Chinese Steamed Rolls

MAKES 15

450 g/1 lb/4 cups plain (all-purpose) flour
15 ml/1 tbsp light brown sugar
1 sachet of easy-blend dried yeast
5 ml/1 tsp reduced-salt soy sauce
15 g/¹/₂ oz/1 tbsp low-fat sunflower or olive oil spread, melted
175 ml/6 fl oz/³/₄ cup hand-hot water

Mix the flour and sugar with the yeast. Add the soy sauce, low-fat spread and the water. Mix to form a soft· but not sticky dough, adding a little extra hand-hot water, if necessary. Knead gently on a lightly floured surface for 4 minutes until smooth and elastic. Return to the bowl, cover with a damp tea towel (dish cloth) and leave in a warm place for about 45 minutes until doubled in size. Re-knead and shape into 15 small balls. Place on baking parchment on a wire rack and leave in a warm place for 15 minutes to rise. Bring a large roasting tin (pan) of water to the boil. Shape a large dome of foil over the rack so it doesn't touch any of the rolls but will keep the steam in. Place the rack over the pan of simmering water and steam for 15 minutes. Serve warm.

* 120 calories per roll
* Medium fibre

Boiled Fruit Salad Slab Cake

MAKES 1 CAKE

100 g/4 oz/¹/₂ cup low-fat sunflower or olive oil spread
175 g/6 oz/³/₄ cup dark brown sugar
120 ml/4 fl oz/¹/₂ cup pure orange juice
75 ml/5 tbsp water
250 g/9 oz/1 small packet of dried fruit salad, chopped, discarding any stones (pits)
5 ml/1 tsp bicarbonate of soda (baking soda)
10 ml/2 tsp mixed (apple-pie) spice
225 g/8 oz/2 cups self-raising (self-rising) flour
5 ml/1 tsp baking powder
1 large egg, beaten
30 ml/2 tbsp skimmed milk

Wet an 18 cm/7 in square cake tin (pan) and line with baking parchment. Put everything except the flour, baking powder, egg and milk in a saucepan. Bring to the boil and boil for 1 minute. Remove from the heat and leave to cool for 5 minutes. Stir in the flour, baking powder, egg and milk. Turn into the prepared tin and bake in a preheated oven at 180°C/350°F/ gas mark 4 for about 1 hour 10 minutes or until a skewer inserted in the centre comes out clean. Cool for 10 minutes, then turn out, remove the paper and leave to cool. Serve cut into 18 fingers.

* **135 calories per finger**
* **High fibre**

Light Wholemeal Scotch Pancakes

MAKES 12

100 g/4 oz/1 cup wholemeal flour
A pinch of salt
15 ml/1 tbsp caster (superfine) sugar
1 egg, separated
150 ml/¹/₄ pt/²/₃ cup skimmed milk
Low-fat sunflower or olive oil spread for cooking

Mix together the flour, salt and sugar. Beat in the egg yolk and milk. Whisk the egg white until stiff and fold into the mixture with a metal spoon. Heat a very little low-fat spread in a frying pan (skillet). Pour off the excess. Add spoonfuls of the mixture and cook until golden underneath and fluffing up. Turn over and cook the other sides. Keep warm in a napkin on a plate over a pan of hot water while cooking the remainder. Serve warm.

* **55 calories per pancake**
* **High fibre**

Light Rye Scotch Pancakes

MAKES 12

Prepare as for Light Wholemeal Scotch Pancakes, but substitute rye flour for wholemeal.

* **55 calories per pancake**
* **High fibre**

Teacup Loaf

Use the same teacup to measure all the ingredients.

MAKES 1 LOAF

1 teacup raisins
1 teacup sultanas (golden raisins)
½ teacup currants
½ teacup light brown sugar
½ teacup pure apple juice
½ teacup cold black tea
¼ teacup low-fat sunflower or olive oil spread
2 teacups self-raising (self-rising) flour
5 ml/1 tsp mixed (apple-pie) spice

Put all the ingredients except the flour and spice in a saucepan and heat gently until the fat melts, then bring to the boil and boil for 2 minutes. Leave until lukewarm, then stir in the flour and spice. Turn into a 900 g/2 lb non-stick loaf tin (pan), base-lined with baking parchment. Bake in a preheated oven at 180°C/350°F/gas mark 4 for 1¼ hours or until risen, golden and a skewer inserted in the centre comes out clean. Leave to cool in the tin for a few minutes, then turn out on to a wire rack, remove the paper and leave to cool. Serve cut into 12 slices.

* **155 calories per slice**
* **High fibre**

Rosemary Teacup Loaf

MAKES 1 LOAF

Prepare as for Teacup Loaf, but add a large sprig of rosemary when boiling the fruit. Remove before mixing in the dry ingredients.

* **155 calories per slice**
* **High fibre**

Minted Currant Loaf

MAKES 1 LOAF

Prepare as for Teacup Loaf, but substitute all currants for the raisins, sultanas and currants and add 10 ml/2 tsp dried mint to the mixture.

* **155 calories per slice**
* **High fibre**

Garam Garbanzos

SERVES 4 OR 6

425 g/15 oz/1 large can of chick peas (garbanzos), thoroughly drained
15 ml/1 tbsp garam masala
A pinch of salt

Dry the chick peas on kitchen paper (paper towels). Spread on a non-stick baking (cookie) sheet. Mix the garam masala with the salt, sprinkle over and toss to coat. Bake in a preheated oven at 180°C/350°F/gas mark 4 for about 50 minutes until the beans are brown and crunchy. Cool, then store in an airtight container.

* **18 calories per 15 g/1 tbsp**
* **High fibre**

Carob and Walnut Brownies

MAKES 12

50 g/2 oz/¹/₂ cup plain (all-purpose) flour
15 ml/1 tbsp wheat bran
1.5 ml/¹/₄ tsp baking powder
50 g/2 oz/¹/₂ cup walnuts, chopped
65 g/2¹/₂ oz/generous ¹/₄ cup low-fat sunflower or olive oil spread
50 g/2 oz/¹/₂ cup carob chips
175 g/6 oz/³/₄ cup dark brown sugar
2 eggs, beaten
2.5 ml/¹/₂ tsp vanilla essence (extract)

Wet a 28 cm x 18 cm/11 x 7 in shallow baking tin (pan) and line with baking parchment. Mix together the flour, bran, baking powder and nuts. Melt the low-fat spread with the carob and sugar. Cool slightly, then beat in the eggs and vanilla essence. Pour into the flour mixture and mix well. Turn into the prepared tin and bake in a preheated oven at 180°C/ 350°F/gas mark 4 for 35 minutes until risen and the centre springs back when lightly pressed. Leave to cool in the tin, then cut into squares.

* **180 calories per square**
* **Fairly high fibre**

Carob and Raisin Brownies

MAKES 12

Prepare as for Carob and Walnut Brownies, but substitute raisins for the walnuts.

* **165 calories per square**
* **Fairly high fibre**

Low-fat Jam Shortcake

MAKES ABOUT 12

350 g/12 oz/3 cups self-raising (self-rising) flour
50 g/2 oz/¹/₄ cup low-fat sunflower or olive oil spread
100 g/4 oz/¹/₂ cup caster (superfine) sugar
A few drops of vanilla essence (extract)
Skimmed milk
Any flavour jam (conserve)

Sift the flour into a bowl. Rub in the low-fat spread, then stir in the sugar and vanilla essence. Mix with enough milk to form a soft but not sticky dough. Knead gently and roll out to about 5 mm/¹/₄ in thick. Cut into rounds or squares using a biscuit (cookie) cutter. Place on a non-stick baking (cookie) sheet. Prick with a fork and bake in a preheated oven at 220°C/425°F/gas mark 7 for about 15 minutes until golden. Cool on a wire rack. Sandwich together in pairs with a little jam.

* **160 calories per shortcake**
* **Medium fibre**

Devil's Food Cake with Marshmallow Frosting

SERVES 12

For the cake:
*75 g/3 oz/¹/₃ cup low-fat sunflower or
    olive oil spread*
225 g/8 oz/1 cup dark brown sugar
2.5 ml/¹/₂ tsp vanilla essence (extract)
2 eggs
75 g/3 oz/³/₄ cup carob chips, melted
15 ml/1 tbsp instant coffee powder
*150 ml/¹/₄ pt/²/₃ cup cultured
    buttermilk*
*150 g/5 oz/1¹/₄ cups self-raising (self-
    rising) flour*
*2.5 ml/¹/₂ tsp bicarbonate of soda
    (baking soda)*
For the frosting:
225 g/8 oz marshmallows
20 ml/1¹/₂ tbsp skimmed milk
2 egg whites
*40 g/1¹/₂ oz/¹/₃ cup low-fat drinking
    (sweetened) chocolate powder*

To make the cake, wet and line two 20 cm/8 in sandwich tins (pans) with non-stick baking parchment. Beat together the low-fat spread and sugar with the vanilla until light and fluffy. Beat in the eggs, one at a time. Whisk the carob and coffee into the buttermilk. Sift together the flour and bicarbonate of soda. Fold the buttermilk mixture into the sugar mixture alternately with the flour. Turn into the prepared tins and bake in a preheated oven at 190°C/375°F/gas mark 5 for about 20 minutes or until risen and the centres spring back when pressed. Cool slightly, then turn out on to a wire rack, remove the paper and leave to cool.

To make the frosting, melt the marshmallows in the milk in a saucepan. Whisk the egg whites until stiff. Whisk in the chocolate powder and whisk again. Fold into the marshmallows, then leave to stand for about 10 minutes before using. Sandwich the cakes together with a little of the frosting, then place on a plate and spread the remainder all over the cake.

* 200 calories per slice
* Medium fibre

Quick Home-made Bread

MAKES 2 SMALL LOAVES

*450 g/1 lb/4 cups plain (all-purpose)
    flour*
20 ml/4 tsp baking powder
*25 g/1 oz/2 tbsp low-fat sunflower or
    olive oil spread*
300 ml/¹/₂ pt/1¹/₄ cups skimmed milk

Sift the flour and baking powder into a bowl. Rub in the low-fat spread. Mix with enough of the milk to form a soft but not sticky dough. Divide the dough in half. Shape each piece into a loaf and place in two 450 g/1 lb loaf tins (pans) lined with baking parchment. Bake in a preheated oven at 230°C/450°F/gas mark 8 for 20–25 minutes until risen and golden and the bases sound hollow when tapped. Turn out on to a wire rack, remove the paper and leave to cool.

* 50 calories per slice
* Medium fibre

Quick Wholemeal Bread

MAKES 2 SMALL LOAVES

Prepare as for Quick Home-made Bread, but substitute wholemeal flour for the white flour.

* **50 calories per slice**
* **High fibre**

Quick Brown Bread

MAKES 2 SMALL LOAVES

Prepare as for Quick Home-made Bread, but use half wholemeal and half plain (all-purpose) flour.

* **50 calories per slice**
* **Fairly high fibre**

Savoury Brown Onion Loaf

MAKES 1 LOAF

350 g/12 oz/3 cups self-raising (self-rising) flour
1 packet of dried brown onion soup mix (to make 600 ml/1 pt/2½ cups soup)
285 ml/scant ½ pt/1 medium carton of cultured buttermilk
30 ml/2 tbsp skimmed milk
Low-fat sunflower or olive oil spread, to serve

Mix together the flour and soup. Stir in the buttermilk and milk to form a soft, slightly sticky dough. Turn into a wetted 450 g/1 lb loaf tin (pan) lined with non-stick baking parchment. Bake in a preheated oven at 200°C/400°F/gas mark 6 for about 30 minutes until risen and golden and the base sounds hollow when tapped. Serve cut into 10 slices with a scraping of low-fat spread.

* **120 calories per slice**
* **Medium fibre**

Savoury White Onion Loaf

MAKES 1 LOAF

Prepare as for Savoury Brown Onion Loaf, but substitute a packet of white onion soup mix for the brown onion soup.

* **120 calories per slice**
* **Medium fibre**

Savoury Asparagus Loaf

MAKES 1 LOAF

Prepare as for Savoury Brown Onion Loaf, but substitute a packet of asparagus soup mix for the brown onion soup.

* **120 calories per slice**
* **Medium fibre**

Savoury Tomato Loaf with Sun-dried Tomatoes

MAKES 1 LOAF

Prepare as for Savoury Brown Onion Loaf, but substitute a packet of tomato soup mix for the brown onion soup and add 4 soaked sun-dried tomatoes, finely chopped, to the mixture before adding the buttermilk.

* **130 calories per slice**
* **Medium fibre**

Date and Walnut Loaf

MAKES 1 LOAF

225 g/8 oz/2 cups self-raising (self-rising) wholemeal flour
225 g/8 oz/2 cups self-raising white flour
25 g/1 oz/2 tbsp low-fat sunflower or olive oil spread, plus extra to serve
45 ml/3 tbsp clear honey
75 g/3 oz/¹/₂ cup chopped stoned (pitted) dates
75 g/3 oz/³/₄ cup walnuts, chopped
375 ml/13 fl oz/1¹/₂ cups skimmed milk
5 ml/1 tsp bicarbonate of soda (baking soda)

Mix together the two flours in a large bowl. Rub in the low-fat spread. Stir in the honey, dates and nuts. Mix a little of the milk with the bicarbonate of soda and add to the bowl with enough of the remaining milk to form a soft dough. Turn into a non-stick 900 g/2 lb loaf tin (pan), base-lined with non-stick baking parchment. Bake in a preheated oven at 190°C/ 375°F/gas mark 5 for about 1 hour or until risen, golden and a skewer inserted in the centre comes out clean. Cool slightly, then turn out on to a wire rack, remove the paper and leave to cool. Serve cut into 12 slices with a scraping of low-fat sunflower or olive oil spread.

* **225 calories per slice**
* **High fibre**

Figgy Nut Loaf

MAKES 1 LOAF

Prepare as for Date and Walnut Loaf, but substitute chopped dried figs for the dates and chopped mixed nuts for the walnuts.

* **225 calories per slice**
* **High fibre**

Almond Shortbread Fingers

MAKES 18

100 g/4 oz/¹/₂ cup low-fat sunflower or olive oil spread, plus extra for greasing
50 g/2 oz/¹/₄ cup caster (superfine) sugar
50 g/2 oz/¹/₂ cup plain (all-purpose) flour
50 g/2 oz/¹/₂ cup wholemeal flour
75 g/3 oz/³/₄ cup ground almonds
A few drops of almond essence (extract)

Beat together the low-fat spread and sugar until light and fluffy. Work in the remaining ingredients to form a soft dough. Press into a lightly greased 18 x 28 cm/7 x 11 in Swiss roll tin (jelly roll pan). Prick all over with a fork. Bake in a preheated oven at 160°C/325°F/ gas mark 3 for about 40 minutes until a pale golden brown. Mark into wide fingers with a knife, then leave until completely cold before removing from the tin. Store in an airtight container.

* **95 calories per finger**
* **Fairly high fibre**

Hazelnut Shortbread Squares

MAKES 15

Prepare as for Almond Shortbread Fingers, but substitute hazelnuts (filberts) for the almonds, vanilla essence (extract) for almond and cut into 15 squares instead of 18 fingers.

* 105 calories per square
* Fairly high fibre

Chewy Carob Bars

MAKES 12

50 g/2 oz/¹/₄ cup light brown sugar
30 ml/2 tbsp golden (light corn) syrup
75 g/3 oz/¹/₃ cup low-fat sunflower or olive oil spread
225 g/8 oz/2 cups rolled oats
45 ml/3 tbsp carob powder
5 ml/1 tsp vanilla essence (extract)
25 g/1 oz/¹/₄ cup chopped mixed nuts
50 g/2 oz/¹/₃ cup sultanas (golden raisins)

Put the sugar, syrup and low-fat spread in a saucepan and heat, stirring, until melted. Stir in the remaining ingredients. Turn into a non-stick 28 cm x 18 cm/11 x 7 in shallow baking tin (pan), base-lined with baking parchment. Press down well. Leave to cool, then chill overnight. Cut into fingers and store in an airtight container.

* 115 calories per bar
* High fibre

Anzacs

MAKES 24

100 g/4 oz/¹/₂ cup granulated sugar
50 g/2 oz/¹/₂ cup plain (all-purpose) flour
50 g/2 oz/¹/₂ cup wholemeal flour
40 g/1¹/₂ oz/¹/₃ cup chopped hazelnuts (filberts)
40 g/1¹/₂ oz/¹/₃ cup desiccated (shredded) coconut
50 g/2 oz/¹/₄ cup low-fat sunflower or olive oil spread
15 ml/1 tbsp golden (light corn) syrup
2.5 ml/¹/₂ tsp bicarbonate of soda (baking soda)
15 ml/1 tbsp skimmed milk

Mix together the sugar, flours, hazelnuts and coconut in a bowl. Put the low-fat spread and syrup in a saucepan and heat, stirring, until the fat melts. Blend the bicarbonate of soda with the milk. Add the liquids to the flour mixture and mix thoroughly. Shape into 24 small balls and place well apart on baking (cookie) sheets lined with non-stick baking parchment. Bake in a preheated oven at 180°C/350°F/gas mark 4 for about 20 minutes until spread and golden. Cool slightly. Transfer to wire racks to cool and harden. Store in an airtight container.

* 75 calories per Anzac
* High fibre

Lemon Fingers

MAKES 24

50 g/2 oz/¹/₄ cup low-fat sunflower or olive oil spread
50 g/2 oz/¹/₄ cup caster (superfine) sugar
2 egg whites, lightly beaten
100 g/4 oz/1 cup plain (all-purpose) flour
2.5 ml/¹/₂ tsp baking powder
A pinch of salt
Finely grated rind of 1 small lemon

Beat together the low-fat spread and sugar until light and fluffy. Beat in the egg whites. Sift the flour, baking powder and salt over the surface, sprinkle over the lemon rind and fold in with a metal spoon. Shape the dough into a soft ball, wrap in clingfilm (plastic wrap) and chill for 30 minutes. Roll out thinly on a lightly floured surface and cut into fingers. Transfer to baking (cookie) sheets lined with non-stick baking parchment and bake in a preheated oven at 180°C/350°F/gas mark 4 for about 15 minutes or until a very pale biscuit colour. Do not allow to over-brown. Cool slightly, then transfer to a wire rack to cool completely. Store in an airtight container.

* **40 calories per finger**
* **Medium fibre**

Orange Fingers

MAKES 24

Prepare as for Lemon Fingers, but substitute the finely grated rind of a small orange for the lemon.

* **40 calories per finger**
* **Medium fibre**

Mixed Citrus Fingers

MAKES 24

Prepare as for Lemon Fingers, but use 5 ml/1 tsp each of finely grated orange, lemon and lime rind instead of all lemon rind.

* **40 calories per finger**
* **Medium fibre**

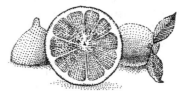

Mighty Mixed Cereal Biscuits

MAKES ABOUT 14

100 g/4 oz/1 cup wholemeal flour
50 g/2 oz/¹/₂ cup barley flour
25 g/1 oz/¹/₄ cup plain (all-purpose) flour
2.5 ml/¹/₂ tsp salt
5 ml/1 tsp baking powder
25 g/1 oz/¹/₄ cup fine oatmeal
75 g/3 oz/¹/₃ cup low-fat sunflower or olive oil spread
50 g/2 oz/¹/₄ cup light brown sugar
90 ml/6 tbsp skimmed milk

Mix the dry ingredients in a bowl. Rub in the low-fat spread and stir in the sugar. Mix with enough of the milk to form a firm dough. Knead gently on a lightly floured surface. Roll out thinly and cut into large rounds using a 7.5 cm/3 in biscuit (cookie) cutter. Transfer to a non-stick baking (cookie) sheet and prick in a pattern with a fork. Bake in a preheated oven at 190°C/375°F/gas mark 5 for 15–20 minutes until golden. Cool slightly, then transfer to a wire rack to cool. Store in an airtight container.

* **100 calories per biscuit**
* **High fibre**

Amaretti Biscuits

MAKES ABOUT 24

90 g/3¹/₂ oz/scant 1 cup ground almonds
175 g/6 oz/³/₄ cup caster (superfine) sugar
2.5 ml/¹/₂ tsp vanilla essence (extract)
2 egg whites
30 ml/2 tbsp amaretti liqueur
Flaked (slivered) almonds
Icing (confectioners') sugar, for dusting

Beat the almonds with the sugar, vanilla essence and one of the egg whites until smooth. Beat in the liqueur. Whisk the second egg white until stiff and fold into the mixture with a metal spoon. Divide the mixture into walnut-sized balls. Place on a baking (cookie) sheet lined with baking parchment and press a flaked almond on top of each one. Bake in a preheated oven at 180°C/350°F/gas mark 4 for about 25 minutes or until golden brown. Leave the biscuits (cookies) on the baking sheet for 5 minutes, then dust with sifted icing sugar and transfer to a wire rack to cool. Store in an airtight container.

* **60 calories per biscuit**
* **Medium fibre**

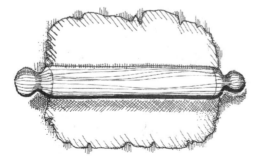

Cigarettes Russes

MAKES ABOUT 16

100 g/4 oz/¹/₂ cup caster (superfine) sugar
2 egg whites, lightly beaten
50 g/2 oz/¹/₄ cup low-fat sunflower or olive oil spread, melted
50 g/2 oz/¹/₂ cup plain (all-purpose) flour, sifted
4 drops of vanilla essence (extract)

Whisk the sugar into the egg whites until smooth. Stir in the low-fat spread and flour and add the vanilla essence. Spread spoonfuls into small rectangles well apart on a baking (cookie) sheet lined with non-stick baking parchment. Bake in a preheated oven at 200°C/400°F/gas mark 6 for 5–6 minutes until lightly golden. Remove from the oven, remove from the baking sheet and place upside-down on the work surface. Quickly roll each one tightly round a wooden spoon handle and hold firmly with the hand until it sets. Cool on a wire rack. Repeat with the remaining mixture. Store in an airtight container.

* **60 calories per biscuit (cookie)**
* **Medium fibre**

Brandy Snaps

MAKES 16

50 g/2 oz/¹/₄ cup low-fat sunflower or olive oil spread, plus extra for greasing
50 g/2 oz/¹/₄ cup caster (superfine) sugar
30 ml/2 tbsp golden (light corn) syrup
50 g/2 oz/¹/₂ cup plain (all-purpose) flour
2.5 ml/¹/₂ tsp ground ginger
5 ml/1 tsp brandy
Finely grated rind of ¹/₂ lemon (optional)

Line two baking (cookie) sheets with non-stick baking parchment. Melt the low-fat spread and syrup in a saucepan over a gentle heat. Sift in the flour and ginger and add the brandy and lemon rind, if using. Mix thoroughly until well blended. Drop 5 ml/1 tsp amounts of the mixture 10 cm/4 in apart on the baking sheets. Bake in a preheated oven at 180°C/350°F/gas mark 4 for 7–10 minutes until golden brown and bubbly. Meanwhile, grease the handle of a wooden spoon with a little low-fat spread. Remove the first sheet of snaps from the oven, quickly lift off the baking sheet with a fish slice and mould loosely around the wooden spoon handle, one at a time, then cool on a wire rack. If the biscuits (cookies) harden before you can mould them, return to the oven for a few minutes to soften. Store in an airtight container for up to 1 week.

* **35 calories per brandy snap**
* **Medium fibre**

Brandy Snap Baskets

MAKES 8

1 quantity of Brandy Snap mixture
Fresh fruit, to serve

Prepare as for Brandy Snaps, but put 10 ml/2 tsp quantities of the mixture well apart on the lined baking (cookie) sheets. Mould over a greased orange or small individual bowl instead of a spoon handle. Serve filled with fresh fruit.

* **70 calories per basket**
* **Medium fibre**

Speciality Flapjacks

MAKES 18

75 g/3 oz/¹/₃ cup low-fat sunflower or olive oil spread
25 g/1 oz/2 tbsp light brown sugar
30 ml/2 tbsp clear honey
175 g/6 oz/1¹/₂ cups crunchy-style muesli
50 g/2 oz/¹/₂ cup plain (all-purpose) flour

Melt the low-fat spread, sugar and honey in a saucepan. Stir in the remaining ingredients until well mixed. Turn into a non-stick 18 cm/ 7 in square baking tin (pan) and press down well. Bake in a preheated oven at 190°C/375°F/gas mark 5 for about 12 minutes or until golden. Cool slightly, then mark into 18 fingers. Leave until completely cold before removing from the tin. Store in an airtight container.

* **85 calories per finger**
* **High fibre**

Hazelnut Macaroons

MAKES 10

Rice paper
1 egg white
75 g/3 oz/³/₄ cup ground hazelnuts (filberts)
75 g/3 oz/¹/₃ cup caster (superfine) sugar
15 ml/1 tbsp ground rice
1.5 ml/¹/₄ tsp vanilla essence (extract)
10 whole blanched hazelnuts

Line a non-stick baking (cookie) sheet with rice paper. Whisk the egg white until very frothy but not stiff. Beat in the ground hazelnuts, sugar, ground rice and vanilla essence. Spoon 10 mounds of the mixture well apart on the rice paper and top each with a whole hazelnut. Bake in a preheated oven at 160°C/325°F/gas mark 3 for about 25 minutes until pale golden brown. Leave to cool. Carefully cut round each one with scissors. Store in an airtight container.

* **90 calories per macaroon**
* **Medium fibre**

Coconut Macaroons

MAKES 10

Prepare as for Hazelnut Macaroons, but substitute desiccated (shredded) coconut for the ground hazelnuts (filberts) and top each with a halved glacé (candied) cherry.

* **90 calories per macaroon**
* **Medium fibre**

Almond Macaroons

MAKES 10

Prepare as for Hazelnut Macaroons (page 369), but substitute ground almonds for the hazelnuts (filberts), almond essence (extract) for the vanilla, and top each with a halved blanched almond instead of a hazelnut.

* **90 calories per macaroon**
* **Medium fibre**

Light Digestive Biscuits

MAKES ABOUT 20

100 g/4 oz/1 cup wholemeal flour
100 g/4 oz/1 cup fine oatmeal
5 ml/1 tsp baking powder
40 g/1½ oz/3 tbsp light brown sugar
50 g/2 oz/¼ cup low-fat sunflower or
*   olive oil spread*
Skimmed milk

Mix together all the dry ingredients. Rub in the low-fat spread. Mix with enough milk to form a firm dough. Knead gently on a lightly floured surface. Roll out to about 5 mm/¼ in thick and cut into rounds using a 5 cm/2 in biscuit (cookie) cutter. Place on a non-stick baking (cookie) sheet and prick in a pattern with a fork. Bake in a preheated oven at 190°C/375°F/gas mark 5 for about 15 minutes until golden brown. Cool slightly, then transfer with a fish slice to a wire rack to cool completely. Store in an airtight container.

* **60 calories per biscuit**
* **High fibre**

Raspberry Angel Cake

SERVES 6 OR 8

50 g/2 oz/½ cup plain (all-purpose)
*   flour*
100 g/4 oz/½ cup caster (superfine)
*   sugar*
4 egg whites
2.5 ml/½ tsp cream of tartar
2.5 ml/½ tsp vanilla essence (extract)
45 ml/3 tbsp raspberry jam (conserve)
5 ml/1 tsp icing (confectioners') sugar
A few fresh raspberries, to decorate
*   (optional)*

Sift the flour twice. Sift the caster sugar to make sure there are no lumps. Whisk the egg whites until frothy but not stiff. Whisk in the cream of tartar, then whisk until stiff and glossy. Lightly whisk in the sugar and vanilla. Sprinkle the flour over and fold in very gently with a metal spoon. Turn into an ungreased 18 cm/7 in deep round cake tin (pan). Bake in a preheated oven at 140°C/275°F/gas mark 1 for 30 minutes. Turn up the heat to 160°C/325°F/gas mark 3 and cook for a further 40 minutes until risen, golden and the centre springs back when lightly pressed. Cool slightly, then turn out on to a wire rack to cool completely. When cold, split in half, sandwich together with the jam, then sift the icing sugar over the top. Decorate with a few fresh raspberries when available.

* **145 or 110 calories per slice**
* **Medium fibre**

Strawberry Angel Cake

SERVES 6 OR 8

Prepare as for Raspberry Angel Cake, but substitute strawberry jam (conserve) for the raspberry and decorate with a few fresh strawberries if available.

* **145 or 110 calories per slice**
* **Medium fibre**

Apricot Almond Angel Cake

SERVES 6 OR 8

Prepare as for Raspberry Angel Cake, but substitute almond essence (extract) for the vanilla and sandwich together with apricot jam (conserve) instead of raspberry. Fill with a few chopped no-need-to soak apricots as well, if liked.

* **145 or 110 calories per slice**
* **Medium fibre**

Chocolate Angel Cake Deluxe

SERVES 6 OR 8

Prepare as for Raspberry Angel Cake, but use half low-fat drinking (sweetened) chocolate powder and half plain (all-purpose) flour. Sandwich together with 45 ml/3 tbsp chocolate-flavoured very low-fat fromage frais.

* **130 or 100 calories per slice**
* **Medium fibre**

Apricot Cut-and-come-again Cake

MAKES 9 SQUARES

100 g/4 oz/1 cup self-raising (self-rising) flour
50 g/2 oz/¼ cup low-fat sunflower or olive oil spread
75 g/3 oz/⅓ cup light brown sugar
1 egg, beaten
2.5 ml/½ tsp almond essence (extract)
30 ml/2 tbsp skimmed milk
410 g/14½ oz/1 large can of apricot halves in natural juice, drained
15 ml/1 tbsp flaked (slivered) almonds

Sift the flour into a bowl. Rub in the low-fat spread. Stir in 50 g/ 2 oz/¼ cup of the sugar. Mix with the egg, almond essence and enough of the milk to form a soft, dropping consistency. Wet an 18 cm/7 in square sandwich tin (pan) and line with baking parchment. Turn the mixture into the prepared tin. Level the surface and arrange the apricots, cut-sides down, over the surface. Sprinkle with the remaining sugar and the almonds. Bake in a preheated oven at 180°C/350°F/gas mark 4 for about 40 minutes until the cake springs back when lightly pressed. Leave to cool slightly, then remove from the tin, discard the paper and leave to cool on a wire rack. Store in an airtight container and serve cut into squares.

* **125 calories per square**
* **Medium fibre**

Cherry Cut-and-come-again Cake

MAKES 9 SQUARES

Prepare as for Apricot Cut-and-come-again Cake (page 371), but substitute 225 g/8 oz fresh stoned (pitted) cherries or 410 g/14 oz/1 large can of cherries, drained, halved and stoned (pitted), for the canned apricots.

* **125 calories per square**
* **Medium fibre**

Apple Cut-and-come-again Cake

MAKES 9 SQUARES

Prepare as for Apricot Cut-and-come-again Cake (page 371), but substitute vanilla essence (extract) for the almond, 3 cooking (tart) apples, peeled, cored and sliced, for the apricots and omit the flaked (slivered) almonds.

* **125 calories per square**
* **Medium fibre**

Jam and Cream Sponge

SERVES 6

Prepare as for Jam Sponge, but spoon 60 ml/4 tbsp low-fat crème fraîche on top of the jam before topping with the second sponge round.

* **135 calories per serving**
* **Medium fibre**

Jam Sponge

SERVES 6

2 eggs
50 g/2 oz/¹⁄₄ cup caster (superfine) sugar
A few drops of vanilla essence (extract)
50 g/2 oz/¹⁄₂ cup self-raising (self-rising) flour
40 ml/2¹⁄₂ tbsp raspberry jam (conserve)
5 ml/1 tsp icing (confectioners') sugar

Put the eggs, sugar and vanilla essence in a bowl. Whisk with an electric beater until thick and pale and the whisk leaves a trail when lifted out of the mixture. Sift the flour over the surface and fold in gently with a metal spoon. Do not over-mix. Turn into two non-stick 18 cm/7 in sandwich tins (pans) base-lined with non-stick baking parchment. Bake in a preheated oven at 200°C/400°F/gas mark 6 for about 8–10 minutes until risen, golden and the centres spring back when lightly pressed. Cool slightly, then turn out on to a wire rack. Remove the paper and leave to cool. Sandwich the cakes together with the jam, transfer to a serving plate, sift the icing sugar over the surface and serve sliced.

* **125 calories per serving**
* **Medium fibre**

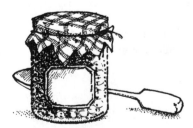

Crispy Oatcakes

MAKES 20

175 g/6 oz/1¹/₂ cups fine or medium oatmeal
50 g/2 oz/¹/₂ cup plain (all-purpose) flour
25 g/1 oz/2 tbsp low-fat sunflower or olive oil spread, melted

Mix together the oatmeal and flour. Stir in the melted spread and enough boiling water to form a firm dough. Knead gently on a lightly floured surface. Roll out very thinly to a rectangle, trim the edges and cut into 10 squares. Cut each square in half diagonally to form triangles. Carefully transfer to non-stick baking (cookie) sheets and bake in a preheated oven at 180°C/350°F/gas mark 4 for about 30 minutes until pale golden. Transfer to a wire rack to cool. Store in an airtight container.

* **45 calories per biscuit (cookie)**
* **High fibre**

Chocolate Indulgence

SERVES 6

2 eggs
40 g/1¹/₂ oz/3 tbsp caster (superfine) sugar
50 g/2 oz/¹/₂ cup self-raising (self-rising) flour
20 g/³/₄ oz/3 tbsp low-fat drinking (sweetened) chocolate powder
5 ml/1 tsp instant coffee powder
100 ml/3¹/₂ fl oz/scant ¹/₂ cup low-fat crème fraîche
5 ml/1 tsp icing (confectioners') sugar

Put the eggs and sugar in a bowl and whisk with an electric beater until thick and pale and the whisk leaves a trail when lifted out of the mixture. Sift together the flour, drinking chocolate and coffee and fold gently into the mixture with a metal spoon. Do not over-mix. Turn into two 18 cm/ 7 in non-stick sandwich tins (pans) base-lined with baking parchment. Bake in a preheated oven at 200°C/400°F/gas mark 6 for about 10–12 minutes or until risen and the centres spring back when lightly pressed. Cool slightly, then turn out on to a wire rack, carefully remove the cooking paper and leave to cool. Sandwich together with the crème fraîche and sift the icing sugar on top.

* **115 calories per serving**
* **Medium fibre**

Vanilla Tea Biscuits

MAKES 28

100 g/4 oz/1 cup ground rice
100 g/4 oz/1 cup self-raising (self-rising) flour
50 g/2 oz/¹/₄ cup low-fat sunflower or olive oil spread
50 g/2 oz/¹/₄ cup caster (superfine) sugar
2.5 ml/¹/₂ tsp vanilla essence (extract)
Skimmed milk

Mix the ground rice and flour in a bowl. Rub in the spread. Mix in the sugar and vanilla essence and enough milk to form a firm dough. Knead gently on a lightly floured surface. Roll out fairly thinly and cut into squares with a 5 mm/2 in fluted biscuit (cookie) cutter. Transfer to non-stick baking (cookie) sheets and prick in a pattern with a fork. Bake in a preheated oven at 180°C/350°F/gas mark 4 for about 20 minutes until pale golden. Cool slightly, then transfer to a wire rack to cool completely. Store in an airtight container.

* **40 calories per biscuit**
* **Medium fibre**

Ginger Drops

MAKES ABOUT 24

100 g/4 oz/1 cup self-raising (self-rising) flour
2.5 ml/¹/₂ tsp cream of tartar
5 ml/1 tsp ground ginger
2.5 ml/¹/₂ tsp ground mace
5 ml/1 tsp caster (superfine) sugar
50 g/2 oz/¹/₄ cup low-fat sunflower or olive oil spread
30 ml/2 tbsp clear honey

Sift the dry ingredients into a bowl. Melt together the low-fat spread and honey and add to the bowl. Mix until the mixture forms a stiff paste. When cool enough to handle, shape into a roll and divide into 24 equal pieces. Roll each piece into a small ball. Place well apart on non-stick baking parchment on baking (cookie) sheets. Flatten each slightly. Bake in a preheated oven at 190°C/375°F/gas mark 5 for about 15 minutes until golden and slightly cracked on top. Cool slightly, then transfer to a wire rack to cool completely. Store in an airtight container.

* **35 calories per biscuit (cookie)**
* **Medium fibre**

Dry-roasted Nuts

Peanuts are cheapest, but I love a mixture of almonds, hazelnuts (filberts) and cashews.

Put 45 ml/3 tbsp raw, shelled peanuts (or other nuts) in a ring on a piece of kitchen paper (paper towel) on a plate. Microwave on High for 3–4 minutes or until golden, stirring once or twice. Cool and repeat with as many nuts as you like. Store in an airtight container. Alternatively, you can dry-fry a single layer of nuts in a heavy-based non-stick frying pan (skillet), tossing over a moderate heat until golden. Remove from the pan as soon as they are golden or they will continue cooking and may burn.

* **45 calories per 15 ml/1 tbsp**
* **High fibre**

Hot Spicy Nuts

Prepare as for the Dry-roasted Nuts, but sprinkle with a few drops of reduced-salt soy sauce before cooking. Then, as soon as they are cooked, sprinkle them with equal quantities of chilli powder and mixed (apple-pie) spice and toss well before cooling and storing.

* **45 calories per 15 ml/1 tbsp**
* **High fibre**

Crispy Potato Skins

Place scrubbed potato peelings in a single layer on a baking (cookie) sheet and sprinkle very lightly with salt. Bake at the top of a preheated oven at 200°C/400°F/ gas mark 6 for about 20 minutes or until crisp and golden. Cool, then store in an airtight container.

* **10 calories per small handful**
* **High fibre**

Sauces, Dressings and Relishes

It is often the sauce, dressing or relish that turns a boring meal into a gourmet experience. Unfortunately, they are also often loaded with fat in one form or another. All the recipes in this chapter are cleverly devised to have maximum flavour with minimum fat and are low in calories too!

Low-fat White Sauce

SERVES 4

45 ml/3 tbsp plain (all-purpose) flour
300 ml/½ pt/1¼ cups skimmed milk
A small knob of low-fat sunflower or
*   olive oil spread*
1 bouquet garni sachet
A pinch of salt
Freshly ground black or white pepper

Put the flour in a saucepan and gradually whisk in the milk. Add the low-fat spread and bouquet garni sachet. Bring to the boil and cook for 2 minutes, stirring all the time, until thickened and smooth. Squeeze the bouquet garni sachet against the side of the pan to extract the maximum flavour, then discard. Season the sauce to taste with salt and pepper. Use as required.

* **50 calories per serving**
* **Medium fibre**

Ultra-smooth White Sauce

SERVES 4

300 ml/½ pt/1¼ cups skimmed milk
1 bay leaf
1 slice of onion
45 ml/3 tbsp cornflour (cornstarch)
Salt and freshly ground black pepper

Put all but 45 ml/3 tbsp of the milk in a saucepan. Add the bay leaf and onion and bring to the boil. Turn off the heat and leave to infuse for 15 minutes. Blend the cornflour with the remaining milk in a separate pan. Strain in the infused milk, bring to the boil and cook for 2 minutes, stirring all the time. Season with salt and pepper.

* **50 calories per serving**
* **Low fibre**

Parsley Sauce

SERVES 4

Prepare as for either of the white sauces, but add 30 ml/2 tbsp chopped parsley to the sauce when cooked.

* **50 calories per serving**
* **Medium fibre**

Mushroom Sauce

SERVES 4

Stew 4–5 finely chopped button mushrooms in 30 ml/2 tbsp water in a covered pan for 3 minutes. Remove the lid and boil rapidly, if necessary, to evaporate any remaining liquid. Stir into either of the cooked white sauces and add a squeeze of lemon juice, if liked.

* **50 calories per serving**
* **Medium fibre**

Cheese Sauce

SERVES 4

Prepare as for either of the white sauces, but add 50 g/2 oz/½ cup grated strong reduced-fat Cheddar cheese after cooking.

* **90 calories per serving**
* **Medium fibre**

Onion Sauce

SERVES 4

Gently stew 2 finely chopped onions in a saucepan with 45 ml/3 tbsp water for 10 minutes until really soft. Stir into either of the cooked white sauces and re-season, if liked.

* 60 calories per serving
* Medium fibre

Creamy Tomato and Basil Sauce

SERVES 4

Prepare as for either of the white sauces (page 376), but add 15 ml/ 1 tbsp tomato purée (paste), 2 skinned and chopped tomatoes and 15 ml/ 1 tbsp chopped basil to the cooked sauce. Serve with ham, fish or chicken.

* 60 calories per serving
* Medium fibre

Caper Sauce

SERVES 4

Prepare as for either of the white sauces (page 376), but add 30 ml/ 2 tbsp chopped capers before seasoning the sauce. Serve with lamb or fish.

* 55 calories per serving
* Medium fibre

Cucumber and Dill Sauce

SERVES 4

Prepare as for either of the white sauces (page 376), but add ¼ cucumber, finely chopped, and 5 ml/1 tsp dried dill (dill weed) to the sauce. Serve with fish or chicken.

* 55 calories per serving
* Medium fibre

Blusher

SERVES 4

Prepare as for either of the white sauces (page 376), but add 1 grated cooked beetroot (red beet) to the sauce with a pinch of caster (superfine) sugar and 5 ml/1 tsp white wine vinegar. Serve with fish or vegetables.

* 60 calories per serving
* Medium fibre

Green Cress Sauce

SERVES 4

Prepare as for either of the white sauces (page 376), but add 1 bunch of finely chopped watercress to the sauce and a pinch of cayenne. Serve with fish or chicken.

* 55 calories per serving
* Medium fibre

Fresh Tomato Sauce

SERVES 4

1 large onion, finely chopped
15 g/¹/₂ oz/1 tbsp low-fat sunflower or olive oil spread
450 g/1 lb tomatoes, skinned and chopped
15 ml/1 tbsp tomato purée (paste)
15 ml/1 tbsp chopped basil or parsley
Salt and freshly ground black pepper

Fry (sauté) the onion in the low-fat spread in a large saucepan for 2 minutes, stirring. Add the tomatoes and tomato purée. Bring to the boil, reduce the heat, part-cover and simmer gently for 6–8 minutes until pulpy, stirring occasionally. Stir in the parsley or basil and season to taste.

* 30 calories per serving
* Medium fibre

Barbecue Sauce

SERVES 4 OR 6

1 garlic clove, crushed
1 small onion, very finely chopped
10 ml/2 tsp low-fat sunflower or olive oil spread
100 g/4 oz/¹/₂ cup tomato purée (paste)
300 ml/¹/₂ pt/1¹/₄ cups fruity dry white wine
10 ml/2 tsp reduced-salt soy sauce
30 ml/2 tbsp clear honey
30 ml/2 tbsp white wine vinegar
A few drops of Tabasco sauce
Salt and freshly ground black pepper

Put the garlic, onion and low-fat spread in a small saucepan. Cook for 2 minutes, stirring, until the onion has softened. Add the remaining ingredients, bring to the boil, reduce the heat and simmer for about 20 minutes until thick. Taste and re-season, if necessary. Serve with any grilled (broiled) meats, fish or vegetables.

* 50 or 35 calories per serving
* No fibre

All-year Tomato Sauce

SERVES 4

1 onion, finely chopped
1 garlic clove, crushed (optional)
15 g/¹/₂ oz/1 tbsp low-fat sunflower or olive oil spread
400 g/14 oz/1 large can of chopped tomatoes
15 ml/1 tbsp tomato purée (paste)
2.5 ml/¹/₂ tsp caster (superfine) sugar
Salt and freshly ground black pepper

Fry (sauté) the onion and garlic, if using, in a saucepan in the low-fat spread for 2 minutes, stirring. Add the tomatoes, tomato purée and sugar. Bring to the boil and boil rapidly for about 5 minutes until pulpy. Season to taste and serve hot.

* 35 calories per serving
* Medium fibre

Herby Tomato Sauce

SERVES 4

Prepare as for All-year Tomato Sauce, but add 2.5 ml/¹/₂ tsp dried oregano, basil or mixed herbs when adding the tomatoes.

* 35 calories per serving
* Medium fibre

Sweet and Sharp Mustard Sauce

SERVES 4

250 ml/8 fl oz/1 cup white wine vinegar
175 ml/6 fl oz/³/₄ cup made English
   mustard
¹/₂ onion, finely chopped
3 garlic cloves, crushed
75 ml/5 tbsp water
60 ml/4 tbsp tomato ketchup (catsup)
10 ml/2 tsp light brown sugar
15 ml/1 tbsp paprika
2.5 ml/¹/₂ tsp chilli powder
Salt and freshly ground black pepper

Put all the ingredients in a saucepan. Bring to the boil and simmer gently for 20 minutes until thick and pulpy. Serve warm or cold with grilled (broiled) meats or fish.

* 25 calories per serving
* Low fibre

Simple Pesto

SERVES 4

20 basil leaves
1 large sprig of parsley
50 g/2 oz/¹/₂ cup pine nuts
1 large garlic clove, halved
30 ml/2 tbsp olive oil
30 ml/2 tbsp grated Parmesan cheese
Salt anf freshly ground black pepper
30 ml/2 tbsp hot water

Chop the herbs, nuts and garlic in a blender or food processor. Gradually add the oil with the machine running to form a thick paste, stopping the machine to scrape down the side. Add the cheese, salt and some pepper and run the machine again, adding the water to form a glistening paste. Store in a screw-topped jar in the fridge for up to 2 weeks.

* 185 calories per serving
* Fairly high fibre

Red Almond Pesto

SERVES 4

1 large garlic clove, halved
50 g/2 oz/¹/₂ cup ground almonds
15 basil leaves
4 sun-dried tomatoes in olive oil,
   drained
30 ml/2 tbsp sun-dried tomato oil
30 ml/2 tbsp grated Parmesan cheese
30 ml/2 tbsp hot water
Salt and freshly ground black pepper

Put the garlic, almonds, basil and tomatoes in a blender or food processor and run the machine briefly to chop. Gradually add the oil with the machine running to form a thick paste, stopping the machine to scrape down the side. Add the cheese, water, salt and some pepper. Run the machine again to form a paste. Store in a screw-topped jar in the fridge for up to 2 weeks.

* 190 calories per serving
* Fairly high fibre

Light Coriander Pesto

SERVES 6

50 g/2 oz/¹/₄ cup low-fat sunflower or
   olive oil spread
1 large garlic clove, quartered
25 g/1 oz/¹/₄ cup pine nuts
6 large sprigs of coriander (cilantro)
A sprig of parsley
15 ml/1 tbsp grated Parmesan cheese
Salt and freshly ground black pepper

Put the low-fat spread in a blender or food processor and, with the machine running, drop in the garlic, then the pine nuts, then the herbs. Stop and scrape down the side as necessary. When well blended, add the cheese and salt and pepper to taste. Use as required.

* 190 calories per serving
* Medium fibre

Minted Yoghurt and Cucumber

Use this as a dip with pitta breads, to top jacket-baked potatoes, or to serve with curries.

SERVES 4

5 cm/2 in piece of cucumber, grated
5 ml/1 tsp dried mint
1 small garlic clove, crushed (optional)
150 ml/¹/₄ pt/²/₃ cup low-fat plain yoghurt
Freshly ground black pepper

Squeeze the cucumber to remove excess moisture. Place in a bowl. Add the remaining ingredients and mix thoroughly. Chill until ready to serve.

* **20 calories per serving**
* **Low fibre**

Low-fat French Dressing

SERVES 4

15 ml/1 tbsp olive oil
30 ml/2 tbsp red or white wine vinegar
30 ml/2 tbsp water
1.5 ml/¹/₄ tsp Dijon mustard
A pinch of salt
A pinch of caster (superfine) sugar
Freshly ground black pepper

Shake together all the ingredients in a screw-topped jar until well blended. Use as required.

* **40 calories per serving**
* **No fibre**

Honey Nut Dressing

SERVES 4

30 ml/2 tbsp clear honey
15 ml/1 tbsp sunflower oil
15 ml/1 tbsp lemon juice
15 ml/1 tbsp water
30 ml/2 tbsp finely chopped mixed nuts
15 ml/1 tbsp chopped parsley
Freshly ground black pepper

Shake together all the ingredients in a screw-topped jar until well blended. Use as required.

* **90 calories per serving**
* **Medium fibre**

Gran's Light Dressing

SERVES 4

15 ml/1 tbsp light brown sugar
30 ml/2 tbsp skimmed milk
30 ml/2 tbsp cultured buttermilk or low-fat crème fraîche
2.5 ml/¹/₂ tsp made English mustard
A pinch of salt
Freshly ground black pepper
Malt vinegar, to taste

Whisk together the sugar, milk, buttermilk or crème fraîche, mustard, salt and lots of pepper in a small bowl or jug. Whisk in vinegar to taste. Use as required.

* **30 calories per serving**
* **No fibre**

Light Cheese Dressing

SERVES 4

60 ml/4 tbsp low-fat soft cheese
10 ml/2 tsp snipped chives
10 ml/2 tsp chopped parsley
30 ml/2 tbsp skimmed milk
5 ml/1 tsp dried onion granules
Freshly ground black pepper

Whisk together all the ingredients, adding pepper to taste. Thin with a little more milk, if necessary. Use as required.

* **30 calories per serving**
* **Medium fibre**

Creamy Garlic Dressing

SERVES 4

15 ml/1 tbsp olive oil
75 ml/5 tbsp low-fat crème fraîche
30 ml/2 tbsp lemon juice
1 garlic clove, crushed
15 ml/1 tbsp chopped parsley
A pinch of salt
Freshly ground black pepper
5 ml/1 tsp clear honey
A little skimmed milk

Whisk together all the ingredients, adding enough milk to thin to a pouring consistency. Chill until ready to serve.

* **55 calories per serving**
* **Low fibre**

Non-oil Vinaigrette

SERVES 4

45 ml/3 tbsp white wine vinegar
30 ml/2 tbsp water
1 shallot, very finely chopped
2.5 ml/¹/₂ tsp Dijon mustard
10 ml/2 tsp chopped parsley
5 ml/1 tsp caster (superfine) sugar
A pinch of salt
Freshly ground black pepper

Shake together all the ingredients in a screw-topped jar until well blended. Chill until ready to serve.

* **10 calories per serving**
* **Medium fibre**

Spiced Crème Fraîche Dressing

SERVES 4

100 ml/3¹/₂ fl oz/scant ¹/₂ cup low-fat crème fraîche
5 ml/1 tsp curry paste
Salt and freshly ground black pepper
5 ml/1 tsp lemon juice
5 ml/1 tsp light brown sugar (optional)
15 ml/1 tbsp water

Whisk the crème fraîche with the curry paste, salt and pepper to taste and the lemon juice. Sweeten, if liked, with the sugar and thin with the water.

* **30 calories per serving**
* **Low fibre**

Honeyed Basil Dressing

SERVES 4

30 ml/2 tbsp lemon juice
30 ml/2 tbsp balsamic vinegar
15 ml/1 tbsp clear honey
Freshly ground black pepper
12 large basil leaves, very finely
chopped

Shake together all the ingredients in a screw-topped jar until well blended. Chill until ready to serve.

* **20 calories per serving**
* **Medium fibre**

Piquant Tomato Drizzle

SERVES 4

2 large ripe tomatoes, roughly
chopped
15 ml/1 tbsp Worcestershire sauce
15 ml/1 tbsp olive oil
15 ml/1 tbsp water
4 basil leaves, chopped
Salt and freshly ground black pepper

Purée the tomatoes in a blender with the Worcestershire sauce, oil, water and basil. Season to taste. Strain through a sieve (strainer) to remove the skins and seeds. Use as required.

* **45 calories per serving**
* **Medium fibre**

Ravishing Relish

MAKES ABOUT 900 g/2 lb

5 ml/1 tsp pickling spice
450 g/1 lb ripe pears, finely chopped
50 g/2 oz/¹/₃ cup dried dates, stoned
and chopped
150 ml/¹/₄ pt/²/₃ cup malt vinegar
60 ml/4 tbsp apple juice
1 small ripe melon, chopped
1 small marrow (squash), chopped

Tie the spice in a piece of clean muslin (cheesecloth) or disposable dish cloth. Put the pears and dates in a saucepan with the vinegar, spice and apple juice. Bring to the boil, reduce the heat and simmer very gently for 1 hour. Add the melon and marrow and simmer for a further 30 minutes until really soft, adding a little more apple juice if the mixture is becoming too dry. Remove and discard the pickling spice. Spoon into clean, warm jars. Cover and seal. When cold, store in the fridge. Serve with cold meats.

* **40 calories per 15 ml/1 tbsp**
* **High fibre**

Cucumber and Dill Salsa

SERVES 4

$^1/_4$ cucumber, very finely chopped
1 shallot, very finely chopped
30 ml/2 tbsp chopped dill (dill weed)
15 ml/1 tbsp caster (superfine) sugar
15 ml/1 tbsp cider vinegar
Salt and freshly ground black pepper

Mix the cucumber and shallot in a small bowl. Stir in the dill and sugar. Moisten with the vinegar. Season to taste and add a dash more vinegar, if liked. Leave to stand for at least 30 minutes to allow the flavours to develop.

* 10 calories per serving
* Medium fibre

English Dressing

SERVES 4

60 ml/4 tbsp skimmed milk
1.5 ml/$^1/_4$ tsp made English mustard
15 ml/1 tbsp clear honey
Malt vinegar, to taste
A pinch of salt
Freshly ground black pepper

Whisk together the milk, mustard and honey. Stir in vinegar to taste (don't worry if it curdles very slightly), then season with the salt and some pepper.

* 20 calories per serving
* No fibre

Hot Chilli Salsa

SERVES 4

1 small onion, very finely chopped
1 small red chilli, seeded and finely chopped
3 ripe tomatoes, skinned and finely chopped
30 ml/2 tbsp ketchup (catsup)
15 ml/1 tbsp chopped parsley

Mix together all the ingredients and chill until ready to serve.

* 25 calories per serving
* Medium fibre

Fiery Cucumber Salsa

SERVES 4

$^1/_4$ cucumber, grated
$^1/_2$ bunch of spring onions (scallions), finely chopped
1 green chilli, seeded and finely chopped
Grated rind and juice of $^1/_2$ lime
2.5 ml/$^1/_2$ tsp ground cumin
15 ml/1 tbsp chopped coriander (cilantro)
7.5 ml/$1^1/_2$ tsp clear honey
A pinch of salt
Freshly ground black pepper

Squeeze the cucumber to remove the excess liquid. Mix together all the ingredients and chill until ready to serve.

* 10 calories per serving
* Medium fibre

Minted Yoghurt Dressing

SERVES 4

90 ml/6 tbsp low-fat plain yoghurt
1 small garlic clove, crushed
15 ml/1 tbsp chopped mint
A pinch of salt
Freshly ground black pepper

Whisk together all the ingredients. Cover and chill for at least 1 hour before using to allow the flavours to develop.

* 15 calories per serving
* Low fibre

Light Soy Dressing

SERVES 4

30 ml/2 tbsp reduced-salt soy sauce
15 ml/1 tbsp medium-dry sherry
30 ml/2 tbsp water
Freshly ground black pepper

Whisk together all the ingredients and use as required.

* 10 calories per serving
* No fibre

Sweet and Sour Dressing

SERVES 4

60 ml/4 tbsp pineapple juice
15 ml/1 tbsp reduced-salt soy sauce
10 ml/2 tsp lemon juice
5 ml/1 tsp tomato ketchup (catsup)
Freshly ground black pepper
15 ml/1 tbsp water

Whisk together all the ingredients and use as required.

* 20 calories per serving
* No fibre

Green Herb Dressing

SERVES 4

60 ml/4 tbsp cider vinegar
15 ml/1 tbsp chopped tarragon
15 ml/1 tbsp chopped parsley
15 ml/1 tbsp chopped sage
15 ml/1 tbsp snipped chives
5 ml/1 tsp caster (superfine) sugar
A pinch of salt
Freshly ground black pepper
30 ml/2 tbsp water
A few drops of Worcestershire sauce

Shake together all the ingredients in a screw-topped jar until blended. Leave to stand for at least 30 minutes to allow the flavours to develop.

* 10 calories per serving
* Medium fibre

Extra-light Mayonnaise

SERVES 4

30 ml/2 tbsp low-calorie mayonnaise
30 ml/2 tbsp low-fat plain yoghurt
2.5 ml/¹/₂ tsp lemon juice
Freshly ground black pepper

Blend together all the ingredients and chill until ready to serve.

* **30 calories per serving**
* **No fibre**

Rosy Dressing

SERVES 4

Extra-light Mayonnaise
10 ml/2 tsp tomato ketchup (catsup)
2.5 ml/¹/₂ tsp Worcestershire sauce
A few drops of Tabasco sauce

Mix together all the ingredients and use as required.

* **35 calories per serving**
* **No fibre**

Curried Mayo

SERVES 4

Extra-light Mayonnaise
15 ml/1 tbsp curry paste
15 ml/1 tbsp sultanas (golden raisins)
15 ml/1 tbsp chopped coriander
  (cilantro), optional

Mix the Extra-light Mayonnaise with the curry paste and stir in the sultanas. Add the coriander, if liked.

* **40 calories per serving**
* **Medium fibre**

Orange and Mango Salsa

SERVES 4 OR 6

1 large just ripe mango
4–6 spring onions (scallions), finely
  chopped
2 oranges
1 small red chilli, seeded and chopped
15 ml/1 tbsp chopped mint
2.5 ml/¹/₂ tsp grated fresh root ginger
A pinch of salt
Freshly ground black pepper
5 ml/1 tsp lemon juice

Peel the mango and cut all the fruit off the stone (pit). Dice finely and place in a bowl. Add the spring onions. Finely grate the rind from one of the oranges. Cut off all the peel and pith from both. Slice the fruit, then cut into small pieces. Add to the mango and onion. Add all the remaining ingredients and mix well. Cover and chill for at least 1 hour to allow the flavours to develop. Serve with barbecued fish or chicken.

* **40 or 25 calories per serving**
* **Medium fibre**

Orange and Pineapple Salsa

SERVES 4 OR 6

Prepare as for Orange and Mango Salsa (page 385), but substitute 300 g/11 oz/1 medium can of crushed pineapple, well drained, for the mango.

* 40 or 25 calories per serving
* Medium fibre

Brown Onion Salsa

SERVES 4 OR 6

450 g/1 lb onions, chopped
25 g/1 oz/2 tbsp low-fat sunflower or olive oil spread
30 ml/2 tbsp light brown sugar
Salt and freshly ground black pepper
15 ml/1 tbsp chopped parsley

Cook the onions in the low-fat spread, stirring, for 5 minutes until softened. Add the sugar, turn up the heat and continue cooking until a rich golden brown. Purée in a blender or food processor and season to taste. Stir in the parsley. Reheat gently, if liked.

* 85 or 60 calories per serving
* Medium fibre

Horseradish Crème

SERVES 4

90 ml/6 tbsp low-fat crème fraîche
15 ml/1 tbsp horseradish relish
A pinch of salt and white pepper

Mix the crème fraîche with the horseradish and season with the salt and pepper. Chill until ready to serve.

* 35 calories per serving
* Low fibre

Sweet Vanilla Sauce

SERVES 4

45 ml/3 tbsp cornflour (cornstarch)
300 ml/¹/₂ pt/1¹/₄ cups skimmed milk
1.5 ml/¹/₄ tsp vanilla essence (extract)
15 ml/1 tbsp caster (superfine) sugar

Blend the cornflour with a little of the milk in a saucepan. Stir in the remaining milk, the vanilla and sugar. Bring to the boil and cook for 2 minutes, stirring until thickened and smooth.

* 60 calories per serving
* Low fibre

Sherry Sauce

SERVES 4

Prepare as for Sweet Vanilla Sauce, but add 15 ml/1 tbsp sweet sherry to the cooked sauce.

* 65 calories per serving
* Low fibre

Luscious Mint Custard

SERVES 4

Prepare as for Sweet Vanilla Sauce, but add a few drops of peppermint essence (extract) and green food colouring and omit the vanilla.

* 60 calories per serving
* Low fibre

Velvet Chocolate Sauce

SERVES 4

30 ml/2 tbsp cornflour (cornstarch)
30 ml/2 tbsp low-fat drinking
(sweetened) chocolate powder
300 ml/¹/₂ pt/1¹/₄ cups skimmed milk

Blend the cornflour and drinking chocolate with a little of the milk in a saucepan. Blend in the remaining milk. Bring to the boil and cook for 2 minutes, stirring all the time, until thickened and smooth.

* 65 calories per serving
* Low fibre

Low-fat Custard

SERVES 4

45 ml/3 tbsp cornflour (cornstarch)
300 ml/¹/₂ pt/1¹/₄ cups skimmed milk
5 ml/1 tsp vanilla essence (extract)
15 ml/1 tbsp caster (superfine) sugar
A few drops of yellow food colouring
(optional)

Blend the cornflour with a little of the milk in a saucepan. Stir in the remaining milk, the vanilla essence and sugar. Bring to the boil and cook for 2 minutes, stirring all the time, until thickened and smooth. Colour with a few drops of food colouring, if liked. Serve hot.

* 60 calories per serving
* Low fibre

Chocolate Custard

SERVES 4

30 ml/2 tbsp cornflour (cornstarch)
30 ml/2 tbsp low-fat drinking
(sweetened) chocolate powder
300 ml/¹/₂ pt/1¹/₄ cups skimmed milk
15 ml/1 tbsp clear honey

Blend the cornflour and drinking chocolate with some of the milk in a saucepan. Stir in the remaining milk and add the honey. Bring to the boil and cook for 2 minutes, stirring all the time, until thickened and smooth. Serve hot.

* 80 calories per serving
* Low fibre

Hot Lemon Sauce

SERVES 4 OR 6

15 g/¹/₂ oz/2 tbsp cornflour (cornstarch)
25 g/1 oz/2 tbsp caster (superfine)
sugar
300 ml/¹/₂ pt/1¹/₄ cups water
Juice of 2 lemons

Blend the cornflour and sugar with a little of the water in a saucepan. Add the remaining water and the lemon juice. Bring to the boil and cook for 2 minutes, stirring until thickened and clear. Serve hot.

* 45 or 30 calories per serving
* Low fibre

Hot Chocolate Caramel Sauce

SERVES 4

1 low-calorie chocolate caramel bar
90 ml/6 tbsp skimmed milk
15 g/¹/₂ oz/1 tbsp low-fat sunflower or olive oil spread
15 ml/1 tbsp low-fat drinking (sweetened) chocolate powder

Cut the bar into pieces and place in a saucepan. Add the remaining ingredients and heat gently, stirring all the time, until smooth and thickened. Serve hot over profiteroles, ice cream or fruit.

* 50 calories per serving
* Low fibre

Lemon Honey Sauce

SERVES 4

60 ml/4 tbsp clear honey
Grated rind and juice of 1 lemon

Mix together in a saucepan and heat gently, stirring, until hot and well blended. Serve hot.

* 65 calories per serving
* Low fibre

Hot Honey Sauce

SERVES 4

15 g/¹/₂ oz/2 tbsp cornflour (cornstarch)
300 ml/¹/₂ pt/1¹/₄ cups skimmed milk
15–30 ml/1–2 tbsp clear honey

Blend the cornflour with a little of the milk in a saucepan. Blend in the remaining milk. Add half the honey and bring to the boil, stirring. Cook for 2 minutes, stirring all the time. Taste and add more honey, if liked. Serve hot.

* 65 calories per serving
* No fibre

Syrup Sauce

SERVES 4

90 ml/6 tbsp golden (light corn) syrup
30 ml/2 tbsp lemon juice

Heat the syrup and lemon juice in a saucepan until hot but not boiling. Serve hot.

* 95 calories per serving
* No fibre

Maple Syrup Sauce

SERVES 4

Prepare as for Syrup Sauce, but substitute maple syrup for the golden (light corn) syrup. Serve over pancakes.

* 80 calories per serving
* No fibre

Apricot Jam Sauce

SERVES 4 OR 6

60 ml/4 tbsp apricot jam (conserve)
30 ml/2 tbsp caster (superfine) sugar
Finely grated rind and juice of ¹/₂ lemon
75 ml/5 tbsp water

Finely chop any pieces of fruit. Blend with all the ingredients in a saucepan and heat gently, stirring, until the sugar has dissolved. Simmer for 5 minutes. Serve hot.

* 75 or 50 calories per serving
* Low fibre

Strawberry Jam Sauce

SERVES 4 OR 6

Prepare as for Apricot Jam Sauce, but substitute strawberry jam (conserve) for apricot.

* 75 or 50 calories per serving
* Low fibre

Raspberry Jam Sauce

SERVES 4 OR 6

Prepare as for Apricot Jam Sauce, but use sieved (strained) raspberry jam (conserve) or seedless raspberry jelly (clear conserve) instead of apricot jam.

* 75 or 50 calories per serving
* Low fibre

Blackcurrant Jam Sauce

SERVES 4 OR 6

Prepare as for Apricot Jam Sauce, but substitute blackcurrant jam (conserve) for apricot and use the finely grated rind and juice of ½ orange instead of the lemon juice and rind.

* 75 or 50 calories per serving
* Low fibre

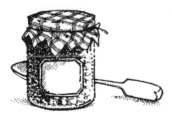

Marmalade Sauce

SERVES 4 OR 6

Prepare as for Apricot Jam Sauce, but substitute marmalade for the jam (conserve) and use the finely grated rind and juice of ½ lemon and ½ orange. Use only 45 ml/3 tbsp water.

* 85 or 60 calories per serving
* Low fibre

Plum Jam Sauce

SERVES 4 OR 6

Prepare as for Apricot Jam Sauce, but substitute sieved (strained) plum jam (conserve) for the apricot jam and use the finely grated rind and juice of ½ orange instead of the lemon.

* 75 or 50 calories per serving
* Low fibre

Fresh Raspberry Sauce

SERVES 4 OR 6

225 g/8 oz raspberries
25 g/1 oz/3 tbsp icing (confectioners')
  sugar
15 ml/1 tbsp lemon juice

Purée the raspberries with the sugar and lemon juice in a blender or food processor. Pass through a sieve (strainer) to remove the seeds. Use as required.

* 45 or 30 calories per serving
* Low fibre

Raspberry Jelly Sauce

SERVES 6

1 raspberry-flavoured jelly (jello) tablet
30 ml/2 tbsp redcurrant jelly (clear
conserve)
200 ml/7 fl oz/scant 1 cup water
5 ml/1 tsp arrowroot

Break up the jelly and place in a saucepan with the redcurrant jelly and most of the water. Heat gently, stirring, until dissolved. Blend the arrowroot with the remaining water and stir into the mixture until slightly thickened and clear. Serve hot.

* **110 calories per serving**
* **No fibre**

All-year Raspberry Sauce

SERVES 4 OR 6

390 g/13½ oz/1 large can of
raspberries
10 ml/2 tsp cornflour (cornstarch)

Purée the raspberries and their juice in a blender or food processor. Pass through a sieve (strainer), if liked, to remove the seeds. Blend a little of the purée with the cornflour in a saucepan. Stir in the remainder. Bring to the boil and cook for 2 minutes, stirring, until thickened and clear. Serve hot or cover with a circle of wetted greaseproof (waxed) paper to prevent a skin forming and leave to cool.

* **90 or 60 calories per serving**
* **Low fibre**

Brandied Loganberry Sauce

SERVES 4 OR 6

225 g/8 oz fresh or frozen loganberries
45 ml/3 tbsp brandy
15 ml/1 tbsp water
Icing (confectioners') sugar, to taste

Gently stew the loganberries in the brandy and water for 8 minutes. Purée in a blender or food processor, then pass through a sieve (strainer) to remove the seeds. Sweeten to taste with sifted icing sugar and serve cold.

* **50 calories per serving**
* **Low fibre**

Apple and Strawberry Sauce

SERVES 6

450 g/1 lb cooking (tart) apples, sliced
60 ml/4 tbsp strawberry jam
(conserve)
15 ml/1 tbsp water
5 ml/1 tsp lemon juice
Caster (superfine) sugar

Simmer together all the ingredients except the sugar in a covered saucepan until the apple is pulpy. Pass through a sieve (strainer) or purée in a blender or food processor. Return to the pan and sweeten to taste. Serve hot.

* **100 calories per serving**
* **Low fibre**

Smooth Strawberry Sauce

SERVES 4 OR 6

225g/8 oz strawberries, quartered
15 ml/1 tbsp crème de cassis or
*   blackcurrant cordial*
15 ml/1 tbsp icing (confectioners')
*   sugar*
A few drops of vanilla essence (extract)

Purée all the ingredients in a blender or food processor until smooth. Chill until ready to serve.

* **40 or 30 calories per serving**
* **Low fibre**

Fresh Apricot Sauce

SERVES 4

450 g/1 lb apricots, halved and stoned
*   (pitted)*
150 ml/¹/₄ pt/²/₃ cup sweet white wine
50 g/2 oz/¹/₄ cup granulated sugar
Finely grated rind of ¹/₂ lemon
30 ml/2 tbsp kirsch

Put the apricots in a saucepan with the wine, sugar and lemon rind. Heat gently until the sugar melts, then boil for 4 minutes. Purée in a blender or food processor, then stir in the kirsch. Serve warm or cold.

* **140 calories per serving**
* **Low fibre**

Greengage Sauce

SERVES 4

Prepare as for Fresh Apricot Sauce, but substitute greengages for the apricots and sweeten with honey instead of sugar, if preferred.

* **150 calories per serving**
* **Low fibre**

Red Plum Sauce

SERVES 4

Prepare as for Fresh Apricot Sauce, but substitute ripe red plums for the apricots.

* **145 calories per serving**
* **Low fibre**

Smooth Cherry Sauce

SERVES 4

Prepare as for Fresh Apricot Sauce, but substitute ripe cherries for the apricots and port for the sweet white wine.

* **145 calories per serving**
* **Low fibre**

Orange Sauce

SERVES 4

Finely grated rind and juice of 1 orange
Juice of 1 lemon
15 ml/1 tbsp arrowroot
Caster (superfine) sugar

Make the fruit rind and juice up to 300 ml/½ pt/1¼ cups with water. Blend a little with the arrowroot in a saucepan. Stir in the remainder. Bring to the boil, stirring all the time, until thickened and clear. Sweeten to taste. Serve hot.

* **35 calories per serving**
* **Low fibre**

Pineapple and Orange Sauce

SERVES 6

300 g/11 oz/1 medium can of crushed pineapple
10 ml/2 tsp arrowroot
150 ml/¹/₄ pt/²/₃ cup pure orange juice

Put the contents of the can of pineapple in a saucepan. Blend the arrowroot with a little of the orange juice and add to the pan with the remaining orange juice. Bring to the boil and cook for 2 minutes, stirring, until thickened and clear. Serve hot.

* **35 calories per serving**
* **Medium fibre**

Jewelled Pineapple Sauce

SERVES 4 OR 6

300 g/11 oz/1 medium can of crushed pineapple
25 g/1 oz/2 tbsp caster (superfine) sugar
25 g/1 oz/2 tbsp chopped glacé (candied) cherries
30 ml/2 tbsp chopped angelica
15 ml/1 tbsp currants
10 ml/2 tsp cornflour (cornstarch)
60 ml/4 tbsp water
Finely grated rind and juice of 1 lemon or lime

Put the contents of the can of pineapple in a saucepan and add the sugar, cherries, angelica and currants. Blend the cornflour with the water and add to the pan with the lemon or lime rind and juice. Bring to the boil and cook, stirring for 2 minutes. Serve hot over ice cream.

* **110 or 70 calories per serving**
* **Fairly high fibre**

Dark Rum Sauce

SERVES 4 OR 6

20 g/³/₄ oz/3 tbsp cornflour (cornstarch)
25 g/1 oz/2 tbsp dark brown sugar
300 ml/¹/₂ pt/1¹/₄ cups milk
30 ml/2 tbsp dark rum

Blend the cornflour with the sugar and a little of the milk in a saucepan. Stir in the remaining milk. Bring to the boil and cook for 2 minutes, stirring. Blend in the rum. Pour into a warm sauce boat and serve.

* **95 or 65 calories per serving**
* **Low fibre**

Real Caramel Sauce

SERVES 4

175 g/6 oz/³/₄ cup granulated sugar
65 ml/4¹/₂ tbsp cold water
150 ml/¹/₄ pt/²/₃ cup lukewarm water

Put the sugar and cold water in a saucepan and heat gently, stirring, until the sugar has dissolved. Bring to the boil and boil rapidly until the mixture is a rich brown colour but not burnt. Remove from the heat and pour in the warm water (take care as it will splutter). Return to the heat and stir until the caramel melts, then boil rapidly until syrupy. Leave to cool. If the mixture is too thick when cooled, stir in a little warm water.

* **175 calories per serving**
* **No fibre**

White Rum Sauce

SERVES 4 OR 6

25 g/1 oz/2 tbsp granulated sugar
120 ml/4 fl oz/¹/₂ cup water
Grated rind of ¹/₂ lemon
25 g/1 oz/2 tbsp low-fat sunflower or olive oil spread
5 ml/1 tsp cornflour (cornstarch)
120 ml/4 fl oz/¹/₂ cup white rum

Put the sugar, water and lemon rind in a saucepan. Heat gently, stirring, until the sugar dissolves. Whisk in the low-fat spread. Blend the cornflour with the rum and stir into the sauce. Boil for 2 minutes, stirring all the time. Serve hot.

* **125 or 85 calories per serving**
* **Low fibre**

Brandy Sauce

SERVES 4 OR 6

Prepare as for Dark Rum Sauce, but substitute caster (superfine) sugar for the dark brown sugar and brandy for the rum.

* **95 or 65 calories per serving**
* **Low fibre**

Red Wine Sauce

SERVES 4

15 ml/1 tbsp caster (superfine) sugar
150 ml/¹/₄ pt/²/₃ cup water
30 ml/2 tbsp redcurrant jelly (clear conserve)
Thinly pared rind of ¹/₂ lemon
5 ml/1 tsp arrowroot
45 ml/3 tbsp red wine

Put the sugar, water, redcurrant jelly and lemon rind in a saucepan. Simmer gently, stirring, for 5 minutes. Blend the arrowroot with the wine and stir in. Bring to the boil and cook for 1 minute, stirring all the time. Serve hot with steamed sponge puddings or plain poached fruit.

* **35 calories per serving**
* **Low fibre**

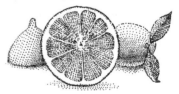

Light Chantilly Cream

SERVES 6 OR 8

1 egg white
300 ml/¹/₂ pt/1¹/₄ cups low-fat
  whipping cream
15 ml/1 tbsp icing (confectioners')
  sugar
5 ml/1 tsp vanilla essence (extract)

Whisk the egg white until stiff. Then, without washing the beaters, whip the cream with the icing sugar and vanilla until peaking. Fold in the egg white with a metal spoon. Turn into a serving bowl and chill for at least 30 minutes before serving.

* **125 or 95 calories per serving**
* **No fibre**

Fluffy Brandy Cream

SERVES 6 OR 8

Prepare as for Light Chantilly Cream, but omit the vanilla essence (extract) and whisk in 15–30 ml/ 1–2 tbsp brandy to taste.

* **135 or 105 calories per serving**
* **No fibre**

Fluffy Cointreau Cream

SERVES 6 OR 8

Prepare as for Light Chantilly Cream, but omit the vanilla essence (extract) and whisk in 15–30 ml/ 1–2 tbsp Cointreau to taste.

* **155 or 115 calories per serving**
* **No fibre**

Fluffy Crème de Menthe Cream

SERVES 6 OR 8

Prepare as for Light Chantilly Cream, but omit the vanilla essence (extract) and whisk in 15–30 ml/ 1–2 tbsp crème de menthe to taste.

* **155 or 115 calories per serving**
* **No fibre**

Tia Maria Cream

SERVES 6 OR 8

Prepare as for Light Chantilly Cream, but flavour with 15–30 ml/1–2 tbsp Tia Maria or other coffee liqueur to taste.

* **155 or 115 calories per serving**
* **No fibre**

Framboise Cream

SERVES 6 OR 8

Prepare as for Light Chantilly Cream, but omit the vanilla essence (extract) and whisk in 15–30 ml/ 1–2 tbsp framboise (raspberry liqueur) to taste.

* **155 or 115 calories per serving**
* **No fibre**

No-sugar Apple and Cinnamon Spread

MAKES ABOUT 225 g/8 oz

2 large eating (dessert) apples, chopped
100 g/4 oz/²/₃ cup dried dates, stoned (pitted) and chopped
2.5 ml/¹/₂ tsp ground cinnamon
175 ml/6 fl oz/³/₄ cup water

Place all the ingredients in a saucepan. Bring to the boil and simmer for 15 minutes or until soft. Purée in a blender or food processor. Turn into a clean screw-topped jar and store in the fridge for up to 2 weeks.

* **40 calories per 15 ml/1 tbsp**
* **High fibre**

No-sugar Apricot Spread

MAKES ABOUT 225 g/8 oz

175 g/6 oz/1 cup dried apricots
1 eating (dessert) apple, chopped
5 ml/1 tsp lemon juice

Put the apricots in a bowl with just enough water to cover. Leave to soak overnight. Toss the apple in lemon juice to prevent browning. Place the apricots with their water and the apple in a blender or food processor and blend until smooth. Turn into a clean screw-topped jar and store in the fridge for up to 2 weeks.

* **40 calories per 15 ml/1 tbsp**
* **High fibre**

Index

Everyday Eating made more exciting

			QUANTITY	AMOUNT
New Classic 1000 Recipes	0-572-02575-0	£5.99		
Classic 1000 Chinese	0-572-01783-9	£5.99		
Classic 1000 Indian	0-572-02807-5	£6.99		
Classic 1000 Italian	0-572-02848-2	£6.99		
Classic 1000 Pasta & Rice	0-572-02300-6	£5.99		
Classic 1000 Vegetarian	0-572-02808-3	£6.99		
Classic 1000 Quick and Easy	0-572-02330-8	£5.99		
Classic 1000 Cake & Bake	0-572-02803-2	£6.99		
Classic 1000 Calorie-counted Recipes	0-572-02405-3	£5.99		
Classic 1000 Microwave Recipes	0-572-01945-9	£5.99		
Classic 1000 Dessert Recipes	0-572-02542-4	£5.99		
Classic 1000 Low-Fat Recipes	0-572-02804-0	£6.99		
Classic 1000 Chicken Recipes	0-572-02646-3	£5.99		
Classic 1000 Seafood Recipes	0-572-02696-X	£6.99		
Classic 1000 Beginners' Recipes	0-572-02734-6	£5.99		

Please allow 75p per book for post & packing in UK • POST & PACKING
Overseas customers £1 per book.

TOTAL

Foulsham books are available from local bookshops. Should you have any difficulty obtaining supplies please send Cheque/Eurocheque/Postal Order (£ sterling only) made out to BSBP or debit my credit card:

☐ ACCESS ☐ VISA ☐ MASTER CARD

EXPIRY DATE   SIGNATURE

ALL ORDERS TO:
Foulsham Books, PO Box 29, Douglas, Isle of Man IM99 1BQ
Telephone 01624 836000, Fax 01624 837033, Internet http://www.bookpost.co.uk.

NAME

ADDRESS

Please allow 28 days for delivery.
Please tick box if you do not wish to receive any additional information ☐
Prices and availability subject to change without notice.